P9-ANY-196

Harry C. Trexler Library
Muhlenberg College

THE STATE AND AGRARIAN CHANGE IN ZIMBABWE'S COMMUNAL AREAS

The State and Agrarian Change in Zimbabwe's Communal Areas

Michael Drinkwater

St. Martin's Press   New York

© Michael Drinkwater, 1991

All rights reserved. For information, write:
Scholarly and Reference Division,
St. Martin's Press, Inc., 175 Fifth Avenue,
New York, N.Y. 10010

First published in the United States of America in 1991

Printed in Hong Kong

ISBN 0–312–05350–9

Library of Congress Cataloging-in-Publication Data
Drinkwater, Michael.
The state and agrarian change in Zimbabwe's communal areas/
Michael Drinkwater.
p. cm.
Based on the author's thesis (Ph. D.)—University of East Anglia.
Includes bibliographical references (p.   ) and index.
ISBN 0–312–05350–9
1. Agriculture and state—Zimbabwe. I. Title.
HD2131. Z8D75 1991
338.1'86891—dc20   90–8934
                                                        CIP

To Sebastien and Caroline
the miracle twins

Contents

List of Figures

List of Maps

List of Tables

Preface

This book is an exploratory exercise. As one who has lived in Zimbabwe for a considerable part of my life, I welcomed the coming of independence in 1980 for the opportunity I anticipated it would bring for the full flowering of the lives of all individuals in the country, and hence the country itself. This idealistic expectation has naturally been tempered, but is one, I hope, that shall not wither completely with time. There is a great deal of human potential which lies as yet creatively caged, especially among the rural peoples. If this book makes any contribution to securing the conditions for the release of this potential it will have served its purpose.

The research project was conceived whilst I was working in the area of rural development for the Zimbabwean Government's Department of Physical Planning in Masvingo province. One periodic struggle I fought whilst setting up and conducting the work was to obtain the funds to complete it. The John Wakeford Scholarship Fund in Zimbabwe provided the initial impetus; later assistance came via a UK Overseas Research Student Award and from Misereor, a West German based episcopal organisation for development cooperation.

This research was written initially as a PhD thesis. A common complaint of those conducting such research is that in their lonely task they receive little assistance. This feeling is probably inevitable given that writing a research thesis transforms not only one's ideas but one's life. At the end, I am aware that this particular research exercise has been completed only because of the innumerable people who have assisted in smaller and larger ways.

Within the School of Development Studies, University of East Anglia, Sholto Cross stayed the course as a supervisor, requiring of him both faith and patience. John Harriss, Nick Abel and Ian Thomas also provided valuable support at different stages. Norman Long, of the Department of Rural Sociology, Wageningen Agricultural University, provided some time and space for the turning of a thesis into a book.

At the University of Zimbabwe, Angela Cheater of the Department of Sociology acted as a facilitator, and particularly during my first period of fieldwork, exercised much tolerance. In Zimbabwe too, Andrew Mlalazi, Bob Vaughan-Evans and Gertrud Scheu were invaluable enablers and I cannot thank them enough for their mutual enthusiasm for the project.

Within the Midlands province, all Agritex staff I encountered were, without exception, positive in their contribution to the research. Many also acted on occasion as interpreters or research assistants, particularly Mrs Mazonde and Aaron Nduku in Chiwundura and Msasanuri in southern Chirumhanzu. Douglas Muburinga of CADEC also interpreted for me during the valuable series of interviews I held with community leaders in the Maware area of southern Chirumhanzu. And without the people of Ture ward, Chiwundura and Chirumhanzu, especially the members of the case-study households, there would be no book. In a few instances I have used pseudonyms for farmers, but generally I have left them as real people. I should like to feel that even a little of what I gained from them has been returned.

Finally, great thanks go to Ken Wilson, who provided enthusiastic support everywhere, to Dorothy, who provided the finance when I was desperate, and to Catherine, who cared enough to kick me when I needed that too.

MICHAEL DRINKWATER

Abbreviations

AEO	Agricultural Extension Officer
AFC	Agricultural Finance Corporation
Agritex	Department of Agricultural Technical and Extension Services
CADEC	Catholic Development Commission
CIMMYT	International Maize and Wheat Improvement Centre
CNC	Chief Native Commissioner
DERUDE	Department of Rural Development
DR&SS	Department of Research and Specialist Services
EW	(Agricultural) Extension Worker
FSR	Farming Systems Research
FTL	Farmer Training Leader
LHA	(Native) Land Husbandry Act
MLGRUD	Ministry of Local Government, Rural and Urban Development
MLRRD	Ministry of Lands, Resettlement and Rural Development (now defunct)
NAD	Native Affairs Department
NC	Native Commissioner
NFAZ	National Farmers Association of Zimbabwe
PAEO	Provincial Agricultural Extension Officer
RAEO	Regional Agricultural Extension Officer
RF	Rhodesian Front
SMS	Subject Matter Specialist
UDP	United Democratic Party
VIDCO	Village Development Committee
WADCO	Ward Development Committee
ZANU (PF)	Zimbabwe African National Union (PF)

1 Introduction: The Past, Present and Future in Zimbabwe's Communal Areas

This book examines the impact government policy has had on agrarian change in Zimbabwe's peasant farming areas over the course of this century. My intention is to find a means of linking an analysis of past and present change with a practical interest in the future. Since such a task accords with the telos of critical theory, that of Jürgen Habermas has been used to inform the theory and method used in this study.[1]

THE RESEARCH ELEMENTS: EMPIRICAL ANALYSIS, PRACTICAL INTEREST AND METHOD

Zimbabwe's communal areas occupy 41.8 per cent of the country's total land area, or just under 50 per cent of the agricultural land. The communal areas contain, however, a disproportionately large percentage of Zimbabwe's population; in 1987, 56 per cent of some nine million people.[2] A large proportion of the remainder of the population are, moverover, tied to the areas, either directly as migrant workers or more indirectly by kinship relations and support networks. The future of Zimbabwe and the majority of its people are therefore closely linked to processes of social and economic change in the communal areas. This is particularly so as greater human and ecological vulnerability is experienced within these areas, which are diverse socially and environmentally, than anywhere else in the country.

The depth and spread of this vulnerability is a comparatively recent historical phenomenon. Before this century, Zimbabwe's Shona societies were by no means static; far from it, as Beach (1971, 1977, 1983, 1986) especially has shown, they were surprisingly dynamic. However, this flux was an indicator of the resilience rather than the

1

vulnerability of these societies. Environmental, economic and social fluctuations and changes did create social stress on occasion, but societies were usually able to adapt and survive. It is only in this century, since the advent of the colonial state, that the parameters of social and environmental change have altered radically and transformed the scale of insecurity that is experienced. Women, children, the poor, the elderly, and the less educated, are the groups particularly affected.

It is beyond dispute, therefore, that the impact on indigenous societies of the structures of the modern state and capitalist economy has been immense. What is disputed is exactly *how* change has occurred, *how much* has occurred, and how much scope rural peoples have in their responses to external interventions. With regard to all three questions, the structuralist approaches of the 1970s, which largely wrote off the ability of peasantries to make any significant choices in their lives, are now being increasingly discredited. In Africa, as Hyden (1980, 1983) among others has stressed, peasantries are far from having become powerless. Zimbabwe is atypical, however, for there was a larger settler population than elsewhere in sub-Saharan Africa except South Africa. This means the indigenous population was forced into a particularly intimate relationship with the colonial state. The state could not be avoided. Some response – resistance, deception, active or passive accommodation – was necessary. And as will be shown, quite how in different areas people responded and the state counter-responded influences peoples' attitudes and actions today.

Those whose lives are referred to in this book are drawn from a study region which covers the central and southern parts of the Midlands province of Zimbabwe (Maps 1 and 2). Historical material was gathered from documentary sources, with less use of oral accounts than I would now desire.[3] Actual fieldwork was carried out in two phases. During a preparatory period from November 1984 to February 1985, work was carried out in the Ture ward of the Runde communal area, Zvishavane district. More detailed comparative research was then performed during the 1986/7 growing season in the Chirumhanzu communal area, Mvuma district, and the Chiwundura communal area, Gweru district. In this work, which is historically contextuated, the production relationships within and between selected case-study households, farmer organisations and government institutions, particularly the Department of Agricultural Technical and Extension Services (Agritex), which is used as an institutional case study, are analysed.

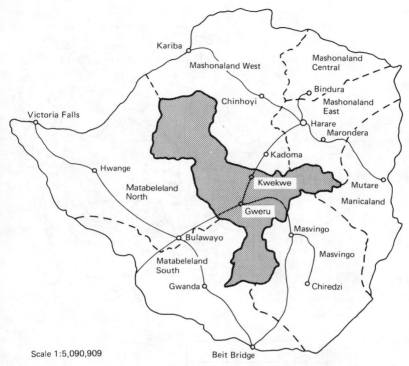

Map 1   Midlands Province – location map

Although an analysis of the impact of government policies on social and economic change in Zimbabwe's communal areas is the primary substantive task of this study, it is not the sole reason for the investigation. The research also has a normative aim.

Social science fieldwork requires one to engage others in inter-action, hence demanding time and commitment from them. If one places such a demand on people there is a responsibility attached to the way in which one uses the material so gleaned, although frequently reseachers are in a position to ignore this. One manner of acknowledging a responsibility towards those one works with, espe-cially people in such disadvantaged circumstances, is to have a practical interest in advancing social justice, or 'radically improving human existence'. This is a fundamental precept of critical theory (Bernstein, 1976, p. 180). Admitting such an interest in those one is working with, however, creates a serious methodological problem: in

Natural region	
I	High rainfall
IIa & b	Moderate rainfall
III	Moderate but erratic rainfall
IV	Low rainfall
V	Low and erratic rainfall

Map 2   Study areas

a research exercise how does one integrate a practical interest with an empirical analysis which is both rigorous and open to evaluation?

The second part of the question shall be dealt with first. In much qualitative anthropological or sociological research this question, which turns on the central role that the researcher's *interpretation* of empirical data performs, is surprisingly underplayed. It is assumed the researcher can play a double role, that is, one that is simultaneously participatory and objectivating. The participant observer, although engaging in interaction, can still report on the research as a 'disinterested observer'. The degree to which the researcher's interpretation of her/his subjects' views of the world is coloured by already-held concepts and feelings, is an issue which has received little inquiry in agrarian research. Occasionally when an interpretation becomes particularly controversial, for instance, as with some of Margaret Mead's work, attention is cast on the issue. But it is not the focus of methodological attention it is in other areas of social science – for instance, educational research.[4]

This hermeneutic issue is one Habermas tackles in his main work, his 'theory of communicative action', and is one of the reasons I have drawn upon his work here. He envisages the role of the social scientist becoming that of a *'virtual* participant' rather than a participant *observer*. The distinction between the two terms is defined more clearly later in the chapter. What is of importance here is Habermas's claim that a social scientist adopting the stance of a 'virtual participant' can reach an interpretative understanding which is rationally defensible. This would seem to suggest, too, a possible way of dealing with the first question that was raised. This is the tension identified between analytical and normative interests – what is and what might (ought to) be.

To summarise, then, the three main areas of investigation in the book are:

(1) the nature of the relationship between government policy and agrarian change in Zimbabwe's communal areas since the beginning of the colonial era;
(2) whether there are possibilities for improving the nature of this relationship in order to improve the quality of the outcomes;
(3) the type of methodology, and consequently also epistemological (and indeed, theoretical) perspective, appropriate for examining these two interconnected analytical areas of what is and what might be.

CRITICAL THEORY AND AGRARIAN CHANGE

A note is needed as to why I have seen critical theory as pertinent to the above areas of investigation. This is especially so considering the empirical emphasis of Habermas's work is on what he perceives as the 'legitimation crisis' occurring within the advanced capitalist societies of Western Europe. Nevertheless Habermas claims universal applicability for aspects of his work and I believe there are insights to be gained from employing some elements in the Zimbabwean context. First, Habermas's development of Max Weber's argument on the nature of post-Enlightenment processes of societal rationalisation, will be used to illuminate the empirical analysis. Second, as stated, critical theory provides a means of connecting the analysis with a practical interest in the future. Third, the concept of researcher as 'virtual participant' provides a model of how the social scientist might carry out social research in a way which is both objectivating and cognisant of the researcher's prior beliefs and values. Fourth, Habermas has maintained the interdisciplinary orientation favoured by the Frankfurt School (Held, 1980, p. 33), from which he comes, and this meets the requirements of my own project.

It should be noted that the decision to employ aspects of Habermas's critical theory in this research project was made subsequent to the project being started. I came to use critical theory because it appeared to provide an appropriate way of dealing with the paradigmatic and procedural problems I was encountering. Initially my intention was to carry out the difficult task of trying analytically to link present reality with future possibilities, through a development planning framework based on John Friedmann's concept of 'social learning' (1973, 1978, 1979). A development or research strategy would emphasise a 'mutual learning' relationship of dialogue between planner or researcher and the local community. Mutual learning about present social conditions would stimulate an attitude of reflection. This would help participants understand their social world and so be in an enhanced position to act upon it. Paulo Freire's (1972, 1974) adult literacy concept of 'consciousisation' is similar. However, attempting to develop a normative-analytic framework and test it simultaneously is unsatisfactory: how does one evaluate whether or not one is seeing in a situation simply that which one wants?[5] After failing to find a satisfactory solution to this dilemma, I concluded it was less schizophrenic to use an already conceived theory, and from it to generate a series of claims about the phenomena at issue. Once tested, these claims can then be modified as felt appropriate.

In the remainder of this introductory chapter, the arguments relating to the three areas to be investigated in the book are sketched out in more detail.

THE PEASANTRY AND THE STATE

As a means of introducing the book's central argument regarding the relationship between government policy and agrarian change, I wish to draw attention to some conclusions of recent debates on the relationship between the peasantry and the state elsewhere in Africa. Country reference shall be limited to the Tanzanian case. Tanzania is instructive as, like Zimbabwe, it has a declared socialist ideology, but having attained independence in 1961 has had a significantly longer post-independence experience. The discussion highlights in a comparative context some of the reasons why I believe critical theory has potential to throw insight on state–people relations. It will also enable me to introduce Habermas's concepts of purposive-rational action and purposive rationality, which are central to the argument that shall be outlined here.

The Penetration of Capitalism

Most of the leading debates in the last twenty years on the nature of social change in Africa have focused on the structural issue of class formation and development. Macro-level theories deal with 'imperialism, *dependencia* and international centre–periphery relations' (van Binsbergen and Geschiere, 1985, p. 1). This focus on national and international economic and political relations is, however, at a level too removed to be helpful in illuminating the complexities of social change within rural societies.

At the level of rural societies themselves, theorising centres on what is happening to them, what should or should not be done to (or for) them, or a combination of both. Theorising about what is happening to them commonly has looked at how capitalist relations of production introduced by colonial regimes have affected the indigenous societies (e.g. Seddon, 1978; and van Binsbergen and Geschiere, 1985). The theorising about what should or should not be done to peasant societies frequently has been part of a search to identify ways of achieving a socialist transformation of society (e.g. for Zimbabwe, Riddell Commission, 1981; Bush and Cliffe, 1984; Cliffe, 1986; Munslow, 1985). Among theorists who have combined both elements, Hyden (1980; 1983) (and see the debate between Kasfir, 1986; Cliffe, 1987; Williams, 1987; and Hyden, 1986, 1987; as well as Geschiere, 1984) is perhaps the most well known. These theoretical debates all take place within the paradigm of production. From them the following conclusions are pertinent to the argument I wish to construct here.

One of the most influential schools of debate about the nature of agrarian change in Africa has evolved around the work of the French

Marxist anthropologists, particularly Rey, Terray, Meillassoux and Godelier. Notwithstanding their differences, the research of the French anthropologists has centred on the conceptualisation of how the advent of capitalism in Africa (predominantly in conjunction with colonialism) has resulted in an *'articulation'* of the capitalist mode of production with indigenous lineage modes of production. Variations in the nature of both in different contexts has resulted in a wide variety of outcomes, but all are characterised by the fact that there has been no complete *replacement* of previous lineage modes of production. Van Binsbergen and Geschiere (1985) summarise the French Marxist anthropologists' concept of an articulation of modes of production as follows:

> in their view, modes of production do not replace each other in the development of a society; instead, a new mode of production can develop – can 'establish its dominance' – on the basis of the continued functioning of older, 'subordinate', modes of production. To put it more concretely, in this view the modern history of Africa can be characterised as a process during which the dominance of the capitalist mode of production was established all over the continent. But this capitalist expansion certainly did not bring about the immediate demolition of the old modes of production in Africa. On the contrary, the old relations of production were 'used', as it were, for the further expansion of capitalism. It is precisely because of the continuing cohesion of the old production communities (no matter how transformed) that specific forms of capitalist exploitation are possible – notably the withdrawal of relatively cheap labour and market products from the village economy. (pp. 4–5)

The Marxist concept 'mode of production' is conventionally differentiated into two components, the forces and relations of production:

> *Productive forces* consist in the labour power of producers, technical knowledge insofar as it is converted into means and techniques that heighten productivity, and organisational knowledge insofar as it is employed for the mobilisation, qualification, and organisation of labour power. The *relations of production*, on the other hand, are the institutions and social mechanisms that determine how labour power can be combined with the available means of production at a given level of productive forces. (McCarthy, 1978, pp. 238–9)

The relations of production as 'an expression of the distribution of power' are established through the form of social political organisation – the 'principle of organisation', as Habermas terms it (McCarthy, 1978, pp. 239, 242). The capitalist form of social political organisation – the modern capitalist state – if it is to become hegemonic has to destroy entirely lineage-based social political structures. In Africa this has not been achieved. Hyden (1980, p. 21) makes this point in his examination of the impact of capitalism on African economies by stressing the distinction between *penetration* and *integration*. Penetration – the process of articulation, to use the French Marxist terminology – implies the juxtaposition, but not necessarily the assimilation or integration of different cultural meaning systems. The predominant occurrence of penetration rather than integration – even in francophone Africa where there was a greater colonial stress on assimilation – suggests there has been little open communication between the societies that brought capitalism and those it was imposed upon. And if different groups have different worldviews and do not communicate with each other, then they do not understand each other either.

A consequence of this lack of understanding is the tendency throughout Africa, first by colonial elites and then by their western-educated indigenous replacements, to regard as backwards and 'irrational' the efforts of peasant societies to adhere to and reproduce some form of lineage or client-oriented principle of organisation. By assuming rural societies to be backward and irrational those within government bureaucracies are then provided with an excuse to deal with them in a high-handed and instrumental way. In countries such as Tanzania, new local institutions – councils, cooperatives, development committees – have been established to create, in principle, a more participatory and democratic government structure. These institutions are, however, often paid no more than lip-service. An example is provided by Finucane (1974), who was informed by officials in the Mwanza region that the role of these institutions should be geared to the 'development understanding' of the people: 'officials should not alter their approach until the people have become more "rational"' (p. 62).

Such reasoning provides a ready enough excuse for a reversion to – or a continuation of – an authoritarian style of government. When Finucane carried out his study in the late 1960s, some seven or eight years after Tanzania's independence in 1961, he concluded from his observations of 'the innumerable actions of officials ... that the approach of the bureaucracy was in no way different from that of the colonial officials in the 1950s' (p. 62).

This issue of bureaucratic style (and hence also the nature of policy actions) is obscured by many Marxist writers who focus instead on the interests of civil servants. The penchant for political and bureaucratic elites to use their positions of power to further their own and their patrons' interests has led to a dilemma for such theorists. How should these elites' interests be construed in class terms? (Cliffe, 1977). For Tanzania, Shivji (1976) coined the phrase 'bureaucratic bourgeoisie' and connected their economic interests with those of the petty bourgeoisie. Debates since then have revolved around whether the term is appropriate (Saul, 1979; Gibbon and Necosmos, 1985), and whether this elite has sufficient economic power to be considered a class capable of controlling the state (Cliffe, 1977). Whilst this debate has some substance, it also obscures the fact that what and how policy actions are performed by government officials is not necessarily directly contingent upon the particular class interests of the officials.

Pratt (1979, p. 206) develops this theme further. He points out, with reference to the failure of the ujamaa villagisation policy in Tanzania, that it is mistaken to assume that the actual or alleged consequences of a policy were those intended by the policy-makers. Furthermore, people – even bureaucrats – frequently do face real dilemmas in deciding how to act. Whilst they are neither 'saints nor aesthetes', in 'an inefficient and resource deficient bureaucracy' officials, even if willing, face huge problems in getting things done and hence maintaining any enthusiasm for the job (Pratt, 1979, pp. 213–14, 227–32). In such resource-stressed situations, labelling the peasantry ignorant and irrational becomes an expedient justification for being authoritarian. Administrators justify autocracy as 'saving' already constrained time and resources.

To summarise, then: although all indigenous societies in Africa have been penetrated by capitalism, none of these societies have been entirely transformed. They are not fully capitalist, but neither has a lineage organisational principle proved impervious to market and bureaucratic forces. It is appropriate therefore to speak of *forms* of production, in which the influence of the lineage or client-based organisational principle persists, existent within an overall capitalist mode of production.[6]

New, educated indigenous elites have inherited a commitment to the particular process of societal modernisation that is peculiar to western societies. This commitment contains a positivistic attitude towards questions of truth, knowledge and rationality. The peasantry, who have a somewhat different outlook, are cast as inferior, and this justifies, across the divide of independence, continuities in agrarian policy approaches.

This literature, I suggest, supports the argument that it is a specific process of *social rationalisation* which is responsible for continuities in bureaucratic style and agrarian policy approaches in many African countries. This process has occurred with the rise of the modern state and the spread of capitalism in Africa.

As the core argument of Habermas's theory of communicative action begins with such an assertion about the correlation of modernisation and rationalisation processes, it is to this argument that I shall now turn.

Purposive Rationalisation and Policy Continuities

The task of critical theory as seen by Habermas and his forerunners in the Frankfurt School was to oppose, through critique, the spread of a technocratic consciousness and associated forms of 'purposive-rational' rationalisation in the modern era. (Horkheimer, 1968, p. x; Thompson and Held, 1982, p. 5; McCarthy, 1978, pp. 8–12). An important starting-point for the Frankfurt School theorists was Max Weber's central thesis that the form of rationalisation process which Weber took to be basic to modernisation, *Zweckrationalitat*, has too often led to the curtailment of political self-determination and freedom (Bernstein, 1985, p. 21). 'Purposive-rational rationalisation' (henceforth largely referred to as 'purposive rationalisation'), which approximates Weber's concept of *Zweckrationalitat*, means the rationalisation of either of two types of goal-directed actions. *Instrumental* actions are concerned with the technical efficiency of an intervention into a 'complex of circumstances and events' (Habermas, 1984, p. 285). *Strategic* actions are concerned with the consistency of choice between suitable means, according to (implicitly) chosen values and the likely efficacy of influencing the decisions of others (p. 285).

With the process of modernisation which has occurred in the Occidental world since the Enlightenment, these two forms of purposive-rational action have been institutionalised in the structures of the modern capitalist state (Habermas, 1984, p. 217). The development of the apparatus of the modern state leads to the transformation of social (or 'practical') concerns into technical issues. Decisions regarding these issues then become the preserve of politicians or senior officials. The public sphere is at best able to legitimise the polity, but the nature of policy decisions themselves remains beyond 'the authority of rational discussion in the public sphere' (McCarthy, 1978, p. 11).

In Zimbabwe the modern state did not develop from within the Shona societies which predominated in the country, but was externally imposed by the white settlers. This in itself was unexpected for the Shona. Even more so was the way this new government made decisions affecting them, without involving their leaders in the decision process. The Shona peoples had had virtually no previous cultural exposure to the values of capitalist modernisation,[7] and hence the purposive-rational approach of the new bureaucratic administration was incomprehensible to them (Vambe, 1972). But since the modern bureaucratic consciousness places no value on the development of social understanding, this lack of comprehension was denigrated by the colonial administration as the outcome of being primitive. Likewise, the reluctance of the Shona peoples to accept the rightness of this imposed approach was taken as evidence of their adherence to irrational superstition.

Since independence there has been a large turnover of administration personnel, but the value placed on formal education and the modern attitudes, skills and scientific knowledge it inculcates, is perhaps even greater than previously. The new bureaucrats may be more aware of the nature of rural societies through their lineage links, but this factor will not by itself result in government agencies operating in a less purposive-rational manner.[8]

From the above synopsis four assertions will now be made concerning the nature of agrarian change in Zimbabwe, which are in accord with Habermas's interpretation of the concept of *Zweckrationalitat*. The first, a starting premise, is that, through the expansion of the power of the state, it is government policy that has been the most important determinant of social and economic change within the communal areas this century.

The second assertion is that there are many similarities in the content of the post-independence agrarian policies of the 1980s – for instance, in the areas of land use, conservation, pastoral management, afforestation and agricultural extension – with those of the pre-independence period.

The third assertion is that since the rise of the modern state agrarian policies have been formulated and implemented according to a purposive rationality.

The fourth assertion is that this attitude has ensured that through-out this century policy actions[9] have been carried out in ignorance of the local environmental knowledge peasant farmers possess and utilise in their production systems. In the renewal of policy actions, learning from the social, economic and environmental consequences of previous experience has been neglected.

Taken together, these assertions are used to construct the argu-ment that it is because successive agrarian policies implemented by pre-and post-independence governments have been pervaded by a purposive rationality that there are strong similarities in these policies. This is despite their failure to alleviate agrarian problems and despite the continued offering of forms of resistance to them by the rural population.

For this argument to be granted credibility there are several claims attached to it which need to be upheld. These are:

(1) that there are similarities between pre-and post-independence policies (Chapters 2 and 3);
(2) that these policies have tended to create or aggravate, rather than alleviate, communal area environmental, economic and social problems (Chapters 2, 4 and 5);
(3) that the rural population has withheld legitimation of these policies (Chapters 2, 5 and 6).
(4) that policy initiatives have been rationalised in a purposive-rational manner (Chapters 2, 3, 4 and 7).

The chapters indicated are those in which empirical evidence and theoretical argumentation are advanced concerning each of these claims.

THE PEASANTRY AND THE STATE: ALTERNATIVE POSSIBILITIES

The above argument dealing with the first subject area examined in the book does not, however, provide a basis for the second, the connection of an analysis of what has and is occurring to what might be possible in the future. In this second area of concern, whether there are possibili-ties for improving the nature of the relationship between state and peasantry, the application of critical theory is again important.

In his empirical usage of the concept of purposive-rational action, Habermas's position is similar to that of Weber's. Where Habermas differentiates his position clearly is in the way he proceeds and goes on to integrate empirical and normative theoretical elements. He does this by making his most important sociological claim. That is that:

> What has happened in modern societies (and continues to happen at an alarming rate) is a *selective* process of rationalisation – where purposive-rational rationalisation prevails, encroaches upon, and deforms the lifeworld of everyday life. (Bernstein, 1985, p. 23; my emphasis)

Habermas is thus claiming that the process of purposive rationalisation that has become institutionally dominant in the modern capitalist state is not the only possible form of societal rationalisation. He holds that the particular course of events which has led to the systematic domination of forms of purposive-rational action, must be distinguished from the 'horizon of possibilities' to which 'modern structures of consciousness' have given rise (Habermas, 1984, p. 221).

These 'structures of consciousness' have resulted from our 'disenchantment' with mythical and religious-metaphysical world views. Disenchantment with such unified world views set in with our ability to differentiate between three 'worlds' – an external *objective* world, an external *social* world, and an internal *subjective* world (Habermas, 1984, pp. 48–53). Differentiation means that we are able to vary the nature of our action orientations depending on the attitude we assume. If actions are oriented towards the objective material world, they are cognitive-instrumental in nature and concerned with technical or factual knowledge. When we act socially, we are concerned with social values, behavioural norms and moral-practical knowledge. And when we are concerned to express our inner feelings and experiences, we draw upon aesthetic-practical knowledge.

To each of these three worlds or cultural value spheres pertain not only particular modes of action but also rationality types. *Selective* rationalisation occurs when one value sphere 'predominates to such an extent that it subjects [the others] to a form of rationality that is alien to them' (Habermas, 1984, p. 240). In the west, the process of societal modernisation given rise to by the Englightenment was hijacked by the *particular* event of the growth of capitalism. And it is capitalism which has promoted

> a pattern of rationalisation such that cognitive-instrumental rationality penetrates beyond the economy and the state into other spheres of life and there enjoys a pre-eminence at the expense of moral-practical and aesthetic-practical rationality. (Habermas, 1984, p. 233)

It is the penetration of the private sphere, the 'lifeworld', by the 'systemic' that Habermas is particularly concerned about. The *lifeworld* is the 'taken-for-granted universe of daily social activity . . . within which everyday conduct unfolds' (Giddens, 1985, p. 101). By providing a source of 'situation definitions' (Habermas, 1984, p. 70) or 'implicit knowledge' (p. 335), the lifeworld enables social actors to reach understanding in their interaction. The attainment of understanding and subsequent action-orienting decisions is the object of a 'communicative rationality'. Thus the lifeworld facilitates such a rationality. The 'colonisation' of the lifeworld by the institutions of capitalist (and now state socialist) societies has resulted in the suppression of a communicative or moral-practical rationality. In this so-called post-Enlightenment era, this has resulted not only in the development of authoritarian and coercive institutional structures, but threatens social reproduction itself. Habermas develops this prognostication and the response to it – that there are alternative possibilities – through the following argument.

Modern structures of consciousness are characterised by our ability to reflect upon and examine the rationality of actions. When we do not understand or accept something we may seek clarification or challenge it through communication and the use of language. In the objective world of 'existing states of affairs', we can challenge *validity claims* of *truth*; in the 'social world of norms' we can challenge validity claims about *normative rightness*; and we can challenge validity claims about the *truthfulness* or *sincerity* of expressions of inner feelings and desires (Habermas, 1984, p. 51). In all the cultural value spheres, therefore, claims can be challenged through processes of argumentation or 'discourse', which are oriented to reaching understanding. Discourse is a special type of what Habermas terms 'communicative action'.

> the concept of *communicative action* refers to the interaction of at least two subjects capable of speech and action who establish interpersonal relations (whether by verbal or extra-verbal means). The actors seek to reach an understanding about the action situation and their plans of action in order to coordinate their actions by way of agreement. (Habermas, 1984, p. 86)

This means that communicative action is oriented to others; it is 'intrinsically dialogical' (Bernstein, 1985, p. 18). Furthermore, Habermas claims that without this other-oriented activity, social life would break down. Communicative action is essential to social reproduction:

> If we assume that the human species maintains itself through the socially coordinated activities of its members and that this coordination is established through communication then the reproduction of the species also requires satisfying the conditions of a rationality inherent in communicative action. (Habermas, 1984, pp. ix and 397)

In contrast to communicative action, purposive-rational action, which is either instrumental or strategic in nature, is oriented to self only – that is, is intrinsically monological. The systemic institutionalisation of forms of purposive-rational action has assisted the development of modern class structures. Thus the constraints to communicative action and achieving a better balance between 'system' and 'lifeworld' orientations lie in the 'relations of force' that are embedded in and distort 'structures of communication'. In contrast to the rationalisation of purposive-rational actions – the process of *Zweckrationalitat* that Weber took to be basic to modernisation – the rationalisation of communicative action is 'radically and categorically different':

> Rationalisation here means extirpating [rooting-out] those relations of force that are inconspicuously set in the very structures of communication and that prevent conscious settlement of conflicts and consensual regulation of conflicts by means of interpsychic as well as interpersonal communication. (Habermas, 1979, pp. 119–20; in Bernstein, 1985, p. 21)

In short, possibilities for the improvement of the participative decisiveness of people in society depend on how much these relations of force and systematic distortions of communication can be overcome.

That there are alternative possibilities for societal rationalisation is the most challenging sociological claim Habermas makes in his theory of communicative action. How can such a claim be grounded, in order for it to be explored, in the Zimbabwean context?

In the general context of sub-Saharan Africa, reference has been made to the current broad agreement on the mode of production debate that although the capitalist mode of production has been articulated with (and hence penetrated) lineage forms of production, no all-encompassing integration or assimilation has occurred. In

Africa, Hyden sees this lack of assimilation as a constraint to 'national development':

> It is because I do not recognise capitalism as already prevalent in Africa that I am ready to consider it as a progressive force. The peasant mode of production is unable to satisfy Africa's longer-term needs and it needs to be transcended and transformed. (1987, p. 665)

Hyden's argument derives from his belief that the persistence of patron–client relations – what he terms the 'economy of affection'[10] – is responsible for the continued inefficiencies of market and bureaucratic operations. In effect, the economic market place has been replaced by a political one (Hyden, 1980, p. 220) and healthy economies cannot be generated this way. Hyden's conclusion to this argument is that there has therefore been too little rather than too much capitalism in sub-Saharan Africa. There is

> an urgent need to strengthen those forces in society that enable the development of a ruling class who [*sic*] is free from the constraints imposed by the present pre-capitalist formations. As argued in this book, the only force capable of addressing this issue in a relatively short perspective is the market. The latter promotes the rise of a local bourgeoisie, encourages greater effectiveness in the public sector through the diversification of structural mechanisms for development, and promotes behavioural changes throughout society, leaving people on different backgrounds more ready for alternative social action. (1983, pp. 197–8)

What Hyden is advocating is the very process of societal rationalisation which Weber and the Frankfurt School philosphers are so pessimistic about. For if such a process merely involves the institutionalisation of a purposive rationality, then, whether it is state-led or market-led, the net effect will be the same – the constriction of peasant societies' remaining autonomy and ability to exercise initiatives of their own. As Williams (1982a; 1987) points out, Africa has not been short of attempts to achieve national development through the panacea of transforming the peasantry. 'Both capitalist and socialist development strategies require peasants to provide the resources necessary for the development of the urban industrial economy' (1982a, p. 80). Such strategies almost inevitably end up to the peasants' detriment, and when they fail 'will, in all probability, be blamed on the peasants and their inherent backwardness' (1987, p. 653).

It would appear, therefore, that the ground-rules from which Hyden develops his argument are ill-conceived. His analysis is consequently insightful but misguided. For there is little new he has to offer Africa's peasant societies apart from yet further emasculation. This is no solution to overcoming the deficiencies of the 'economy of affection'. As occurred in Zimbabwe in the early years of this century, the peasantry are likely to contribute more to the national economy through incentive than through threat. When options in the formal economy are devalued, as Robert Bates (1983) argues, then peasants retreat and 'seeking refuge in the most private of all institutions – the family – pursue private solutions to the problem of economic welfare' (p. 133). If governments wish to turn the peasantry outwards then institutionalised dialogue as a way of encouraging 'alternative social action' is preferable to institutionalised force. This is the counter-argument which can be derived from Habermas's critical theory.

Hyden (1983) recommends Korten's concept of a 'learning organisation' which 'tries to build on what people already know and the resources they already possess' (p. 157–8). To do so, to build on the knowledge and resources peasants already possess, requires, however, a commitment to dialogue which is absent from the task-oriented behaviour typical of most bureaucracies. The development of learning structures is dependent therefore on the transformation of the institutional structures of African political economies rather than the transformation of the peasantry.

The likelihood of this occurring may seem remote, but are there other alternatives for improving the welfare of Africa's rural societies? If critical theory is to offer hope rather than to be dismissed out of hand, then one must examine whether there are possibilities of developing within institutions a commitment to dialogue. Here these issues are investigated from Chapter 4 onwards through use of the method of critique Habermas recommends, namely the challenging of validity claims through argumentation, and through an evaluation of the activities of Zimbabwe's agricultural extension agency.

CRITICAL THEORY AND METHOD

In the previous two sections, the two interlinked areas of the empirical analysis have been laid out. The final area inquired into in the thesis is the nature of an appropriate methodology and epistemological perspective for the analysis. There are several reasons why I have posed methodology and epistemology as subjects of investigation. First, because after the preparatory stage of the fieldwork I became dissatisfied with the quantitative method I had used and the positivist theory of knowledge it implicitly upholds. Second, this dissatisfaction prompted my interest in applying critical theory, with its specific emphasis on challenging claims of truth, norms and intention. Third, because it examines relations, critical theory demands the use of an 'interactive' methodology. The researcher must be concerned to provoke engagement with the subjects of investigation. Fourth, a methodology oriented to learning is never complete. Further refinement is always required, both from the lessons of experience and in order to adapt to each new context. Thus in this research project the methodology employed for the second and main component of the fieldwork was at best an exploratory exercise in how one might use critical theory to inform research practice.

These four reasons for treating methodology as a subject of inquiry will be taken together in a brief discussion. To begin, a comment is necessary on the initial stage of fieldwork. This work consisted of investigating, on behalf of the Midlands Provincial Development Committee, a proposed land use scheme in the Ture ward of the Runde communal area, Zvishavane district. Support was obtained in particular from the Department of Physical Planning and the Department of Agricultural Technical and Extension Services. This support was essential for my attempt to analyse the effects of agrarian policy.

The initial fieldwork itself consisted of a census survey carried out in the ward during November–December 1984, followed up by three sample arable land use surveys and discussion meetings with village development committees (VIDCOs), farmer groups, women's project groups and local political leaders. A final project report was prepared for the Midlands Provincial Development Committee in March 1985.

The aim of the questionnaire survey was to obtain 'scientifically valid' social and economic information about the ward. In the event I doubt the method would stand up to rigorous evaluation, although the information gathered was more accurate than the 1982 official census data which had been used to delineate ward and VIDCO boundaries.

However, what was most unsatisfactory about the questionnaire survey was that although it provided information *about* the world of the people in Ture ward, only rarely were glimpses provided *into* their world. The various discussions held were more enlightening but only sharpened my perception that I was an externality to the community. I was consuming people's time and offering little in return. Moreover my knowledge base was wrong. I was approaching issues from a perspective foreign to the people I was dealing with and it was blocking my desire to penetrate and understand their world.

Once one starts considering one's status as a researcher, further questions follow. What should one's role be in interactions with those one is researching? How should one interpret and react to their actions – what they say and do? And, can I play a role which is sufficiently relevant to them for me to be able to penetrate their world and come to understand it?

In social science research, these questions can only begin to be answered through the use of qualitative methods. None of these questions are original, but as they have no certain answers they are always worth repeating. Perhaps the major problem with research methodology and the subsequent so-called knowledge that is produced, is that they are not often enough considered controversial issues. In much social science data-gathering work, even if the data is to be collected from people, any debate on methods focuses on technical matters rather than the issue of how one interacts with people.

There is still a mythology that empirical social science research can be objective and 'value free' (Fay, 1975; Bernstein, 1976). This belief is part of the purposive-rational consciousness I wish to critique. In other words, the belief in the value of 'objective', quantitative information is linked to the belief that such information will enhance technical control (Fay, 1975, p. 44). Consider the Ture ward research exercise again. Information about livestock numbers was collected in the census questionnaire survey I conducted. The area defined by Agritex as land appropriate for grazing was mapped and measured by them. Then according to recommended stocking rates a judgement could theoretically be made as to whether there was sufficient land for grazing purposes in the ward, and whether additional land should also be sought. In this case the device served the purpose; it enabled a recommendation to be made that the ward development committee (WADCO) be supported in efforts to acquire adjacent ranchland.[11] But the 'promise' of technical control inherent in the exercise of collecting livestock numbers, mapping grazing land, and working out stocking rates, is a delusion. For instance, Ian Scoones has shown from research he has carried out in

Mazvihwa communal area, Zvishavane district, that animals obtain much of their fodder from key resource areas *outside* those demarcated for grazing schemes (Scoones, 1987). The concept of stocking rates based on *fixed* carrying capacities also has no ecological grounding when one examines the issue.

This example supports the argument presented by Heron (1981) that

> questionnaires and all such instruments unilaterally designed by researchers will simply rest on their prior norms and values. And if the researchers make no attempt to determine whether these norms and values and hence the design of the questionnaire, are acceptable to those who are invited to fill it in,[12] then any statements about the respondents made by the researchers on the basis of the questionnaire results will have indeterminate validity . . . grossly distorted conclusions may emerge . . . For if the researchers are not themselves the respondents, then the conclusions will be 'truths' that hang in a curious void – alienated from the values of the researchers, and from the actual and different values of the respondents. (p. 33)

But what are the alternatives? Subjectivism, and therefore relativism? In much anthropological and sociological work, if the attempt is made to escape this trap it is through emphasising the 'disinterested' aspect of the researcher as 'participant observer'. This model was originally formulated by Schutz, a phenomenologist. Schutz also introduced the concept of 'Lebenswelt' or lifeworld, which is redefined by Habermas: 'All interpretation of this world is based on a stock of previous experiences of it, our own and those handed down to us by parents or teachers; these experiences in the form of "knowledge at hand" function as schemes of reference' (in Bernstein, 1976, p. 146). Schutz thus acknowledges that a researcher who participates in the culture of others is in danger of employing a very different reference scheme in her or his interpretation of events and speech acts in that culture. Nevertheless, Schutz still holds that objectivity may be achieved if the researcher 'adopts a *theoretical attitude* that enables him to raise himself above the lifeworld perspective of both his everyday practice and that under investigation' (Habermas, 1984, p. 122).

The model of the disinterested observer or participant observer requires the social scientist to engage in schizophrenic behaviour. One is expected to break with a 'natural' or 'performative' attitude and, by adopting a theoretical attitude, seen by Schutz as 'the value system of the sciences', to take up a position beyond one's own or any lifeworld (Habermas, 1984, pp. 122–3).

The first of three principal objections to this model is that it is impossible to achieve. We cannot shed our own private skins quite so simply. Schutz himself acknowledges that 'this ideal is a strenuous one that is frequently violated in practice' (Bernstein, 1976, p. 167). Furthermore, if the researcher did practise rigorously the attitude of a disinterested observer, the researcher's role would be reduced to a merely descriptive one. Any judgement or critical evaluation of the social world being perceived would have to be avoided. This is because such interpretations of social situations, which are in fact made all the time in research, are coloured by the values and pre-interpretations one brings into the situation (Bernstein, 1976, p. 168). But if one holds to the model, and restricts analysis to description of why people do what they do, then 'the upshot . . . is profoundly conservative, because it leads to reconciling people to their social order' (Fay, 1975, p. 91).

On these two of the three objections, Fay (1975, pp. 93–6) suggests that a critical social science should have three characteristics. One, it should be interpretive in nature, and therefore oriented to understanding a social world from the viewpoint of the actors concerned. Two, it should recognise that many of the actions people perform are caused by social conditions they have little control over, and that people are also unconscious of many of the implications of their actions. A critical theory therefore has to seek understanding of the nature of social relations. Three, a critical social science has to recognise that social theory is interconnected with social practice and therefore 'the truth or falsity of these theories will be partly determined by whether they are in fact translated into action' (p. 95).

If these characteristics are to be used to guide a field research methodology, then the interpretive requirement can only be achieved through *interaction* between the researcher and social actors concerned. For the researcher to penetrate the understanding others have of their own world, the first requisite of interaction is the build-up of 'mutual trust'. To seek understanding of the nature of social relations, the second characteristic, requires a *process of critique*. The third characteristic implies the researcher should have a commitment towards *'enabling change'* – 'change towards better relationships, towards a more just and rational society' (Gibson, 1986, p. 2).

In Africa, most of the critical theorists who have carried out field research have been Marxists. The praxis of Marxist theory (characteristic three) is class formation and struggle, and to understand these there is more emphasis in Marxist research on critique (characteristic two) than on interpretive (or hermeneutic) understanding (characteristic one). This leads to the danger of abstraction which has occurred in much debate about mode of production concepts and class change. Van Binsbergen and Geschiere (1985, pp. 235–89) in discussing 'Marxist theory and anthropological practice' are concerned to find

> ways that save us from relegating to one-dimensionality the rich reality which the anthropologist was privileged enough to share in the course of field-work. Only thus can we hope to impart, in the course of our research, real meaning to such concepts as class and class struggle. (pp. 258–9)

Van Binsbergen and Geschiere identify the danger of arrogance in a researcher presuming to know what is the 'objective' reality. But they do not go far enough. To see class as underlying *all* social conflict is still an *a priori* judgement about the diverse nature of local disputes anywhere. Van Binsbergen sees the role of the researcher as 'the production of a more penetrating and thus liberating form of knowledge and consciousness' (1985, p. 223). But is this knowledge only to be about class issues?

It is on this issue of imposing concepts that Habermas raises the third objection to any model in which the researcher maintains some form of third-person 'observer' status. He argues that a researcher can only fully understand social action by adopting the 'performative' attitude of a first person. Critique should be carried out as an intersubjective process of challenging validity claims about truth, normative rightness and sincerity. Habermas conceives of a researcher as a 'virtual participant':

> In the model of communicative action, social actors are themselves outfitted with the same interpretive capacities as social-scientific interpreters; thus the latter cannot claim for themselves the status of neutral, extramundane observers in their definitions of actors' situations. They are, whether consciously or not, virtual participants whose only plausible claim to objectivity derives from the reflective quality of their participation. But this reflexivity is in principle open to the actual participants as well; it does not exempt the social scientist from having to take a position – however

reflective and however implicit – on the validity claims relevant to the definition of the situation. (McCarthy, in Habermas, 1984, p. xiii)

The virtual participant differs from the full participant in that:

> Those immediately involved in the communicative practice of everyday life are pursuing aims of *action*; their participation in cooperative processes of interpretation serves to establish a consensus on the basis of which they can coordinate their plans of action and achieve their aims. The social-scientific interpreter does not pursue aims of action *of this kind*. He participates in processes of reaching understanding for the sake of understanding [only]. (1984, pp. 113–14)

The model of the virtual participant is supposed to answer the question: 'How can the *objectivity of understanding* be reconciled with the performative attitude of one who participates in a process of reaching understanding?' (Habermas, 1984, p. 112). In practice the model has its own difficulties. How to draw the line between a participant observer and a virtual participant on the one hand, and between a virtual participant and a full participant on the other hand, is extremely tricky. All human communication is fraught with tensions. In interpreting and understanding others one has to proceed with sensitivity and cannot merely proceed according to a rational method. The language of another culture trips one up constantly; the need for local interpreters, invaluable to perceive nuances of meaning even if one has a basic command of the other language, makes one dependent. These difficulties will be discussed more fully later in the book.

In the second phase of fieldwork my inquiry was guided by principles of critical theory, and in particular the three requirements of a critical theory that Fay outlines. I attempted to combine quantitative and qualitative research techniques in an 'interactive' methodology, accepting Giddens's (1984) indictment that all 'quantitative' data is at root based on composites of 'qualitative' interpretations (p. 333). In setting up the work, I began by using the concept of form of production as a methodological device. I decided I would investigate the nature of the production systems of different types of households and the relationships underlying resource access within and between households (including the relationships between households and farmer groups). Into this picture was drawn the influence of government agencies, particularly the agricultural extension agency, Agritex. Agritex was selected as a case-study organisation because it deals with all agrarian policy issues and because, since 1982, it has attempted to be an innovative agency. In each of the Chiwundura and Chirumhanzu communal areas, the areas of two farmer groups were selected as study areas. The areas were selected on the basis of my interest in exploring group dynamics and linkages between households, farmer groups, and extension agency. Selection was carried out in conjunction with Agritex, and in Chirumhanzu also in conjunction with the Catholic Development Commission (CADEC), as in this communal area CADEC has been responsible for the establishment, training and auditing of local savings clubs. My research took in the activities of three of these clubs.

The comparative nature of the research was extended downwards by the selection of six to eight case-study households in each of the four study areas. The households were selected on the basis of differentiating characteristics which I had identified as key ones in my own earlier work, through discussions with other researchers, and through discussion with the local farmer groups themselves. The actual households who agreed to participate were then chosen by the farmer groups. Their range in all four areas included farmer group (and savings club) member and non-member households, relatively wealthy to poor households, and households of a variety of compositions (that is, at least one headed by a woman, at least one whose male head was a migrant worker, and others where both the husband and wife were living in the area).

The semi-structured methodology I used during the six months of fieldwork I carried out from November 1986 to April 1987 (with a return visit to each area being made in July/August 1987) will be discussed in Chapter 5. I did find, however, that much of the time I was with the selected households was spent in understanding the household production system and in establishing a relationship with the people concerned. The extent to which I was able to participate with farmers in occasions of reflection and critique were minimal. However I was able to engage with Agritex staff in this way. At different stages of the work I wrote two progress reports and a paper. The issues in these, especially where they contained challenges to the claims inherent in Agritex's policies, were then raised and debated with Agritex staff from all levels of the organisation in a variety of discussions and meetings. Encouraging dialogue and critical reflection in this way, contributes to 'enabling change'. It also helps fulfil the requirement of a critical theory that its claims 'can only be validated partially in terms of the responses that the social actors themselves have to the theory' (Fay, 1975, p. 109). This work with Agritex is discussed in Chapter 7.

In the final chapter of the thesis, the experience of applying and testing aspects of Habermas's critical theory and a derivative research methodology, will facilitate an evaluation of both theory and method.

CONTENTS AND STRUCTURE

In the next chapter colonial government policy, particularly during the 'technical development phase' from the late 1920s to the early 1960s, will be examined. The empirical data used relates mainly to the three study communal areas in the Midlands province. My aim is to analyse the nature of the policies and to interpret the rationale which is used by the colonial authorities for justifying them.

In Chapter 3 the account of policy initiatives is taken into the post-independence period. In both this and the preceding chapter, material is also introduced which allows a more accurate account of the impact of government policies to be gradually built up than is acknowledged within the official perspective.

These different accounts begin to illustrate how wide the contrasts are in the outlooks held by government officials and peasant societies themselves on the nature of the environment and peasant production activities. The extent to which different attitudes develop and persist, including at different levels of government agencies, is enlarged upon as an issue in Chapter 4. Here one particular policy issue, that of pastoral land use management, is looked at in more detail. In this analysis the differences are identified and examined in the claims made by policy-makers and peasant farmers in their respective interpretations of environmental processes and appropriate economic uses of the land.

In Chapter 5, the farming systems and general economic activities of the twenty-nine case-study households in the Chirumhanzu and Chiwundura communal areas are analysed. This shows the resource constraints experienced by different categories of farmer households and their struggles to overcome these in order to ensure their survival.

Chapter 6 looks beyond the household to the level of the collectivity. Critical issues regarding the efficacy and legitimacy of local institutional structures are considered through an analysis of instances where collective action to improve household access to resources has been attempted. Some of these instances – the cases of early season herding in Chirumhanzu and a group credit scheme initiative in Chiwundura – have been controversial failures. Others – the Chirumhanzu savings clubs and fragile local initiatives to establish *mushandirapamwe* resource sharing schemes – bear the genetic requirements of more sustainable local organisational initiatives.

The debate I provoked with Agritex staff based on the improved understanding I had gained of the lifeworld of these peasant societies, is evaluated in Chapter 7. Issues arising from the contrasts between the agency's formal policy, actual practice and the impact of that practice, were communicated to Agritex in reports and in meetings. This acted to stimulate reflection and dialogue among staff throughout the organisation on the contents of policies and the nature of policy practice. The result is to enable me to make a sharper assessment of the principle normative concern of the study: whether there is realistic potential for improving the quality of communication between rural peoples and government agencies, in order to improve the outcomes of policy actions.

Finally, the concluding chapter contains a synthesis of the insight gained from the analysis of agrarian change in Zimbabwe and the value of critical theory in undertaking such an analysis. What are the limitations of Habermas's critical theory? Are there ways of developing his theoretical and methodological framework, whilst keeping faith with the epistemology of a critical theory, in order to make it more appropriate for African contexts? Can one say that there are possibilities of applying the principles of a critical theory, in order to improve mutual understanding between leaderships, administrators and peoples, through an intersubjective process of critique? And, moreover, can this be institutionalised sufficiently for there to be hope that change towards more satisfying human relationships in the troubled circumstances of contemporary Africa, will be enabled?

2 The Colonial State and the Penetration of Purposive Rationality

> So, with increasing urgency, we are led to ask, whether there may not be hidden in our experience of the world a primordial falsity; whether, in our linguistically transmitted experience, we may not be prey to prejudices or, worse still, to necessities which have their source in the linguistic structuring of our first experience of the world and which would force us to run with open eyes, as it were, down a path whence there was no other issue than destruction.
> (H. G. Gadamer, 1975, p. 481)

Zimbabwe's ninety-year colonial experience is one of a journey down the path of linguistically – and hence socially – transmitted prejudices of which Hans-Georg Gadamer writes. But this path, I shall argue, must be understood as the result not primarily of racial prejudices *per se*, but rather of the prejudiced belief of the new settlers in the superiority of their western material and technical culture. This chapter explains the importance of this distinction.

The ninety years of colonialism which came to an end in 1980 has had an extraordinary effect on the shaping of the country and its peoples today; so much so that most agrarian policy research of this period simply portrays the working-out of agrarian policies as being a 'straightforward contest between European and African producer interests subject to intervention by the metropolitan power' (Mosley, 1983, p. 2).[1] Later research, including by Mosley himself, provides evidence to the contrary. With regard to the white 'settler–producer group' Mosley shows how conflict between competent and incompetent farmers affected policy choices (1983, pp. 234–5). And Cheater (1984), in her study of a black small-scale freehold area, illustrates how sharp were emerging distinctions between black freehold and communal area farmers in the pre-independence period. She argues that such internal differentiation is significant 'even by comparison with the major class cleavage between White capital and Black labour' (p. 176).

Recognising that neither white nor black economic interests were monolithic does not, however, affect the assumption that the most crucial legacy of the colonial period is still the racially drawn economic divide between white and black. It is to this assumption that I propose an alternative. Rather, the most important legacy of the colonial period was the transformation which occurred in the nature, role and power of the state. This transformation was that of the institutionalisation of purposive rationality. It left the state at independence as the dominant source of power in the country and its generally centralised institutions in the habit of exercising this power through purposive-rational action. Taken together, these mutually reinforcing characteristics have resulted in continuities in approach between pre-and post-independence agrarian policies which cannot be explained simply through a white–black class thesis.

The latter part of this argument – the continuities in attitudes and policy style – will be explored in Chapter 3. Here, the first part of the argument, which deals with the transformation which occurred in the nature of the state, will be established through an analysis of the nature, grounds and impact in the study region, of colonial agrarian policy. This analysis is organised in the following way. An introductory sketch on the latter years of the pre-colonial period provides a prelude to an account of the early colonial period from 1890 to nearly 1930, during which the colonial state was being established. The importance of this account is to show how, from the outset, white and black misunderstood each other. The way in which colonial officials perceived environmental and economic change to be occurring is contrasted with the rather different actual experience of the rural population.

This already existent misunderstanding forms the context, then, for what S. E. Morris, Chief Native Commissioner (CNC) from 1956 to 1964, termed the 'technical development phase' of colonial agrarian policy (CNC, Annual Report 1961). This phase, which ran from the late 1920s to 1962, Morris contrasted with the 'protective phase' of the early colonial period. During the technical development phase a profound increase in the scale and coercive nature of state intervention took place. Its impact on the shaping of contemporary Zimbabwe cannot be overemphasised. Accordingly, the analysis of the four major policies of this period – agricultural demonstration, centralisation, destocking and land husbandry – forms the core of this chapter. In this analysis I examine not only the policies in themselves, but also seek to interpret the rationale used by the administration to justify the journey down the path to unmitigated coercion. A key claim I make is that this rationale was founded in an ideology which was a translation into social terms of Darwin's evolutionary theory of natural selection.

The technical development policies generated resistance which became more open as the degree of coercion was raised. The eventual outpouring of physical opposition to the policies led to a brief period of policy review in 1961–2. Why this review was short-lived is the subject of the final part of the chapter.

NINETEENTH-CENTURY STATES AND PRODUCTION RELATIONS

The acknowledged starting-point of the colonial period in Zimbabwe is with the arrival of the British South Africa Company's Pioneer Column[2] in Zimbabwe in 1890. At this time the study region lay on the periphery of the area which had come under predominantly Ndebele influence since their arrival under Mzilikazi in the south-west of Zimbabwe in the late 1830s. The Ndebele arrived towards the end of a period of major demographic shift amongst the Shona peoples themselves. The challenge to established dominant lineages threatened by the swelling number of inmigrating *vatorwa* (stranger) groups (Beach, 1977, p. 43) had created a complex entanglement of political relationships (Beach, 1986, p. 30). The impact of the Ndebele served to heighten already acute political tensions in the area – and resulted in a variety of political and economic relations between them and the Shona.

In the north of the study region, for instance, the leaders – for whom the word 'chief' shall be used, albeit with caution[3] – whose people now live in the Chiwundura communal area, actively collaborated with the Ndebele (Beach, 1979, p. 406). In the south, Chief Wedza, whose Dumbuseya people, like the Ndebele, had also been immigrants in the 1830s, was also a collaborator (Zachrisson, 1978, pp. 52–4). Most peoples in the region, however, co-existed more uneasily with the Ndebele (Beach, 1971, p. 215). In the Chirimuhanzu chiefdom, for example, apart from a brief period in the late 1880s and early 1890s (Beach, 1986, p. 72), tribute was paid in the form of labour. Similarly, in the Mberengwa, Zvishavane and Shurugwi areas, all to the south-west of Chirimuhanzu, young men had to be supplied as recruits for the Ndebele *lozwi* regiments (Beach, 1971, pp. 126–7).

Other chiefdoms still, such as that of Chivi further away to the south-east, had never formally submitted to the Ndebele. Living in the natural hill strongholds provided by the steep-sided granite outcrops that sweep this region (Wallis, 1954, pp. 114–15) these people were subjected to both sporadic raiding by groups of Ndebele bandits, and occasionally to larger raids ordered by Lobengula himself (Beach, 1971, p. 215). This meant that, aside from Wedza's Dumbuseya, the people in the Zvishavane area, who lay in the path of both Ndebele bandits and armies, lived a particularly precarious existence. The Ndebele took most of their livestock so that in this erratic rainfall area they had to live off a solely arable production system. Access to land in the localised wetland vlei (*makuvi*) areas was therefore not only important for survival, but also provided the major source of local power.[4]

> Late nineteenth century 'chiefly' power stemmed from their owner-ship of these refuges, their ability to mobilise labour (for war and agriculture) and their ownership of the largest granaries: which were filled from their *makuvi* (vleis). These elements interacted strongly. They owned the vleis because of their political authority, which was maintained by the dependent men clustered around them, as sons and sons-in-law doing *ugariri* (bride service) for their daughter. The rulers were big polygamists: during famines com-moners had to pledge (*kuzvarira*) their daughters in return for the 'chiefs' grain: grain that was produced from the vleis by the wives, sons-in-law and children. (Wilson, 1986c, p. 1)

Cultivation was thus primarily intensive. The system of 'land rotation cultivation' (Allan, 1965) that Palmer (1977) and others refer to, although practised, was of only subsidiary importance in this region (Wilson, 1989a). It is the wetland system of cultivation to which travellers such as Thomas Leask, who visited this area in 1876, refer (Wallis, 1954; in Wilson 1986a, p. 2). And as Ken Wilson illustrates above, *makuvi* cultivation required control over a large labour force, because the task of constructing the ridges (*mipanje*) that were integral to the system, was arduous and labour-intensive.[5] Social relations, such as the vassalage nature of the practice of bride service, have a feudal ring to them.

The Ndebele created sufficient flux and insecurity for this late nineteenth-century period to be recalled in the Zvishavane area as one of acute poverty (Wilson, 1986a, pp. 1–5). Many peoples thus welcomed the arrival of the whites because of the opportunity they afforded as a potential ally.

NEW MARKET RELATIONS AND STATE EXPANSION: THE
RISE AND FALL OF PEASANT PROSPERITY, 1890–1933

The arrival of the white settlers did actually bring two net benefits to
peoples in the study region – peace and a new economic prosperity.
The benefit was, however, unevenly distributed and shortlived. For
the parallel rise of the colonial state, and particularly the peculiar
perception that those who administered the state had of the rural
world, set in motion a policy process that terminated this brief period
of prosperity. In illustrating this process here, reference shall be
focussed on the Zvishavane and Chirumhanzu areas.

The peace established in the late nineteenth century was the
outcome of conflict with the Ndebele. Its price was European control,
although the adverse effects of this only began to be felt with full
force from 1930 onwards. At first many of the Shona groups regarded
the whites as useful allies. In the 1893 Ndebele war and again in the
First Chimurenga of 1896–7, six 'chiefdoms', Gutu, Chirimuhanzu,
Zimuto, Banka, Chivi and Matibi, all in the outer periphery of the
Ndebele sphere of influence, combined with the British against
the Ndebele. More proximate tributary chiefdoms such as in the
Mberengwa, Shurugwi and Gweru districts, refrained from playing
any direct role, as many of their young men were already in the
Ndebele *lozwi* regiments (Beach, 1971, p. 345; 1986, pp. 68–89).

In the Mberengwa–Vishavane area,[6] the eventual ending of hostili-
ties between the Ndebele and the local peoples had several significant
economic effects. To begin with, people were able to spread their
settlements out from their former hill refuges (Zachrisson, 1978,
pp. 50–1). They could also reaccumulate cattle, for after expropriation by both the Ndebele and the whites there were only a few
thousand head left in the district.[7] These two processes, together with
a sharp increase in the adoption of the plough from 1914 (Zachrisson,
1978, p. 203) led to an escalation of the area under cultivation. Intra-
and inter-district grain and cattle trading assumed a revived vitality.
Barter exchange of cattle and grain – and women and sons – were
balancing mechanisms long used among producers to even out the
wide variation in yields which often occurred because of uneven
rainfall distribution between even proximate locations.

The establishment of relative peace and stability was a precondi-
tion for these economic processes to take place. And by themselves
these processes might have reduced some of the inequalities of the
late nineteenth century, whilst largely preserving the power of

lineage leaders. The introduction of a monetary economy, facilitated by the growing power of the settler state ensured, though, that far more traumatic social and economic change occurred. The introduction of taxes, wage labour, consumer goods and the marketing opportunities offered by the incipient settlements established by the whites, were all precipitatory mechanisms.

Economic trends in the first three decades of the twentieth century were affected by short-term 'moments' as well as longer-term changes. Moments had a variety of causes. They could be the result of drought, as in 1902, 1911–12, 1916 and 1922–3. Others were of an economic nature – the depressions of 1914–18 and 1922–3, and the years of growth in the 1900s, and then between 1919–21 and 1925–9. Or the moments could be of a political nature, such as the introduction of a ten-shilling hut tax in 1898 and its subsequent raising to £1 in 1904.

The coalescence of moments increased their combined impact. The introduction of a hut tax by the colonial government was initially received by male elders with profound shock. It was the first indication for the Shona peoples that under white control they would lose not only their autonomy but all ability to represent their interests (Vambe, 1972, pp. 105–6). At first the tax was erratically collected and often in kind, but increasingly in times of drought the need to pay taxes forced men in the Mberengwa district to supply their labour to the Shabani and Belingwe mines (Zachrisson, 1978, pp. 194–5). In the first fifteen years of the century local migration rates did rise gradually, although labour supply was still nowhere near demand.[8]

Several indicators can be used to show that there was a general rise in prosperity at this time. First, there was a dramatic growth in the purchase of consumer goods – clothing, sugar, salt, iron utensils and equipment – during the first decade of the century (Wilson, 1986a, p. 3), particularly in areas near the new mine or town markets. Seasonal regulation was again apparent: it is in the good agricultural years of 1910, 1913, 1917 and 1918 that the CNC refers specifically to rises in the sales of goods to the rural population (Zachrisson, 1978, p. 196). Second, apart from the drought years of 1911–12, the demand for labour on the mines exceeded supply until 1932. Only then did the trend reverse itself until 1948 (Mosley, 1983, p. 127).

Third, average levels of cattle ownership continued to rise until the end of the 1920s. Thus, although Palmer (1977b, pp. 227–30) terms the period between 1890 and 1908 as 'the era of peasant prosperity' in colonial Rhodesia, in the Zvishavane area the late 1920s, and in

Table 2.1   Runde communal area: population and cattle 1927–57

Year	Pop'n	Area (ha)	Density (ha/person)	Cattle	Density (ha/head)	Head/ h'hold
1926	5682	62880	11.07	19705	3.19	17.35
1931	7838	62880	8.02	19309	3.26	12.31
1933	8195	62880	7.67	17498	3.59	10.68
1934	8406	62880	7.41	16805	3.74	10.00
1938	8583	62880	7.26	17449	3.60	10.16
1942	9795	62880	6.36	17242	3.65	8.80
1946	12239	62596	5.09	15805	3.96	6.46
1948	11991	62596	5.22	12933	4.84	5.39
1951	15010	63868	4.56	12956	4.92	4.62
1954	14875	63868	4.29	12900	4.95	4.34
1955	14875	63868	4.29	8390	7.61	2.82
1957	13690	63868	4.62	9518	6.71	3.48
1984 (Ture ward)	3265	8630	2.64	2284	3.78	4.33

Sources: 1927–46 NC Belingwe and ANC Shabani, Annual Reports;
1948–57 Director of Native Agriculture, Annual Reports;
1984   Ture Ward survey, Drinkwater 1985.

Note: The following additional figures are provided in the annual reports of
the NC Belingwe and ANC Shabani:
Total cattle pop'n: Belingwe + Shabani   Shabani only
1924   54950   1927   29619
1925   87309   1929   30200
1926   108708
1930   135206

Mberengwa perhaps even the early 1930s, appears to have been the zenith of prosperity. Cattle accumulation reached its peak in the Runde area, in both gross and average terms, probably between 1926 and 1928 (see Table 2.1). Although no figures for the Runde area are shown prior to 1926 the peak would not have preceded this date, as for the district as a whole cattle numbers proliferated from 1924 until the late 1920s.[9] Zachrisson (1978) records the gross cattle total for the Mberengwa area as having increased from around 50 000 head in 1923 to 150 000 head by 1934 (p. 201). However, to the extent records are provided in the annual reports of the Native Commissioner (NC) Belingwe, the bulk of this growth occurred between 1924 and 1926, when the number of head doubled from 55 000 to nearly 109 000 head (see footnote to Table 2.1). After this, growth slowed considerably. This was partly because of increased cattle sales. Following the slump of the early 1920s, a rise in demand for meat by the expanding mines led to an improvement in cattle prices from 1925 until 1930, and from 1928 a substantial increase in sales occurred throughout the Mberengwa district (Zachrisson, 1978, pp. 200–1; NC Belingwe, Annual Report 1929).

In Chirumhanzu, the peak of peasant prosperity was probably also attained in the late 1920s. During this period of good crop and cattle prices, cattle sales reached their highest levels in the Chirumhanzu communal area this century – higher even than during the late 1940s and mid-1950s, the years of enforced destocking. The average herd size reached a peak (considerably lower than in the Runde communal area) before the drought of 1933. In this year cattle owners were forced to sell or barter cattle to obtain grain, and thereafter, although the aggregate number of cattle in Chirumhanzu continued to rise until the advent of destocking in 1945, the average size of herds declined (Table 2.2). This was because the periodic influxes of people into Chirumhanzu, as a consequence of the Land Apportionment Act, were ensuring an even faster population growth.

The importance of cattle to the relative rise in rural prosperity was recognised by the native commissioners. For instance, the NC Belingwe comments on the ability of people to meet their food requirements in several adverse seasons through the bartering of cattle for grain.[10] Statements such as 'we all know that the native's whole prosperity has been largely dependent on his cattle' (NC Belingwe, Annual Report 1923) occur often in district administration reports of this period.

After describing this period of the late 1920s as the zenith of peasant prosperity, some qualification is needed, however. First, this wealth was not generated solely from agricultural and stock sales; in fact, over the course of the three decades from 1900, the wage earnings of migrant workers had steadily become the dominant source of rural wealth. Figures that Arrighi (1973) quotes show the extent of the transition. In 1903 the marketed sale of grains, other produce and stock accounted for some 70 per cent of the total cash earnings of the indigenous African population. But by 1932 these sales accounted for less than 20 per cent of earnings (p. 207). The turning-point in this shift of the primary source of African income came perhaps around 1914. The real wage level of this year was not reached again until 1956 (Mosley, 1983, pp. 119, 129–30) – and then it was because of the effect of black trade-union activity coupled with a new demand for semi-skilled labour (Arrighi, 1973, pp. 216–18).

Table 2.2   Chirumhanzu communal area: population and cattle 1923–61

Year	Pop'n	Area (ha)	Density (ha/person)	Cattle	Density (ha/head)	Head/ h'hold
1923	14000	129628	9.26	15753	8.23	5.63
1925	14523	129628	8.93	17170	7.87	5.83
1927	15185	129628	8.54	18354	7.06	6.04
1929	17423	129628	7.44	23100	5.61	6.63
1930	17767	129628	7.30	24975	5.19	7.03
1933	18036	129628	7.19	27958	4.64	7.75
1934[a]	13926	110172	7.91	19102	5.77	6.84
1935	14810	110172	7.44	20103	5.48	6.79
1937	17500	110172	6.30	23230	4.74	6.64
1939	21517	110172	5.12	22639	4.87	5.26
1941	21182	110172	5.20	26831	4.11	6.33
1943	22783	110172	4.84	24929	4.42	5.47
1945	24889	110172	4.43	26860	4.10	5.40
1946	25260	110172	4.36	23384	4.71	4.63
1947	25570	110172	4.31	21507	5.12	4.21
1948	26790	110172	4.22	22575	4.88	4.21
1951	27260	102898	3.78	23891	4.31	4.38
1954	30100	102898	3.42	27202	3.79	4.52
1955	33870	102898	3.04	25669	4.01	3.79
1957	37500	102898	2.75	27395	3.76	3.65
1958	38690	102898	2.66	21433	4.81	2.77
1959	40314	102898	2.55	19038	5.41	2.36
1961	41156	102898	2.50	19901	5.18	2.42
1982	42144	104200	2.47			

[a] Figures prior to 1934 for both Chirumhanzu and Serima communal areas.

Sources: NC Chilimanzi, Annual Reports; 1982 Population census.

Second, an important qualification needs to be noted about the use of the rise in cattle holdings as an indicator of a general growth in rural prosperity. This is that these holdings were even more unevenly distributed than they had been in the late nineteenth century. The very success of cattle as a means of economic accumulation and exchange meant that capital reinvestment seems to have occurred largely in yet further purchase of livestock. With cattle being used to purchase wives as well as food in drought years, those with cattle increased their labour force and thus, too, their control over land and production. This process served to strengthen inequalities within the relations of production, but often along new divisions (Wilson, 1986a, p. 2). For the new *hurudza*, or land barons, who had prospered from the expansion of dryland grain cultivation were mostly younger men than the old male patriarchs (Wilson, 1986c, p. 3).

The introduction of wage labour and a monetary and 'consumer' economy provided a means whereby young men sought to escape from patriarchal control. By partly substituting cash for the payment of cattle they could avoid absolute dependence on male elders for bridewealth (Weinrich, 1979, pp. 94–101), though if they wanted rural wives they could not escape the framework of lineage relations. Wage employment was still primarily a source of income to pay taxes (NC Belingwe, Annual Report 1923; NC Chilimanzi, Annual Reports 1931–3), rather than as an alternative form of economic accumulation. Moreover, after the decline of real wages during the First World War, senior men re-tightened their control over women and young men by demanding higher initial cash payments for bridewealth (Jeater, forthcoming).

To the colonial state, though, it was not an unevenly distributed growth in rural prosperity that the rise in cattle numbers signified. Instead, by the late 1920s the administration was becoming alarmed at what it perceived as the threat to the environment caused by the rise in livestock densities. To understand the administration's reaction and subsequent role in the process of rural economic change, we need now to turn from the empirical account to an examination of the perspective held by government officials.

The Rise of the Dominant State

The colonial state's intervention in the indigenous political economy began in earnest when the expropriation and redistribution of land and livestock to settlers occurred in Matabeleland after the 1893 Ndebele War. The distribution of land was the central agrarian concern of the new state over the next thirty years and a vital source of its growing power stemmed from the control it gained over land use and tenure during this process. This policy of land redistribution was undertaken along racial lines: it was thus a policy of land segregation.

Land segregation, or land apportionment as it came to be formally labelled, was a more hypocritical version of the South African apartheid system (Lessing, 1957, p. 106). In essence the policy came into being with the creation of the first 'reserves' in Matabeleland, following the Matabeleland Order-in-Council of 1894. This Order was a protective reaction by the Imperial government to the wholesale grabbing of land by the white 'conquerors' which ensued following the 1893 war. Any protective intention was, however, undermined by the hasty and careless work of the 1894 Land Commission. Its recommendations that two reserves in the Gwaai and Shangani areas be assigned to the Ndebele served only to support the settler land seizure (Palmer, 1977a, p. 38). Existing Ndebele settlement in both areas was minimal for they contained infertile, sandy Kalahari soils. 'Far from excluding African villages from European farms, the lands of the Ndebele were expropriated in toto' (Palmer, 1977a, p. 38).

This discriminatory allocation established a pattern which was largely followed in the remainder of the country after the Southern Rhodesia Order-in-Council of 1898. Much of the more productive arable and ranching areas were alienated by the state for settler use, often despite attempts by local native commissioners to have these areas proclaimed reserves if they were already important areas of African occupation (Palmer, 1977a, pp. 251–76). A reason for the lack of concern of the Imperial government and British South Africa Company officials,[11] was that both believed that the reserves were only a 'temporary makeshift'. They assumed the role of the reserves would diminish as the agrarian population was absorbed into the colonial economy and education saw their assimilation within colonial 'society'. This ungrounded assumption was also made by the 1914–15 Native Reserves Commission, and it was only when the Commission's report was attacked, particularly by missionaries, that the assumption dissolved (Palmer, 1977a, pp. 56–8, 108).

There persisted, however, a Boserup-type thesis[12] that any failure of agricultural production to keep pace with African population growth could be resolved simply through the technical development of the reserves (Palmer, 1977a, p. 108). This meant the reserves were kept as small as native commissioners could be pressured to accept and the missionary protests would allow.[13] Nevertheless, by the early 1920s, advancing population and livestock densities were already attracting worried comment from some native commissioners.[14] They feared that, contrary to official belief, the demand for the return of their land by the black peoples would become an escalating and not a diminishing phenomenon. In this atmosphere, when attention was drawn to the subject of environmental degradation it was certain to generate official alarm. If it took place, degradation would threaten the whole land policy of squeezing the blacks into reserves. Hence, when in 1920 a Native Department official wrote of imminent disaster, he set a tone that was to be echoed repeatedly in government reports on environmental conditions over the next forty years:[15]

> Deterioration of the reserves has assumed such proportions that even lay men can note it and present methods of agriculture cannot continue . . . the soil is being exhausted . . . while the extensive destruction of timber should be checked . . . one of the first needs is an instructor to demonstrate with a plough what should be done . . . Without better methods of agriculture it will be impossible for the native reserves in the future to accommodate the native population. This applies equally to animal husbandry. (Native Department official reporting to the CNC in 1920; in CNC, Annual Report 1961, p. 21)

And so began the 'rising tide for development' (CNC, Annual Report 1961, p. 21). This tide was to come in for the remainder of the 1920s. An increment was added in 1924 by the Wooley Commission, set up to investigate the cost of administering the colony, following the granting of responsible government in 1923.[16] The Commission's concern was centred on the fact that the 1921–2 drought had cost the government £50 000 in famine relief: 'the natives are still so improvident and so little disciplined that the failure of their crops for one season can bring about such disastrous results' (in CNC, Annual Report 1961, p. 20). There has been 'too much shepherding and not enough discipline' (p. 20) moralised the Commission.

The next rise in the tide occurred the following year. The Carter Land Commission concluded that the 'increase in the number of cattle cannot be maintained' (para. 228), and that land tenure reform was required in the reserves if animal husbandry and agricultural production methods were to be improved (paras 244–7).

It was these accumulating feelings that led to what S. E. Morris described as the shift from the 'protective phase' to the 'technical development phase' in the administration's agrarian policy (CNC, Annual Report 1961, pp. 19–30). In 1926, E. D. Alvord was appointed the Native Affairs Department's (NAD) first Agriculturalist. To him fell the responsibility for 'developing the native reserves so as to enable them to carry a larger population, and so avoid, as far as possible, the necessity for acquisition of more land for native occupation'.[17] In 1927, after three years of training, the first eleven black agricultural demonstrators were deployed. In this year, too, the Native Affairs Act empowered native commissioners to introduce measures for the conservation of natural resources and the improvement of grazing and farming land in their districts (Robinson Commission, 1961, para. 72). Two years later, in 1929, the Native Development Act was passed, its primary aim being the promotion of technical training. And in the same year Alvord initiated the policy of centralisation in the Selukwe Reserve (now Shurugwi communal area). Then in 1930 the policy of land segregation that all this subsidiary activity was designed to support was formally enacted as the Land Apportionment Act.

Palmer (1977a) aptly describes the Land Apportionment Act as 'the most contentious piece of legislation passed by a Rhodesian government' (p. 178). Its passing signified that the tide for development had come in fully. The most controversial phase of colonial agrarian policy, the phase of technical development, had begun.

TECHNICAL DEVELOPMENT AND SOCIAL DARWINISM, 1930–62

The 'technical development phase' of colonial agrarian policy comprised four main activities: agricultural extension, centralisation, destocking, and land husbandry. It has been noted that behind the launching of these policies was the felt need of the colonial authorities to manipulate people into raising production levels in the reserves. Raising production output would enable the increased population densities brought about by land apportionment to be justified, and demands by lineage leaders to have their people's land returned, to be resisted.

Whatever the misgivings he expressed in retrospect about the technical development policies, Morris, in his 1961 historical review, nevertheless still uses the term 'development' in his characterisation of the years of their implementation. This is not how the rural peoples themselves viewed the policies. They felt that the aim of their implementation was simply to enable yet more land to be taken away from them (NC Belingwe, Annual Report 1931; Godlonton Commission, 1944, para. 63; Wilson, 1986a, p. 14). Indeed, as shown by the statistics in Tables 2.1 and 2.2 for the Runde and Chirumhanzu communal areas, communities experienced in general an ongoing decline in both the land available per person and the average size of cattle holdings. By the taking of their two most important resources, land and cattle, people were made 'in their own eyes "poor"' (Weinrich, 1964, p. 37).

At this level of the discussion, then, the policies as 'straightforward contest between European and African producer-interest' thesis, appears to be vindicated. Certainly this is what many people in the rural areas feel themselves. For example, from the oral history research he conducted in the Runde and Mazvihwa areas of the Zvishavane district, Wilson (1986a, pp. 14–18; and personal communication) emphasises that almost all the people he interviewed felt that these policies were designed to oppress rather than benefit them in any way. They were simply part of the government's aim to gain 'total control' over the rural population.

Furthermore, even before the technical development policies had been launched in any significant way, the colonial government's Maize Control Acts, in combination with a drought and the Depression, had already had a crippling effect on the rural economy. The 1931 Maize Control Act was introduced for two main reasons. European producers wanted protection against the falling price of maize – the international depression had resulted in a slump in the export price from 11/- in 1920 to 3/4d in 1931 (Palmer, 1977a, pp. 210–11) – through an artificially controlled domestic price Keyter, 1978, p. 3). But, in addition, European producers also wanted protection against the fear of African competition – a fear more imagined than real, according to Keyter, since black producers sold to regional markets rather than the national market supplied by white farmers (p. 21).

For black producers, maize control resulted in a dramatic worsening of their terms of trade (NC Belingwe, Annual Reports 1931–6; Keyter, 1978, pp. 5, 24). Traders were given by the 1931 Act a monopoly to purchase maize. This, coupled with the impact of the Depression, caused the maize prices fetched by farmers to plummet from the 1928–30 level of 6/- to 7/6d per bag to as low as 2/- to 2/6d per bag in 1932 (Keyter, 1978, pp. 5, 10; Palmer, 1977a, p. 212).

In the Mberengwa district, because the Shabanie Mine depots were still able to offer good prices for the unregulated millets and sorghum, producers switched their production away from maize to the smaller grains. Even after the maize price improved in 1940 they only made a gradual return to the crop (NC Belingwe, Annual Reports 1944–5).

The economic shock for households in Chirumhanzu during the early 1930s was even greater than in the Zvishavane area. Maize control reduced the maize price to 2/- in 1932 (see Table 2.3). The price of other grains also slumped. A foot-and-mouth-disease outbreak

Table 2.3   Chirumhanzu grain production 1923–45

Year	Season	Maize price	Grain production (bags)			Grain sold (bags)		
			Maize	Other grains	Total	Maize	Other grains	Total
1923	Good	6/- to 10/-			120 000			4 000–5 000
1924	Poor	8/- to 10/-			75 000			2 500–3 000
1925	Too wet				82 000			1 500–2 000
1926	Good				102 500			3 000
1927	Fair		8 000	84 000	92 000	500	4 000	4 500
1928	Fair	7/6 (1)	9 000	85 000		1 000	6 500	7 500
1929	Poor	7/- (1)	4 000	55 000	59 000	0	3 000	3 000
1930	Good							
1931	Fair							
1932	Good	2/-						
1933	V.poor							
1934	Good	5/- (Central estates) 3/- (Traders)				3 000	600	
1935	V.poor							300
1936	Good					MCB 1 499 T 500	5 000	6 999

1937	Fair		MCB 3327 / T 500		3500	7327
1938	Poor	5000	MCB 350 / T –		2000	2350
1939	Fair	7000	MCB 621 / T 450	72000 / 79000	1500	2571
1940	Good	8000	MCB – / T 2500	75000 / 83000	2750	5250
1941	Fair	6500	MCB 33 / T 2290		2500	4823
1942	Poor	5000	MCB 205 / T 383		2231	2819
1943	Good	10000	MCB 2214 / T 1630		4216	8060
1944	Good	18000	MCB 4039 / T 13025		4216	
1945			MCB ? / T 12951		4209	

(1) Prices in Zvishavane area (NC Belingwe, Annual Reports 1928–29).
MCB = Maize Control Board
T = Traders

Sources: NC Chilimanzi, Annual Reports 1923–45.

in 1931–2 prevented people from selling cattle to European buyers. The Depression reduced employment and wage levels. A poor harvest in 1933 resulted in some non-cattle-owning households being granted drought relief maize on credit. Judging from his reports, however, what the NC Chilimanzi felt most keenly through these years was the 'great trouble' experienced in collecting taxes (NC Chilimanzi, Annual Reports 1930–33).[18]

This blinkered, officious reaction leads us into an explanation of why the 'straightforward contest' argument does not entirely hold. For a start, even at the local level the rural social and economic trends portrayed here were not well understood by colonial officials. Even the reports of native commissioners, the NAD officials closest to the black peoples, are riddled with contradictory and confused statements. Take the above-mentioned reports of the NC Chilimanzi. In his 1932 report he acknowledged the severe difficulties felt by the rural population: 'Cattle movements were prohibited and there was no demand for grain, and employment could not be found.' But under the heading 'Political Situation', the NC still stubbornly states: 'It is difficult to fathom the Native mind. Notice may be taken of the only outstanding attribute of the natives and that is their reluctance to listen to or accept advice on Administrative or commercial matters.'

Those more removed from the local level lacked even the basic understanding of rural economic trends. For instance, in 1924 when the Wooley Commission spoke of there being 'too much shepherding and too little discipline' they added to this, '. . . for we learn that standards of living and civilisation generally in their kraals is little or no better than it was forty years ago' (CNC, Annual Report 1961, p. 20). The commissioners' ignorance is revealed by the fact that their report was published immediately after the economic slump of 1921–3, during which the maize price had halved, sales had fallen by 78 per cent, and the price of cattle had slumped dramatically.[19]

Even someone like Alvord, who was responsible for the agricultural demonstration and centralisation policies and who actually spent considerable time in the reserves, was ignorant of the economics of agrarian production. In 1929 when average levels of cattle ownership were the highest they have been this century, Alvord saw a very different rural world:

Today a great majority of our rural native population is merely existing, doing no good for themselves or for the country, and wearing out the natural resources of the land. Periodical famines result . . . not so much due to unfavourable seasons as they are due to poor farming [and] lack of foresight . . . Because of their poor farming method, the lives of the great mass of our Rhodesian natives are filled with poverty. They have worn-out lands, poverty-stricken cattle, poorly constructed huts and under-nourished, naked children. (1929, pp. 10–11)

There are thus two dimensions to the attitude of those representing the state towards the peasantry. At one level the attitude is quite ruthless: squeeze the black population and prevent them from competing with white producers. But at another level it is to regard them as impoverished, primitive and incompetent. The first dimension represents the policy impulse of the state in its central objective of meeting settler interests. The second dimension is the moral–practical aspect – how the state justifies its actions as actually being in the interests of the black peoples themselves. This ideological element of the argument shall now be introduced.

The point of departure in explaining how the government attempted to justify its agrarian policies was that the practices urged upon black farmers were those used by white farmers. In 1907 a party of British South Africa Company directors had toured the country and decided that it was time to put an end to the myth which had motivated the trek of the Pioneer Column, that Rhodesia could be a 'Second Rand' (Palmer, 1977a, p. 80). The following year the Company subsequently launched the 'white agricultural policy'. This was based on offering would-be settlers incentives to become farmers. A Director of Agriculture was appointed; specialist advisors recruited; a Land Bank established to provide low-interest loans for the purchase of farms, livestock, equipment, and for land improvements such as fencing and irrigation works; and the minimum price of ranching and agricultural land was reduced until 1912 (Palmer, 1977a, pp. 80–2).

As the development of white commercial agriculture began, the reserves policy, with the reserves being predominantly situated away from the main white settlement areas, provided a mechanism to ease black farmers away from the markets it was intended the new white farmers should supply. However, if white farmers did not want black producers competing with them on the formal local market, nor did the state want the latter to be hit too hard (Mosley, 1983, p. 41). It had to be shown that the reserves did provide sufficient land for at least food subsistence needs. Besides, the government preferred to be seen as actually having the interests of the indigenous peoples at heart, and the policies to modernise agriculture could be shown in this light.

For a start, indigenous production techniques were oriented to coping with the vagaries of the environment rather than towards obtaining ever higher yields. It was also the low-yielding and extensive dryland cultivation practices, widespread only since the adoption of the plough, that the colonial government was mistakenly judging to have been the basis of nineteenth-century agricultural production. These practices were regarded as technically backward and producers' adherence to them the consequence of ignorance. This constituted, as Floyd wrote in 1961, 'a theme of rejection', 'a general denial that there was anything good in the former systems of native cultivation and resultant ways of life' (p. 290). Thus if, as producers claimed, their interests were now being jeopardised, it was the fault of their own backwardness and not the actions of the new settler state.

An important element in this reasoning of the state was the belief that the African peoples did not know what their own 'real' interests were. This meant that it was necessary for the state to now redefine these for them – and to then enforce acceptance of appropriate measures. There could be no admitting that anything other than modernisation (seen as the extension of a purposive rationality) was desirable, as the white political economy that was being developed depended on this belief for its maintenance and growth.[20] In this sense, coercion of blacks in the name of technological progress was also a means of preventing in-group questioning amongst whites themselves about how their own interests were being defined and pursued.

This ideological rationale was thus mainly for the internal consumption of the white population, as well as its European connections. It was a self-justification of their colonising actions. Its fiction helped maintain the gulf between the ways in which the white and black peoples perceived the world.

The black peoples who were the victims of the colonial state's peculiar definition of reality could hardly be expected to appreciate it. They saw their own worldview as being entirely more rational than that of the whites. This theme is returned to repeatedly by Lawrence Vambe in his novel, *An Ill-fated People* (1972). His own people, the vaShawasha, found the behaviour of whites as 'wielders of power and insatiable land-grabbers' (p. 97) not only constantly threatening, but also bewildering: 'The white community in Southern Rhodesia is a complete puzzle to me, a concentration of irrationality. I cannot repeat this fact too often' (p. 142).

As an inheritor of a pre-capitalist culture, it is a feeling that there is something restrictive and perverted about the type of value system the whites had introduced, that Vambe expresses. This is the same argument that Habermas makes – that a purposive rationality is an incomplete rationality. In their turn, the whites felt that the rationality they invoked was not only sensible but unquestionable. The rightness of their views could be validated even by laws of science! These laws, in particular, were those of natural selection. The ideology the colonial government invoked, although without recognising it as an ideology, was therefore that of social Darwinism.

A good illustration of the colonial state's use of social Darwinism is provided by J. F. Holleman. Holleman, perhaps the most perceptive social scientist of the colonial period, examines how the commission which paved the way for the 1951 Land Husbandry Act, the 1944 Native Production and Trade Commission (Godlonton Commission), appeals to the theory of natural selection. The Commission's report proceeds, he states (1968, pp. 45–6), from the premise of 'possessory segregation' between white and black.[21] To justify this premise the Commission develops a line of reasoning which uses this principle of natural selection. 'Change, progress and adaptation' are considered to be 'natural laws which inexorably govern human existence. Failure to comply with such laws will in nature lead to extinction' (p. 46). The 'inexorable natural law' to which Africans as 'backward peoples' would have to adapt, was the intrusion of civilised, 'forward' European peoples. This situation was one which, according to the Commission, imposed duties on both peoples:

> forward people while preserving their settled economy have a duty by all reasonable and proper means to assist backward peoples to progress and *for that purpose to enforce discipline without oppression*. It is also the duty of forward peoples to adapt themselves to the presence of such backward peoples in their midst; it is the duty of backward peoples to contribute to their own advancement to the limit of their powers *and to observe proper discipline*. (p. 46; my emphasis)

These duties could, of course, only be carried out through legislation and the determined enforcement of appropriate government policies. So the circle was completed. Europeans 'being identified with progress and progress being enshrined in an inexorable law of nature, the legitimacy of white progressive leadership now becomes fully sanctioned by both law and logic' (p. 46).

This assimilation of social theory to natural science theory is not, however, solely an idiosyncrasy of the colonial mind. It is, Habermas feels, a key component of the whole Occidental mentality, and thus one of the basic features of modernisation that he wishes to critique:

> From this perspective (a combination of Newtonian physics, bourgeois social philosophy and economics, Darwinian biology and contemporary systems theory), the attributes of mind – knowing, acting for an end – are transformed into functions of the self-maintenance of subjects that, like bodies and organisms, pursue a single 'abstract' end: to secure their continued (and contingent) existence. (1984, p. 388)

Habermas critiques this type of reasoning because its proponents appeal to 'science' to disguise its ideological nature, and because it lacks a normative value base which can be evaluated rationally. With the breakdown in the Occidental world of religious-metaphysical worldviews, capitalism, now entrenched as an economic system, has been disengaged from an ethically grounded value system. Instead the 'spirit of capitalism' has been attached to evolutionary theories of natural selection. Self-preservation of the human species requires survival of (or adopting the methods of) the fittest, and this means the technically advanced and economically efficient. These two criteria have then become the goals of modern political and economic institutions. Action is oriented instrumentally towards technical ends, or strategically through the selection of means which involve the manipulation of people but are consistent with the way goals have been justified. Socialisation leads people to adopt the attitudes of 'representation' and 'action' towards other external and social objects. 'The subject relates to objects either to represent them as they are or to produce them as they should be' (Habermas, 1984, p. 387). The belief that man can, and in fact is destined to, dominate nature, becomes repeated in society. Man is to dominate man. People exist to be manipulated not understood.

> The structure of exploiting an objectivated nature that is placed at our disposal repeats itself within society, both in interpersonal

relations marked by the suppression of social classes and in intraphysic relations marked by the repression of our instinctual nature. (1984, p. 389)

Oliver Tambo, president of the African National Congress of South Africa, has summed up in direct terms this ideological argument and its practical consequences in the Southern African context:

The theoreticians of racism in our country draw on the gross perversions of science which assume their clearest forms during the second half of the last century in Europe and the United States. In these centres of imperialist power, there grew up theories that biology and social anthropology provided the basis, to justify the notion that all black people carried with them both an innate and a cultural inferiority to the white, giving the latter the right and the duty of guardianship over the former. (1986, p. xiv)

It can be understood, then, why the behaviour of the whites should have appeared so 'irrational' to Vambe. For someone such as the NC Chilimanzi to have made in 1932 the statement referred to earlier about 'the Native mind', he must be able to divorce totally technical considerations from the process of spatial and economic squeezing to which he also drew attention. For rural people themselves it is understandable that they could only interpret this bewildering behaviour of the colonial authorities as being aimed at depriving them of their independence. But as Wilson (1986a) argues, it was a particular kind of control over the black peoples that the colonial state wanted; it wanted people recruited into 'modernity' (p. 15). Thus he suggests the technical development policies were,

not so much the government simply trying to force people to do particular things – rather it was part of a strategy of illegalising Africanness: creating 'criminality' which itself could be used for continual authority supporting punishment. (1986: personal communication)

In the context of the colonial state's ideology, this remark can be taken further: the colonial authorities were able to justify the use of force because they perceived the values and production methods of African societies to be 'wrong'. To use Habermas's terms introduced in Chapter 1, the colonial authorities not only had a strategic political aim in manipulating peasant producers to adopt new practices so as to serve white interests, but at the normative level they believed they were right in doing so. This means that in challenging the technical development policies of the colonial government through an application of critical theory, one should go beyond illustrating merely why it was in the interests of the government to control the autonomy of the indigenous peoples. Ideally, one should also examine the actual technical basis of these policies: were the colonial authorities justified in condemning Shona production methods as not only inefficient, but also damaging to the environment, and therefore entitled to be considered 'criminal'?

This question can be answered in two ways: by relating technology to farmers' ecological circumstances, and to their social and economic circumstances. In my own fieldwork I concentrated on the latter area, although by using the work of others I shall integrate the ecological aspect into my overall argument. These subjects will be discussed in more detail in later chapters. First, in order to lay the basis for this examination, it is necessary to understand more about the technical development policies themselves and the nature of the claims made by the colonial government that are inherent in the policies. In so doing I seek to validate the argument I have presented in this section.

THE TECHNICAL DEVELOPMENT POLICIES

(i) Agricultural Demonstration

The first black agricultural demonstrators were deployed in the reserves in 1927. Alvord, the NAD Agriculturalist under whose jurisdiction they came, having originally been a missionary took pride in terming himself 'the first Agricultural Missionary to be appointed in Africa' (Director of Native Agriculture, Annual Report 1947). He certainly approached the task of modernising peasant agricultural production methods with evangelical zeal. Alvord believed infinitely in the superiority of modern technology and culture, accrediting no importance to the environment in which both were to be transplanted. Whites found it difficult to communicate with blacks not because they were too prejudiced to seek to understand them, but because, he felt, of their cultural superiority. This was why it was necessary to train black agricultural demonstrators if peasant farmers were to be taught successfully modern agricultural practices. In 1947 he wrote retrospectively of the judgement he made in the 1920s:

He soon discovered that in spite of high qualifications, a white man could not teach agriculture to the superstition steeped African who attributed high crop yields to *divisi, muti,* witchcraft charms and favour of the ancestral spirits. He made the discovery that – 'The African must see things demonstrated on his own level, within his reach by Demonstrators of his own black skin and kinky wool.' (Director of Native Agriculture, Annual Report 1947, p. 2)

This statement might seem obnoxious to us today but the belief on which it rests – that nothing can be learned from peasant farmers – is still commonly held in Zimbabwe, as the next chapter will show. For Alvord:

Agriculture to the Native, is not a trade or an occupation. It is a mode of life. And, because of the low type of agriculture around which their lives are centred, the economic and social standards of the Natives are low and primitive. They cannot be raised to a higher plane unless their agriculture is improved. They have developed a clearly defined practice spoken of by Europeans as 'Kaffir farming'. Their methods are wasteful, slovenly and un- necessarily ineffective, and if continued, will be ruinous to the future interests of Rhodesia. (Alvord, 1929, p. 9)

To play up the deleterious nature of these practices, Alvord preached mythical rather than actual examples. He exemplified what the good farmer should do, either by drawing idealised pictures of the peasant farmer who had seen the light about the advantages of modern methods (e.g. Alvord, 1958, in Ranger, 1985, p. 71), or purely through parables (e.g. Alvord, 1928, pp. 35–43). In the parable 'the Great Hunger', the term is employed initially in a literal sense to indicate the outcome of poor farming methods in good seasons. It is then transformed into a figurative 'Great Hunger', as farmers are disillusioned by the inadequacy of their old methods and come 'begging the Demonstrator to do plots for them' (1928, p. 43).

It was the colonial authorities who experienced the greater disillusionment, however, because of farmers' slow adoption of the demonstrators' 'propaganda'. This perplexed the authorities who could not understand why farmers would not adopt techniques which would they believed, enable the farmer to assume control over the environment. The newly deployed demonstrators were tasked to persuade farmers to cultivate 1–2 acres of land as 'demonstration plots'. On these plots farmers were supposed to use manure, plough and harrow before planting, row-plant selected seed, keep the crop weed-free, and carry out crop-rotation. But such was the disappointing demand of farmers to be plotholders, coupled with the rate at which they dropped out, that in 1939 demonstrators were restricted to managing only ten plotholders each. This meant that in 1942/3, sixteen years after the start of agricultural extension, there were in the whole country just 843 plotholders (see Table 2.4 later in the chapter) and 3456 'cooperators' – the latter being those who used some of the recommended practices but did not rotate their crops (Godlonton Commission, 1944, para. 59).[22]

Because they blamed 'superstition' and 'tradition' for the failure of farmers to embrace 'modern' methods, it was rare for the white administrators to consider that there might also be rational reasons for this failure. In the annual reports of native commissioners for the 1930s and 40s observations are occasionally made which reveal flaws in the conventional wisdom. But rarely were the consequences of these anomalies in the logic of the colonial worldview considered. When the native commissioners did think further their views made little impress on national policy. An example of this concerns the use of the plough and maize cultivation.

One of the more obvious constraints to peasant households taking on 'modern' methods is that they necessitated more labour than many households could supply. Because it helped overcome such labour constraints the plough became a rapidly adopted innovation. It was in fact used ubiquitously before Alvord's first demonstrators were even deployed. In the Chirumhanzu district the native commissioner reported 1100 ploughs being used in 1923 and 1600 ploughs in 1928; in the Mberengwa–Zvishavane area widespread adoption occurred during the 1920s and 30s (NC Belingwe, Annual Reports 1923–40). However, the plough was used in isolation of other recommended techniques. Its technological importance to peasant households was that it enabled them to compensate for the loss of males who had migrated to earn a cash income in order to pay taxes. This was because it enabled arable cultivation to become more extensive.

During the 1920s and 30s a large expansion in the area under cultivation took place in the Mberengwa–Zvishavane area (Wilson, 1986a, p. 2). This caused the Belingwe native commissioner to bemoan that 'good cultivation is sacrificed for a larger area' (Annual Report 1926). The ANC Shabani observed that there were 'large tracts of worked out land . . . (because) with the growing and general use of the plough extensive tillage takes place' (Annual Report 1934).

Yields dropped (Yudelman, 1964, p. 238 estimates that nationally peasant production yields decreased by half between 1900 and 1950[23]) but the additional area planted compensated for this. The plough permitted the same output to be produced for a reduced labour input.

In the Chirumhanzu area, as late as 1943 the native commissioner commented that: 'there is still a tendency to be land greedy; large tracts of land being ploughed up resulting in inability by the owner to care for his crops efficiently and consequently the stand gives a poor yield' (NC Chilimanzi, Annual Report 1943). Much of this area put under the plough was probably given over to growing maize. This was a crop that men controlled, using it for tax-paying purposes as well as for food. Women devoted more of their own labour time to rapoko and groundnuts, since they more directly controlled the crop output and the proceeds received from sales (NC Chilimanzi, Annual Report 1935).[24]

This was also the period when maize prices had fallen because of the Depression and the discriminatory Maize Control Acts. The decline in maize income had forced more men to seek wage employment in order to pay their taxes (NC Chilimanzi, Annual Reports 1931–3). Men were consequently in short supply in the reserves: in 1942, for instance, the NC Chilimanzi suggested that over a third of the 'able-bodied males of this district are at work in other districts' whilst many others were employed in the district itself (NC Chilimanzi, Annual Report 1942).[25]

Yet despite the cogent reasons the native commissioner identifies for agricultural labour not being devoted wholeheartedly to maize production, he still will not acknowledge the logicality of this behaviour:

> The Chilimanzi Reserve . . . is very backward. The people seem to be full of superstition and reluctant to take advice. The old demonstrator was discharged in August for misdemeanour and a new man appointed. The new man is endeavouring to court their confidence and has this year about 30 plots under his supervision. Great difficulty is experienced in turning out the natives to till as directed, especially mealie lands. (NC Chilimanzi, Annual Report 1935)

The new demonstrator had no more success. In 1940 he was moved to Chief Hama's area in the southern part of the Chirumhanzu communal area 'owing to the apathy of the natives in Chief Chilimanzi's area' (NC Chilimanzi, Annual Report 1940).

Nevertheless, apart from the use of the plough, there were some general changes occurring in production methods during this period. Nationally, for the first 22 years that demonstrators were deployed in the reserves, from 1926–7 to 1947–8, there was minimal change in the yields of farmers.[26] This suggests that at least a halt was brought to the decline in yields to which Yudelman refers; a decline which, for one thing, the forced shift to sedentary methods of cultivation would have brought about.

One of these changes that was occurring was the switchover from indigenous, multi-coloured, dwarf maize varieties, to white maize varieties producing larger-sized grains. Seed for these was obtained from white farmers (ANC Shabani, Annual Report 1926; NC Gwelo, Annual Reports 1927, 1929). Another shift was to the use of manure. In the late 1920s very little cattle manure was used as fertiliser (NC Chilimanzi, Annual Report 1928; NC Gwelo, Annual Report 1929). Farmers complained they did not have the carts to transport the manure from their cattle kraals to their fields (NC Gwelo, Annual Report 1924; NC Chilimanzi, Annual Report 1928), and besides, the manure 'produces too great a crop of weeds' (NC Gwelo, Annual Report 1928). A decade later, however, manure was used throughout the study region by nearly all the farmers who had access to it (NC Belingwe, Annual Report 1938; NC Chilimanzi, Annual Report 1938; NC Gwelo, Annual Report 1940).

By this time in the late 1930s, though, administrative attitudes were changing. It was soil conservation rather than soil fertilisation that was the agricultural activity of greatest concern. In particular, an end was being sought to the expansive practices of the 'plough entre-preneurs' (Ranger, 1985). The opening-up of new lands and the erosion being created by better stumping and consequent straighter ploughing 'up and down hills', were creating alarm because of their threat to the implementation of the Land Apportionment Act:

At several Native Board, Native Farmers' and public meetings, the necessity for conservation of arable lands has been discussed . . . The object in view is to control indiscriminate and wasteful ploughing, and reduce native lands to accommodate a larger population in the Reserves. The very mention of limiting lands roused a storm of protest, but the more intelligent natives are already realising that proper control is necessary, and the quickest course to it is by fertilising and correct methods. (NC Gwelo, Annual Report 1933)

It ws to deal with these issues of land use that the second of the major technical development policies to be launched was introduced. This was the policy of centralisation.

(ii) Centralisation

Centralisation was the first state policy to intervene directly in the nature of the lineage land tenure system. Alvord, the policy's architect, intended it to end the 'haphazard distribution of agricultural and grazing lands, which he saw as wasteful and injurious' (Godlonton Commission, 1944, para. 19). The policy involved the selection and separation out of land deemed suitable for arable and grazing purposes, with 'village lines' and roads 'centralised' between the two. Implementation began in the Shurugwi communal area in 1929. In Shurugwi, population expansion had already created problems. Cattle passing through arable fields to reach dip tanks were a particular source of friction. So after an initial experimental scheme had helped resolve some of the associated conflicts, Chief Nema requested that the whole reserve be centralised (Palmer, 1977a, p. 220).[27]

At first, as Table 2.4 shows, centralisation was pursued cautiously. By 1933 just seven reserves and some 480 103 acres had been affected (Agriculturalist, Native Affairs Department, Annual Report 1933, p. 13). There were two reasons for this. First, the number of agricultural demonstrator staff in the reserves was still very limited: by 1936, nine years after the first eleven demonstrators had been deployed, Alvord still only had an extension staff of four whites and 87 blacks (Palmer, 1977a, p. 202). Second, the imperially imposed Southern Rhodesian Constitution afforded protection against arbitrary settlement removal within the reserves. As people were being trucked on occasion over considerable distances to new settlement sites, the claim was made that the policy was being implemented on a 'voluntary' basis (Holleman, 1968, pp. 54–5). Until the 1951 Land Husbandry Act there was no direct statutory provision permitting this type of resettlement to be enforced. Long before this, however, the slippage to overt compulsion had taken place.

In some areas Alvord decided that the end justified the means: 'conditions on some reserves can only be remedied by making centralisation compulsory' (Agriculturalist, NAD, Annual Report 1933; in Palmer, 1977a, p. 221). Owing to the staff shortage several schemes were steamrollered through with minimal explanation

Table 2.4   Agricultural demonstration and land use reform: numbers performance 1929–62

Year or season	No. of demonstration plotholders	No. of master farmers	Area centralised or demarcated under land husbandry* (acres)
1928/29	44 (1)		
1929/30			145 000 (3)
1933/34	320 (1)		480 103 (3)
1936			1 203 637 (4)
1938/39	1 054 (1)		2 400 000 (4)
1942/43	843 (1)		7 386 250 (5)
1946			
1948	2 017 (2)	764 (2)	
1950/51	3 287 (2)	1 665 (2)	8 200 000 (6)
1955	4 582 (2)	5 322 (2)	140 000 *(6)
1960	5 327 (2)	8 966 (2)	15 046 000 *(6)
1962			16 726 000 *(6)

Sources: (1) Godlonton Commission, 1944; para. 61.
(2) Johnson, 1964, p. 181.
(3) Agriculturalist, NAD, Annual Report 1933, p. 13.
(4) Palmer, 1977a, p. 22.
(5) Godlonton Commission, 1944; para. 19.
(6) Bulman, 1973.

'regardless of African wishes and sometimes in the teeth of outright opposition'. Where this happened the people affected simply regarded the schemes as another device for reducing their collective land holding (Palmer, 1977a, p. 221).

In the study areas the native commissioners admit in their annual reports that implementation did not proceed altogether smoothly. Their comments on how rural communities had 'accepted' the scheme are tempered by juxtaposed statements on associated conflicts. For example, the Lower Gweru and Chiwundura (Que Que reserve) communal areas were centralised in 1935 and the native commissioner reported that: 'The centralisation of the Reserves into agricultural, pastoral and living areas was carried out very easily, occupants adapting themselves readily to the new order' (Annual Report 1935). Yet the following year the native commissioner was stating: 'Considerable difficulties have been experienced in getting them to make lands in the areas denoted for this; they keep trying to plough their old lands in the grazing areas' (Annual Report 1936).

During the 1930s, though, the degree of coercion employed in implementing centralisation was still muted. In 1933, the agricultural demonstrators were supplemented by community demonstrators whose work lay in the new village 'lines'. Households were encouraged to build their new homes from burnt kimberley bricks instead of the old pole and dagga, and to make compost pits for the fertilisation of small vegetable gardens. An idyllic picture was painted by the Gweru native commissioner:

A journey through the areas in which these Demonstrators are operating affords a striking view of the progress which is being made. Better housing, cleaner surroundings, small vegetable and even flower gardens, with the improved methods of agriculture and tilth, together with the centralisation of pastural and arable areas, are a striking testimony to the policy of this Department. (NC Gweru, Annual Report 1939)

One factor spoilt this contemplation: 'In the Que Que Native Reserve there is a need for soil conservation' (NC Gweru, Annual Report 1939). In the 1940s, as communal area population and livestock densities increased (see Tables 2.1 and 2.2), the emphasis of the centralisation exercise switched to the implementation of conservation works. Blocks of arable land began to be contoured, the new individual holdings standardised in size and reallocation made, not by the lineage leaders, but by the Native Affairs Department. Opposition grew.

In the Runde communal area, centralisation was carried out in 1938–9. No opposition was reported then, but nor did the land use demarcation exercise appear to have affected farmers' activities greatly: 'Efforts to discourage ploughing up and down gradients are being continued, with rather indifferent results' (ANC Shabani, Annual Report 1939). In 1945, mechanical conservation measures – the digging of contour ridges, drain strips, storm and road drains, and the protection of gullies – were begun. Progress was slow and expensive. In 1946 the ANC Shabani not entirely facetiously remarked that unless they received tractors to assist, 'the Lundi Reserve will still have its contouring gang pegging away in 2000 AD' (Annual Report 1946).

A tractor did arrive and costs escalated. Nationally £106 171 was spent on soil conservation works between 1936 and 1946 (Agriculturalist, NAD, Annual Report 1947), but the bulk of the conservation works were constructed after this date. In 1948 the Native

Development Fund (NDF) was established to provide the funding for all 'development' work in the reserves. Over the thirteen-year period until 1961, about one-third of the fund's capital came from a 'development levy' on formal sales of cattle and crops from the reserves (Johnson, 1964, p. 213). Peasant farmers participating in the formal economy were therefore paying directly for the implementation of the conservation works. In the Zvishavane area in 1951 and 1952, 31 per cent and 32 per cent respectively of NDF expenditure was spent on soil conservation works, and in Chirumhanzu it was 28 per cent for each of those two years.

The construction of these works was not appreciated. 'In the Lundi Reserve, failure by landholders to maintain demarcations on lands and the ploughing across contours by others resulted in a number of prosecutions under the Natural Resources Act' (ANC Shabani, Annual Report 1951). The NC Chilimanzi called soil conservation the 'least popular' development work and recorded that labour for the conservation gangs was hard to obtain (ANC Shabani, Annual Report 1952). However, if they observed it, the native commissioners played down the underswell of resentment that was building up. Wilson (1986e, p. 1; 1988c) records that farmers in the Zvishavane area hold that the digging of conservation works accelerated erosion. The concentrated run-off which occurred when a contour ridge broke, or from water flowing out the end of a poorly sited and constructed contour, led to gully erosion and stream development on a scale not previously experienced.

No local research was carried out into the comparative effectiveness of different conservation techniques. Instead it is likely that the specific concept of mechanical conservation was imported from America, where Alvord and other officials visited in the mid-1930s. This was part of a general trend in which the Southern African region was becoming increasingly open to technical ideas being dispersed from the international scientific arena (Beinart, 1984, pp. 67–9). This 'developing technical discourse', as Beinart terms it, was taking place in a period when the activity of planning was assuming a central role in the operation of bureaucratic states. Increasingly, 'more total intervention as a means of solving the political and technical problems that arise from limited intervention' was being advocated (Beinart, personal communication, 1988). Thus local political trends were being fuelled not only by their own discourse but by international trends as well.

By 1950, however, rural peoples' physical experience of the

hardening of attitudes within the administration towards agrarian policy was not merely limited to the slow but relentless march of conservation works. For by this time the destocking programme of the mid to late 1940s had been enforced rigorously and comprehensively.

(iii) Destocking

From 1943 implementation of the centralisation policy eased up (Table 2.4) as the NAD emphasis switched to the environmental evils being wrought by 'overstocking'. In 1942, the Natural Resources Board (NRB) was established following the passage of the Natural Resources Act the previous year. The Board, concerned with what it viewed as escalating land degradation in the reserves, began its life by pushing vigorously for the promulgation of destocking regulations (Passmore, 1972, p. 26; CNC, Annual Report 1961, p. 25). This demand was backed up by a broad official consensus. Morris (CNC, Annual Report 1961) comments that the only arguments between the NRB and H. D. Simmonds, then Chief Native Commissioner, were 'not over the objects in view, but the speed and methods by which they might be achieved'. The Board was 'solidly behind technical advice and planning as against sociological views' and as such favoured coercive action (p. 25). They got it. In 1943 regulations were enacted for the compulsory destocking of animals in areas 'where this was necessary' (Passmore, 1972, p. 26), and in 1945 a five-year destocking plan was launched to enforce the regulations.

The 'need' for destocking was established on what was presented as a rigorous technical basis. From 1946, statistics on population and livestock 'concentrations' in the reserves appear in the annual reports of the Director of Native Agriculture. Livestock carrying capacities were simply decided on the basis of whether an area was in a 'high', 'medium', or 'low' rainfall area:

High rainfall   (+28"):   10 acres per animal
Medium rainfall (20–24"): 13.5 acres per animal
Low rainfall   (−20"):   16.67 acres per animal

In individual reserves the only concession made to factors affecting land quality was that extremely rocky areas were excluded. Carrying capacities were defined by estimating the total area of a reserve and that suitable for grazing and arable purposes, and then dividing this by the appropriate acreage deemed necessary per animal (see

Table 2.5 Livestock concentrations: the technical basis for destocking 1946–50

Area	Year	Total area (acres)	Area for grazing (& arable)	Cattle	Total in large stock equivalent	Carrying capacity for stock	% Over- or under-stocked
Chirumhanzu	1946	275 431	259 809	23 384	27 186	25 980	+4
	1947	275 431	259 809	21 570	24 833	25 980	−4
	1948	275 431	259 809	22 575	25 103	25 980	−3
	1949	257 470	244 557	24 570	27 105	24 456	+10.8
	1950	257 470	244 557	24 193	26 719	24 456	+9
Chiwundura	1946	47 100	47 100	5 628	6 524	3 541	+84
	1948	47 100	44 475	4 826	5 932	3 355	+77
	1949	44 830	42 800	4 401	5 050	3 205	+57.5
	1950	44 830	42 800	4 501	5 252	3 205	+63
Runde (Lundi South)	1946	156 490	150 605	15 805	17 595	11 292	+55
	1948	156 490	150 605	12 933	14 310	11 295	+27
	1949	159 670	153 361	12 403	13 653	10 952	+24.6
	1950	159 670	153 361	13 106	14 428	11 290	+27

Sources: Director of Native Agriculture, Annual Reports 1946–50; NC Chilimanzi, Annual Report 1947.

Table 2.5). The figure obtained for the carrying capacity of the reserve as a whole was then compared with the actual estimate for the 'large stock equivalent' (that is, including donkeys, goats and sheep) to determine the '% overstocked' figure. The validity of this technical basis for assessing 'overstocking' will be commented upon in Chapter 4.

In early 1945 destocking plans were approved for those 49 out of the total of 93 reserves that were declared overstocked. The time spread and number of stock to be affected in each plan were determined by the exent of overstocking and overpopulation. The herds of individual owners were to be reduced on a percentage basis according to herd size. Owners with small herds were in theory to be exempt initially (CNC, Annual Report 1945, p. 8), although over the five-year period the correct stocking rate was nevertheless supposed to be achieved (CNC, Annual Report 1948, p. 12).

The course of the destocking exercise in the Chirumhanzu communal area is well described by the NC Chilimanzi (Annual Reports 1944–8). In 1944 the reserve was declared 22.7 per cent overstocked. The people were warned of the 'evils':

> Every effort has been made during the year and in the past to persuade natives to reduce their holdings of stock, special meetings of natives were called at which the evils resulting from overstocking were explained to stockowners and they were warned that unless they reduced their stock compulsory measures would have to be taken. (NC Chilimanzi, Annual Report 1944)

Yet despite this 'propaganda' formal sales of cattle dropped by 758 head in 1944 compared with the previous year. The reasons for this were that the season had been a good one with a large grain harvest, and prices were up on what they had been in the 1930s. In his 1944 Annual Report the NC acknowledged these factors, but failed to acknowledge that from his statement on the condition of the veld (grazing land) he had no grounds for speaking of the 'evils' of overstocking. 'The past season was a good one in so far as native stock was concerned. Grazing was fair throughout the year and there was no shortage of water' (Annual Report 1944). There was thus no need for stock owners to increase their sales.

The following year, 1945, was another 'good one for native stock', wrote the NC (Annual Report 1945). Nevertheless at the end of the year destocking began in earnest. Stock owners were informed that their herds would have to be reduced to nine animals in order to meet the destocking requirements. According to the NC:

> Natives have accepted destocking with a fatalistic equanimity; there were always arguments and replies to propaganda in its favour, but the fact that talk has been followed by action seems to have shocked them into mute acceptance. (NC Chilimanzi, Annual Report 1945)

Well, not quite: 'There has been a large increase in the numbers of native-owned cattle in the European area from 9998 to 14 401 in 1945.'

In the period 1944–7, as Table 2.6 shows, cattle figures fell by 21 per cent in the Chirumhanzu communal area through destocking. In

Table 2.6   Destocking in Chirumhanzu 1944–7

	1944	1945	1946	1947
Cattle numbers	27 287	26 860	23 384	21 507
(Cattle sales)	(1 685)	(1 710)	(2 815)	(3 769)
Total animal units*	31 798	32 035	27 186	24 833
No. allowed GN 62/44		25 980	25 980	25 980
Excess		6 055	1 206	−1 147

* Including donkeys, sheep and goats.

Source: NC Chilimanzi, Annual Reports 1944–7.

1946 there was a drought and in 1947 an even more serious one.[28] The maize harvest fell in 1947 to 2000 bags compared with 23 000 bags in 1945. Cattle were either sold (3769 head in formal sales) for grain or cash, or slaughtered for food (2779 head). Small stock were likewise consumed for food (NC Chilimanzi, Annual Report 1947). The drought combined with the destocking programme meant that the Chirumhanzu communal area was now understocked by over 1000 head. A year later it was still in the same position (NC Chilimanzi, Annual Report 1948) and in fact the average level of stock ownership never recovered to the level it had been before (Table 2.2). The effect of the destocking programme was that it curtailed the common mechanism employed by Shona peoples until then for ameliorating the impact of drought, the trading of grain for cattle.

Destocking had one other highly significant social impact. In order to 'save' animals from destocking, a great deal of redistribution of cattle took place through *kuronzera*, the pre-colonial system of loaning to clients for safekeeping. But because these cattle were then registered with the new owners, a *de facto* equalising of cattle holdings took place (Floyd, 1961, p. 150).

In the Runde and Chiwundura communal areas destocking was also implemented, though with less zeal than in Chirumhanzu. The livestock figures remained above the stipulated carrying capacities (Table 2.5). The ANC Shabani reported for 1946:

Despite record sales, stock continue to increase and the Lundi Reserve is now overstocked by 6517 head. Reduction of stock to the carrying capacity of a Reserve is doubly difficult when such Reserve is also overpopulated (by 37 per cent). During the year 3831 head of cattle were sold. This increase was only achieved by the application of the destocking regulations. (Annual Report 1946)

Chiwundura was considered even more overpopulated – by a whole 182 per cent in 1946! – so that although destocking quotas were met the reserve was still 57.5 per cent over the official carrying capacity at the end of 1949 (NC Gweru, Annual Reports 1946–9).

Effectively, the equalisation of cattle holdings meant that destocking had not been as successful in reducing the numbers of animals on the land as the NAD had anticipated. It was virtually inevitable, therefore, that the next problem to come onto the technical development policy agenda was that of 'overpopulation'. The policy designed to incorporate this issue with the established concern for land use was that of land husbandry.

The land husbandry era of the 1950s was to prove the apogee of the technical development phase. During this period the coercive enforcement of technical development ran amok to such an extent that by the early 1960s even the colonial administration was forced to question the logic of its approach and to question some of the human costs.

(iv) Land Husbandry

For a while the drought of 1946 and the even more severe one the following year took the sting out of the destocking programme.

Destocking was naturally assisted through both increased mortality rates and 'voluntary' sales of stock to provide cash for food purposes. This allowed the CNC to report in July 1948 that the 'excess' in the now 52 overstocked reserves had been reduced by 70.4 per cent – 10.4 per cent more than the actual target set for this time (CNC, Annual Report 1948, p. 12).

Following the two consecutive drought years recognition was occurring, even in the higher reaches of the NAD, that destocking was having a negative effect on the rural economy, 'in some cases reducing individual holdings to an uneconomic figure' (CNC, Annual Report 1948, p. 12). This recognition only earned, though, a paternalistic reference to irresponsibility:

> Few however are able to see beyond their own individual interests or fully appreciate the necessity of keeping stock holdings down to the carrying capacity to preserve the natural resources of their land for future generations. (Annual Report 1948, p. 12)

By now, too, the pseudo technocratic juggling of figures, definitions and alternative courses of bureaucratic action had become firmly embedded within the NAD's approach to the formulation and amendment of policy. Trapped within this constrictive purposive rationality, it was considered that policy 'improvements' could only be made by increasing the technical scope and refinement of the policy framework.

> whilst certain improvements [in the destocking policy] may be made in administration, for example by redefining land units and reassessing carrying capacity, new regulations and possibly new legislation may be required to achieve a proper balance between economic stock holdings and the natural resources. It is envisaged that individual holdings of stock therefore be reduced to, but not below, the figure fixed as a minimum economic stock holding for any particular area . . . To achieve this however, without undue damage to the land, some means must be found of relating stockholdings to the human carrying capacity and this can only be done by limiting the number of stockowners. (CNC, Annual Report 1948, pp. 12–13)

From the mid-1940s, such thinking as this, that the introduction of fully coercive measures was the only way the 'native' could be taught to look after 'his' own interests, was gathering ground. By 1944 even Alvord had become despairing:

We have wasted our time for 17 years in conducting agricultural demonstration work . . . average yields on plots have been 10 times the yield on ordinary native lands. The lessons to be learned have been preached for the past 16 years, yet the vast majority . . . have made no change . . . It is now quite evident that they will never change without compulsion and control. (in Passmore, 1972, p. 25)

The time of Alvord, the agricultural evangelist, had however passed. The nature of the figure who replaced him as the chief architect of land use policy is symbolic of the shift, following the Second World War, in international, as well as national, development policy mood. In the same year that Alvord wrote the above, the Report of the Native Production and Trade Commission (Godlonton Commission) was published. This report laid the foundation for the 1951 Native Land Husbandry Act (LHA). Secretary of the Godlonton Commission was Arthur Pendered, and it is he whom Holleman identifies as the prime mover behind land husbandry. Unlike Alvord, Pendered remained a remote manipulator. Operating from a key-position in the departmental structure, he acted as a spokesman for the 'progressive' technical branches rather than for the 'conservative' administrative branch from which he originated.[29] Skilfully marshalling his forces and arguments, and backed by the necessary finance and a vast service organisation, he gained wide support for the execution of his ideas during the 1950s, thereby manoeuvring the administrative branch ('controlling power') of the Division into a position in which, albeit reluctantly, it had by and large to follow his lead (Holleman, 1968, pp. 53–4).

In the Godlonton Commission report is illustrated clearly the involuted, selective and often contradictory thinking employed by the colonial state in its claim that to bring the benefits of 'civilisation' to the African peoples, coercion had to be used. The Commission notes that in the evidence taken Africans had 'frankly exposed their fears and suspicions' (para. v). They were informed that a principle reason for the rejection of new agricultural techniques was the fear that any raising of production levels would countenance yet further land appropriation (para. 63). Yet in its key recommendations on 'good husbandry', the Godlonton Commission's members ignored this insight totally. Instead they advocated command planning:

In our opinion, the maximum benefits, both for the State and for the Natives from Native agriculture and animal husbandry, can only be obtained by compulsory planning of production, whereby a statutory body should be empowered to direct what crops, acreages and areas should be planted and what livestock should be kept, to enforce good husbandry conditions, and to control the distribution and marketing of the consequent products. (para. 95)

In his 1961 review Morris described the Godlonton Commission's report as the 'decisive point of departure towards compulsory powers' (CNC, Annual Report 1961, p. 26). Its recommendations for a 'Good Husbandry Act' came to fruition in 1951.

The Native Land Husbandry Act was conceived as a 'large-scale agrarian development scheme' which would 'transform agriculture in the African reserves' (Bulman, 1973, p. 2). Towards this end, especially once an accelerated five-year plan was launched in 1955, the entire technical and administrative resource base of the NAD was committed. Between 1950 and 1958 the Act cost over £15 million, 'at the expense, let it be admitted, of most of the other facets of administration' (CNC, Annual Report 1961, p. 26).

The purposive rationality which underlay the LHA can be gleaned even from the title of the government document which sets out the Act's objectives: 'What the Native Land Husbandry Act means to the rural African of Southern Rhodesia' (1955). In short, the Act was to be imposed whatever the rural African thought of it. Indeed a Select Committee of black leaders warned in 1951 that the authoritarian nature of the Act could only aggravate antagonism between African farmers and European administrators (Floyd, 1961, pp. 244–5). The administration disregarded such warnings, as had the Godlonton Commission seven years previously.

The main assumptions and principles of the LHA, as extracted from the above-mentioned government document and reports of the CNC, were:

(1) The natural environment of the reserves had to be protected, and to ensure this, measures of good husbandry enforced.
(2) This required limiting stock holdings since farmers themselves could not be expected to see 'beyond their own individual interests', and therefore would not 'preserve the natural resources of their land for future generations' (CNC, Annual Report 1948, p. 12).
(3) 'Economic holdings' should be allocated and registered on an individual basis, so as to provide security of tenure and hence

maximise producer incentive. (This principle thus runs counter to (2), in which 'individual interests' are denigrated.)

(4) As there was not enough land for 'economic holdings' to be provided for even all the rural adult *male* population, those without land should emigrate to the urban areas and find secure employment.

These assumptions and principles depend for their valdiity on the adequacy of the concept of an 'economic holding'. The definition of this concept can be evaluated in technical and economic terms, and its appropriateness in social terms. For the moment I will confine myself to discussing the technical and economic aspects.

The concept of an economic unit is first mooted in the Godlonton Commission's report:

> under optimum conditions of high rainfall, the practice of crop rotation, the use of manure, and proper marketing facilities, a peasant with 6 acres and a herd of 6 head of cattle could reap 10 bags per acre and expect a cash return of between £18 and £23 per annum after his subsistence needs had been met. (in Weinrich, 1975, p. 25)

The grain crop economics are worked on the assumption that the average family (size unstated, but probably taken as 4–5 people) needs 20–25 bags of grain for its subsistence for a year, leaving 30–40 bags from the 6 acres for sale (assuming that the whole area is planted under grain). An average sale price of 10/- per bag is used, which would fetch £15–20 (para. 61). The remaining £3 is presumably from the sale of an animal. The Godlonton Commission did recognise that in the drier parts of the country, where arable farming was extremely hazardous, farmers should be permitted to maintain larger herds (para. 74).

The 'standard' or 'economic holding' set down in the land husbandry policy followed both this latter principle and the Commission's basic definition of an economic unit (Table 2.7). However, the economic and technical bases of the model do not stand up to scrutiny. Consider just one aspect of the definition, yield.

The figure for yield, which is crucial to the whole calculation, is obtained from a table included in paragraph 61 of the report. The table shows that the average yield for demonstration plotholders varied between 9.5 and 10.9 bags per acre over four seasons between 1928 and 1943. Apart from the narrowness of the data base,[30] this

Table 2.7   'Standard' or 'economic' holding sizes

Ave. annual rainfall	Areas of arable land (acres)	No. of livestock units	Stocking rate (acres/LU)	Approx. total acreage per holding (1)
28″+	8 (2)	6	10	68
24″–28″	8	6	12	80
20″–24″	10	10	15	160
16″–20″	12	15	25	390
–16″	15	20	30	620

Notes: (1)   'Total acreage per holding' is not a real concept, since grazing areas were not enclosed but remained communal. Grazing rights were for stock, not for area.

(2)   In the high rainfall areas 6 acres were meant for cultivation and the additional 2 acres were meant for legumes or fodder production.

Source: Government of Southern Rhodesia, 1955, in Bulman, 1973, p. 11.

means that the Godlonton Commission is calculating the necessary yield figure for an economic holding from the average yields of probably less than 0.5 per cent of farmers.[31] The average crop returns of most farmers, as the Commission also records, were then less than 2 bags per acre. In sum, with over 99.5 per cent of cultivators then producing at yield levels far lower than those required to meet their definition of an 'economic holding', the Godlonton confidence in the concept was rather fantastic.[32]

If this faulty definition of an 'economic holding' was not sufficiently problematic, when implementation of land husbandry began an additional 'technical' hitch was exposed: there was not enough arable land in the reserves. When the registration exercises for the implementation of the LHA were carried out in the 1950s, it was found that full holdings could only be created for about two-thirds of those deemed eligible for them.[33] Faced with the nominal possibility of creating 100 000 landless families (plus those not able to register), it was decided the 'solution' to this would be to treat the 'economic holding' as an ideal 'economic and viable unit' (CNC, Annual Report 1959, p. 11). In areas where there was land scarcity, less than the full holding would be allocated, in most cases by reducing the stock holding. In other words, the already non-economic concept of an 'economic holding' was being devalued still further. Floyd, a researcher at the time, in fact calculated that as many as 61.2 per cent of land allocations would have to be made in terms of the 'intermediate or tight formulae' regulations (1961, p. 223).

Beinart (1984, p. 79) suggests the strategy of delimiting economic units was yet another import from the USA. In the communal areas the attempt to implement it created considerable trauma. And in their warning that resistance would be generated to the LHA the black Select Committee proved right. The NC Chilimanzi provides an evocative illustration of this in his annual reports.

In 1943 the NC drew attention to a problem that was looming because the area immediately south of the Chilimanzi reserve had been designated under the Land Apportionment Act as an African Purchase Area:

> The Zinyaningwe Purchase Area has not yet been surveyed into farms and at present there are some 267 native tenants with an established population of 2146. The tenants own 2838 head of cattle and when the time comes for them to be moved off Zinyaningwe, it will be difficult to settle them in the Reserve, more especially will it be difficult to decide where to put their cattle because the Reserve is already overstocked. (Annual Report 1943)

Over the next eleven years the native commissioner tried unsuccessfully to obtain permission to have the Zinyaningwe area declared part of the communal area. Eventually in 1955, the by now 500 families and 4800 Large Stock Equivalent (LSE)[34] were moved into the southern Chirumhanzu area, considerably exacerbating pressures on the land.

Real disaster was initiated on 27 August 1957, when the NLHA Assessment Committee sat at Mvuma. Its recommendations, gazetted in November, were drastic. Until then, as shown in Table 2.7, the carrying capacity for livestock in Chirumhanzu had been set at a rate of approximately 10 acres per LSE, and for the calculation of the area's overall carrying capacity the only land that had been deducted from the total area was that delimited excessively rocky. Now the Assessment Committee readjusted the figures. The stocking rate was set at 1 LSE per 11 acres,[35] and 69 000 acres were subtracted as being under arable cultivation. At a stroke of a pen it was decided 14 306 LSE would have to go – some 47 per cent of the livestock in the communal area! The native commissioner could only make a gesture of protest: 'In spite of this apparent overstocking cattle remained in fairly good condition throughout the year' (Annual report, 1957). The axe fell the following year. In 1958 the number of LSE fell by 12 183 – 12 347 head of cattle alone went (4660 head sold, 5677 head slaughtered for consumption, 222 head died, 1788 head removed from district). 'The stock owners took this unpleasant manoeuvre very well', the NC tried to bluff (Annual Report 1958). He was wrong. They were incensed. Forced to resell at low prices to neighbouring white farmers, people felt that their cattle had been 'taken' (Weinrich, 1964, p. 19).

The NC did become worried. In 1959 he requested funds for the 'intensive development' of the southern half of the Chirumhanzu communal area, saying that unless this development was carried out people would need to be moved out. But by 1961, no funds had arrived, no families had been moved, and people were openly expressing their resentment of the administration. Throughout the Chirumhanzu communal area and especially in the south, there was an outpouring of resistance to the implementation of the LHA:

> It was confidently expected that land allocation would have been finished this year and that (as a concomitant) the total farmed extent of the two Reserves[36] would have been reduced to the calculated required acreage, and wholesale intensive extension work undertaken in an endeavour to rehabilitate the Chilimanzi Reserve in particular: but determined non-cooperation on the part of the husbandmen resulted in only about 400 acres being dealt with instead of an estimated 27 000 acres.[37] (NC Chilimanzi, Annual Report 1961)

The nature of this non-cooperation was specified more clearly later in the report:

> this office's complacency was severely jarred when the first pre-allocation meeting disclosed how much antipathy to the Act had grown (fomented by widespread political agitation). Passivity turned to overt and active opposition, and physical attacks were made on Native Development Fund staff and on demonstrators and others, and intimidation was rampant and effective. Over a score of criminal prosecutions followed (including that of the cousin of Chief Chilimanzi). (Annual Report 1961)[38]

The breaking-out of overt opposition to the LHA in Chirumhanzu was part of the culmination of a substantial national protest raised against the LHA (CNC, Annual Reports, 1959–62). The most surprising thing about this protest is that the administration did not expect it. Seventeen years previously the Godlonton Commission had been warned that protest might arise because people feared further land appropriation. And although no further reductions of the communal areas had occurred, if the administration had comprehended economic trends in the areas they could not have been so astonished. First, the coupling of population growth with the periodic removals of people into the communal areas, had led, as shown in Tables 2.1 and 2.2, to the steady rise of population densities. But more crucially, the rigid implementation of destocking regulations in the late 1940s and again in the mid-1950s had drastically reduced livestock holdings – to the extent, for instance, that after commenting in the late 1930s on the widespread use of fertiliser, by 1956 the NC Gweru was stating that farmers no longer had 'the means to manure the lands'. Consequently, soil fertility was being depleted so that he doubted 'whether the majority will ever make an independent living from the land' (Annual Report 1956). This belief was echoed by the NC Chilimanzi (Annual Reports 1959, 1961). The NC Shabani, after overt opposition to the LHA had also occurred in the Runde communal area in 1961, acknowledged:

> One realises that during the past four years while the Act was in the process of being applied . . . people have been subjected to a lot of pressure . . . and have not seen any real benefits. In their minds the Act has resulted in small pieces of land, destocking, and hard work in the form of digging contours. (Annual Report 1961)

There were clear signs therefore that the implementation of the Land Apportionment Act and the technical development policies was placing the rural economy under stress. However, for as long as they could, the administration's officials postponed interpreting the signs. In 1958 the NAD sharply rejected the charge by the short-lived African National Congress[38] that the Act was 'a vicious device whose principal aims and objectives are to uproot, impoverish and disperse the African people' (in Floyd, 1961, p. 268).[40] Even as late as 1959, Morris, as yet an unshaken Chief Native Commissioner, was reporting a senior NAD official who claimed to have found in the districts 'nothing but enthusiasm and a welcome for the consolidated and secure tenure [the LHA had] brought among the people' (CNC, Annual Report 1959, p. 2). Morris continued further:

> Undoubtedly, the severest critics of the Act are to be found among the 'landless' who live in the towns. It is surprising how they

cherish the ancient sentiment that everyone, be he businessman, skilled worker or head waiter, has a natural right to cultivate a piece of land . . . Of course, the facts are that no man who is actually tilling land or grazing cattle on the day the Act is applied to his particular area is deprived of his right to till or graze his cattle . . . If there is any move on his part to town, it will be predominantly the attraction of conditions there which move him, not a pushing out at the rural end. (Annual Report 1959, p. 2)

The CNC therefore understood very little about the way in which migrant labour and agricultural production were necessarily interconnected in rural relations of production. He was not acknowledging that urban wage levels for most black workers were insufficient for them to support an urban family (Arrighi, 1973, p. 216) and that instead most black workers were under obligation to remit money or goods to help support a rural-based household.[41] He was also ignorant of just how many people had *not* been allocated land during the implementation of the LHA, as for instance was reported by the Mangwende Commission in 1961.[42]

Throughout the technical development phase, the Native Affairs Department had therefore remained confident and complacent about the presumed benefits of the policies they were enforcing. This complacency was completely shaken by the overt opposition to the LHA which erupted in many parts of the country in 1961. This was the first physical resistance the colonial state had experienced from the rural populace since the 1896–7 First Chimurenga. It initiated a brief but quite remarkable period of reflection. No significant policy change took place, however, for the admissions made by the NAD and the then United Federal Party government served instead to bring down the government in December 1962. Why this occurred is the topic of the final section of this chapter.

REFLECTION AND COLLUSION, 1962–5

The brief flurry of debate generated by the shock of the overt opposition to the LHA was extraordinarily open. It also became extraordinarily heated, forging a sharp polarisation of white political viewpoints. The net outcome was not liberalisation but the entrenched conservatism of the Rhodesian Front (RF).

In the early 1960s the 'winds of change' were gathering strength in

Africa.[43] Morris's soul-searching but optimistic historical review was thus written against this background. Having now become convinced of the need for policy change, he readily admitted that the naive perceptions so long trotted out by the NAD staff needed to be discarded:

> The year 1961 has been a crisis year in that old usages and concepts have been shaken up, examined in detail by working parties and discussed interminably in the light of appreciations and recommendations made by three objective commissions. (CNC, Annual Report 1961, p. 29)

The three commissions were the Quinton, Mangwende and Robinson Commissions.[44] The four working parties were set up to examine the proposals of the Robinson Commission. And in 1962 two more commissions, the Paterson and the Philips,[45] also produced reports. Collectively these reports called into question the efficacy of the state's use of coercion to implement policies (Holleman, 1968, pp. 219–20). The Mangwende Commission, of which Holleman was a member, in particular, questioned in strong terms some of the crucial assumptions that underlay the land husbandry strategy. Questioning too the social desirability of using force to brush aside conflicting views, the Commission called for unforced communication as a means of seeking common ground between the discrepant world-views of white and blacks. This theme in the Commission's report, which strikes a chord with elements of Habermas's theory of communicative action, is returned to in the next chapter. What I shall briefly refer to here is the Commission's comments on the social and economic assumptions contained in the LHA.

The key assumption that the Mangwende Commission undermined was that the LHA was improving the individual's security of land tenure in the communal areas. The Commission pointed out that the notion of a fixed land right which the Act had imposed on the Shona peoples, was an alternative interpretation of what constituted secure tenure to that already embraced by the Shona land system. In Shona societies rights of access to land were attached to a person's membership in a particular territorial community; security thereby lay in a member's 'vested right to claim a share' (para. 82). However, under the LHA, rights were 'related to actual occupation (lawful cultivation) at an arbitrarily appointed date line. This condition is foreign and wholly irrelevant to land rights in indigenous society' (para. 88). According to the Mangwende Commission it was this conflicting interpretation of what constituted secure tenure that was the 'understandable cause of public discontent', since the Act had deprived 'a considerable portion of the recognised rural village membership of its basic right to land':

> Among these people, many of whom are young migrant wage earners preparing for a married rural life, this sudden deprivation is likely to engender a feeling of insecurity and a sense of injustice, which is not easily dispelled by arguments, however pertinent, of an economic or legalistic nature. The issue touches such a sensitive field of African thought and ambition, that the utmost consideration for the human aspect would have to be exercised in this approach . . . in this respect, however, the Land Husbandry Act is sadly lacking. (para. 90)

Women's usufruct land rights to which under the lineage system all women were entitled, even if their labour was exploited, were similarly affected, although the Mangwende Commission did not draw attention to this. What is to be noted here is the colonial administration's reaction to the reports of the various commissions and working parties.

In the case of Morris, his response as Chief Native Commissioner was to be stimulated and innovative. He accepted the conclusions of the commissions: the coercive imposition of alien technical policies was non-productive:

> It is now obvious that imposed technical planning has had its day . . .
>
> The problem is not a technical one, nor is the crux of it the extent to which capital, management and labour are there to develop the land, as the economist would have it. It seems clear that the more a technical approach is adopted, the more technicians try and reinforce their objectives with modern mass-media, the greater becomes the cultural resistance. We must see it as a human problem . . . What we have been seeking is a transformation of a whole society, using influences from outside to do it and concentration on individuals and one specific aspect of their lives. (CNC, Annual Report 1961, pp. 26–7)

Morris decided that what was necessary was the introduction of a community development policy. In this the government was once more influenced by policy fashions in the United States. In May 1962 a project agreement was signed between the Southern Rhodesian government and US AID (CNC, Annual Report 1962, p. 1). At this juncture, though, the white electorate intervened. In December 1962 Whitehead's United Federal Party (UFP) was voted out of power and replaced by the Rhodesian Front. In the same month the dissolution of the Federation of the Rhodesias and Nyasaland was agreed. This reaction against the UFP was because of white fears of what its move towards liberalisation would entail (Holleman, 1968, pp. 271–2). The UFP's acceptance in principle of the recommendation of the Second Quinton Report of 1960 to repeal the Land Apportionment Act created the breaking-point (Rifkind, 1969, p. 155). The debate within both the NAD and the UFP directly threatened the rationale which had been employed by the state for pursuing white interests at the expense of black interests. Inevitably such questioning, if it continued, could lead only to a breakdown in the solidarity of the white settler group, and the maintenance of this was essential to the continuity of white political and economic power. The white electorate believed in 1962 that it faced a choice between the alternatives

> either to put one's faith in the rather obscure prospect of seeking cooperation with an African leadership that vociferously challenged white supremacy; or to stick to entrenched positions which, no matter how heavily besieged they might be in times to come at least represented all the familiar and fondly cherished values and benedictions of the 'European way of life'. (Holleman, 1968, p. 272)

The RF election victory brought to an end the period of reflection. In 1963, Morris complained that community development was now being regarded as 'some strange obsession' of the Ministry of Internal Affairs (Secretary for Internal Affairs, Annual Report 1963, p. 1).[46] When the community development policy was eventually launched in July 1965, it was used by the RF not to ameliorate but to reinforce the policy of segregation (Holleman, 1968, p. 276). The Land Apportionment Act, far from being abolished, was replaced in strengthened form by the 1969 Land Tenure Act.

The government no longer sought to justify in public its segregationist policies, as the previous Southern Rhodesian governments had done, through appeal to a social Darwinist ideology of white superiority. The debates of the early 1960s had revealed the pitfalls of being open, so the RF simply sought to stifle further political debate. They were supported by the majority of the white electorate, for whom reflection was a supremely uncomfortable exercise. Growing nationalist opposition was repressed in mid-1965 by the detention or restriction of most active nationalist leaders – a move which helped to catalyse the switch to a military strategy. The belief by whites in their cultural superiority, and hence moral rectitude, remained however unshakened.

Unquestionably the vast majority of Rhodesian whites were deeply convinced of their superior judgement in these matters. Quite apart from wishing to protect their own interests they also genuinely felt that they had at least a moral right, if not an obligation, to ensure that they could exercise and enforce this judgement in order to protect 'the black masses against irresponsible and self-seeking leadership'. And the only effective means of achieving this was, in their view, the continuance of white political supremacy 'for the time being' (Holleman, 1968, p. 287).

This type of behaviour is described by Bates (1983) as 'collusive behaviour'. As a minority group, white Rhodesians needed to prevent any internal dissent over the measures used to contain the black population from rising to levels which might endanger white collective interests. Thus in-group processes of socialisation, which worked to prevent questioning of the assumptions of colonial ideology, had to be maintained and strictly enforced (Lessing, 1957). As Bates argues, collusive behaviour among the minority holding political and economic power has played an important role in the perpetuation of colonial states in general:

> Colonialism is a political system which is designed to bring eco-nomic benefits to foreign nationals. Political systems allocate access to force and they provide mechanisms for altering the operation of markets. Clearly, politics provides a means whereby groups can use coercion to levy resources from others: colonialism led to the redistribution of resources from indigenous to foreign interests. But, less obviously, access to state power also provides a means whereby the members of a group *can coerce themselves*; and it is by coercing themselves that they attain the capacity for collusive behaviour. *In so far as state institutions apportion access to coercive power, they then allocate the means to organise.* The importance of the political order is that it provides differential access to the means of organising economic interests – groups can then act to bias the operation of markets to their advantage. (Bates, 1983, pp. 90–1)

In its agrarian policies, the colonial state in Zimbabwe kept the power to organise policy in its own hands. In this chapter, I have shown how the colonial state used this power to implement a technical development strategy which was justified through appeal to evolutionary theory. This policy was implemented in a purposive-rational manner, with the state retaining sole control over policy actions. Apart from serving white interests, this meant the belief in the superiority of formal scientific knowledge was institutionalised in dogmatic form. It was never understood, for instance, that the indigenous societies might possess greater wisdom about their natural environment than newcomers whose experience was negligible. As Vambe (1972, p. 56) points out, the whites through adopting racialist rather than democratic strategies failed to tap the full energies of the black people. In the brief period of open reflection during 1961–2 it was recognised how empty was the contact between government officials and rural people, because of the inherent prejudice in the outlook of the former. But thereafter, to invoke the opening quote of Gadamer's, the whites forcefully chose to continue 'to run with open eyes, as it were, down a path whence there was no other issue than destruction'.

Unfortunately the tragedy of this path of destruction has not ended with the coming of independence. This is because the prejudices of the colonial administrators were not simply racial, but also the outcome of the purposive rationality which those employed within the institutional structures of the modern capitalist state are encouraged to adopt in how they think and act. Hence, as will be developed in the following chapter, the post-independence government has still not abandoned this path. And should a turn not be made and the end ever reached, the destruction that awaits would not this time be of the colonial regime, but of the rural peasantry and their environment.

3 The Socialist State and the Peasantry

> Rather than assume that governments attempt to maximise social or economic welfare but fail to do so, it might be more suitable to assume that governments have quite different objectives and generally succeed in achieving them. Rather than criticising governments for failing to attain, or offering advice on how to attain a non-goal, it would be instructive if more time were devoted to analysing what governments actually do and why. (Griffin, 1975, in Clay and Schaffer, 1984, p. 2)

The question that Griffin addresses – why do governments do what they do? – is the complex essense of policy analysis. To answer it requires, at the empirical level, an identification of how government agents actually act, as opposed to how they say they act. To explain these actions, the ideological justifications governments provide for their policy actions then need to be separated from the 'real' (and possibly partly unconscious) motives that operate at different levels of the polity and bureaucracy. Making a distinction between 'levels' is a reminder that governments are not undifferentiated entities. Conflicts over policy directions between the political leadership and government agencies, and between and within government agencies, occur because of people's different interests, perceptions and beliefs.

In Zimbabwe, the colonial government did not overtly state it was pursuing a particular ideology, and hence it was generally blatant in stating its agrarian policy intentions. In the post-independence period there are, however, more subtle distinctions between what policies are made out to be and what other intentions might be behind them. Nevertheless, the attributes of the analysis in this chapter are similar to those in the previous chapter on the pre-independence period. In order to identify the major underlying themes in the relationship between the post-independence state and the rural population there is need to explore the interplay between interests, attitudes, ideology and actual policy actions. As the post-independence period is the subject of the remainder of the book, in this chapter my aim is to lay only a framework for this exploration.

The analysis is divided into five sections. The first deals with the two dilemmas being faced in the establishment of an ongoing policy framework. One relates to the question of the capitalist to socialist transformation of the economy. The other is the conflict of interests that exists in the relationship between the state and the peasantry.

The outline of these two dilemmas is followed by a review of the main agrarian policy thrusts since independence. As in the previous chapter, this presentation will show also how the policies have been justified. This raises the question, important to the thesis, of the link between ideology, attitudes and policy actions.

The third part of the analysis turns to this question. It will be argued that although the ruling party, ZANU (PF), has adopted Marxist-Leninist principles, its policy practice reflects more closely populist (in the appeal to nationalism, pragmatism and national development planning) and technocratic attitudes. It is for this reason, I suggest, and as is proposed in the first hypothesis of the thesis, that there are strong continuities between pre- and post-independence agrarian policies, notwithstanding the stated radical shift in ideology to Marxism-Leninism from social Darwinism.

In the fourth part of the analysis some of these continuities in policies will then be identified. Reference will also be made to critical theory to suggest why they have occurred. It will be argued that the new government, like the old, has not yet sought to pursue policy actions which genuinely seek to promote an atmosphere in which accord between peasantry and state can be struck. All measures pursued since 1980 can still be characterised as either instrumental or strategic actions; the difference being that thus far the government has used forms of manipulation rather than coercion in their implementation.

One agency in which there has been some recognition of the deficiencies of a purposive rational approach, especially with regard to the stifling of initiative, is Zimbabwe's agricultural extension agency. The final part of the chapter, therefore, outlines and places within the general context of post-independence agrarian policy, a policy initiative first launched by Agritex in the Midlands province in 1983. Since then an attempt has been made to spread implementation more widely. This initiative seeks the improvement of rapport between agency staff and communal area farmers. Some comparison is made here with the 1962–5 period of reflection, when too there was a concern for the development of a communicative rationality, distinct from the purposive rationality normal to bureaucratic action.

This contextual analysis of post-independence policy then leads into the more detailed discussion in Chapter 4 of post-independence policy initiatives affecting the control and use of land in the study region. In this later discussion, the clash between the different aims and worldviews of peasant societies and the administration is explored more thoroughly.

THE TWO DILEMMAS IN POST-INDEPENDENCE POLICY

Zimbabwe attained formal independence from Britain on 18 April 1980. Thus ended ninety years of colonial rule. The first elections to be held on the basis of universal suffrage brought into power Robert Mugabe's ZANU (PF) party, which won 57 of the 80 contested seats (20 being reserved for whites under the 1979 Lancaster House agreement).

The new government inherited two legacies from its colonial predecessors: the institutional structures of a modern capitalist state and a very unequal society. ZANU (PF) accepted the first legacy – the capitalist economy and the regulatory state – but announced its intention of ameliorating the second. ZANU (PF) is not a communist party and nor have any of its members been communists,[1] but the party has officially adopted the principles of Marxism-Leninism as its guiding motifs. The party has thus formally committed itself to the establishment of a socialist society in Zimbabwe.

ZANU (PF) sees the state's role as that of enabling the transition from capitalism to socialism. And as with other socialist countries this is to be fulfilled through the execution of national development plans. Socialism and national development planning are consequently two of the identifying fetures of the new government's approach to policy:

> Our firm belief is that it is only within the framework of a planned economy that Government is better able to influence and purposefully direct development, create appropriate institutions, and establish the magnitude of investment and its allocation as well as the formation of a pattern of income and wealth distribution in harmony with socialist objectives. (Mugabe, in Government of Zimbabwe, 1982, p. 1)

The third guiding theme is that of nationalism. And as it is the cause upon which the black liberation movement was founded and the Liberation War fought, nationalism is the oldest and most deeply rooted of the themes that guide ZANU (PF). But the old theme of nationalism and the new theme of socialism, for reasons that will shortly be explained, are not necessarily compatible in the party's ideological constitution. They are, however, presented as such. At independence, the inherited economic imbalances were declared to be manifest in the 'ownership structure' of productive resources and the 'institutional structure' built to support it. Ownership was vested in the hands of 'a small proportion of the local population, and foreign capitalists'. Thus a key requirement in the creation of a socialist economy is that ownership of the means of production comes under Zimbabwean control, whether held by the state, local authorities, private companies or individuals (Government of Zimbabwe, 1986a, p. 2).

In achieving this transfer the government acknowledges that it faces a dilemma. Radical change would create 'massive disruption of economic activity' and the 'damage would take a long time to repair' (Government of Zimbabwe, 1986b, p. 8). The policy framework within which the themes of socialism, national development planning and nationalism have been expressed has been popularised under the catch-phrase 'Growth with Equity', the title of the government's first economic policy statement, published in 1981. But, warned Bernard Chidzero, then Minister of Economic Planning and Development,[2] 'Growth with Equity' had to be implemented with caution. The rural sector required greater levels of investment but *without* sacrificing growth in other sectors (*The Herald*, 26 February 1981). Capitalism should be 'purposefully harnessed, regulated and transformed as a partner in the overall national endeavour to achieve set national plan goal's, and a 'delicate balance' observed in moving from the old to the new social order (Mugabe, in Government of Zimbabwe, 1986b, p. i). The process is one of gradual, planned change (Government of Zimbabwe, 1982, p. i; 1986b, p. 8).

The dilemma that is admitted to here in the government's formal presentation of its post-independence policy and planning framework, namely that of how to ameliorate the inequalities inherent in ownership and institutional structures, is however not the only dilemma the government faces. Beneath it runs another, which although also crucial is considerably less emphasised. This dilemma concerns the government's relations with the peasantry.

ZANU (PF) won the 1980 elections because it had gathered the support of most of the Shona peasantry during the Liberation War (Astrow, 1983, p. 158). And the peasantry supported ZANU because they wanted to recover the land taken from them and to eject administrative coercion (Ranger, 1985, p. 284). The dilemma the government thus faces is that on the one hand it needs to appease the peasantry in order to retain their support, but on the other hand it fears a peasantry, led by the old lineage leaders, being permitted access to most of the agricultural land. If the latter scenario took place the state's power would be severely weakened. From the large-scale farming sector the state can reliably accrue surpluses at the national level and for reasons of national and regional food security it is reluctant to lose the certainty of this marketed output.

The relationship that has developed between the peasantry and the state since independence is, therefore, more insecure than either side readily acknowledges. Various aspects of this relationship will be considered through the remainder of the book. To begin with, let us look in more detail at the context of the above dilemma.

One of the arguments presented in the previous chapter is that the colonial government failed to incorporate the communal area population fully within the formal economy, notwithstanding its use of force. The abandonment of the Land Husbandry Act meant the government fell far short of ending the migrant labour system, which is necessary if full economic integration of the peasantry is to succeed. It succeeded neither in creating a yeoman farming class on the one hand, nor a permanent urban working class on the other. And without these two lower tiers of a capitalist class structure coming into being, a capitalist mode of production has fallen short of fully assimilating a kinship-based system.

Coming into power at independence on a tide of nationalism, ZANU (PF) has understandably been committed to the creation of a single, national economy, and thus still to the goal of a firmly integrated peasantry. ZANU (PF)'s adoption of Marxism-Leninism has also meant it has expressed an intention to transform the peasantry according to the tenets of a socialist rather than a capitalist philosophy. According to ZANU (PF)'s 1985 election manifesto, an ideal socialist agricultural system in Zimbabwe would have two 'arms': large-scale state farming and the cooperative farming movement (1985, pp. 20–1).

Where does this leave the peasantry? As a party intellectual phrased it, it leaves them theoretically as a 'residual sector'.[3] In its outline of an agrarian reform programme, ZANU (PF) proposes that the country's prime arable farming regions, natural regions I and II, be left for the above two sectors.[4] The resettlement strategy for the peasant farming population (discussed in the following section) would be concentrated in natural region III. But these resettlement schemes – and the communal areas themselves – are not intended to remain as individual farming areas. The manifesto advocates the encouragement initially of service cooperatives in these areas for input provision and marketing. And although the manifesto does not specify beyond this, the government's policy on cooperative development is that such marketing or 'elementary' cooperatives should be seen only as a stage in the progression to 'advanced collective cooperatives' (Ministry of Lands, Resettlement and Rural Development (MLRRD), 1983, pp. 6–8).

In the short term, the new government is reconciled to the existence of the peasantry by its emphasis on increasing the marketed output of production from this sector. But in terms of ideology this is only an 'emotional attachment' (Interview, 28 April 1988). ZANU (PF)'s socialist programme can only be achieved through imposing upon the peasantry once more and eventually breaking down completely the lineage form of production. Here, unlike the colonial state, the new government is handicapped by the importance of the peasantry as constituents. Because too, as is shown in Chapter 5, the value of migrant labour remittances to rural security has not diminished, the urban working class will retains a vested rural interest. Thus in the communal areas, any commitment to establishing an integrated and socialist national economy has to be balanced against the populist commitment to deliver to the peasantry more land, more social services, and less coercion.

It is not surprising that to date the outcome of this dilemma is that the relationship between the new government and the peasantry has been uneasy and varied. This will be illustrated in Chapter 4 in the discussion on land use policy in the study region. In the remainder of this chapter, at a more general level, I wish to analyse the nature and context of the agrarian policy framework that has developed in the first seven years of independence.

AGRARIAN POLICY DIRECTIONS, 1980–7

At independence I have suggested the government faced two dilemmas: how to reduce the economic control of local whites, and more especially foreign companies, without disrupting the economy; and how to improve the access of the peasantry to land, productive resources and social services and at the same time extend control over them. Whilst the second dilemma is implicit in ZANU (PF)'s intention to construct a socialist state, the first has been explicitly stated and tackled. The 'Growth with Equity' policy framework was conceived as providing a general orientation for its address through the embracement of a 'balanced' approach. At the ZIMCORD[5] donors' conference, held in March 1981 to attract foreign aid for Zimbabwe's post-war recovery and development programme, an overall economic policy of 'moderation and reconciliation' was emphasised (Government of Zimbabwe, 1986b, p. 9).

In the rural sector, translating this approach into practice required the implementation of a land distribution policy sufficient to appease land hunger, but cautious enough not to disrupt the major contribution agriculture made to the national economy. Land resettlement, as the first major agrarian policy of the new government, was intended to exemplify the balanced approach. In gathering aid at ZIMCORD, Chidzero

> warned delegates that the society could not hold together without a successful land distribution programme. The poor and the weak – those who had borne the brunt of the war and sanctions – were owed the means to improve their lot. (*The Herald*, 25 March 1981)

Nevertheless, in accordance with the 1979 Lancaster House Conference agreement, land would only be acquired by the state for resettlement purposes on a willing-seller/willing-buyer basis. There would be no expropriation of land. Furthermore, the whole resettlement process would be planned and controlled by the state. Whatever the poor were 'owed' the government was not going to go so far as to extend to them control over the means of production.

In late 1980 a three-year intensive resettlement programme was launched, its planned budget of Z$60 million to be shared between the Zimbabwean and British governments (Kinsey, 1983, p. 170; MLRRD, 1981, p. 21). The programme's aim was to resettle 18 000 families on 1.1 million hectares of former commercial farmland. These people would be, in order of priority, war refugees, the landless (including former farm workers living on purchased farms), and the poorest families from the most overcrowded communal areas. At ZIMCORD the programme attracted further assistance and in the 1982 Transitional National Development Plan (TNDP) its scope was greatly enlarged. The time period was extended to five years, that is until the end of the 1982/3–1984/5 TNDP period, and its target was expanded to the resettlement of 162 000 families on 9 million hectares of land (MLRRD, 1981, p. 2).

The programme, however, fell far short of its target. As far as the 'numbers game' is concerned (Bush and Cliffe, 1984, pp. 84; Simon, p. 83), by August 1985 only 36 000 families had been settled and 2.48 million hectares of land purchased (Government of Zimbabwe, 1986b, p. 126), at a total cost of Z$157.8 million (Mbwanda, 1985, p. 37). The government officially blamed the slow progress on 'drought and financial constraints' and the fact that the willing-seller/ willing-buyer basis had made it difficult to acquire land for resettlement in large enough blocks for development purposes (Government of Zimbabwe, 1986b, p. 28). Within government, though, it was also admitted that there was a shortage of trained manpower for planning the schemes and that the bureaucratic task of coordinating 'the activities of 20 Ministries, 12 departments and a host of non-governmental organisations' was monumental (DERUDE, MLRRD, 1983, p. 11).

In the 1985 Land Acquisition Act the government has dealt with the complaint about land availability. The Act permits the government to designate for resettlement purposes blocks of land near or adjacent to communal areas. In these areas, if owners had not already offered their land to the government they would be encouraged to do so, with compulsory acquisition only a last resort (Government of Zimbabwe, 1986b, p. 125; *The Financial Gazette*, 10 August 1984).

With the Land Acquisition Act the government set its resettlement target for 1986–90 at 15 000 families annually, double the average achieved between 1980 and 1985, but well below the 1980–5 target of 162 000 families. In fact, so far as the numbers' game is concerned, through setting its 1980–5 target at such an unrealistic level, the government has hidden what it has achieved. The 2.56 million hectares purchased to September 1987 forms a significant 6.6 per cent of Zimbabwe's total land area, and the large-scale commercial farming area has been reduced by nearly 20 per cent over what it was in 1969 (Table 3.1).

Nevertheless, with the rural population growth rate in the region of 3.6 per cent (World Bank, 1983, p. 14; MLRRD, 1985, table 1),[6] the communal areas have experienced little alleviation of population

Table 3.1   Land distribution 1930–85

	1931 (1)	1953 (1)	1969 (2)	1983 (3)	1985 (1)
			(hectares in millions)		
Communal areas (5)	8.64	9.99	16.19	16.35	16.35
Small-scale commercial areas (6)	2.98	2.26	1.49	1.42	1.42
Large-scale commercial areas (7)	19.67	18.96	15.61	13.41	12.51
Individual resettlement areas (Model 'A')				1.67 ⎤	2.64
Cooperative resettlement areas (Model 'B')				0.07 ⎦	(4)
State farms				0.08	0.08
National park and forest areas	0.24	1.58	2.96	5.88	5.88
Unassigned land	7.12	5.68			
Other areas	0.03	0.02	2.80	0.19	0.19
Total land area	38.68	38.51	39.05	39.07	39.07

Sources: (1) World Bank/Government of Zimbabwe (1985).
  (2) World Bank (1983).
  (3) Weiner *et al.* (1985).

Notes: (4) Resettlement statistics as at 31/8/87 were:
    Model 'A': Land acquired/set aside – 2.45 mill ha.
          Land settled – 2.16 mill ha.
    Model 'B': Land acquired/set aside – 0.18 mill ha.
          Land settled – 0.14 mill ha.
    Model 'C': Land acquired/set aside – 0.01 mill ha.
          Land settled – 0.01 mill ha.
    Model 'D': Land acquired/set aside – 0.19 mill ha.
          Land settled – 0.06 mill ha.
          (MLGRUD, 1987).
  (5) 'Native Reserves' 1896–1962.
    'Tribal Trust Lands' 1962–80.
  (6) 'Native Purchase Areas' 1930–62.
    'African Purchase Areas' 1962–80.
  (7) 'European' Area 1930–80.

densities and land pressure. This was the conclusion of a 1985 World Bank Land Subsector study:

> It is now generally recognised that even had the government's previously held land resettlement target been achieved, it would not in all likelihood have had much impact on land use conditions in the communal areas. (p. 26)

The government itself has conceded this point, but not just because of the failure of the resettlement policy to live up to expectations. Perhaps even more significant has been the effect of the 1982–4 drought. For the drought has led the government to shift the emphasis of its economic policy as a whole. 'Growth' is now a greater concern than 'equity'.

The facts of what happened to agriculture during the drought provide the reason for the policy change. The agricultural sector forms the backbone of Zimbabwe's economy (Government of Zimbabwe, 1986a, p. 25). Since independence it has steadily provided about a third of Zimbabwe's exports, as well as providing inputs for other sectors and more than 90 per cent of Zimbabwe's food requirements (Government of Zimbabwe, 1986b, p 43). In 1979/80 and 1980/1 Zimbabwe had good agricultural seasons. This, together with the impetus provided by independence and the end of the war, led to two years of rapid economic growth. However, then came the three drought seasons, accompanied also by rising inflation and balance of payment problems. The economy stumbled badly. GDP which had averaged a 12.2 per cent growth over the two good years, went into a decline during the drought and only rose again following the good 1984/5 season (Government of Zimbabwe, 1986b, pp. 13–16).

Perhaps the biggest shock the government received during the drought was the drop which occurred in food production, particularly with respect to maize, the staple food crop. Strategically, Zimbabwe has been perceived to have the structural and environmental capacity to be the food basket for the nine member countries of the Southern African Development Coordination Conference (SADCC) region. SADCC was established in 1980 in order to lessen regional economic dependence on South Africa, and the chief responsibility allocated to Zimbabwe was for regional food security. Zimbabwe then proceeded to show it had its own problem. Marketed maize fell from a record of 2.25 million tonnes in the 1980/1 delivery period[7] to 1.2 million tonnes in 1981/2, 610 000 tonnes in 1982/3, and 900 000 tonnes in 1983/4 (Government of Zimbabwe, 1986b, pp. 116–18; *The Financial Gazette*, 11 May 1984; *The Herald*, 6 September 1984). This led to the country importing maize in 1984 for the first time since the Second World War and post-war years of 1942–53 (Bock Commission, 1962, para. 15). Even more galling for the Zimbabwean government was that these imports had to be railed through South Africa.

Accordingly since the drought, increasing food production,

marketed output and storage facilities, to ensure not only national food self-sufficiency but also a surplus for both adverse season reserves and export purposes, have become highly conscious political and government priorities.[8] However, such a commitment to food self-sufficiency would require, according to the Minister of the then distinct Ministry of Agriculture,[9] Zimbabwe having 'to double its present level of food production within the next 17 years' just in order to cope with the anticipated population growth (*The Herald*, 27 September 1984). To achieve this would require shifting attention away from resettlement at the margins back to the 16.35 million hectares of the communal areas themselves. A paper delivered at a conference in May 1984 by J. W. Hayward, then Director of the Department of Agricultural Technical and Extension Services (Agritex), drew attention to the cost of not improving the communal area production base:

> unless we can develop rapidly a large, growing, ecologically sound agricultural base in the communal areas, the chances are that our rural development strategy will fail. (NAER conference report, 1984, p. 200)

As occurred fifty years earlier when the Wooley Commission reported, it was not just the drop in production during the drought that was focusing government concern, but more directly the cost of drought relief. Between 1980 and 1985 the land resettlement programme officially cost Z$157.8 million. In the three financial years 1982/3–1984/5, drought relief cost the government Z$101.1 million, with an additional Z$10 million being spent on drought relief public works (Government of Zimbabwe, 1986b, p. 124).

The drought then resulted in a shift in agrarian policy from an emphasis on land redistribution at the margins of the communal areas, to increasing production output in both resettlement and communal areas. The new drive to achieve this picked up in two policy areas once the drought was over. First, in the area of inputs, 'Green Revolution' style pressure was placed on farmers to adopt, particularly for maize, input packages consisting of hybrid seed, fertiliser and pesticide. To finance their use of these packages, farmers were encouraged to apply for credit. For the 1984/5 season, the Agricultural Finance Corporation (AFC), the parastatal responsible for extending agricultural credit, increased its lending to communal and resettlement farmers to Z$35.1 million from Z$14.7 million the previous season (Government of Zimbabwe, 1986b,

p. 107). In 1985 (for 1985/6) this amount rose again to an estimated Z$53.9 million (DANIDA, 1985, p. 15).

On the surface the government has had some success with this credit package policy. Even in the poor 1983/4 season it was encouraged by late deliveries from the communal area sector, which boosted the season's maize delivery from the first estimate of 560 000 tonnes to the final 900 000 tonnes. Much was made of the fact that in the period from 1965 to 1980 (that is, the UDI and war period), official sales by communal farmers only averaged 55 000 tonnes a year (Chavunduka Commission, 1982, para. 127). Then, the communal share of marketed production had only been 10–15 per cent; now, it had risen from 13.85 per cent in 1980/1, to 23 per cent in 1981/2, 25 per cent in 1982/3 and 35 per cent in 1983/4 (Hayward, 1984, p. 200). From here, the 1986 Five-Year Development Plan document picks up the story – 45 per cent in 1984/5 and an estimated 57 per cent in 1985/6 (Government of Zimbabwe, 1986a, p. 25).

There are two facts which these statistics do not reveal though. The first is that much of this increase in marketed output is coming from a small proportion of farmers in the small proportion of communal areas in the higher rainfall natural regions.[10] Second, the increase in credit use means farmers have to market more to stay solvent. In the Midlands, most of those I worked with are running into problems. At the national level the picture might look encouraging, but at the household level it is commonly debts not profits that are on the rise.

The implications of this extension of crop and credit packages will be analysed more closely from Chapter 5. It is time, here, to return to my interpretation of the official account of agrarian policy and the second of the two policy areas given greater attention after the drought. This area is that of land use and land management. A comparison of the 1982 and 1986 National Development Plans reveals the switch that has occurred.

In the TNDP period, the land policy was 'redistribution and development of land and resettlement of the maximum number of families possible over the plan period' (Government of Zimbabwe, 1982, p. 23). In the 1986–90 First Five-Year Development Plan this has altered to 'land reform and efficient utilisation of land'. 'During the Plan period, Government will give priority to land reform and proper land utilisation, in order to change the present ownership relations as well as promote proper land management' (Government of Zimbabwe, 1986a, pp. 3, 10–11).

With the elevation to the political agenda of a concern for

improving land management, 'land reform' is now conceived not only as an exercise in land redistribution, but also as one of internal reorganisation within the communal areas:

> In addition to the translocation resettlement which utilises purchased former large-scale commercial farms, the re-organisation of settlement patterns in the Communal Areas will become part and parcel of the resettlement programme. This entails replanning of land-use patterns in order to attain optimum exploitation of the agricultural resource potential on a sustainable basis and to ensure adequate provision of economic, social and institutional infrastructure. (Government of Zimbabwe, 1986a, p. 28)

It is therefore intended that in addition to the annual resettlement target of 15 000 families, another 20 000 families should be affected annually by the communal area reorganisation exercise (p. 28).

The policy of internal land use reform within the communal areas was actually launched in 1986, with a pilot 'villagisation' programme. In each of the 55 district council areas, one village was to be selected by the District Administrator, in conjunction with the District Council. Within the boundaries of the village area, Agritex were to be responsible for demarcating arable and grazing areas, and for assessing water requirements for human, stock and irrigation purposes. The Department of Physical Planning was to plan a consolidated village settlement (Cousins, 1987, pp. 20–1).[11] It is ironic that the need for this villagisation programme has been justified through appeal to the inequity of the colonial land apportionment policy:

> The misallocation resulted in inefficient use of land and low per capita income for the majority of the population. Because of the relatively small areas of land allocated and consequent population pressure in communal lands, the poor quality of the land and poor agricultural support services resulting in relatively unimproved traditional farming practices, the productivity of land progressively declined over the years. (Government of Zimbabwe, 1986b, p. 5)

What is therefore being acknowledged by the government in this shift in policy emphasis, is that the land resettlement programme cannot continue to be promoted as the predominant component in a balanced 'Growth with Equity' approach in the rural sector. And indeed, in practice, resettlement has been scaled down to a far greater degree than the plans acknowledge. By 31 July 1987, the number of families resettled had risen only to 39 823 (MLGRUD,

1987, p. 15) – an increase of just 3800 in the two years since mid-1985. Thus with the switch from resettlement to villagisation the government has changed its whole approach to solving the two rural sector dilemmas it faces. On the one hand, pressure on the commercial farmers is being eased, and on the other hand, a familiar squeeze on the communal farmers, absent for the first five years of independence, is being reapplied.

The introduction of the Land Acquisition Act might seem to belie that pressure on the commercial farmers is being relaxed. In practice though, this Act has had little impact; a 1987 official report labelled it 'a paper tiger' (MLGRUD, 1987, p. 59). For a start, as will be illustrated by an example in Chapter 4, much more land 'at the margins' (that is, adjacent to communal areas) has been offered to the government than it has purchased – and these are the areas government has said it will favour in the declaration of designated areas under the Land Acquisition Act. But, in addition, the commercial farming sector is no longer the group of 6000 whites who owned or managed farms at independence. Many white farmers have moved to the more productive Mashonaland area (Natural Region II), whilst others have sold up and either left the land or prefer the security of being paid a salary as a manager of a black-owned farm. Official figures on the extent of this transfer of ownership do not exist, although Moyo (1987) estimates that by 1986 some 300 blacks had joined a remaining 4000 whites as freehold title owners of large-scale commercial farms.[12] Whatever the ownership structure now is, in a joint World Bank/Zimbabwean Government land subsector study carried out in 1985, the need to safeguard a large-scale commercial farming sector was vehemently argued:

in the Communal Areas there is land scarcity due to population pressure, increasing land degradation, the reduction in the commons, growing numbers of livestock, and continuing subdivision of land through inheritance.

. . . If land from the Commercial Areas is redistributed to relieve pressure in the Communal Areas, the trade-offs in terms of productive capacity would need to be considered.

The evidence suggests that the trade-offs would be quite steep. At present the Commercial Areas are highly productive, accounting for about 60 per cent of the country's marketed food production, 76 per cent of the country's agricultural export earnings, and 87 per cent of the total marketed offtake from the national herd. It is quite clear, therefore, that these farmers make much more than a proportionate contribution to the nation's welfare and general development . . . The evidence suggests that any attempt to reduce the land holdings of the commercial farmers through compulsory means would have to be weighed against the almost certain losses in productive capacity. The price to pay would be very high. Thus the path of growth with equity would likely suggest a different course of action. (1985, pp. 26–7, 37)

This joint study is thus arguing that in the Zimbabwe of the late 1980s growth and equity are incompatible goals. Immediate needs suggest productivity should be emphasised over equity. In fact, the contention made in the study that production would suffer if greater land redistribution occurred, is highly debatable. Differences in average yield levels between the sectors[13] are largely the result of differential access to productive resources (Chavunduka Commission, 1982, para. 131). Any claim that commercial farmers are 'better' or more efficient farmers is simply not proven by the evidence available – although counter claims also need greater substantiation.[14] The evidence that the joint study is more certainly appealing to is that despite the growth in the proportion of the communal areas' contribution to the marketed output of specific crops (most notably maize and cotton), this output is not yet reliable. The further drought of 1986/7, with an estimated cost to the government of Z\$87 million for drought relief and public works projects (*The Herald*, 25 June 1987), emphasises this. The droughts have made more likely a process warned of by Williams (1982b) in a statement he makes which amplifies a paragraph of the 1981 Riddell Commission report[15]:

Deprived of their monopoly of political power the rich (predominantly whites) are likely to have to concede some redistribution at the margin. Once they are joined by a substantial number of politically influential blacks, redistributive measures will be resisted more effectively. Hence the importance of making changes now, otherwise '. . . only a minority (albeit with a different racial composition and probably only a slightly larger minority) will continue to enjoy stable and adequate levels of consumption' (para. 378). (pp. 114–15)

What may be concluded from this discussion on post-1980 agrarian policy directions, is that the commitment of the post-indepedence government to socialism is not as is professed. In fact, as will be detailed more fully in Chapter 4, implementation of the internal land use reform programme would result in many places in a recommendation to return to something closely resembling the 1950s land husbandry land use patterns. However, rather than falling foul of Griffin's dictum by simply criticising the government for failing to keep considerations of social and economic justice high on its agrarian policy agenda, I should prefer now to examine the nature of the ideology to which the government is actually adhering in practice. In what sense, if any, is it Marxist-Leninist? – and what is the role of 'ideology' in policy practice? An attempt to answer these questions will illuminate why there are continuities between pre- and post-independence policies.

THE 'NATIONAL DEMOCRATIC REVOLUTION': IDEOLOGY AND POLICY PRACTICE

In spite of ZANU (PF)'s declared commitment to principles of Marxism-Leninism,[16] quite how Marxism-Leninism is supposed to guide and justify the government's pursuit of specific policies has remained unclear. A fundamental difficulty with both Marx and Lenin is that they were neither always consistent nor compatible thinkers. This makes possible various interpretations of what Marxism-Leninism actually entails. For instance, the distinction discussed in Chapter 6 between 'orthodox' and 'critical' Marxists, is not just one of interpretation but even of epistemology. Consequently, if a government genuinely wishes to apply Marxist-Leninist principles, it has first to spell out how these are to be interpreted in order to create a consistency. If Marxism-Leninism is merely invoked through the use of such terms as 'scientific socialism' and 'revolutionary theory', as occurs in ZANU (PF)'s 1985 election manifesto, it is an ideology without specific content.

In an application of elements of Habermas's critical theory to an analysis of Soviet bureaucratic socialism, this is what Andrew Arato argues. He holds that since Stalin's repression, Marxism-Leninism has become an 'empty and ritualistic' ideology. 'The classical dogmas of Marxist-Leninist orthodoxy, especially those concerning the transition to communism, are held increasingly cynically' (1982, pp. 211–12). Nevertheless, Marxism-Leninism still performs as a 'symbolic system' which justifies the existence of the 'monolithic party', formally separate from yet closely linked to the state. The 'party' justifies itself because it is crusading for greater social justice and solidarity. The state is identified as the party's executive in the carrying out of this crusade. Furthermore, the socialist crusade requires the state to act against the capitalist class controlling the economy. Hence the coalition of the 'party-state' is now legitimised, and 'the domination of the *prerogative state* over society' (Arato, 1982, p. 202) thoroughly justified.

But because the *content* of Marxism-Leninism has been emptied, in order to *act* the party-state has to employ other ideologies.

> Marxism-Leninism cannot be the *sole* means for the ideological legitimation of society: as a ritualised dogmatic quasi-religion, it is too impoverished; as a rational ideology, it is constantly endangered by the reality to which it is increasingly irrelevant. But it is still an indispensable component of the identity of the institutional core, and its dominating role in philosophy and political theory guarantees the exclusion of serious public discussion about society. Thus within the limits of the system, it can only be supplemented, not replaced. (p. 212)

Arato believes that the three additional ideologies employed in the pre-Gorbachev Soviet Union have been an ideology based on memories of the New Economic Policy, a nationalist–traditionalist ideology and an authoritarian–technocratic ideology (p. 211).

This supplementation has also occurred in Zimbabwe. In its policy and planning framework, the Zimbabwean government has bolstered Marxism-Leninism with one additional ideology. This ideology – or set of attitudes, if one wishes to avoid vulgarising the term (Bernstein, 1976, p. 107) – is that of populism.[17]

The proclivity to endorse pragmatism, nationalism, and national development planning are described by Robertson (1984, pp. 221–31) as three of the main features of state populism. The Zimbabwean government's 'Growth with Equity' policy approach which embraces all three, thus sits firmly within the populist mould. Governments themselves do not describe themselves as populist, but a sense of grounded teleology in Zimbabwe's 'socialism' is as absent or as wishful as in Tanzania's ujamaa socialism. The latter, Worsley (1984, p. 113) describes as the classic twentieth-century expression of populist themes.

Historically, populism has favoured 'a society composed of self-sufficient small producers, preferably associated via the community or some form of co-operative linkage, which enables them to constitute themselves into a force powerful enough to ensure that they will receive the just reward for their labours' (1984, pp. 112–13). This century, in countries such as Argentina under Peron, populism has been oriented towards an urban working-class electorate. But within many Third World countries populism has become more essentially a mode of self-presentation by the state. The state represents itself as pursuing a purpose which is in the interest of all citizens, that of national economic and social development. It does this by representing all divisions within the country as only the legacy of the arch dividing factor of imperialism.

> The populist asserts that there are no divisions in the community, or that if they are discernible, they are 'non-antagonistic'. Thus class-divisions can then be dismissed as *external* ('imperialist') intrusions, alien to the society. Ethnic differences can equally be dismissed as consequences of 'divide and rule' or as vestigial, disappearing legacies of the past ('tribalism' or 'feudalism'), though, of course, in this case, it is necessary to accept that ethnicity *did* divide society in the past: only *now* is a truly homogeneous society emerging. All these divisions, it is held, will soon disappear, leaving a united society. (Worsley, 1967, in Robertson, 1984, p. 229)

This populist stance has been adopted by ZANU (PF). A mention of a key feature of the history of the party shows why this is so. This feature is that, like the other parties that constituted at various times the pre-independence nationalist movement, ZANU (PF) was primarily that – a nationalist rather than a socialist organisation. Only for a brief period from November 1975 through to January 1977, when a military leadership, the Zimbabwe Peoples Army (ZIPA), controlled ZANU's guerrillas in Zimbabwe, could it be said that a fervently left-wing leadership controlled either of the guerrilla armies (Astrow, 1983, pp. 94–108, 135–44; Mandaza, 1987, p. 31–3).[18] ZANU's political leadership, once it reasserted control over its military wing, remained a nationalist and generally non-radical movement, despite an endorsement in the late 1970s of anti-imperialist media rhetoric (Mandaza, 1987, p. 32). 'National independence was the central goal; the methods whereby to attain it . . . could be neither justified or condemned in the light of whether or not this central goal was attained' (Mandaza, 1987, p. 29).

Within ZANU, as with the other nationalist organisations, the range of political views held by leaders meant there was little consensus over a future political programme. What did exist was a broad agreement that after independence, Zimbabwe, whether or not it eventually became socialist, would have to go through a stage of capitalist development – in the terminology of the South African Communist Party, the 'national democratic revolution' (Astrow, 1983, pp. 136, 147).

Since independence, the subject of the 'national democratic revolution' has formed within ZANU (PF) the focus of an internal, unpublicised debate over ideology.[19] A vital part of this debate is the issue of whether ZANU (PF) should continue as a mass party (that is, a nationalist party), or a vanguard party (that is, a revolutionary Marxist-Leninist socialist party). Although still a mass party, ZANU (PF) does have a strong leadership core as most of its current leaders have been in the party's central committee since ZANU's formation in 1963. This does not mean, though, that the entire leadership is socialist. Since independence, the national democratic state of the revolution has been considered essential for the achievement of national unification and post-war reconciliation and rehabilitation. Internal party debate is thus over how ZANU (PF) should now proceed. There are three areas of policy concern in this debate – those of the party, the state, and the economy. At the level of the party, a vanguard leadership is required to guide overall party policy, but at the level of the state, a 'democratic' policy (of nominations) is required to ensure all sectors of society are represented in parliament. It is thus a system of democratic centralism that is being projected, in which the party justifies its leadership of the state.[20] Following the 1985 elections and the unification in 1987 of ZANU (PF) with Joshua Nkomo's PF party, Mugabe reshuffled his cabinet to create a supervisory system. Senior ministers now oversee groups of ministries – the divisions being those ministries connected primarily with the economy, party, and state and local government, respectively. Such an arrangement accords with a party-state structure in which major decision-making is concentrated within a politburo. The whole of the preceding is also exactly in accordance with Arato's argument of how the party-state uses Marxism-Leninism to legitimise itself.

As part of the move towards democratic centralism, the post-independence government has established a national development-planning machinery. This is presented as being a decentralist system, but as it is subsumed under state structures it can be easily controlled and circumscribed by the political centre:

The National Planning Machinery, which has been approved by the Central Committee of the Ruling Party and by Cabinet, will consist of Cabinet and its Committee on Development, Planning Commission, Sectoral Planning Committees, Provincial Councils and Provincial Planning Committees, District Councils and District Planning Committees, Village Development Committees and Ward Development Committees. (Government of Zimbabwe, 1986a, p. ii)

This development planning structure is thoroughly populist. It is presented as a 'bottom-up' planning system, but as though the country has no political, economic and ethnic divisions. An obvious issue too, when committees are proliferated bureaucratically in this way, is whether those at district and local (or even provincial) levels have any significant power and control over resources. In Chapter 1 reference was made to Finucane's (1974) research in Tanzania, in which he comments on the condescending attitude government officials often display towards local development committees (p. 61). In Chapters 4 and 6 I will illustrate that in Zimbabwe too these committees have little real power.

In a populist approach a government seeks to purvey an impression of being at one with all the people. As a result it may, because policy practice is often reduced to a safe and indecisive muddling-through, exacerbate rather than resolve major societal conflicts.

The land issue and the government's attitude towards the peasantry in Zimbabwe, is a case in point. The much publicised land resettlement policy has neither resolved the government's dilemma of how to deal with the peasantry nor satisfied the land hunger of the latter. The government's response has been to introduce an initiative for land reform within the communal areas. Thus far the government has not decided on a definite method for implementing this policy. If it proceeds with the populist development committee approach it may become frustrated by the lack of take-up of the policy at the local level, as occurred in Tanzania in the mid-1970s (and for which Stalin's and Mao's collectivisations form the original model). Any acceleration of the policy would then require the use of power in some form. The hardline approach would be to turn the national development planning machinery into a command planning system and couple this with an authoritarian–technocratic ideology, again as occurred in Tanzania. The way of such an approach forms part of the colonial legacy, even if it were brought in through the thoroughly different channel of a vanguard party and Marxism-Leninism was used to justify the prerogative state.[21]

Another alternative to either muddling on with populism or regressing to authoritarianism, would be to turn the populist approach into a more genuinely liberating one. As will be shown in the next section and developed more fully in the final part of the chapter, this would require, however, a fundamentally different approach to the policy dilemmas the government faces than those currently contemplated.

NEW POLICIES IN OLD CLOTHES

An examination of the government's land resettlement policy and the proposals made to 1987 for land tenure reform in the communal areas, shows the type of policy continuities that have occurred since independence. It also allows an explantion to be offered as to why this is the case.[22]

From 1980, when it was established specifically for the purpose, until its amalgamation with the Ministry of Agriculture in July 1985, the Ministry of Lands, Resettlement and Rural Development (MLRRD) was responsible for the overall direction of the land resettlement programme. Resettlement, as well as the redistribution of land, provided also the obvious point of departure for the government's intention to transform rural relations of production:

> The new land schemes are seen as establishing new cohesive and stable communities out of the many individuals from different areas of the country and with different social backgrounds . . . Through farming cooperatives in agriculture, the first steps towards socialisation in farming will be taken. (DERUDE, MLRRD, 1983, p. 1)

Practice has, however, been much less radical than the intention. After consultations, mainly between the Ministry of Agriculture and the MLRRD, three models were chosen for implementing resettlement schemes. Of these, Model 'B' – 'intensive settlement (of usually 50-plus people) with communal living and cooperative farming' (MLRRD, 1981; Kinsey, 1983, p. 174) – was the farming system the MLRRD was particularly keen to promote. This model, together with Model 'C' – 'intensive settlement combined with a centralised estate farm, the latter providing central services in return for labour'

(MLRRD, 1981; Kinsey, 1983, p. 175) – accord with the two 'arms' of ZANU (PF)'s declared ideal socialist agrarian strategy.

However, of the three models, and those subsequently added,[23] it is Model 'A' which has been implemented over the largest area and incorporates the most people. By July 1987, 35 244 families had been settled on 1.99 million hectares under Model 'A', 2842 people on 0.14 million hectares under Model 'B', 507 families on one Model 'C' scheme, and 1417 families on 0.17 million hectares in 'accelerated' Model 'A' schemes (MLGRUD, 1987, pp. 8–13). Model 'A' is defined as 'intensive village settlement with individual arable units and communal grazing areas' (MLRRD, 1981; Kinsey, 1983, p. 172). It is the simplest and easiest model to implement because settlers can be placed without the scale of social, managerial and infrastructural organisation the other two require. The model also bears close relation to the economic farming unit which firstly the centralisation scheme and then land husbandry aimed to establish. The village settlements are nucleated; individual families are allocated about 5 hectares of arable land; and a permit for five to fifteen livestock units depending on natural region, allows a family to have livestock in the communal grazing area. It has been to Model 'A' schemes that most of those resettled from communal areas have gone. The limited Model 'B' cooperatives have been established largely by groups of young war veterans.[24]

Just as the form of Model 'A' resembles the LHA economic holding, so has the control exercised over the schemes by the state resembled the colonial precedent. Settlers are issued permits for arable, grazing and residential land, which up until August 1987 were still renewable on an annual basis. Permit enforcement is the responsibility of the government resettlement officer and farmers can be evicted for not following 'correct' agricultural practices. In Chirumhanzu a ZANU (PF) district chairman stated that seven people had been 'kicked out' of the neighbouring Tokwe resettlement area for not farming properly, leaving them landless (Interview, 15 April 1987). If this is the case, it affirms the point made by Gaidzanwa (1981):

The law and order component in the resettlement permit suggests great control over the producers by the government. This is not likely to go down well with the poorest people who have just been liberated from other more direct control measures from the previous regimes. (p. 113)

The government has nevertheless kept sacrosanct its desire to keep control of the land in the resettlement areas. It seems that when the government talks about ownership of the means of production becoming 'Zimbabweanised', in the case of the peasantry this means nationalisation and not any form of local ownership. Two reasons have been put forward to justify the government's desire to control resettlement tightly. First, the state – and party – wish to head off any conceivable extension of conservative authority over land by the lineage leaders. Second, they wish to prevent any continuation of what are seen as the backward farming practices of the lineage system.

> The resettlement process discourages spontaneity in settlements and fights against attempts at reversion back to traditional methods and systems of agriculture . . . [Thus] resettlement can never be about . . . extending the boundaries of existing communal areas . . . creating new power bases for those clamouring for the restoration of traditional authorities, such as chiefs, headmen etc. (DERUDE, 1983, pp. 1–2)

As occurred with land husbandry, it is the rights of women and children, in particular, that have been prejudiced, because the resettlement scheme permits are predominantly expressed in the names of married males. If families are moved from a communal area to a resettlement area, they rarely forgo the land to which they have access. Some members remain behind to continue cultivating it (Callear, 1982, E4).

In the communal areas, although the government has failed to involve peasant communities themselves in discussions about tenure, it has recognised that security of tenure is an important requisite in the development of a productive agricultural system. An as yet unresolved debate on tenure in these areas was begun by the 1981 Riddell Commission, and followed up shortly after by the 1982 Commission of Enquiry into the Agricultural Industry (Chavunduka Commission).[25]

Neither of these commissions' perspectives on the communal areas included much that was refreshing. Both were 'left in no doubt whatsoever about the extent of land hunger in the communal areas' (Chavunduka Commission, para. 264; also Riddell Commission, para. 119). But their responses offered the perennial brush-off to rural opinion. The response of the Riddell Commission was to describe the present cultivation of small, 'individual' holdings as an 'inefficient use of land' and on this premise prescribed the need for 'a substantial restructuring and transformation of agricultural production within the peasant sector' (paras 682 and 686). This recommendation, although coupled with support for the provision of more and better land, has since served as a basis for the separation of the question of land access from that of land use. For whilst a general consensus exists that land should be made available for resettlement, this may be ignored in any specific internal land use planning exercise. The Riddell proposal for 'blocks of land to be given to each village, dividing the land into arable, grazing and (consolidated) residential areas' (para. 687), is distinct from the land husbandry model only in terms of the larger scale of the 'village'. This is fundamentally the model embraced by the internal land use reform policy.

The Chavunduka Commission was even more dismissive of the peasantry's demands. Its report merely reiterated the old refrain: 'the main problem facing many communal areas in this country is one of land husbandry' (para. 264). What the Commission did note was that any proposed change in tenure system must be recognised 'in practice' as well as in law. The implication of this was that in the communal areas the government would have to replace its instrumental approach to resettlement with one that was more strategically concerned with winning people's support:

> In order to provide communal farmers, including those in newly settled areas, with both the status and the means to acquire a personal responsibility for the land in their care, it will be essential for farmers individually or as groups to become identified with their land and livestock. In regard to land, means must be found of ensuring security of tenure so that there is a clear link between an area of land and an individual or a group, which will be recognisable in practice and in law . . . The Commission therefore recommends that the government initiate, as a matter of urgency, a study to identify existing land tenure systems in the communal lands with the objective of defining the future pattern of land tenure in those areas and the resettlement areas. (para. 270)

This recommendation was taken up by the Ministry of Lands, Resettlement and Rural Development.[26] In February 1985 the Ministry produced draft proposals for a fifteen-year communal lands development plan, which it envisaged would become a major policy document for the communal areas.[27] The draft plan reiterates the need for a 'more appropriate land tenure system in the communal areas' in order to control the 'two ecologically undesirable effects of the traditional land tenure system: that of the sub-division of the arable land into ever-smaller, non-viable units, and that of the constant over-stocking of the grazing land' (MLRRD, 1985, p. 79).

The recommendations in the draft plan, however, acknowledged no need to gain any local acceptance for policy measures. Indeed, the plan's authors appeared to have learned little from the history of land husbandry. In the style of their presentation there is a close resemblance to the way the Southern Rhodesian government presented the objectives of the Land Husbandry Act (MLRRD, 1985, pp. 79–80; Government of Southern Rhodesia, 1955, p. 4).[28] Once again it is recommended that land be subdivided into economic units for allocation. Leasehold tenure is, however, preferred to the land husbandry policy's idea of bringing into being a land market (of closely prescribed form). Allocation too should be to groups or cooperatives, as well as to individuals. Nevertheless all land, whether for arable, grazing or residential purposes, should only be 'allocated by the State subject to cadastral surveying, proper land use planning and demarcation' (MLRRD, 1985, p. 80).

At the time the MLRRD was preparing this authoritarian proposal another concept for land reform was being formulated within the Ministry of Agriculture. This proposal was for a 'National Land Use Programme' (Reynolds and Ivy, 1984). Its objective would be:

> To develop a voluntary community based land use reform programme capable of integrating elements of local decision-making, renewed village institutions and matched technical, managerial and financial support. (p. 1)

This proposal is more subtle and less control oriented than the MLRRD draft development plan. It advocates the negotiation of a development contract between an administering agency and the 'community' for a demarcated land area. Individual use rights, as in the lineage form of social integration, would be distinct from the actual individual, group, or communal exploitation of them, with, for instance, a negotiable quota system being suggested for the regulation of arable and livestock grazing rights (1984, pp. 1–6). This is a more sophisticated version, guaranteeing equal rights for women and men, of the land husbandry 'market' system for land and livestock units.

With the amalgamation of the two ministries in July 1985 neither of these plans came to any immediate fruition. As stated earlier, although the 1986–90 First Five-Year Development Plan has now officially endorsed a land reform programme in the communal areas, the mechanics of the strategy are still being explored. In 1986 Lionel Cliffe produced an FAO consultancy report on agrarian reform, the preparation of which was conducted under a steering committee chaired by a Deputy Secretary within the Ministry of Lands, Agriculture and Rural Settlement (Cliffe, 1986, p. 111). This report has been debated by representatives from several ministries and Zimbabwe's three agricultural unions (*The Financial Gazette*, 13 November 1987), although by early 1989 no formal decisions had resulted from it.[29]

On the subject of communal land tenure, Cliffe dismisses the proposal in the MLRRD draft plan for leasehold tenure. Policing of a leasehold system could only be carried out through increasing bureaucratic powers and so would only fuel insecurity (Cliffe, 1986, p. 80). Cliffe's preferred option is in fact simply to tidy up the land allocation system which has come into being since independence. Land allocation and use would be legally controlled by Village Development Committees (VIDCOs) on behalf of the District Council, which is the formal local authority. The tidying-up Cliffe proposes is to ensure 'the other disadvantaged groups or poorer peasants' are represented, as women already are, by having members on the VIDCO (p. 81). However, when local political realities are taken into account, as even the cursory examination in the following chapter shows, the degree of power most VIDCOs actually hold is extremely limited. To implement the 'democratic' system would require the government to step in to enforce it, thus contradicting its intention.

This means, in conclusion, that none of the policy options which have been considered to date can easily be implemented without extensive intervention on the part of the government. In most districts in the Midlands, government has, until now, been cautious because of this. District Councils have been encouraged to urge VIDCOs and WADCOs (Ward Development Committees) to accept land reform schemes, with the delicate matter of land allocation issue being left aside. The grazing schemes which are being implemented have historically been tried on various occasions since their origin with centralisation in the 1930s. The last instances were the veld management schemes of the 1970s (Dankwerts, 1975). Where 'villagisation' is being encouraged, what officials promoting the scheme have in mind is that those who used the war and the 'freedom' of independence to settle on and cultivate grazing area land, should now return to the settlement lines and arable blocks of land husbandry. It should be surprising if voluntary take-up of internal land reform is anything other than extremely slow. Where some take-up is occurring, as in the Zvishavane area, a great deal of manipulation has taken place.

The reason the government faces a potential impasse here, I propose, is because the only policy options that have been considered, as in the colonial period, are purposive-rational in nature. There has been little change over time in official attitudes towards the definition and solving of communal area land use problems. This can be illustrated concisely by a comparison of three statements:

(1) 'Deterioration of the reserves has assumed such proportions that even laymen can note it and present methods of agriculture cannot continue . . . the soil is being exhausted . . . While the extensive destruction of timber should be checked.'

(2) '. . . it is no exaggeration to say that at the moment we are heading for disaster. We have on the one hand a rapid increase taking place in the African population and on the other a rapid deterioration of the very land on which these people depend for their existence . . .'

(3) 'If soil erosion rates are allowed to continue at existing levels the soil over large areas of Zimbabwe will be destroyed within our own lifetime. Crop failures will become the norm, water will become scarce, and most of our resources will go towards feeding a vast, starving rural population.'

Each of these three statements predicts imminent disaster. But now compare their dates:

(1) 1920. (Native Department official reporting to the Chief Native Commissioner)

(2) 1954. (Extract from the Annual Report of the Natural Resources Board)

(3) 1985. (H. A. Elwell)

Each of these three statements is made from physical observation. The exaggerated conclusions reached are not based on rigorous survey, as their repetition over 65 years illustrates. Yet physicalist intervention policies have been developed throughout this period on the basis of these or similar statements. The interrelationship between environmental and economic problems and social relations of production are inadequately understood and hence not tackled. The result is the persistence of the problems which are the physical outcome of social inequalities. Even since independence, an accept-ance that land apportionment has caused the fundamental inequali-ties in the communal areas had had little impact on the physicalist and technocratic approach to production constraints in these areas. At no time has there been any active attempt to initiate dialogue with peasant community leaders in order to find out if any more mutually acceptable land policy options can be opened up. Innovation has been lacking because these people, who have a different and more intimate view of their world to offer, have remained only the objects of policy practice. Where their views have been cursorily sought – for instance, the 1944 Godlonton Commission or the 1982 Chavunduka Commission – they have then been largely ignored, because they cannot be easily incorporated within existing attitudes and approaches to policy. This is not to suggest that peasant communities have readily available answers themselves to policy dilemmas; rather that there is a wide gap between how the state officially views the rural world, and how peasant societies view it themselves. In the bridging of this hermeneutic gap there is much that can be learned by participants on either side.

'Bridge-building' is a key feature of populism (Robertson, 1984, p. 222), but only in a very superficial way. For Habermas, the development of understanding through communicative action is the way we resolve apparent or real conflicts in order to coordinate social actions. But he holds too that communication is everywhere distorted because of the relations of force that are built into the social struc-tures of communication. In Zimbabwe I use his theory to advance a two-part argument. First, that the development of agrarian policies capable of yielding environmental, economic and social benefits requires a radical improvement of communication between state and peasantry. But, second, the major constraint to achieving this lies in the way administrative (and economic) structures operate, and the way those within the party-state complex think. Bureaucratic and economic structures force people to conceive of their interests in narrow senses: maintaining a bureaucratic job and hence a certain lifestyle requires obeying hierarchically set rules. Is genuine dialogue about policy issues therefore inconceivable in a country such as Zimbabwe?

In the last part of this chapter I want to ground this question, so that it can be examined later on, by referring to two people who have already thought about the problem in the Zimbabwean context. The first person, J. F. Holleman, figured prominently in the official period of reflection that occurred in the early 1960s. The second, a senior officer in Agritex, was the driving force behind an attempt begun in 1983 to redirect Zimbabwe's agricultural extension strategy.

COMMUNICATION AND AGRICULTURAL EXTENSION

In the previous chapter the 1961 Mangwende Commission report was mentioned as pre-eminent among several published in 1961 that questioned the nature and effects of the technical development policies of the previous thirty years. One of the Mangwende commissioners was J. F. Holleman, to whose analysis of the 1962–5 transitional period (Holleman, 1968) reference has already been made. The epilogue of Holleman's book provides a personal account of how the commission's report was completed.

The final paragraphs were written some time after two a.m. one April morning in 1961. Holleman had been standing looking out over Jameson Ave in Salisbury (now Samora Machel Ave in Harare), reflecting on the report's conclusions and recommendations. He was unsettled by the fact that the report omitted any reference to something which all the commissioners had been conscious of in taking evidence from both white and black witnesses. This lacuna was, 'a clear focus on one vital but elusive factor which had been a major cause of estrangement and conflict: the lack of understanding between white and black' (1968, p. 372). Eventually Holleman added five more paragraphs to the report. 'Their scientific value might be slight and they might look somewhat out of place in an official report; but I felt they touched the heart of the matter and that my fellow commissioners would feel the same' (p. 373). These paragraphs were on communication. Their crux is as follows:

> In almost every aspect of our enquiry we have been struck by the desperate need for better communications between Administration and people. It was with profound sadness that time and again, we found that misunderstanding, frustration and even conflict, arose because at some crucial stage, communications had been inadequate or altogether lacking. In many cases, the means of contact did exist but were either not, or insufficiently, or wrongly, used.
>
> It struck us there may be something lacking in the understanding of the very concept of communication. We could not fail to notice for instance that Africans were inclined to look upon . . . established

communications channels . . . as a means of bringing 'grievances' to the notice of the Administration; while on the part of the latter there was the tendency to regard these channels largely as a means of disseminating instructions. Surely the concept of communication is wider than this and also involves the need for the pooling of views, attitudes and experiences in search of mutual understanding of individual and communal problems . . .

'Communication' then . . . involves the genuine effort to perceive and understand different views in the spirit and against the background in which they were conceived and formulated, and without the prejudice and critical reservations which are only too often the heritage of the discipline of western thinking. (Mangwende Commission, 1961, paras 456–8)

In these paragraphs Holleman is discussing the distorted nature of communication that had resulted from the 'colonisation of the lifeworld' of the African peoples in Zimbabwe. These thoughts parallel Habermas's own critique of how social communication has become distorted because of the colonisation of the lifeworld that has occurred through the growth of capitalism in general (Habermas, 1984, p. xxi). To overcome this distortion Holleman is recommending that to inform and guide policy practice, knowledge should be pursued, not in the form of scientific observation, but in the form of hermeneutic or interpretive understanding.

One man's written remarks by themselves are hardly likely to have a significant impact on policy practice, unless they pick up and coincide with more widely felt beliefs. In this instance the impact of the Mangwende Commission report was unusually significant because of its role in an eighteen-months review exercise during which an extraordinary amount of rethinking of policy took place. This generated the already described push for a community development programme.

In community development policies, as they were implemented internationally in the late 1950s and early 1960s, lay at least some of the seeds of the populist development strategies that have developed in many Third World countries since. These seeds can be seen in a statement made in August 1961 by Whitehead, the United Democratic Party Prime Minister, about the government's proposed change in political philosophy and policy practice:

It is part of our political duty to obtain support from every village in the country. We do intend to see that we are making an active battle to make democracy work in this country. To make democracy work we have to make the ordinary man in the street, whatever his race, feel that he has a voice in the planning in the early stages of decisions and in building his future. (Holleman, 1968, p. 259)

Such talk, as I suggested at the end of the previous chapter, frightened the white electorate. The election of a Rhodesian Front government in 1962 was as much a reaction by the white electorate against the insecurity and unease engendered by bringing into critical scrutiny the rationalisation employed to defend their political and economic supremacy, as it was a defence of this supremacy itself. After the change in government community development was still taken up and launched by the RF in July 1965. However it was never implemented in the liberal manner it was conceived and the policy was opposed by the black nationalist movement. Black leaders who supported the policy were branded collaborators (Holleman, 1968, pp. 281–5).

One further issue that Holleman raises in his commentary on the 1962–5 period also bears highlighting for it is an issue that will be returned to in the following chapters. Within government organisations there are often sharp differences in attitudes among personnel according to where they work in terms of both spatial and hierarchical distance from central government. Prior to the official launching of the community development programme, training courses for some senior district and central government officers were instituted in 1964. From the assessment remarks written at the conclusion of courses, a clear divergence in attitudes between district administrators and more senior government officials can be detected:

— 'I certainly went home with something to think about' (district commissioner);
— 'I got the lousy feeling I never could do anything right again' (district commissioner);
—'. . . all right then, paternalism is dead. But how exactly do I go from here?' (district commissioner).

— 'I got rather bored, and when I wasn't bored I felt bloody annoyed' (senior research officer);
— 'I find that I am as authoritarian as ever – not that it bothers me' (provincial medical officer);
— '. . . it all remained a bit vague' (senior official at Internal Affairs head office).

(Holleman, 1968, pp. 266–7)

These random outlooks gelled into divergent approaches between many district administrations and the political and state leadership. Holleman remarks that he

> could not escape the odd sensation of watching two currents moving in opposite directions. At the higher level of government and political decision-making, the feebly liberalistic current of the early 'sixties had stopped and was beginning to flow back towards the political and authoritarian right, leading to a polarisation of white and black political attitudes . . .
>
> At the lower level there was the current of administrative and technical activity, the deliberately non-authoritarian efforts towards a better understanding and more effective promotion of African ambitions, involving a steady increase in areas of contact, a search for stronger links of cooperation and for more channels of meaningful communication.
>
> . . . That [these approaches] did seem to continue in opposite directions as late as 1966, may be partly because the full weight of community development efforts was as yet concentrated on all-African communities, but also because of lack of communication between the local operatives and the political top. (pp. 290–1)

If we move on in time now to the 1980s, this tension between those who prefer the 'normal' method of bureaucratic action, that is adhering to a purposive rationality, and those who advocate a more questioning and democratic communicative rationality, can be seen to have re-emerged. In an interview I had in March 1985 with the then Midlands Provincial Agricultural Extension Officer (PAEO), he expressed his own preoccupation with this phenomenon. Early in the interview he introduced a theme to which he returned throughout in his reflection on policy developments in the province since 1982:

> You get that attitude [of commitment] in the grassroots workers and the likelihood is it will work upwards. Then you will meet obstructions through the organisation's top-down approach. (Interview, 21 March 1985)

Robertson (1984, pp. 156–7) suggests that such antipathy between the highest and lowest echelons is a normal occurrence in bureaucracies. In Kenya, David Leonard (1977, pp. 78–80) certainly believed such antagonism existed in their post-independence agricultural extension organisation. The standard response of managers to organised dissatisfaction was repressive – 'to try to crush collective organisations by punishing those who show open opposition and by rewarding those subordinate leaders who seem pliable' (p. 79). This response was deleterious for the organisation. 'It only drives resistance underground and heightens the alienation of subordinates from their work' (p. 79).

In the Midlands the PAEO wished to overcome this typical authoritarian approach, for he believed it was the chief cause of the ineffectiveness of the agricultural extension agency in the communal areas prior to independence. This realisation was brought home to him by a particularly traumatic six-hour meeting held with staff in the Gokwe district in early 1982. 'All I heard was complaints and problems dating back 20 years.' After attending this meeting and visiting farmers in the region, the PAEO concluded that

> there was nothing wrong with the peasant farmer, there was nothing wrong with the people in the organisation, but there was a hell of a lot wrong with the way in which they were being managed and encouraged to develop agriculture . . . I came away totally and utterly convinced in my mind that there was just no limitation to what we could do in peasant agriculture, providing we could correct those basic factors that were wrong. One, that people . . . that peasant farmers were idiots and couldn't think for themselves and weren't capable of achieving higher production, and two, the same attitude was more or less applied to the extension workers. (Interview, 21 March 1985)

The PAEO also thought, as Holleman did, that authoritarianism and paternalism militate against effective communication. Hence he felt that it was both the organisation's management structure and the attitudes of personnel that needed changing:

> [Prior to independence] . . . The felt needs of the people were supposedly determined through processes of consultation. But in practice it was more one of dependence . . . Total and utter dependence to the point where even the [staff] in the organisation depended for almost everything they did upon decisions taken for them. Maybe here and there, there was a spark of an attempt to try and create independence in the people they were working with, but it wasn't possible until after independence for that to emerge . . . But that I saw as the most important thing that had to be done for the staff and for the department. We had to try and create . . . an attitude of mind now which would encourage people to think for

themselves. That's the start. And in turn to encourage the clientele to stand on their own feet and think likewise. (Interview, 21 March 1985)

At this time, the agricultural extension agency was in a period of organisational flux. This provided the PAEO with some opportunity to tackle what he perceived to be the twin problems of structure and attitude. The flux was consequent upon the merger in October 1981 of the two pre-independence agricultural extension organisations – CONEX, which had operated only in the commercial farming areas, and DEVAG, responsible for communal area extension – to form a unified agency, Agritex.

In September 1985, the PAEO was promoted to become Agritex's Deputy Director (Field). In this position he was able to gain acceptance for a proposed new organisational structure in Agritex. In another interview I had with him in 1987, the now Deputy Director described this structure as one of 'teams within teams' (Interview, 10 June 1987). The principle of the structure is that at the operational end of the organisation, staff should work in teams of ideally less than ten people, and that this team should be headed by just one person (rather than a chain), who is given sufficient responsibility to run the team through a collaborative style. The organisation's old conventionally pyramidal structure had been suited to an authoritarian and purposive-rational style, in which orders are passed downwards and staff performance is measured in terms of the efficiency with which orders are implemented. In order to break this structure up, the technical and extension staff have been largely separated out (see Figure 3.1), so that it is only provincial and district officers (and the Director himself) who have direct responsibility over both technical and field staff. The twin aims of this are to give extension teams (under an extension officer) more responsibility, and, by reducing the administrative role of technical staff, to improve their ability to deliver relevant technical support.

The successes and problems encountered in effecting this organisational change, I will only examine in Chapter 7. What I shall examine next is how much Agritex's approach to land use management has changed in practice in the Midlands province. The analysis will have a strong hermeneutic element in that peasant views on land use management will be interpreted and contrasted with the official position. This will illustrate how political and economic issues affect the extent to which the relevance of technical approaches is questioned.

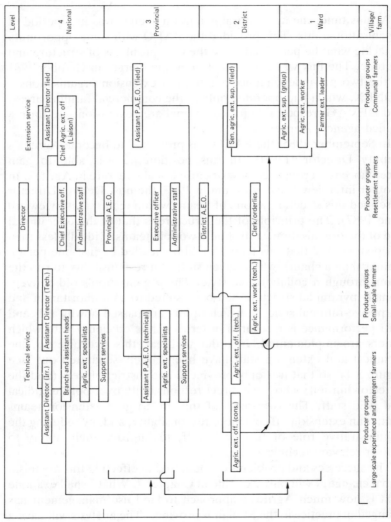

Figure 3.1 Organisational structure: Department of Agricultural Technical and Extension Services

4 Alternative Strategies for Managing Livestock on the Land

It is land and cattle which the Europeans have taken away from the African, and it is land and cattle which an African Government promises to restore to the people. European politicians have reduced the natural resources of the people and made them, in their own eyes, 'poor'. Nationalism promises them traditional wealth . . . Agricultural output in Chilimanzi is low, and this is attributed by the people to Government policies; but the Government attributes it to undue interference of nationalists who persuade people not to comply with the advice given to them by the Agricultural Department. Whatever view is right, one thing is clear: agriculture in Chilimanzi is firmly rooted in politics, and politics are expressed in agricultural terms. (Weinrich, 1964, p. 37)

Conflict over interpretations of how land is used and how it should be used has formed a major barrier to understanding between the peasantry and the state since the origin of the colonial state in Zimbabwe. In Chapter 2 I argued that the colonial state's pursuit of technical development policies was influenced not only by the political ends the government wished to achieve, but also by the purposive rationalisation employed by the state. The white authorities acted collusively and coercively: only in the early 1960s was it briefly acknowledged that the peasantry might hold not only an alternative, but a credible view of the world.

Since independence, the purposive-rational approach to communal area policy has continued. The government would like to see the peasantry fully integrated within the national economy and raising their formally marketed output. Following the 1982–4 drought the government has been less concerned to appease its rural constituents and meet the promises made by the nationalists in the years of the struggle. nstead, its emphasis has been to ensure that Zimbabwe maintains its status as one of the few countries in the SADCC region that produces a food surplus.[1] Thus the government has turned to the offensive by attempting to increase agricultural production output,

113

and by calling for the reform of land management practices within the communal areas.

It is the second of these policy areas that I will deal with in this chapter. And since the thorniest current land use policy issue is that of livestock management (Cliffe, 1986, p. 106), I will focus on this issue.[2] Many people I have spoken to, particularly in Agritex, are apprehensive about the likely response of communal area societies to land use policies which they recognise do not offer anything fundamentally different to the veld management policies of the 1970s – nor even the notorious land husbandry policy itself.

In examining the land use policy issue, there is another central theme of the book to which I wish to return. This is the argument that the fundamental constraint the government faces in pursuing a successful agrarian strategy is that, because of its purposive-rational approach, it is unable to tackle communal area environmental and economic problems in a way that fully acknowledges the perspective that rural societies themselves have of their problems.

The chapter is organised in four sections. In the first two I shall contrast the procedural model for pastoral management that is entrenched in government policy with an interpretative account of the preferred strategy of many communal stock owners. Case-study examples will be used to illustrate how Agritex staff and farmers cope with the problems they face in actually implementing their respective models. This contrast will show why the peasantry do not believe that the pastoral land use management policies that governments in Zimbabwe have promoted until now do lead to the most effective and economic use of land.

In the third section of the chapter the work of other researchers will be drawn into this discussion of communal area livestock economics and ecology. This work will be used to verify that communal area stock owners, given the constraints they face and their economic objectives, do employ livestock management strategies that by and large make efficient use of the restricted land available. Furthermore this work points up the dearth of substantive evidence behind the official assumption that there is ongoing environmental degradation occurring in the communal areas. Nevertheless, the pressures which have been placed on rural societies stemming from the land apportionment policy, population growth, and restrictions placed on the movement of cattle, mean that the livestock management strategies of stock owners are now extremely prone to failure. This was evidenced by the high livestock mortality rates during the 1982–4 drought and again in late 1987.

This explains why many amongst the peasantry believe that they will only be made yet poorer if the government continues to pursue the same type of land use management policy that the colonial government practised. Thus the government may only succeed in provoking anew rural resistance. This re-raises a central question of this study: why has there been such a remarkable lack of genuine communication between the peasantry and the first government in Zimbabwe purporting to represent them?

I have invoked as a reason the purposive rationality that has become institutionalised within the Zimbabwean bureaucracy and which permeates policy actions. The argument outlined so far proceeds as follows. The Zimbabwean government like the Rhodesian, has sought to enunciate in purely technical and economic terms, land use policies which are in fact designed very much for political purposes. The respective ideologies of past and present governments have then been used to justify not only the policies themselves but also, in their implementation, the government's coercion or manipulation of the peasantry. Moreover, these ideologies disguise the interests of those in power and in the government who are responsible for shaping and working out policy.

In the final part of the chapter I shall again use case studies to examine the role that interests play in distorting or preventing communication between peasant communities and senior government officials and politicians. This means the deficiencies in the official understanding of communal areas economic and environmental processes are obscured. And here the argument I have outlined turns full circle. For if the bulk of the peasantry do continue to become poorer, then neither their interests nor those of the state will be served.

THE OFFICIAL PASTORAL MANAGEMENT STRATEGIES: PADDOCKS AND STOCKING RATES

In the next two sections I seek to outline two alternative schemas or strategies for pastoral management. The first is the procedural model utilised by staff within Agritex; the second the normative ideal spoken of by peasant farmers. My role in offering these two accounts is that of an observer who has experienced and discussed at first hand the operation of each schema. I am, however, not a disinterested observer but an interested one – one who believes that the current agrarian policy framework is severely flawed in its inherent assumptions about the environment and rural society. Hence, after attempting to lay open the claims attached to each strategy, I will use the empirical research of others to make my own claim. This is that the strategies peasant stock owners aim towards are better suited for their economic objectives and environmental circumstances than the strategy government would like to see them adopt. I do not imply, however, that local strategies cannot be improved upon.

One further introductory explanation needs to be made about the status of these two schemas. Each until now has been culturally fixed: the attitude adopted depends on whether one is working in a government department or living in a peasant village. This does not mean, for instance, that a member of Agritex may not be aware of – or even use himself on his own land – the strategy of the peasant farmer. However, when performing his official role he adopts the official procedure. Bernstein (1976) in his discussion of Schutz's work on the phenomenology of the social world offers a theoretical explanation of this phenomenon: 'We are continuously ordering, classifying, and interpreting our ongoing experiences according to various interpretive schemes. But in our everyday life these interpretive schemes are themselves essentially social and intersubjective' (p. 145). So the point I wish to suggest is this: despite the anomalies within *both* strategies they are reinforced by the tacit normative acceptance that is granted them in their respective bureaucratic and agrarian environments.

The basic distinction between the respective strategies is seen in the opposition of peasant farmers to the government's proposals, within the context of internal land use reform, to demarcate and paddock grazing areas. This opposition is for two reasons. First, people live in the 'grazing areas' (that is, those areas delimited for grazing under the 1951 Land Husbandry Act), and to where will they move? Second, cattle obtain the greater part of their free-range forage from areas generally excluded from fenced grazing schemes, because these areas are ecologically sensitive. The official view is that it is precisely because cattle are allowed to graze and browse just 'anywhere' that grazing schemes are necessary. This is grazing anarchy not grazing management, and it is anarchy that Hardin holds leads to the 'tragedy of the commons'.[3]

Let us now examine more thoroughly the official pastoral management schema that Agritex plans and promotes. This schema can perhaps best be understood as a procedural model which Agritex staff employ when they are requested to provide a land use plan, either for a grazing scheme or for a more comprehensive land resettlement or internal land reform exercise. A case example of it is the land use mapping and planning exercise carried out in Zvishavane by Agritex in tandem to the survey work I undertook within Ture ward in 1984–5.

The Agritex procedure is based on the defining of land capability classes. This is justified in the Agritex handbook on the subject as follows:

> In land use planning, as practised in Zimbabwe, the planner is concerned with the capability of the land to produce permanently, under specific uses and treatments. The objective of classification is therefore the systematic arrangement and grouping of different kinds of land to show their most intensive safe use and indicate their management requirements and to show the permanent hazards attached to the use of the land, in terms of increasing degree of limitation of use. (Ivy, 1981, p. 1)

The first objective of the land-mapping exercise for Ture was therefore to map out the different land classes. The outcome is given in Table 4.1. There are eight land classes. The first four are designated as suitable for arable production. Class V land consists of 'vleis and watercourses subject to severe wetness not usually corrected and best left under permanent vegetation' (Ivy, 1981, p. 2). In Ture, the class VII land consists of broken granite hills; it is adjudged suitable for rough grazing. And class VIII terrain is not so much 'land' but the area occupied by sheer-sided, round-topped, granite outcrops.

Table 4.1   Land class areas for Ture ward (estimates)

	Ha	*%*
Potential arable	2 500	29.0
Class V (vlei)	380	4.4
Class VI	1 300	15.0
Class VII and VIII (hilly and rocky)	4 400	51.0
Mabwematema Dam	50	0.6
Total land area	8 600	100.0

Source: Drinkwater (1985).

Generally, it is the class VI and VII land which has been delimited as the 'grazing area' since aerial photographs were first used for allocating land uses during implementation of the Land Husbandry Act. Thus the Ture mapping exercise showed Agritex staff immediately where 'encroachment' into the grazing area had occurred. This is where people, practising the same type of 'freedom ploughing' that was a symbol of opposition to the LHA, moved into the grazing areas to cultivate and settle during the war years of the 1970s and immediately after independence. One premise of a grazing scheme is that these encroachers have to be moved out again. How the district council chairmen in Chirumhanzu and Chiwundura attempt to use this sensitive issue politically will be described towards the end of the chapter.

The most difficult task Agritex face in turning a land capability map into a land use plan is the delineation of boundaries. In the Ture exercise grazing areas were supposed to be demarcated for each of the four VIDCOs.[4] Local government and Agritex topographical staff had, though, been put under pressure in the early months of 1984 to rush through the task of establishing VIDCOs. Consequently boundaries were drawn rather arbitrarily, using 1982 census data, and on the ground local leaders disputed both where they had been drawn and when they felt the boundaries should be.[5]

This is not the first time that the government's attempts to draw lines on the map have created disputes. The ward boundary between Ture and Dayataya wards to the south has been an affair of long simmering dispute. The people of Dayataya are predominantly Ndebele, descended from those who moved into the area under Chief Mafala in 1917, after having being evicted from the Fort Rixon area. The Dumbuseya Chief Wedza, in Ture, claims only to have invited them in, and so on occasions, such as when the land husbandry system was being implemented, Wedza's people have clashed with their southern neighbours over grazing land boundaries.[6] There is still no agreed boundary between the wards.

The negotiation of boundaries by Agritex's cartographer was therefore the trickiest component of his mapping exercise. When he had completed his attempt, however, he had the basis for a ward land use plan: each VIDCO area had arable areas, grazing land, village areas, roads and schools.

After the boundaries and land use areas have been set, the next stage of Agritex's procedure for planning and implementing a grazing scheme is the calculation of livestock carrying capacity. Ture lies within natural region IV and for this region Agritex staff in Zvishavane were employing a carrying capacity ratio of 1 LU per 4 ha for class VI land and 1 LU per 10 ha for the combined area of class VII and VIII land. Together this provided the ward with a grazing area of 5700 hectares and an overall carrying capacity of 765 LU. However, even after the three-year drought the actual livestock numbers in the ward exceeded this estimated carrying capacity by about 250 per cent. In the census questionnaire survey the 60 per cent of households which still held cattle were recorded as having 2284 head of cattle (1427.5 LU). And this figure was only two-thirds of the total claimed to have been owned in 1981.

The destocking policy of the late 1940s and 1950s was implemented because once 'carrying capacity' calculations were made alarm was felt at the extent to which in many areas actual livestock numbers on the land exceeded what was believed to be the safe ecological figure. This 'overstocking' is still ubiquitous throughout the communal areas. Cousins (1987, p. 34) reports that of the 83 operating or planned grazing schemes that he collected data on, 70 had a stocking rate in excess of 1 LU per 4 ha. Although not *de rigueur*, for some fenced schemes Agritex have included a sizeable chunk of arable land in their calculations, terming it winter grazing. This is at least in part to appease donor agencies such as the EEC who want grazing scheme committees to honour agreements to reduce livestock holdings to the stipulated carrying capacity.[7]

In Ture too, because according to our survey 53 per cent of households were unable to provide their own draught power, Agritex's Zvishavane district officer did not use the formal figures to suggest that destocking take place in the ward. Rather he supported a proposal by the ward leaders that commercial ranchland adjacent to the ward be purchased and used for grazing purposes. Some of the intricacies involved in negotiations over this proposal I shall discuss in the final section of the chapter.

If there is agreement between local leaders and Agritex over scheme boundaries and the stocking rate that will at least be accepted initially, a grazing scheme may proceed to be implemented. This means delineating paddocks, either by fencing or simply by boundary markers, and the election of a grazing scheme committee to manage the scheme. The committee is encouraged to draw up, in conjunction with Agritex, by-laws for the scheme and to enforce them – another source of local dispute. To conclude this account of Agritex's schema for pastoral management I shall refer to some comments made by

Agritex staff themselves on the subject. In a discussion paper on the issue of communal area grazing Agritex's Assistant Director (Field) summarises the major features of the veld management schemes, popular in Masvingo province in the early 1970s as:

— Planning of the scheme with the people.
— Definition of the scheme boundary on the ground with the people.
— Division of the grazing into five paddocks, with the arable as a fifth area in winter.
— Aerial photographic map and brief project report.
— Formation of management committee and training of members in their responsibilities.
— Levy of grazing fee and fines for wrong-doers.
— Short duration grazing practised on most schemes. (1986, p. 7)

It can be seen that the current format for the establishment of grazing schemes has no substantial changes from this model of the 1970s. The Assistant Director's note on the fate of the 315 veld management projects implemented in Masvingo province is therefore telling: 'Practically all these schemes broke down eventually because of "overstocking" and settlement of people in the grazing areas' (1986, p. 8). This is the situation that pertains today.

And finally two comments from Agritex annual reports for the Midlands province:

Generally there is no veld management practised in communal areas. Gradual land reform programmes may help to bring about grazing management, as more land may be released for grazing. (1984, p. 28)

There are two [EEC micro] projects in Mvuma and Gweru – Zinyoro and Chiwundura respectively . . . The problem of following proper rotation systems still exists and apparently is not appreciated by the community members who prefer to move their animals to paddocks nearest to their homesteads or to poach graze in nearby areas. (1986, p. 28)

Officially Agritex recognises that the implementation of its pastoral management schema in Zimbabwe's communal areas faces near insurmountable constraints. Nevertheless, the agency holds to its procedural model.

THE PEASANT MANAGEMENT STRATEGY

In April 1987, with the assistance of a member of CADEC who acted as an interpreter, I conducted a series of interviews, mostly about land issues, with lineage, VIDCO and ZANU (PF) leaders in the Maware ward of southern Chirumhanzu. When I asked if government officials had come to talk to people in the ward about introducing paddocked grazing schemes, the response of those I interviewed was unanimous. I shall quote from these responses below. In so doing I shall also identify the features they refer to of an 'ideal' grazing strategy. This will serve two purposes. It will help corroborate my account of farmers' normative pastoral management schema, which will be presented on the basis of my fieldwork observations and discussions. And it will provide an immediate impression of the restrictions stock owners face in attempting to operate this schema.

(1) *V/H (sabhuku) Mawindi:*

It has been at least a year since they talked about paddocks, but people are still not interested. When we look at it we can see it would not be possible. It will be killing the cattle. Because there would not be enough grass to eat . . . People in the community are very much crowded. If they introduced paddocks, some of our people would have no place to stay . . . Destocking is something else which would make people very much angry all over. (Interview, 14 April 1987)

Mawindi identifies three reasons why people oppose the introduction of grazing schemes. They fear the area of forage available for grazing will be reduced. They fear the destocking of the 1940s and 1950s will be repeated. And some fear they will be made homeless.

(2) *VIDCO Chairman Mkata:*

There is no cooperation amongst people on this issue [of paddocks]. The reason is that the place is very small and the people are crowded and the grass is not growing. I cannot understand what can be done. We really need land because there are some people who don't even have enough land for fields. (Interview, 15 April 1987)

Here Mkata makes one additional point: 'the grass is not growing'. This is not just a reference to the drought then being experienced, but also to the belief that there is now insufficient grazing area for owners to be able to leave land long enough for the grass to grow. The same concept is expressed below by Mutumiri.

(3)   *H/man Mutumiri:*

Wherever there is grass people will now take their cattle there for grazing. . . In the past when we were planting we would take the cattle with us and leave the grass to grow. Then after planting was finished, we would take them back to where the grass was growing. We would still like to do it, but the problem is that the rainfall is very low.

[On paddocks] We once tried that idea (during Smith's government); Chief Hama accepted the idea, but we later discovered the animals were dying.[8] There was not enough grass . . . By that time there were enough paddocks for the cattle, but what happens is that when the cattle have finished the grass in one areas, it will be difficult for them to feed. There is no possibility of keeping the cattle in one place because they are used to just roaming around. (Interview, 15 April 1987)

Mutumiri points out how their preferred rotations for grazing cattle have been disrupted primarily, in his view, because of a decline in rainfall. This common belief that rainfall has declined will be commented on in the next section. The point about cattle 'just roaming around' implies the animals know where to find the best forage.

(4)   *VIDCO Chairman Mugarisi:*

If you start talking about it [paddocks] at a meeting people will start leaving. It could be that the area does not have enough grass. Personally I don't see many advantages. It could be done but people are very much crowded and to find a place for that is impossible. The only means for cattle to have enough grazing is to take them to the edges of your field and have them grazing there. (Interview, 14 April 1987)

Mugarisi provides a further account of how stock owners are being forced to modify their preferred grazing system. Because there is insufficient grass in the main grazing areas to last the cattle through a poor rainy season, stock owners are forced to bring their animals back to graze on the contours and around the edges of their fields, before harvest.

(5) *V/H Mazhlatini:*

The previous government did not allow people to herd their animals in the vleis. Now they can take their animals wherever they can find grazing. (Interview, 14 April 1987)

Vleis are one of the few other areas where cattle do find forage, but these are areas normally excluded from grazing schemes. In short:

(6) *VIDCO Chairman Gova:*

As you can see there is not enough grass here. How do you think we can introduce paddocks? (Interview, 16 April 1987)

From these quotes it is clear that all the community leaders in Maware believe that if livestock were restricted to a paddocked grazing scheme it would reduce the forage available to the animals. Responses to this belief can be made on the grounds of economic effectiveness and environmental impact. The four main responses possible can be subsetted as follows:

(1) Their belief is mistaken because they are unaware of the advantages of systematically rotating animals through paddocks.
   (a) And if they used the land adequately there would be no need for them to have any further land.
   (b) However, because many families have no cattle the people need more land if they are to implement fenced grazing schemes.
(2) By not restricting livestock to confined areas animals are better able to use all forage available.
   (a) However, allowing animals access to even ecologically sensitive parts of the landscape leads to degradation and it would be better for people to have more land and use conventional grazing management systems.
   (b) And this system is not only more efficient but also ecologically sustainable, as long as people are not so constrained that they are forced into environmental abuse.

The colonial government, in its striving to maintain land apportionment, held by response 1(a). Since 1980, with the implementation of some land resettlement current government policy more closely follows response 1(b), although some local and district extension staff will grant 2(a). That is, they will allow that more forage is available to livestock if they are not confined, and that therefore peasants may have economic efficiency on their side even if not environmental these economic and environmental issues argue that in fact response 2(b) is the most accurate representation of peasant stockowners' management strategy. Their work will be examined in the next section. It is time now, though, to outline the generalised model for pastoral management to which communal stockowners make reference.

Two of the three elemtns in this model are referred to in the above quotes: *livestock*; *forage*. The additional element is *labour*. or each of these elements the following principles underlie the livestock management strategies of most owners:

Livestock (cattle). The daily movement of animals begins from and ends at kraals or pens which are usually located near the home. (Animals are kralled so that their manure can be collected, so they do not have to be watched at night, and so they can be fed supplementary stover in winter.)

During their daily movement cattle must be able to obtain forage; at least three to four times a week obtain acceess to a water supply where they can drink their fill; and at periodic intervals (which vary according to the season) travel to the dip.

The minimum ideal herd size is one that with the right structural balance will ensure the household always has at least two mature oxen for ploughing purposes. (Farmers hold that this is from ten to twelve animals.)

The critical time for animal fitness, particularly the draught stock, is when the first rains arrive, for this is when the ploughing season begins.

Labour. Adult labour time on herding should be minimised.

Forage. All available forage should be utilised (except the crops in people's fields during the growing season).

Some rotation of cattle should take place to 'let the grass regrow'.

If these principles are linked together, then the basic features of farmers' livestock management strategies can be understood. Forage availability determines where cattle will go if left to 'just roam around'. Thus the extent to which livestock are directed to specific areas depends on the labour input. Livestock owners have a range of four decisions they can choose among regarding the allocation of labour to herding:

(a) Animals can be left to graze unattended.
(b) Animals can be left to graze near one or more household members who are engaged in other activities.

(c) One or more household members can be specifically allocated the task of herding.

(d) An agreement can be reached with a number of other owning households to group the animals and rotate herding duties.

Option (a) may be used in winter when there are no vulnerable crops and the grass does not grow. Option (c) is only desirable if there are children to undertake the task, that is, during the school holidays. Option (d) is unlikely to work at periods of the season when labour demand is highest.

Taking these elements and principles, one can now begin to piece them together into a rational, normative (that is, ideal) pastoral management strategy. In spring, before the first rains, animals graze the early flush of grass in vlei areas or along drainage lines, to gain strength for the planting season. At planting, animals accompany owners to the fields and graze nearby, allowing the first grass to come through in the extensive grazing areas. During the growing season animals are herded either by children or, during term-time, under cooperative herding arrangements in the main grazing areas. Some form of rotation (there was in Chiwundura) may be used. After harvest, the animals are returned to the fields to eat crop residues and the grass along contours. Late season grazing is also provided along watercourses, and during winter, stover, predominantly maize but also from crops such as groundnuts, may be used for supplementary feed.

The net result of this strategy is that a few critical areas become vital to the provision of forage at times of the year when general grass cover, even in better seasons, is low. During 1986/7 research on livestock management was carried out by Ian Scoones in the Mazvihwa communal area, south of Zvishavane. He terms these areas of greatest forage availability – vleis, river banks, drainage lines, contours – 'key resources':

> Much of communal area cattles' feeding time, especially in the critical end of dry season period, is spent in small areas (perhaps 5 per cent of the total grazing area); the rest of the grazing area is simply unused for most of the year. These small areas I shall call key resources. A key resource is a patch that offsets critical constraints either of forage quality or quantity. (1987, p. 22)

The actual ability of stockowners to employ their normative pastoral management schema, whatever degree of social organisation exists, is usually highly constrained. As Scoones notes, this makes the key resources vitally important – and vulnerable. As the remarks of the lineage and VIDCO leaders in Maware indicate, social, economic and environmental conflict all impinge on actual livestock management practice. Scarcities, respectively, of labour, cattle and forage aggravate each of these. Thus the battle of stockowners is to acquire and maintain a cattle herd large enough to provide draught power, and in the quest to avoid abusing the environment.

Examples of conflicts experienced in the Maware area have already been hinted at. I shall spell them out further since it will clarify why farmers manage livestock in the way they do, and hence will help a comparison of this strategy with the official grazing scheme model.

To return, then, to southern Chirumhanzu. In Chapter 5 when I examine the farming systems of the extended case households I worked with in Chirumhanzu and Chiwundura, I shall explain the contrasting land use patterns of both areas more fully. What it is necessary to note here is that the open field pattern of the land husbandry era still largely persists in southern Chirumhanzu. Homesteads straggle in village lines along the edge of unfenced arable land blocks. Population density is high because of the large movement of additional people into the area in 1954 that was described in Chapter 2.[9]

In this area the time when the greatest controversy over livestock occurs is in the period between the first rains, when early planting begins, and the main rains which may set in only a month later. Conflict arises between those who plant early and those who do not, since the latter will only start to herd their animals after they have planted. The crops of the early planters (predominantly maize) which germinate in November are therefore highly vulnerable to the still unwatched animals of the late planters.

Three of the factors that influence farmers' ability to plant early – soil texture, soil moisture level, and capacity to winter plough – will be referred to in Chapter 5. The factor that I am concerned with now is labour. If a household is to plant early there must be sufficient available people and draught animals for them to work immediately and rapidly once the first significant rain has fallen. Timing is all important.[10] Then once planting has been undertaken the die is cast. Labour now has to be committed for the rest of the growing season to maintaining the crop[11] and to herding livestock. As is shown in Table 4.2, of the fourteen case households in Maware and Mavhaire, thirteen owned at least one head of cattle by the end of my research period, and ten of these had arrangements for sharing herding duties

Table 4.2 Extended case study households, Chirumhanzu: cattle ownership and management 1986/7
(a) Mavhaire area

Household	Cattle held Nov 1986		Aug 1987	Draught power	Herding arrangement	Winter supplementary feeding
Nhakuza	16 Head		17 Head	own oxen	From Jan to harvest 8 households, 2 days on each	maize and groundnut stover
	2 bulls	5 cows	+1 calf			
	3 oxen	2 heifers				
	3 steers	1 calf				
Mhene	30 Head		31 Head (1)	own oxen	6 households, 2 days on each (1)	maize and groundnut stover
	1 bull	10 cows	+1 calf			
	8 oxen	2 heifers				
	3 steers	1 calf				
W. Mugwisi	37 Head			own oxen	No sharing. Labour hired occasionally on a monthly basis	maize stover
	1 bull	11 cows				
	8 oxen	2 heifers				
Nhambeni	No cattle		1 young bull	own donkeys	3 households, 3 days on each	maize stover
	4 donkeys					
Gonga	21 Head		24 Head	own oxen	2 households, 3 days on each	maize and groundnut stover
	2 bulls	6 cows	+3 calves			
	4 oxen	4 heifers				
Jeke	8 Head		9 Head	own oxen	2 households, 3 days on each	maize stover
	1 bull	2 cows	+1 calf			
	2 oxen	1 heifer				
		2 calves				

Table 4.2 (Continued)

| Household | Cattle held | | Draught power | Herding arrangement | Winter supple-mentary feeding |
	Nov 1986	Aug 1987			
Masocha	2 Head 1 cow 1 calf		Borrowed 4 donkeys from brother-in-law	3 households, 2 days on each	maize stover
Tevera	No cattle	1 heifer	Hired oxen (paid with income earned as a builder)	3 households, 2 days on each	

Note: (1) Of these animals 14 belonged to a son who is professionally employed in Harare. For this reason the household had a double herding turn (i.e. 4 days). The son paid for a full-time hired labourer.

(b) Maware area

| Household | Cattle held | | Draught power | Herding arrangement | Winter supple-mentary feeding |
	Nov 1986	Aug 1987			
Mugarisi	6 Head 2 oxen 2 cows 2 heifers	6 Head 2 large oxen replaced by 2 young oxen	own oxen	none	maize and groundnut stover

K. Mugwisi	3 Head 1 ox 1 cow 1 calf	4 Head +1 ox	own ox and cow	From late Nov to harvest 8 households, 2 days on each	maize stover
Jengwa	7 Head 3 oxen 3 cows 1 calf		own oxen	4 households, 3 days on each	maize stover
Machipisi	9 Head (2) 1 bull 4 oxen 3 cows 1 calf	9 Head +1 calf 1 ox sold to pay 'O' level exam fees	own oxen	none	maize and red sorghum stover
Manyonga	No cattle		hired oxen (paid with income earned as labourer)	—	some maize stover kept for animals they hire
Rangwa	4 Head 1 bull 2 oxen 1 heifer	4 Head	own oxen	2 households, 2 days on each	none

Note: (2) Of these 1 cow and 1 calf belonged to a brother who had moved to the Urungwe area.

with other families. But none of these herding arrangements came into effect until all participating households had planted their fields. For some groups, their sharing arrangements came into effect in mid to late November 1986, but as schools broke up for six weeks holiday in the first week of December, many only commenced the arrangement when schools reopened in mid January.

These arrangements therefore do not solve the early season conflict. An argument that might be advanced in favour of paddocked grazing schemes is that this type of conflict could then be avoided. However this is the time when farmers wish to avoid the limited remnants of the main grazing areas, in order to allow the early grass to come through. They prefer their animals to graze in the places where the early season nutritional value of the forage is highest. One of the Maware farmers who assisted me as an interpreter on occasion explained why people belong to comparatively small sharing groups. In his own group, seven families now rotated herding duties, whereas before the war the whole 'line' had participated – 'so someone ended up herding 200 animals or so'. But now there was no longer sufficient grazing for so many animals in one place. One person could not look after too many and they had had to break up into smaller sharing groups.[12] This change means that there is no longer the land available for paddocked schemes.

The example of one of the non-sharing case households is enlightening in this discussion on farmers' pastoral management strategies. This household was that of the Mugarisis, whose male head, Silvester, was chairman of the Maware farmers' group. Mugarisi only had six animals, but he claimed that if his animals were grazed with those of other people they were looked after inadequately. Mugarisi in fact operated his own mini pastoral system. His farm is the most intensive of any I saw in southern Chirumhanzu. It is focused on a 2.2 ha fenced smallholding area (that is, including home and homefield), in contrast with the more general pattern in the area of village lines and open arable blocks. At the lower end of the smallholding was a stream, across which Mugarisi had constructed a small dam. On the other side of the small dam was a grassed area, the lowest end of a drainage basin which extended up the gentle slope of the land for about a kilometre. Mugarisi's cattle obtained most of their forage from feeding inside the smallholding, from being fed stover, or from this grassed area. Behind his home was a rock-strewn slope which was part of the official grazing area. However, in the poor 1986–7 season the only forage obtainable from this area was leaf browse. Thus the grassed area, through necessity, was being heavily grazed by livestock from the area. It had a 3–4 metres deep gully down one side of it. In the time I was there the soil was often dry and friable, vulnerable to cattle hooves. As I watched, during the season there were places where 1–2 metres wide sections of the sides of the gully collapsed and tumbled in. Mugarisi was worried about his cattle being able to survive the dry winter of 1987. Consequently when I made my last visit to his home in August 1987, he had exchanged his two large oxen for two smaller ones 'because they eat less' (Fieldnotes, 7 August 1987).

Apart from the concern about forage availability, Mugarisi's strategy is satisfactory to him and his wife because, even during the grazing season, their animals generally do not have to be closely herded. They will remain near the stream and an eye can be kept on them from the homefield area. The labour spent on herding is minimised. This is, though, exactly the type of grazing strategy that the grazing scheme concept is designed to prevent. In the exercise undertaken to calculate the grazing area for Ture ward, the 4.4 per cent of 'key resource' class V land was excluded. But, as the Maware leaders comment, in Chirumhanzu, through most of the poor 1986/7 season the bulk of the forage that was available was either in the drainage areas, or in or near fields, where the soils are usually better than in the class VI and VII formal grazing areas.

A brief reference shall be made to the grazing strategy of farmers in the Mtengwa ward of Chiwundura, as a final point to this section. In Mtengwa, the central grazing area forms a patched band down the centre of the ward. This was the area allocated to arable holdings when the Land Husbandry Act was implemented. From the late 1960s, as the land lost fertility, many cultivators had moved off to focus their efforts in cultivating fenced, homefield areas. Thus today, unlike southern Chirumhanzu, the Mtengwa area has a smallholding settlement pattern. The 'patches' in the grazing area are where farmers have retained their former arable holdings. This grazing area, which has dams and key resource areas, in 1986/7 was used by stockowners once they had finished planting until mid-January. At a ward level meeting it was then agreed that animals should be taken off the area until after harvesting. In Phumela, one of the two parts of Mtengwa I worked in, animals were switched to river valleys which ran through the belt of their smallholdings to the Kwekwe river behind. This streambank grazing area was important but small. Thus many farmers during the latter part of the growing season took their animals across the Kwekwe river to commercial farmland beyond.

Here an almost ritualised annual running battle took place with the farmer concerned, resulting on occasion in communal area cattle being impounded and their owners fined.[13]

The threads of this section can now be pulled together. Two pastoral management schemas have been outlined. One, used by Agritex in the planning and implementation of grazing schemes, is a clearly laid out procedure. The other is not. This is the management strategy that communal area stockowners, specifically in Chirumhanzu, but also in other parts of the Midlands,[14] actually attempt to follow. Some of the constraints that effect the practice of each schema I have attempted to illustrate.

The two main criteria which can be used to respond to these respective schemas are those of the effectiveness of the schema in maximising the quantity and quality of forage available to livestock, and the environmental sustainability of the respective strategy. An evaluation of these two strategies will be undertaken in terms of these two criteria, through reference to the research of others.

GRAZING STRATEGIES AND THE ENVIRONMENT

The following series of quotes are taken from the 1923–30 annual reports of the NC Belingwe:

Year	Comments on stock and veld condition	Comments on economic use of cattle
1923	The cattle are now feeling the drought and lack of pasturage... They suffer from long journeys to the dipping tanks and the absence of any pasturage in those trampled-down localities.	More young men have gone out to work, but the elderly or even middle aged native cannot always get work in the few months that it is possible for him to leave his lands. Hitherto he has relied on cattle sales to pay his dues and we all know that the native's whole prosperity has been largely dependent on his cattle.
1924	Cattle on the whole stood the bad season well ... with the new grass they improved rapidly and are now in a splendid condition.	

1927   Cattle fell off in condition early in the year owing to the scarcity of grazing due to a scanty rainfall. A number of cattle died from poverty, especially in the Lundi Reserve which is considerably overstocked.

In some parts of the district practically no crops were reaped but in others the crops were fairly good and by natives exchanging cattle for grain amongst themselves they managed to get sufficient for their own requirements.

1930   Very few deaths occurred from either poverty or disease. This is undoubtedly a splendid cattle district.

There is no doubt, however, the natives are somewhat independent owing to the demand for their cattle by the mines.

These quotes are illustrative of the primary feature of the Zimbabwean savanna environment. This is that the condition of the environment – and hence the animals using it – fluctuates considerably depending on the nature of the season. If the account in Chapter 2 is recalled, the period from which these extracts come was the period of peak peasant prosperity, and cattle were of fundamental importance to this prosperity. Already, however, in the poor season of 1927 overstocking is being bemoaned. But the fact the native commissioner passes over, in spite of his reference to it, is that in this season farmers have an economic strategy of their own for moving cattle from drier to more favourable parts of the district – they barter cattle for grain. Similarly, in another poor season, 1923, he identifies that farmers 'destocked' by selling cattle to pay taxes. The rough statistics in Table 4.3 show this point. The economic destocking of cattle in the very poor seasons of 1934 and 1942 is much higher than the good season of 1944 – and the full internal movement of cattle under the barter and *ruzonzera* systems would accentuate these seasonal trends. From 1945, though, farmers were forced to sell their stock regardless of the nature of the season because of the official destocking policy.

By 1947, when there was a severe drought, the economic situation of the population in the Runde communal area had become considerably less secure. This is fully acknowledged by the ANC Shabani:

The Reserve Native is being forced to maintain a dual existence working away from home and leaving his family behind: particularly when the economy of an overpopulated Reserve such as the Lundi is productive of few marketable surpluses and then only occasionally . . .

Table 4.3   Runde communal area: cattle 'losses' 1928–52

Year	Cattle	% Died	% Sold/ traded	% Domestic slaughter	Destocking	Harvest
1928			3.1[1]			good
1929			3.8[1]			good
1934	16 805	5.4	13.2			v.poor
1935	16 927	1.8	6.2	4.5		poor[2]
1942	17 242	7.0	16.0			v.poor
1944	16 649	1.0	5.9	4.0		good
1945	17 807	0.6	21.5	4.9	x	fair
1946	15 805	1.9	14.8	6.6	x	poor
1948	12 933	1.9	15.2	4.9	x	poor
1949	12 403		+15.0		x	fair
1952	11 911		15.0		x	varied

Notes: [1] Figure for purchases by traders only, and applies to the Zvishavane area in general.
           [2] Foot-and-mouth outbreak in adjacent districts restricted permitted sales.

Source: NC Belingwe and ANC Shabani, Annual Reports 1928–52.

And were a drought such as this to strike the Lundi Reserve with its present economy at a time when it had no bank in the form of excess livestock the results would be more than calamitous. (Annual Report 1947)

Such a drought did strike in 1982–4 and the results *were* calamitous. For Ture ward I mentioned earlier that in the census survey I conducted it was estimated that cattle numbers had decreased by one-third during the drought. Table 2.1 showed that at the end of the drought the stocking density for Ture was about 3.78 ha per head,[15] which was only slightly lower than the peak stocking density of 3.19 ha per head for the whole of Runde between the years 1927 and 1957. But before the drought, in 1981, the density was at its highest ever at an estimated 2.60 ha per head.[16] At this high stocking rate, the average number of head per household was roughly 6.2 head. But by the end of 1984 this average was only 4.33 head[17] – with the net result that 53 per cent of households did not have their own draught power.[18] Stock losses in Ture would also have been much higher if stock-owners had not been able to move animals onto 7800 ha of adjacent commercial ranchland belonging to Garfield Todd and De Beers.[19]

Of this total stock loss in Ture only around 18 per cent were through sales. Scoones (1987) notes from his research in Mazvihwa that: 'People prefer the tactic of movement to destocking through sales and later repurchasing animals because the low prices gained at the onset of drought do not, in their experience, allow repurchase at the end' (pp. 20–1). Thus the high stocking rate in 1981 and the reluctance of farmers to sell animals during the drought, was because they were simply trying to accumulate and hang onto the minimum herd required to maintain draught power.

As Scoones also points out (p. 21), this behaviour accords with Stephen Sandford's model of an opportunistic livestock management strategy. Sandford (1983, pp. 38–41) distinguishes an opportunistic strategy from a conservative one. The latter is a strategy in which livestock stocking rates are kept down to the level which can be supported in all but the poorest seasons. This is the level which in past and present land use policies in Zimbabwe has been reified as *the* carrying capacity of the land. In contrast, an opportunistic strategy is based on an acceptance that environmental conditions fluctuate rather than remain stable. The land has a fluctuating ecological carrying capacity. In good years the numbers of animals on the land may rise, but then, to avoid economic loss, must be sold or transferred elsewhere when forage availability decreases. Thus, 'In more variable environments the costs of underutilisation under the conservative strategy rise and an opportunistic strategy is increasingly favourable' (Scoones, 1987, p. 21).

Most of Zimbabwe's landscape is tropical savanna and if one thing is certain about savanna environments it is that they are subject to extremely wide-ranging and irregular fluctuations in rainfall and hence biological constitution. As Walker and Noy-Meir (1982) comment, savannas are 'amongst the most variable of terrestrial ecosystems' (p. 56). What they also argue is that savanna ecosystems are highly resilient. By *resilience* they mean 'the capacity of a system to absorb disturbance (change) without qualitatively changing its behaviour' (p. 556). Quite how resilient different types of savanna environment are is an issue of much current debate.[20] Abel (1985, personal communication) suggests that, 'Resilience must be looked for in terms of the ability of the soil to carry a variety of successional stages of vegetation without losing its potential productivity, and there must be physical bases for resilience.' Walker and Noy-Meir suggest that a contributory factor to the resilience of savanna ecosystems is that they have multiple equilibria. An equilibrium condition is defined in terms of a particular balance between herbaceous and woody vegetation. An example of two equilibria possibilities in an environment would be that of a higher and lower successional state, each with its own 'domain of attraction' and with an intermediary, unstable equilibrium condition (Walker and Noy-Meir, 1982, p. 557). But what is most vital about savanna environments, Walker and Noy-Meir emphasise, is that 'in all probability' they require temporal variability in order to maintain their resilience (p. 585).

These ecological concepts can be elucidated further through reference to the distinction between conservative and opportunistic livestock strategies. On a commercial ranch, conservative stocking rates and good range management might keep the rangeland ecosystem within the domain of attraction of the higher successional equilibrium. In communal areas, the use of what in effect is an opportunistic strategy may result in the ecosystem declining to a lower successional state but no further.

Yet what is not clear at all is the effect of ecological change on vegetational productivity. Stocking (1984, p. 8) defines plant *productivity* as 'a measure of the *rate* of accumulation of energy, or, in the context of soil (or land or agricultural) productivity, it is the productive potential of the soil system that allows accumulation of energy in the form of vegetation'. In a livestock management system, however, it is not plant productivity that is of greatest value, but livestock biomass. In this regard the quality of the plant biomass in more pertinent than plant productivity *per se*.[21]

On this issue the assumption that has been inherent in all government land use policies in the communal areas since 1930 is that land degradation is occurring. In the last chapter it was shown how this assumption as much underlies the post-1984 internal land use reform initiative as it did the colonial technical development policies. In government reports it is still regularly trotted out.[22] Even a 1984 farming systems research report of the Department of Research and Specialist Services[23] supported the claim that rapid degradation and desertification of the communal areas is taking place (p. 29). Yet although the assumption has so long underlain government land use policy it has never been proved.

The first doubts as to the validity of the degradation thesis were cast by Dankwerts (1975) in his evaluation report of the Masvingo province veld management schemes:

> In support of the view that the optimum equilibrium for tribal cattle may differ from European expectations, the two pasture

specialists frequently professed to be amazed that heavily stocked veld in schemes where grazing control was satisfactory, was at least holding its own against further deterioration. They were also incredulous at the comparatively low stock losses, with present stocking rates and levels of forage production after the exceptionally poor rainy season of 1972/73. (p. 58)

Sandford (1982) has been the most outspoken critic so far of the conventional wisdom in Zimbabwe. Defining environmental degradation as 'an irreversible (except at prohibitive cost) decline in the productivity of land and water resources' (p. 45), Sandford states unequivocally that suppositions of grazing land degradation through overgrazing are not supportable on present evidence:

No long term direct measurement of the productivity of natural grazing in the communal lands of Zimbabwe has been carried out, and the only direct measurement (Kelly, 1973) which has been carried out does *not* support the thesis that degradation has occurred. (p. 3)

Nevertheless Sandford is careful to point out that a counter-argument develped from the multiple equilibria or resilience thesis, also lacks a firm empirical support:

What we do not know is whether the communal area grazing system has now been stabilised under heavy stocking, at a low level of primary production (which can go on being consumed at a high rate) or whether, due to soil erosion and eradication of palatable species through overgrazing, production will continue to decline. (p. 17)

Let us review the economic and environmental parameters of the discussion so far. Economically, the suggestion is that by *de facto* pursuing an opportunistic livestock management strategy, the returns to communal area farmers are greater than if they adhered to the government recommendations on carrying capacity (Dankwerts, 1975, p. 58). If one takes into account all the economic uses of communal area cattle, that this is so seems to be incontestable. Mature oxen perform ploughing, harrowing and cultivating work; travel extensive distances annually drawing manure, crops and firewood in scotch carts; produce manure; and at the end of their working lives can still be sold for beef. Cows often also perform ploughing and other draft work; produce milk, calves and manure; and again may eventually be sold. Using a rough replacement cost method, Scoones (1987, pp. 8–9) argues in fact that the annual economic output of a communal area animal in Mazvihwa (which lies in natural region V) is much higher than that of commercial beef cattle in the same district.

The productivity of communal area cattle *per unit area* may also be higher. Kelly in his earlier research (1973) showed that the quantity and quality of biomass consumed by livestock was higher on communal grazing land than on commercial ranchland (Sandford, 1982, pp. 46–7). Blaikie and Abel (1988, in Blaikie, 1989) conclude that 'both primary production (grass) and secondary production (livestock) have never been higher on the grazing lands of the communal areas' (p. 33). However, Kelly also showed that communal area production was much more volatile within and between years (p. 47). As Sandford (1983, p. 40) stresses, if an opportunistic strategy is to cope successfully with the variability of biomass production, stockowners must be able to reduce, without incurring deaths, and increase livestock numbers, as conditions alter. But here communal area farmers are not only more reluctant than previously to part with animals, because draught power is at such a premium, but their preferred strategy of moving animals is now even more difficult to implement than it was during the 1982–4 drought. The Department of Veterinary Services, in order to meet the EEC standards for Zimbabwe to export beef to Europe, has made the regulations on animal movement harder to avoid. In Chirumhanzu none of the case-study farmers moved animals in the winter of 1987, despite the drought, because of the constraints and costs of movement. For even where owners can still move their cattle – to usually either resettlement or commercial farming areas – grazing levies are now being charged.

All the case-study households with cattle were supplementary feeding their animals during the winter months on maize stover, adding groundnut stover if they had it. Faced with little choice, they could only hope that the 1987–8 rains would arrive early. They did not. The rains came over a month late in December. Agritex reported the occurrence once again of debilitating mortality rates: 'Livestock condition was still very poor, with deaths reported in all provinces and especially the communal areas. Lack of draught power due to the poor condition of stock was affecting land preparation in most areas' (in *Financial Gazette*, 11 December 1987).

If farmers are finding it increasingly difficult to achieve their economic livestock management objectives, what about the environment? Is there a continuing depletion in the productivity of the land or has a levelling-out within a lower successional domain of attraction taken place?

Campbell *et al.* (1986) who have undertaken a recent environmental survey in the Chiweshe communal area which lies within the particularly controversial area of the Save river basin, take issue with Sandford:[24]

> Sandford regards the rate of soil erosion as being an indicator rather than a measure of environmental degradation. This is a matter of semantics in the case of Chiweshe; the erosion need not be quantified for its severity to be appreciated, and even if this degree of erosion only *indicates* environmental degradation then there is nonetheless cause for grave concern over future productivity of the grazing land. (p. 27)

In the Chiweshe area, which has particularly vulnerable sodic soils, this may be, but this is insufficient reason for not accepting as Sandford does that erosion and declining environmental productivity are distinct phenomena. The point remains: evidence on productivity trends is thin. As Scoones (1987) notes 'With the possible exception of erosion assessments the present veld condition measures are inadequate: It is not clear that the presence of "sub climax" grassland or a high density woodland are indicators of permanent degradation' (p. 14).

With respect to the views of peasant farmers themselves, there is the widespread belief, which I referred to earlier, that rainfall has declined. Wilson (1986c), whom Scoones worked with in the Zvishavane area, records that 'people of the area are almost universally of the belief that rainfall patterns are changing and the total falls are declining' (p. 7). Yet his analysis of rainfall patterns for the Zvishavane area (including the Runde communal area) from 1928/9 shows the only change has been a marginally increased variability of starting date since 1969/70. One cause of the belief, Wilson suggests, might be a lowering of the water table and a reduction of soil moisture levels,[25] coupled with the greater economic vulnerability (exemplified by the dependence on drought relief and the high livestock mortality rates in the droughts in the 1980s). There is, however, record of farmers in the Gweru area stating this belief as early as 1950, which supports Wilson's other statement that farmers do tend naturally to paint a 'rosy' picture of the past.[26]

Whether the primary productivity of the pastoral land in the communal areas is continuing to decline and whether this process can be reversed, are therefore open questions (Scoones and Wilson, 1988, p. 16). At the national research level in Zimbabwe, the inadequacies of current environmental knowledge are now being acknowledged by more people, not least because of the myth-breaking role of Sandford's report.[27] Cousins reports that within the DR&SS's farming systems reseach unit it is now acknowledged that a negligible amount is actually known about communal area livestock production (p. 24).[28] Kelly's work on primary productivity, referred to by Sandford above, is also being replicated at the same sites by a University of Zimbabwe student in order to investigate long-term trends (Cousins, 1987, p. 75).

But even if the first signs of recognising that present assumptions about the communal area environment are flawed and that formal existing knowledge is woefully inadequate, it is still a long step to changes in policy actually taking place. What the lacuna in technical knowledge reveals most is that to rely solely on such expertise for the formulation of even the technical aspects of policy is a futile enterprise. And, although both the past and present governments have tended to present land use policies as a technical issue, this is only obscuring their highly political aim: to persuade the peasantry they can make do with their unequal share of the land. The technical perspective also ignores that it is the lives, livelihoods and rights of rural societies that are at stake – even though the rural population made this fact clear in their opposition to the LHA and in the support they lent the guerrillas during the liberation war.

THE POLITICS OF THE GAME: LAND REFORM FOR LAND GIVEN

In the last part of the chapter, I examine the role that the perspectives and interests of different groups play in distorting or preventing communication of how livestock and grazing area management could be improved. The example of the Ture ward project proposal will in particular be drawn upon. This means I shall concentrate on the relations between government officials and the new local political leadership (party and local government structure). The interaction between Agritex and farmer groups will be dealt with in Chapter 7.

To begin with it will help to recap why I was in Ture ward in late 1984. As explained in Chapter 1, a proposal for a land reform project in the ward had been submitted by the Zvishavane District

Development Committee to the Midlands Provincial Development Committee. The first provincial annual plan for the Midlands was being prepared at the time under the aegis of the Department of Physical Planning. It was the time too when internal land use reform within the communal areas was coming onto the national rural development agenda. The significance of the Ture proposal lay in it being one of the first applications for a land use reform project, as opposed to simply a grazing scheme. For this reason I undertook to investigate the proposal's genesis and feasibility.

The Provincial Development Committee accepted the land reform project application as a provincial plan priority because it was reported that within the ward the scheme had 'enthusiastic acceptance'. Within Ture ward, however, the proposal turned out to be not only unsupported but virtually unknown. Prior to my survey the solitary public discussion of the proposal had taken place at a ward level meeting held in August 1983. At the meeting, addressed by local government promotion officers from the office of the Zvishavane district administrator, two government policy proposals were presented. The first was land use reform; the second an associated scheme for building rural housing. According to the VIDCO members who provided me with an account of the meeting, prominence was accorded to the latter proposal and hence to the villagisation component of land reform (Fieldnotes, 2 December 1984). People were told that if they moved into centralised villages the government would construct houses for them. To many this seemed acceptable – if the expense was indeed to be borne entirely by the government and no rent was to be paid for the houses. Quite clearly, though, support for such a speculative and unlikely proposal did not constitute support for land use reform.

How had the proposal for a land reform scheme come to be presented then? The project had been written up by the local government promotion officers, their own enthusiasm being unimpeded by such matters as accuracy. In addition, the ward's district councillor had also had a hand in the promotion, supporting the land use reorganisation proposal at district level although he had no mandate from his constituents to do so. The mandate the councillor did have was to gain government assistance in the purchase, for grazing purposes, of the 5400-hectare portion of Debshan ranch adjacent to Ture. This was part of the ranch land cattle owners in Ture and the neighbouring Mapirimira ward, north of Ture, had been using during the drought.

In discussions with VIDCO members and in larger open meetings, people made it plain to me that it was access to more land, not land reform, that was their aim. One VIDCO secretary's comment to me that the government could be told that when they received more land they could talk about implementing paddocks, summed up this general attitude (Drinkwater, 1985, p. 16). There had in fact already been discussion within Ture and Mapirimira wards as to whether it would be feasible to raise money from families with livestock to contribute to the purchase of the 5400 hectares of Debshan.[29] The interest of the ward leaders in acquiring this additional land meant they would attempt to use the question of internal land reform as a bargaining counter instead of outrightly rejecting it.

In the questionnaire survey people were asked what their attitude was towards improving their management of grazing resources. The land issue clouded their responses, which were roughly equally divided between those for and against wishing to see an improvement in grazing management. But of those in favour many also registered their belief that the ward had insufficient grazing land, whilst of the 46 per cent who were opposed to the improvement of grazing land management half of these stated that it was because there was insufficient grazing area in the ward. Of the remainder opposed, some feared destocking, some did not wish to leave their homes in the designated grazing areas, and some stated it was because they did not want to live in centralised villages. There was only 6 per cent who could be construed as being outrightly opposed to the concept of improving grazing management. But these responses, because of the questionnaire format in which the question was asked, were mostly superficial. Neither in the survey nor in meetings was anything brought out about the fact that stockowners actually manage their cattle in a fundamentally different way to that officially recommended. This issue of what is and is not discussed in meetings, I will raise again later in the chapter and the book because these are the events where nearly all formal contact between outside government officials and farmers occurs.

In Ture, the community's interest in gaining access to further land, I have said, kept the debate on the land reform proposal open. Apart from the district councillor, the other important local political figure in the affair was the ZANU (PF) political commissar for Ture and Mapirimira. The role of Mawena, the political commissar, was pivotal. On the one hand he worked closely with and acted as a facilitator for the local government and other extension staff in the ward, but on the other hand he had also to maintain his power base in the community. He backed, for instance, the consensual view in public meetings. Both Mawena and the councillor, in order to sustain their positions, have to balance conflicting demands. Their authority, for external agents, depends on their capacity to deliver the compliance of the ward population with government and party initiatives. For the ward population it is their capacity to deliver greater access to production resources that is valued. Because of his unauthorised role in supporting land reform, the ward councillor in fact lost his position in early 1985, to a nominee of the political commissar, although by 1987 he had been re-elected.[30]

The Ture project proposal having been placed on the provincial planning agenda has remained there. In my report to the Provincial Development Committee, I concluded the Ture population needed more land for pastoral purposes. Since then the Ministry of Local Government, Urban and Rural Planning has continued to pursue the project. Their implicit offer has been the reverse of that desired by the VIDCO secretary: accept land reform and we will support land purchase.

In March 1987 I revisited Ture briefly. Committees had been formed for both Ture and Mapiramira to raise contributions from cattle-owning households towards the land purchase. In Ture the chairman of the committee – a brother of the councillor – claimed that over 100 households (approximately one-third of those with cattle in the ward) had contributed Z$16 each.[31] But more pressure was being exerted on the VIDCOs to obtain local acceptance for villagisation and land reform. In Mapiramira ward, according to the ward's agricultural extension worker, all VIDCOs had agreed to land use reorganisation taking place. One VIDCO had also accepted the Ministry of Public Construction and National Housing's rural housing scheme. The idea was for building brigades to construct four-roomed houses, which occupiers would pay off at Z$81 a year for thirty years. When one looks at household cash flows (Chapter 5), it is difficult to perceive the government recouping its expenditure if it does proceed with such schemes.

In Ture, the fund-raising committee chairman was more cautious in his comments than the political commissar. The latter stated that people had agreed to land reform; the former, that at VIDCO level meetings in mid-March, people had been asked only to decide afterwards whether their areas were suitable for the organisation of grazing schemes or not. The housing scheme proposal had also been discussed further in Ture but only two villages so far had shown interest. In the political commissar's VIDCO area, however, people in a few villages had knocked down their homes and rebuilt them in the old land husbandry lines – a move paralleled in the village of the ZANU (PF) district chairman who lived in Maware ward, southern Chirumhanzu.[32]

Agritex's regional officer (RAEO) in Zvishavane was worried about the continued attempts to peddle land reform in Ture.[33] He had been requested by the Department of Rural Development within the Ministry of Local Government, Rural and Urban Development[34] via the District Administrator's office to supply figures on stocking rates. His recommendation was that in order to accommodate, at the conventional carrying capacity, the cattle belonging to owners in Ture and Mapiramira, Lot 5 of Debshan plus two additional farms (together roughly equal in size to Lot 5) needed to be purchased. This was an area double that of the area classified by Agritex as grazing land in Ture. The Ministry of Local Government was proposing that a Model D grazing scheme be implemented on this ranchland – the model entailing three or four groups in turn rotating their cattle on the acquired land.[35] The regional officer's concern was that Agritex was being used, and at short notice, merely as a service agency. In other parts of the Zvishavane-Mberengwa area too, he was being asked to perform the technical planning for land use reform projects which were being initiated within the local government framework, rather than by Agritex's extension staff.

There is an irony here to which I shall return shortly. The RAEO was aware that land reform meant returning areas to the land husbandry land use pattern and he feared there was no popular support for this, especially in the more densely populated wards such as Ture. In the Mberengwa communal area, where population densities are considerably lower than in the Runde communal area[36] a large grazing scheme had been implemented at Mataga. The leading local figure behind this scheme is also the largest cattle owner – and the Member of Parliament for Mberengwa–Zvishavane Rural. With no national political position it is in his interest to perform well at the district level. From more than one government source I was informed he was responsible for persuading the Mberengwa and Zvishavane district councils to push land reform in the area. As a policy it had been accorded a higher profile on the local political agenda here than anywhere else in the Midlands.

At this juncture I will make brief reference to the Chirumhanzu and Chiwundura areas. In both places the politics of land again prevented any consideration that the how of land management might form a subject of debate between local leaders and government agents. In both communal areas the public stance of the District Council chairmen was to say land reform schemes could be implemented in their area if the government could supply the land to resettle those families living and cultivating in designated grazing areas.

In Mtengwa ward, Chiwundura, I attended a public meeting in early January 1987 at which this issue was discussed (Fieldnotes, 8 January 1987). The meeting was chaired by the District Council chairman, who is also councillor for the ward. The conventional case for implementing a grazing scheme was presented by Agritex's agricultural extension officer (AEO) for the communal area, and then the councillor spoke against the current practice of refencing old holdings in the grazing area. The AEO subsequently left before the main debate on the subject.

It was mentioned earlier that in Mtengwa the main grazing area was formally the arable land area. Households have, however, not relinquished their claim to land allocated to them here under the LHA, and since 1984–5 a process of redemarcating these old allocations has been taking place. Two reasons were cited to me for this.[37] The first is to do with changes in the farming system since the introduction of the Training and Visit pilot project in the area. This issue I shall return to in the next chapter. The second reason is a fear that soon 'the state' will take control of the land and prevent any of the land in the grazing area from being brought back under cultivation. People face a dilemma. They have insufficient pastoral land, but as one old man expressed succinctly at the public meeting: 'Our families are big, we need land for our sons; if they cannot fence land they will not have sadza to eat and will starve' (Fieldnotes, 8 January 1987). His speech drew a groundswell murmur of agreement. The councillor gained agreement only that until the harvest cattle should be moved out of this main grazing area to let the grass grow. Later, because of the drought and the shortage of forage even this agreement was abrogated prematurely.

The irony I referred to above can now be explained through the following account. At an Agritex Midlands provincial conference in November 1986, the whole subject of land reform was discussed worriedly and at length.[38]

The topic was introduced by Agritex's land use planning specialist in the Midlands: 'Amongst us I think we have the general view that there are serious problems in the communal areas . . . Land is short, the population is overcrowded.' The specialist admitted that Agritex wanted to go back to the land husbandry model with the villages forming a line between the clearly defined arable and grazing areas. No one doubted this model was controversial, but it seemed the most desirable practice. What was needed was more direction on how conflicts over boundaries should be solved, and on the compensation of people forced to move out of grazing areas. The hierarchical planning system – which the land use planner described as 'the half-way, bottom-up, top-down, planning process' – for implementing these schemes was now in place but had to be operationalised more successfully.

In the final plenary session on the conference's key topics, the discussion on land reform captured participants' attention. Perhaps the most lively part of the debate was sparked off by a point made from the floor on the planning of grazing schemes. 'Leaders and councillors understand the need for schemes, but will not move people because those are the people that voted for them.'

One response to this was that the Ministry of Local Government should be more involved, instead of leaving all the 'dirty work' to Agritex. The Zvishavane RAEO then referred to the Ture experience. Land reform 'is a road of pitfalls for councillors'. Mentioning the Ture councillor who had gone too far, he said that if the councillor is asked to take the lead 'he is just going to agree with us, and then when he gets to his area to forget about it'.

The Mvuma RAEO now intervened. 'We are bound to get our fingers burnt in this whole affair . . . We should only come in with a technical input.' Another person described the situation as a 'hide-and-seek game'. 'Local government and the people have different expectations. Local government are hiding behind us. They should be going to generate dialogue.'

And so here is the irony. The general mood expressed was that Agritex should only be responsible for the technical planning work, and that the Ministry of Local Government with the elected councillors should be responsible for the 'dirty' work of selling villagisation. In short, Agritex should wash their hands of the politics of land reform. Yet in Zvishavane this was exactly the situation that later was increasingly worrying the regional officer. He *was* only performing a technical role and he did not like it at all. For he knew that if local opposition did build up, Agritex's extension staff would still be held responsible by farmers for the planning and implementation of land reform.

The final exchange in the discussion on land reform at the provincial conference goes to the heart of many of the issues concerning land reform that I have raised in this chapter. The exchange is between one of the two desk-bound Deputy Provincial Agricultural Extension Officers and two district level officers, the second of whom has a great deal of field experience:

DPAEO: 'If one village wants replanning it should be.'

RAEO, Gweru: 'I disagree, because if there are six villages they will be sharing a grazing area.' (Implying the probable motive of the village accepting land reform is to lay claim to the shared land.)

DPAEO: 'There is nothing stopping us from planning a ward in our offices and then going to sell it to people.'

Senior Extension Supervisor, Gweru: 'This is a very burning issue. It is not a matter of selling a plan drawn up in an office. We are doing here like the colonial government. We are not calling the right people who need to solve the problems . . . For example, the politicians. They need to be taken to task by us. People do not have the country at heart; they have power at heart.' (Notes, 27 November 1987)

I believe that I have now substantiated my claim that the pursuit of strategic interests (including an interest in not becoming involved) by different individuals and groups within and without the Ture ward, means that the issue of land reform, although much tossed about, has failed to become an issue of detailed substantive discussion. In his address at Agritex's 1986 Midlands conference the land use specialist stated that, 'We are in a new era where we have to respect what the people want . . . Improved communication is required with people through district administration and district councils' (Notes, 26 November 1986)

This communication is supposed to be met by the 'half-way, bottom-up, top-down planning process', but where is the location of this half-way? Take for instance the comment made to me by Simplicio Mugarisi, one of the VIDCO chairmen in Chirumhanzu, on what he sees is the difference between the present and the previous government:

For example, on the building of homes. The previous government would have just told people you are going to build here, whilst with the present government, government representatives will hold a meeting and say the government wants to do this, and then the people will have to respond. (Interview, 14 April 1987)

On this account, the envisaged 'half-way' point seems to be well below the actual hierarchical half-way between the peasantry and the central government. Besides, how relevant is it to speak of a 'half-way' meeting point in a *hierarchical* structure? Is this populist administrative structure an appropriate vehicle for farmers and officials, with their different world views and interests, to engage in *genuine* intersubjective communication? I do not believe it is, although I will beg the question for the time being of what might be. Neither in Ture nor anywhere else in the Midlands has there been debate between people and the state on how grazing management, in the context of an overall (that is, including land redistribution) land reform programme, might be improved.

Where does this leave the present situation in the Midlands? During the course of my 1986–7 fieldwork period I participated in two discussion meetings with Agritex staff in Gweru in which progress reports I had written were debated. In the second meeting, held in April 1987, the aforementioned land use planning specialist asked me my general impression of grazing areas: '. . . you know, general conditions of erosion. Is it severely overgrazed; don't they appreciate the conditions in talking to them; you know, the need to kind of embark on better land use practices?'[39]

My answer, in abbreviated form, was that people did understand the conditions, and would like to improve their land use practices. Nevertheless they were severely constrained in their ability to do so. I referred to the conflict of interest that was now taking place in Mtengwa ward with the competing demand for arable and grazing land.

This conflict had already been commented upon in the first of the two discussion meetings, held in February 1987, by Agritex's then Assistant Director (Technical). He suggested that if current trends continued in Chiwundura one of the land settlement formats implemented in Kenya might become appropriate for the area. Under this model, settlers received only a 5 ha land allocation – 3 ha for arable cultivation and 2 ha for cultivating legumes for cattle feed. Thus the pastoral component might necessarily have to become intensive.[40]

In the Mavhaire area of Chirumhanzu, at the end of my time there,

I asked the two oldest and most experienced of the selected case farmers the same question:

MD: 'What will happen to the grazing area?'
Mhene: 'You can see it is going.'
MD: 'What will you do when it is gone?'
Nhakuza: 'We will have to feed the animals on maize stover.'
    (Fieldnotes 8 August 1987)

If one has seen the savanna plains of Zimbabwe – and elsewhere in tropical Africa – seen them under the hot sun, green when the rains come, but very, very often brown and dusty and parched, then one can grasp the magnitude of what Mhene and Nhakuza are expressing. For them and the Assistant Director to speak of peasant pastoral management in such an environment becoming an entirely intensive operation, is to speak of a system which is as far from the conventional model as one can conceive.

Such a future need is, of course, not assured. These three, from their different perspectives are only in agreement on their projection of present trends in the more densely populated communal areas. Radical land reform might take place. AIDS might depopulate the countryside. But what if neither does occur? What then are the environmental, social and economic implications?

In this chapter I have aimed to show that peasant stockowners hold an alternative interpretation to that of the government of what constitutes an efficient and sustainable use of the communal area landscape. I have also illustrated how recent researchers, through accepting savanna ecosystems as fluctuating and usually resilient, have acknowledged that the peasant strategy is the best suited for their economic objectives. However, through the use of case studies I have shown, thirdly, that because of the unalleviated effects of past land apportionment policies and growing population pressures, peasants are now increasingly constrained in their ability to manage stock. Their present options are not ideal by either their or the government's standards. Consequently, although it has yet to be proved that an ongoing decline of environmental productivity is occurring in the communal areas, farmers themselves feel they are now forced to abuse the land. As constraints grow, so often does conflict. In the case of the early season herding issue in southern Chirumhanzu, which will be discussed further in Chapter 6, local leaders express a psychological as well as a real political loss of control.

In addition, discourse between farmers and officials over land use has failed to occur, because at the points of contact it is always already formulated policies that are discussed. People's concerns then narrow down to the realisation of interests centred on and around these policies and the resources at stake, obstructing any opportunity for real communication. But, and here I raise the question for the second time, is it really in anyone's interest if the communal area population continues to become poorer?

At this stage I could be accused of speculating too far. Look at Harare's 'farming miracle';[41] the extent to which communal area farmers have increased their share of national maize output since independence. This is the subject to which I shall now turn: the state of health of the farming systems of the selected households.

5 Maize Production and Household Survival

> This year we might only manage to survive. (Mrs Mkucha, widow, Phumelela area, 14 February 1987)

> This year is going to be a drought year and if you don't use your brains you are going to starve. (Mathe, elderly farmer, Phumelela area, 17 February 1987)

> It looks like God has forsaken us. (Tangwena, elderly farmer, Phumelela area, 16 February 1987)

If misunderstanding and misrepresentation underlies official attitudes towards peasant livestock management strategies, much the same can be said of the government attitude towards the communal area economy as a whole. The subject of this chapter moves from land use to household production activities, and whereas in the previous chapter I juxtaposed the conflicting interpretations of state and peasantry, here my concern is solely to use the field research to examine how households survive.

To place the account in context, I shall begin by summarising the Zimbabwean government's policy position on communal area agriculture. This has three main aspects to it. The first is the foundational assumption that agriculture forms the backbone of the rural and national economy and will continue to do so for the foreseeable future. This assumption is expressed clearly in the 1986–90 First Five-Year Development Plan:

> Agriculture, which has been the backbone of the economy in the past will remain the dominant sector in the economy over the Five-Year Plan Period. This is borne out by the fact that over 70 per cent of the population lives in rural areas[1] and their main source of livelihood is farming. In addition, the growth of the economy is largely conditioned by the performance of the agricultural sector which, in addition to providing more than 90 per cent of the food requirements of our society, accounts for 40 per cent of total merchandise exports. (p. 25)

The second feature of the government's position is its highlighting of the proportional increase in maize and cotton sold to the Grain

Marketing Board (GMB) by peasant farmers since independence, and the credit it claims for this:

> Of great significance is the rapid transformation of the rural areas that has been taking place since independence as a result of deliberate orchestrated Government policy. Peasant farmers have been growing in importance in the production of key crops such as maize and cotton. (p. 25)

The importance of this trend is that it provides statistical support for the third and normative aspect of the government's view towards communal area agriculture. This aspect is rooted in the government's determination since the 1982–4 drought that the peasantry, and hence potentially the country, should not be dependent on food aid in adverse seasons. To avoid dependency communal area agriculture should be commercialised. At the conference convened to discuss the FAO report on land reform produced by Cliffe, the Deputy Secretary of Lands, Agriculture and Rural Settlement expressed this theme succinctly:

> Government aims at developing the *whole* agricultural sector gradually into a *commercially-oriented growth economy* with a continuing export potential on the one hand, and achieving sustained food self-sufficiency on the other. (MLA&RS, 1987, p. 3; my emphasis)

The government paints an optimistic picture. In the First Five-Year Development Plan it is projected that in the communal and resettlement areas agricultural output will grow at an average rate of 7–8 per cent over the plan period. Maize yields in these areas 'will have risen by the end of the Plan period' to 1.75 tonnes per hectare (1986a, p. 25).

In the chapter I challenge the first two aspects of the government's position and thereby question its ability to achieve the third. To begin with, the impression gained from the government's self-congratulation that all or most communal farmers are benefiting from its largesse is an inaccurate one. It will be demonstrated that in fact it is only a small minority of households that have participated significantly in the production increases achieved since independence. Following on from this, it is too simple to say, as the First Five-Year Development Plan does, that in the rural areas 'the main source of livelihood is farming' (p. 25). For the majority of communal area households their agricultural activities are only occasionally viable in

Table 5.1   Crop areas 1986/7

| | Chiwundura | | | | | Chirumhanzu | | | | |
	L ha	M ha	P ha	Total ha	%	L ha	M ha	P ha	Total ha	%
Maize	14.45	9.30	5.45	29.20	74.30	11.55	8.08	4.25	23.88	45.12
Groundnuts	1.95	0.85	0.15	2.95	7.51	1.95	0.50	0.10	2.55	4.82
Rapoko		0.23	0.90	1.13	2.88	1.98	3.00	0.95	5.93	11.20
Sunflowers	2.00	0.30		2.30	5.85	3.80	2.55	0.03	6.38	12.05
Sorghum	0.50		0.35	0.85	2.16	1.95	5.35	2.40	9.70	18.33
Mhunga	0.05			0.05	0.13	1.45	1.60		3.05	5.76
Nyimo	0.90	0.31	0.40	1.61	4.10	0.35	0.48	0.17	1.00	1.89
Nyemba		0.02	0.05	0.07	0.18	0.10		0.10	0.20	0.38
Tomatoes	0.27			0.27	0.69				0.00	
Sweet potatoes	0.05	0.15		0.20	0.51	0.20			0.20	0.38
Beans	0.40	0.05	0.03	0.48	1.22				0.00	
Rice	0.20			0.20	0.51	0.05			0.05	0.09
Total	20.77	11.20	7.33	39.30	100.0	23.38	21.55	8.00	52.93	100.0

L = leading farmer   Rapoko = finger millet
M = middle farmer   Mhunga = bulrush millet
P = poor farmer   Nyimo = bambara nuts
    Nyemba = cowpeas

themselves, and in many seasons have to be subsidised from other income sources.

This argument shall be presented in the chapter through an analysis of the maize production and economic survival strategies of the 29 households which cooperated as case studies. Maize cultivation is selected because it is the chief agricultural activity. In Chiwundura 75 per cent of the land cropped by the fifteen case-study households in the 1986/7 season was given over to maize cultivation, and in Chirumhanzu it was 43 per cent (Table 5.1). For all households in both areas maize was the main food crop grown, and apart from three Chirumhanzu households maize was also their main cash crop.

Nevertheless, amongst those farmers categorised as poor and middle, maize in all but good rainy seasons is commonly an economically subsidised activity. If the farmer is a woman whose husband provides a regular and sizeable wage remittance, the struggle to secure this subsidy may be a relatively untraumatic one. For many, however, the battle to accumulate sufficient money to buy food and agricultural inputs and to pay secondary school fees is a constant worry. It is for this reason that the range of strategies that people employ to earn food and money is the second empirical focus of the chapter.

In the discussion of these subjects, how environmental and social factors bear on production will, I hope, also be conveyed. In Chapter 6 I shall use critical theory to link these themes more explicitly.

As a preface to the empirical analysis, however, the case-study methodology employed in the research will be discussed. It is legitimate for the reader to question the status of the information used in support of the argument I advance. Hence, the rationale of the methodology I employed in working with farmers shall be clarified, as well as the respective roles of all those that participated – farmers, those who assisted me, and myself. Comment can then be made on how the information gathered and discussed during the fieldwork is used here.

THE SELECTED CASE STUDY METHODOLOGY

As outlined in Chapter 1, the households used as case studies in Chiwundura and Chirumhanzu were chosen and their cooperation secured by the farmer group and VIDCO leaders in the four study areas. Meetings were held in each area to explain the purpose and nature of the research. After the research project had been accepted, the range of household types I wished to work with was explained to those present. The criteria were that the range should include from relatively wealthy to poor farmers (the latter explained not as 'poor' but as those without cattle), both members and non-members of farmer groups, and a variation in the structural composition of the households. The latter was specified to mean that the households should include at least one headed by a migrant worker, one where the husband and wife were living in the area, and one headed by a woman. In each area those involved in the selection obliged by meeting these requirements in the range of from six to eight households chosen.

The range of households requested was based on my own prior experience and that of other researchers I consulted. Since no accurate baseline information existed for either communal area, the extent to which the proportional composition of the selected case study households represents the overall household composition in each area can only be roughly estimated. Notwithstanding this, in the analysis I have categorised the 29 households under three headings: leading, middle and poor. This classification (summarised for each of the two areas in Table 5.2 and detailed in Appendix 1), is one of

Table 5.2 Resource access 1986/7

	Arable land (ha)		Labour	Livestock & draught power	Fertiliser management	Investment sources for ag.
Chiwundura						
Leading farmers n = 4	Homefield Dryland Garden Total	1.98 2.91 0.59 5.48	Full: 2–3 Part: 4–6[a] Piecework	10–16 cattle kept at home: surplus in resettlement area & locally	Cmp.D: 12.3[c] AN: 7.3 manure: 0.2–0.5 ha	Mainly credit & reinvestment of maize sales
Middle farmers n = 5	Homefield Dryland Garden Total	1.12 0.98 0.22 2.32	Full: mostly 2 Part: 2–3	1–5 cattle at home. Donkeys used by one; two hire & borrow draught power	Cmp.D: 2.8 AN: 1.8 manure: 0–0.3 ha	Remittances or, if lacking, credit
Poor farmers n = 6	Homefield	1.51	Full: 1–2 Part: 1–2	2 have draught power, remainder rely mainly on borrowing	Cmp.D: 0.5 AN: 0.7 manure: 0–0.15 ha	Craft sales & piece work. Credit no longer used
Chirumhanzu						
Leading farmers n = 4	Total	6.01	Full: 2[b] Part: 2–5 Piecework	6–37 head, all kept at home	Cmp.D: 8.8 AN: 6.5 manure: 0.5–0.6 ha	Reinvestment of income saved from crop sales
Middle farmers n = 6	Total	3.71	Full: 0–2 Part: 0–3	0–18 head. All have sufficient draught power (1 uses donkeys)	Cmp.D: 1.2 AN: 1 manure: 0–0.6 ha	Reinvestment of income from crop sales, remittances, building piecework
Poor farmers n = 4	Total (3 under 2 ha)	2.55	Full: 1–2 Part: 0–2	0–5 head. Draught power borrowed	Cmp.D: 1.3 AN: 0.6 manure: some compost only	Building piecework, craft and beer sales

Notes: [a]One farmer had much less labour.
[b]One farmer had two additional hired labourers.
[c]50 kg bags.

farmers. It takes into account the size and diversity of households' land holdings and the level of their production output, but it does not necessarily relate directly to household incomes. This is because, for many, agricultural income is less than non-agricultural income.

Leading farmers are 'leading' in two senses. They are the farmers with the most land and the highest production levels, and they are the farmer leaders. Middle farmers have less land, are usually no more than irregularly active members of farmer groups, and require income from non-agricultural sources to sustain their farming activities. The poor households are poor in all senses. They have the least land, lack labour, draught power and capital. They eke out a marginal existence, characterised by extremely low returns to labour.

In working with the households I used a semi-structured approach. Each household was visited at least once a month during the 1986/7 growing season. For the few farmers who spoke English I usually conducted the visits by myself, whilst for the remainder I used a variety of assistants to interpret. In Chiwundura two Agritex staff assisted: a recently qualified female extension worker, who became a valued research assistant, and a male research assistant already based in the area because of the pilot Training and Visit project. In Chirumhanzu a greater range of people provided assistance – one extension worker, three local leaders, and one temporary school teacher. All of these people were men. As well as interpreting, they aided by providing a range of views either about the local community or on how Agritex staff worked with farmers.[2]

In the monthly visits no set questionnaires were used. Rather, for each farmer a briefing sheet was prepared of household activities or issues to be followed up. All meetings were arranged in advance with people and were held at times convenient to them. As well as a conversation, each visit involved observing the progress of production activities, and to some extent performing tasks – ploughing, weeding and harvesting. Part of the discussion revolved around activities kept track of through the growing season, such as the progress of different crops. Other subjects raised were those significant at particular stages of the season, such as the herding of livestock during the sensitive period between when some farmers have planted crops and all have planted. Finally, activities and issues pertaining to specific households were followed up, such as the progress of children seeking employment, or the relative success or failure of informal income-earning activities. In this type of semi-structured approach, where the briefing sheet is used to guide the discussion rather than to order it rigidly, there is opportunity for farmers to bring up their own areas of interest. Nevertheless, the interviewer still dictates the shape of the discussion. This means the question of how best the farmers can bring their world into the information exchange remains one I did not resolve during the fieldwork.

In turning to the rationale behind this method of working with farmers, there are three issue areas I wish to raise. The first relates back to the discussion conducted in Chapter 1 on critical theory and method. There I referred to the three characteristics which Fay (1975) argues a critical social science should fulfil. The first has already been stressed several times, that a critical social science should be *interpretive* in nature and thus oriented to understanding a social world from the viewpoint of the actors concerned. Even remotely achieving such understanding is a much harder task than usually imagined, for almost inevitably one seeks to interpret a given situation from one's own already held stock of beliefs and experiences. Wilson, in a discussion I had with him on research methodology, emphasised the extent to which one, in adopting a hermeneutic approach, must be prepared to enter with an open and unencumbered mind. 'The researcher as a participatory person at first is totally dependent on informants; you enter as a humiliated small child' (Discussion, 13 October 1987).[3] The difficulty here is that one must have sufficient self-confidence and experience to negotiate the psychological trauma of letting go the world from which one comes. Anthropologists favour lengthy immersion approaches but the many years required are not always available. This means there are advantages to the use of a selected case-study approach over the course of a single season, in which the researcher actively generates interaction with farmers. But this is only the case if much care is taken and thorough preparatory groundwork carried out.

Undertaking the type of interactive research which hermeneutics requires is, therefore, not as straightforward as superficially it may seem. There is another need: the capacity to express vividly the interaction one has experienced. In Zimbabwe the rural peasantry and the urban proletariat are referred to as the 'povo' or the 'masses'. Those that do the referring are the 'chefs', or more Orwellian, the 'comrade chefs'. The term 'povo' is dehumanising. Describing people in this way makes it easy to utter statements and prescribe policies in which they are regarded as amorphous and malleable. Land reform or raising maize yields become board games played by the bureaucrats and chefs, in which people, as counters, are simply moved around.

The human implications of policies that are fashioned with reference to numbers cannot be understood until the faces and characters of those they apply to are visualised and the proscriber is reflexively aware of those being affected as fellow humans. This is a reason which strongly motivated me to turn to a case-study approach, instead of dealing with farmers merely as statistics in a quantitative sample.

The next issue area to be raised about the rationale behind the case-study method I employed related to the second of the characteristics Fay identifies, that of being critical. Through critique one attempts to penetrate linguistic presentations of reality – 'narrative', as Habermas terms it – in order to understand the undistorted nature of environmental and social relations. This is a goal not an expectation, and if one adheres to Habermas's principles, it is a quest that should be undertaken intersubjectively. Researchers who write as isolates pronouncing solitary judgement on all they have purveyed, leave blank their own role and legacy. Has anyone benefited from their intrusion?

This is not to suggest that the researcher necessarily has to carry the burden of leaving material benefits. If, as a result of her or his presence, people understand their lifeworld more thoroughly and are better able to direct their lives, this is sufficient achievement. Thus the rationale behind the researcher engaging in intersubjective critique is that although people may be very constrained in the activities they perform, because of their lack of control over social conditions, not all of their vulnerability is inevitable. Through failing to reflect in depth on their actions or through lacking alternative ideas, they may fail to improve their circumstances, even in areas where there is potential for them to do so. Wilson remarked of group discussions on the role of trees that, 'The researcher was able to get people to think more abstractly about their world – i.e. to objectify it ... We were struck by how critically people did think about many social norms' (Discussion, 13 October 1987).[4] Nevertheless, fear of new forms of external manipulation may cause people to shy away from challenges which may force them to contemplate changing their production behaviour. Thus the researcher who comes to understand also poses a threat: 'And when once I did know, people became quite worried. They want you to know and they also don't want you to know' (Wilson, discussion 13 October 1987).

If the researcher or fieldworker is to encourage dialogue, then she or he is forced into an active role. But how to undertake this cannot be easily prescribed. Habermas speaks of the 'virtual' participant. This is one who,

> In concentrating as a speaker and hearer exclusively on the process of reaching understanding ... takes part in the observed action system *subject to the withdrawal*, as it were, *of his qualities as an actor*. (1984, p. 114)

In my own work I wanted time for reflection and to diarise the day's experiences. Fearing the situation James Scott describes – 'In the first few months, perhaps half my trips to the outhouse were for no purpose other than to find a moment of solitude' (1985, p. xviii) – I retained some distance from the communities with which I was working. This meant remaining a virtual participant – committed to acting as a social scientist and belonging to an action system lying on a different plane from that of the local people (Habermas, 1984, p. 114).

As I already had knowledge of how Agritex operated, it was within the extension agency rather than with farmers that I attempted most to provoke critical discussion, although there were instances of the latter too. One meeting of this nature was held in Chiwundura to discuss the serious problems (referred to in the next chapter) being experienced with the group credit scheme. In an instance such as this, if one is to play an active role in discussions – and hence local life – one needs to have definite ideas to offer. If one does not or if the ideas are irrelevant, one may disillusion people and be regarded as brash or ignorant.

In our discussion on field methodology, Wilson, who conducted two years of field research, mentioned that an indicator of the transition from 'virtual' to 'full' participant was, 'when the quality of your life is also determined by what the local people think of you. You change the way you behave ... you have to service your relationship with the people in the area' (Discussion, 13 October 1987). As he stressed, this brings its own problems too.

In his research with Scoones, the two of them began to investigate issues which local people themselves were interested in and 'not just what is fashionable for outsiders'. Two consequences of their work have been a household level water development project funded by Oxfam, and a community forestry project managed by ENDA-Zimbabwe and funded by the Ford Foundation. The projects were initially welcomed locally because the communities concerned, through local organisers, were influential in their design.

In conclusion, there is no easy divide between remaining a virtual participant and becoming a more committed participant within the insider community. Much depends on the particular instance – the current social dynamics of that context, the nature of the people concerned and their collective social experience. And then one's character, experience and aims undeniably influences one's own behaviour.

The third issue area to be remarked on concerning the field methodology is that of the representativeness of the case-study households. As already stated, despite the absence of an accurate baseline sample to go on, I have still categorised these households into three groups. This means that although rejecting the anonymity of quantitative methods, I still hold that the names and personalities referred to here do perform as representatives of considerable others who live in communal areas in the Midlands and elsewhere in Zimbabwe. By 'representatives' I imply that the farmers named are like others in the broad structural situations in which they find themselves. Where they differ is in the details of their struggles to ensure their own, their children's and their grandchildren's survival.

In the following section I aim to substantiate this last argument. The analysis will focus on the impact that the environment, culture and resource constraints have on maize production. Where empirical details concerning the environment or cropping activities are referred to, information will simply be reported, though where necessary the basis on which estimates were made shall be stated. However, where I am concerned to interpret and analyse phenomena observed by myself or described by others, reference will be made where possible to those providing the interpretation or corroboratory information. The case-study material is intended to provide the reader with some insight into the rural world and be presented in a way which allows opportunity for independent assessment.

MAIZE PRODUCTION AND THE FIRST RAINS

It is around 10.30 in the morning of Sunday, 23 November 1986. The main body of a Catholic church congregation sits tightly clustered in the shade of a smallish tree on a dusty knoll in the south of Chirumhanzu communal area. The spillover – all men, and including myself – are grouped in the fragile shade of a yet smaller tree, separated from the others by a stretch of hot sunlight. Immediately to our left huddle three stores, a grinding mill and a small warehouse belonging to the Maware savings club. Four hundred metres beyond, a primary school guards the junction with the main gravel road through the communal area. This is Maware.

Afterwards I wrote an article on this day. It was translated and read back to the congregation at another service before the summer's end. People commented on the descriptions of the landscape as much as anything. The two passages quoted below impress how much the timing of the rains affects household maize production strategies.

> This part of Chirumhanzu lies in Zimbabwe's natural region IV, a region declared to be environmentally suitable only for semi-extensive livestock ranching. Such expansive luxury is, however, beyond the reality of the communal areas. To the west and north of Maware, dusty, dry-green and brown plains undulate to blue-hazed hills. Straggly lines of round homesteads, built from locally made bricks and thatched with grass, surround the plain areas. On the plains, the vista of brown fields is broken by low, dotted trees and scrub.
>
> . . . Insignificant white puffballs are appearing in the sky; a sign the air is heating up. The only rain to have fallen in the area so far this season was at the end of October, now a long three weeks back. Past the line of women waiting for confession, the fields are too far for me to pick out details. But I know that about half have been ploughed and planted since the few showers and solitary downpour. The rest wait in suspension for the coming of the rains. Some early maize, already beginning to wither, finger millet and groundnuts, have germinated. If there is no further rain before the month's end, much of the maize will have to be replanted.[5]

If the planting patterns of the farmers I worked with can be generalised, only about 30 per cent, not half, of the land cultivated that season had been planted at this time. The germination rates of this early maize were also poorer than that planted after the brief return of heavier rains in early December. Nevertheless, the early maize outyielded the December crop, on average from 21 per cent for the poorer case-study farmers in Chirumhanzu to 95 per cent for the leading ones.

In Chiwundura the yield pattern was skewed even more in favour of the early plantings. There the leading and middle farmers, especially, have access to wet land 'garden' areas. These gardens occur in areas of impeded drainage, often caused either by the granite bedrock lying shallow and unjointed underneath, thereby supporting a perched water table, or by a clay, hardpan layer. The gardens have open wells, but apart from the watering of a few vegetables in winter and spring, the wells are not used for irrigation purposes. In wetter seasons these areas are prone to waterlogging. Accordingly all farmers intercrop in their gardens, planting maize, rice and cucurbits. In wet seasons conditions favour the rice, in drier years the maize yields best.

Household garden areas in Mtengwa ward are comparatively small. Those of the leading case-study farmers averaged 0.43 ha and the middle farmers 0.3 ha, forming 12 per cent and 16 per cent respectively of the total area planted to maize by the two groups. Yet from these gardens came over 25 per cent of the maize harvested for the poor 1986/7 season.

Table 5.3 presents the basic information for the 29 case-study farmers in Chiwundura and Chirumhanzu on the areas planted to maize, the harvests and the yields obtained by the three different groups of farmers. It should be emphasised that all the figures are estimates only.

The information in the table is sub-divided according to the time of planting in order to illustrate the yield variations. The three planting periods listed are:

(A)   before the first rains, i.e. before the end of October;
(B)   after the first rains, i.e. before mid November;
(C)   after the second rains, i.e. after the end of November.

Between the middle and end of November, the soil was too dry for germination to occur. On the granitic sandveld soils, ubiquitous in Chiwundura and Chirumhanzu, soil moisture is not retained within the topsoil for long. The planting periods were thus dictated by the pattern of rainfall distribution with the best germination rates being attained when planting was carried out immediately following rain. For the 1986/7 season total rainfall figures were among the lowest received this century. In the two communal areas the seasonal distribution is shown in Table 5.4.

The average seasonal rainfall figure over a 25-year period for both Chaka and Muchakata falls between 650 mm and 700 mm. St Joseph's

Table 5.3   Maize yields by planting period 1986/7

	Chiwundura			*Chirumhanzu*		
	L	M	P	L	M	P
Ave. maize area planted (ha)	3.61	1.86	0.91	2.89	1.35	1.06
A. Area planted before rains (before end Oct)	0.43	0.30	0.13			
B. Area planted after 1st rains (before mid-Nov)	1.26	0.65	0.23	0.78	0.35	0.29
C. Area planted after 2nd rains (end Nov onwards)	1.93	0.91	0.55	1.99	1.00	0.78
Ave. harvest (bags)	44.63	12.00	4.47	40.80	11.25	5.25
Planting period A	11.63	3.20	0.54	[a]		
Planting period B	22.75	3.70	1.72	17.63	4.08	1.63
Planting period C	10.25	5.10 [b]	2.21	23.13	7.17	3.63
Ave. yield (bags/ha)	12.35	6.45	4.92	14.11	8.36	4.94
Ave. yield (tonnes/ha)	1.11	0.58	0.44	1.27	0.75	0.44
Planting period A	2.46	0.96	0.39			
Planting period B	1.62	0.51	0.66	2.05	1.05	0.51
Planting period C	0.48	0.50	0.36	1.05	0.65	0.42

[a] Two of the leading Chirumhanzu farmers planted the bulk of their maize in planting period B, and two in planting period C.
[b] One farmer lost crops in planting period B and had a much larger harvest in period C.

Mission, just north of Mavhaire, had an average of 678 mm until 1983, since when rainfall figures have not been collected. It is a common fallacy, though, to compare production in any particular year with a 'normal' season. There is no such thing as a 'normal' season and no two seasons are the same. For example, a good descriptive account of the seasons experienced between 1923 and 1948 in the Zvishavane area, is provided by the NC Belingwe and the ANC Shabani, in their district annual reports.[6] The range of seasons was:

full drought years	6	end season drought	1
early season drought	5	fair or good seasons	8
mid season drought	4	excessive rains	1

This reinforces the point stressed in the previous chapter: savanna ecosystems are tremendously variable. And the fact that seasons are

Table 5.4   Rainfall distribution in Chirumhanzu and Chiwundura 1986/7

| Chirumhanzu | | | Chiwundura | | |
Date	mm	Monthly Total mm	Date	mm	Monthly Total mm
23 October	45		late October	72	72
29 October	24	106			
November		0	November		0
7–10 December	151	151	1–8 December	83	
			15 December	18	101
16–19 January	78	78	2 January	20	
			9 January	20	
			19 January	20	
			25 January	25	75
4–7 February	58	58	5 February	23	23
March		0	9–10 March	25	
			24 March	22	47
	Aggregate	393		Aggregate	318

Note: In southern Chirumhanzu rainfall was lower than at Chaka. In the study area less rain fell in October and December and the overall total was nearer 300 mm.

variable heavily influences farmers' agricultural production strategies. 'Variability' does not mean randomness though, and there are patterns to the rainfall distribution which can be used as a predictive basis for production strategies. As the Zvishavane figures show, early season droughts (in November, after the initial rains) and mid-season droughts (in January) are more common than end of season droughts in February–March. In 1986/7, maize that survived the November dry spell then received sufficient moisture in December, January and early February to produce a harvest. Farmers were growing one or both of two hybrids: R201, which has a growing season of about 120 days, and R215, which reaches maturity in 130 days. This meant that maize planted in early December with the second rains, had ripened insufficiently by early February, when the rains stopped, to produce much. Yields for these late planted crops were in most cases less than 0.5 tonnes per hectare, compared with an estimated average yield of 2.46 tonnes per hectare gained by the leading Chiwundura farmers for their garden maize (planting period A) and 2.05 tonnes per hectare by the leading Chirumhanzu farmers for their early planted maize (planting period B).

In 1985/6 the late maize had paid off because of good rains in March and early April. As a result, six of the eight leading farmers planted some very late maize, on or after Christmas. If there are no late rains this is used as cattle feed. The critical month is January. 'January is the bad month, it is the month we are not sure of the rains. If we get rains we are assured of good crops' (Takavada, fieldnotes, 15 January 1987). Thus crops planted before mid-November can usually manage through a dry spell in January, crops planted in late November or early December cannot, but late December crops will survive if the rains continue until the end of March or early April. Nevertheless, it is the early maize that is the banker crop. In the recent 1987/8 season there was almost no rain until December, but once the rains did arrive they continued well into April. Nevertheless farmers were still hit by a dry spell in January. This was followed by heavy rains in February, which caused waterlogging and soil leaching, and caught the crop at a stage early enough to retard its later development (Mangwalala, fieldnotes, 14 April 1988).

A final resume of the maize yields and production outputs obtained among the case-study households for 1986/7 is now in order. Overall the leading farmers in both areas achieved an estimated yield of 1.18 tonnes per hectare, the middle farmers 0.66 tonnes per hectare, and the poor farmers 0.44 tonnes per hectare. More tellingly, the eight leading farmers (28 per cent of the sample) produced 66 per cent of the maize, at an average of 42.7 bags (3.84 tonnes) each. The eleven middle farmers (38 per cent) produced 25 per cent cent at an average of 11.6 bags (1.04 tonnes) each, and the ten poor farmers (34 per cent) produced just 9 per cent at an average of 4.8 bags (0.43 tonnes) each.

So far, only the direct relation between planting period and yield has been discussed. To comprehend why this highly skewed distribution of production output and yield levels takes place, one must move on to consider the resource situations of each of the three farmer categories.

The key resources to which households require access in order to grow maize are: various types of arable land, permanent and periodic labour, draught power and manure (and hence grazing land), hybrid seed and inorganic fertiliser, capital and equipment. Differing access to these resources is the major characteristic that distinguishes the three categories of farmers. A general access picture for each category is provided in Table 5.2. The relevance of this picture is only grasped, however, through understanding the ways in which resources are combined together and how access to them is controlled.

For example, to illustrate the point about access, to make best use of the first rains, either by dry planting beforehand or planting immediately after the first showers, farmers need fields that are sufficiently yielding to take a plough without requiring a thorough soaking. Fertile soils with a good organic content are most likely to be of this nature. This means farmers must have reasonable quality soils to start with – the leading farmers usually do – or have organic fertiliser to improve the soil structure. The latter requires the livestock to produce the manure and the labour to apply it. Thus the fact that leading farmers can usually manure at least 0.4 ha of their land annually, whilst for middle farmers it is nearer 0.2 ha and for poor farmers, if at all, it is a small area irregularly, makes a large difference to their respective production capacities in dry seasons. The possession of livestock and labour too, enables households to autumn plough their fields after harvest.[8] This assists early planting the next season by helping to conserve moisture, through permitting better infiltration, and by preventing the soil from crusting.

From this one example it can be seen that if one resource – land, labour, or livestock – is limiting, the effect reverberates through the farming system. Moreover, the possession of one resource is often contingent on possession of others and on factors of social history – who one is. These are old points, but their social and economic causes and implications are often not easily grasped by those who view increasing production as merely an instrumental activity. An account of relations of resource access, in the context of maize production, will now be expanded upon through farmers' accounts.

Land, Labour, Livestock and Manure

Amongst those I worked with only the leading farmer households regularly produce more food than they consume. The reason for this phenomenon begins with land. In both Chiwundura and Chirumhanzu all except one of the leading farmer households possess more land than the middle and poor households. The exception is the Mugarisis[9] in Maware, who are the only ones in this category to have less than 5 ha. In addition, all possess at least some land which is amongst the best that can be found in their localities. This land they have acquired by virtue of being either one of the first settlers in their particular area (Chiwundura), or a member of an established lineage (Chirumhanzu).

The Phumelela and Takunda area of Mtengwa ward in Chiwundura have both been settled comparatively recently. The following account of land settlement and land use change in the Phumelela areas was provided by Mangwalala, chairman of the Phumelela farmers' group:

Our family had been living in the Gokomere area. We moved here in 1934–5 when Gokomere became purchase area. We were then living further up the road, on this same side of the road on top of the ridge. In 1958 I was given this stand.

In 1935 centralisation began in the area.[10] The village lines were along this road, although when I was given this stand by sabhuku Majojo there was no one else here except someone where Mai Skosana is now.

Our fields were allocated in the arable area, under Land Husbandry. The garden area I inherited later from my father. Sadunhu Mtengwa allocated my father and his two brothers a block of land which they shared between them. When the Land Husbandry Act was passed, it was stipulated that they should have 6 acres. Before then my father had had about 18 acres. After I had a wife I was given one of the 6 acre pieces into which my father's land was divided. This was in the mid-1950s, before I moved here.

The area west of our homes [sloping down to the Kwekwe river] was the grazing area. In 1962 people started cultivating small gardens around their homes. In 1965 we expanded our homefield [*munda wepamba*] area because the land was not enforced so strictly. By this time there was one person across the road, Mpanzi, and a few other scattered people.

Our land was fenced in 1966 – about two seasons before Mai Skosana moved in. From this time the area began to fill up, the sabhuku allocated more land and people began to fence and cultivate around their homes.

The grazing area was now still mainly on the western side, as there were still few people here, and most people were still cultivating in the land husbandry arable area. In 1978, when the second wave of settlement began nearer the river, the grazing was split into two and the largest area was moved to the east. By this time we only had small gardens in the old arable areas. (Fieldnotes, 16 February 1987)

Mangwalalas's account is corroborated by those of others in the area and by a time series of 1:25 000 aerial photographs (1950, 1964, 1974, 1985). Two distinct periods of movement occurred, as Mangwalala relates. The first movement began around 1966 and took place over the next decade. Mrs Skosana, another of the farmers I worked with, explained the move as such: 'At that time people were cultivating mhunga [bulrush millet] and rapoko [finger millet] on the old worked out fields. They were sandy and fertile and yields were very poor, so people had to move' (Fieldnotes, 12 December 1986).

People gradually abandoned their old land husbandry allocations from the late 1960s, except for the small, wet land garden areas. Cultivation became concentrated around the homestead, and, augmented by new settlers into the area, the smallholding pattern which exists today developed.[11] On the fencing of smallholdings, Mrs Skosana remarked, 'It is like a fashion, once someone starts the rest want to follow' (Fieldnotes, 12 December 1986). The location of cattle kraals adjacent to the holdings facilitated the application of manure and the intensification of crop production. This intensification has had two other implications. One has been a shift over time from small grain to maize production, and the other was people's receptiveness to credit when it was promoted in conjunction with the T and V extension programme in 1984/5. The subject of credit will be taken up in the next chapter.

The second distinct period of population movement occurred in the late 1970s and early 1980s. With the end of the war and then the departure of many whites, former commercial farm employees and domestic workers from Gweru and Kwekwe sought communal land allocations for their families, as did many newly married couples. So a second wave of smallholding land allocation took place within the former grazing area between the original village lines and the Kwekwe river.

These second-wave arrivals have had to pay for their occupation of the land. Mrs Mkucha, a widow who had previously been a domestic worker in Gweru, paid Z$19 for her 2.0 ha in 1979. Land, if available, is now much more expensive.[12] Tangwena, the poorest of the case-study farmers, purchased a 1.9 ha portion of land from the brother of the sabhuku in 1983. He paid Z$220, provided by an employed son-in-law, but has since lost a 0.3 hectare piece reappropriated by the former landholder. Tangwena has not been reimbursed for this, for he lacks the necessary influence to make an issue of a deal which is illicit from the outset. Nevertheless, land purchase, despite its formal illegality, does have local legitimacy. In the Takunda area, a dispute arose because the farmers' group ploughed and planted as a group plot, a portion of land 'given' to them by the sabhuku in whose area the land was ostensibly located. Two years previously a migrant worker, Mudeke, had been cultivating this land. What the sabhuku concerned had failed to reveal was that he had earlier sold the land to another sabhuku, Chikomo, who had since emigrated to farm in Mashonaland. But before leaving, Chikomo had resold the land to Mudeke. Mudeke was relatively wealthy – he was one of only three people in Mtengwa ward to own a tractor – and hence influential. In the end the ward councillor, who was also the District Council Chairman, was called in to adjudicate the dispute and Mudeke, by virtue of his payment, retained control of the land.[13]

In contrast, the second-wave settlers in the Phumelela area have little power. In spite of paying for land their tenure is insecure. The problem is that they are located in part of the old grazing area. Their holdings slope and are susceptible to erosion. However, the colonial practice of constructing contour ridges, originally introduced in the 1940s, is still the only soil conservation technique used. The pegging of the lines for the ridges by agricultural extension staff has therefore long been held to legitimise the use of land for arable purposes. Agritex staff now have to be authorised by the District Council, on the recommendation of the VIDCO, to peg the ridge lines. Two successive VIDCO chairmen have, though, refused to accede to this. 'We have been told the land is for grazing and we will have to move sometime', one woman asserted (Fieldnotes, 19 January 1987).

However, the earlier settlers are also playing a role in the consumption of the grazing area by reclaiming and fencing their abandoned land husbandry allocations. Many such areas were repossessed in 1986/7, often with only a gesture at cultivation. This trend was because of the fear, referred to in the previous chapter, that the old arable land areas might be declared 'state' land. One rumour was that the second-wave settlers would be moved onto this land.

In the last twenty-years, land use patterns in Mtengwa ward have therefore been very fluid. With control over arable land being at once so vital for household survival and comparatively tenuous, the claim to land is first demarcated by the erection of a fence – perhaps no more than a few symbolic strands. Without being able to present any confident data on trends in the size of arable land holdings, the general picture is clear: the new settlers hold less land and they hold it less securely.

In southern Chirumhanzu the land use pattern is very different. There the land husbandry arrangement of the 1950s has altered only through the establishment by some families of homesteads and arable plots in the grazing areas, during the war years of the late 1970s. This movement, carried out as an expression of freedom from colonial authority, has now become controversial for the new government is urging the VIDCO's to persuade people to retreat to the old village 'lines'. In the lines, where most homesteads are still located, people are huddled too close together for fenced small holdings to be established. Thus it is only the households who have moved away from the lines who may have fenced homefields.

In Maware, more so than in Mavhaire, there are very few fenced fields to be seen. An exception is that of the Mugarisis, whose 2.2 ha homefield was described in mid-December by the temporary school teacher who occasionally assisted me, as a 'green island' (Fieldnotes, 19 December 1986). The Mugarisis was the only household in the area that had been able to raise successfully a sizeable area of maize planted with the first rains, because they had the fencing to protect their crop from the depredations of unherded cattle. Roaming animals are the bane of any farmer trying to take advantage of the rains and they are a highly controversial local issue, as shall be seen more fully in the following chapter.

Moving now from land to livestock, the effect of the diminishment of the grazing area in both communal areas, coupled with the effects of the 1982–4 and 1987 droughts, means that households' livestock holdings are falling. In the Shurugwi communal area, for instance, current average household cattle holdings are at a level similar to the previous lowpoint reached at the height – or, perhaps more accurately, nadir – of cattle destocking in the mid-1950s.[14] The situation in the surrounding communal areas of Runde, Chirumhanzu and Chiwundura, for which I have incomplete information for the war years, is likely to be broadly similar. Population densities are however higher in Chiwundura than in Chirumhanzu[15] and consequently cattle ownership levels are lower in the former. Whereas both Mhene and Mugwisi kept over 30 head in the Mavhaire area, none of the leading case-study farmers in Mtengwa ward kept more than 16 head at home. Nhonga, chairman of the Chiwundura area farming committee and vice-chairman of the Takunda group, was the wealthiest farmer with whom I worked. Still he kept only 13 head of cattle at his home, although he had at least another 32 head amongst more than one person in the Masvori resettlement area, north of Chiwundura.

Usually only a few farmers who are members of well-established lineages can, however, manage such an option. Even many in the leading farmer category worry about whether they will be able to maintain their own draught power.

Mangwalala, for example, had two superb oxen, Luxor and Box, as part of the herd of ten animals he had when I arrived in November 1986. With these animals he had won ploughing competitions not only within Mtengwa ward, but within Chiwundura as a whole. By the time I made my last visit in July 1987, Mangwalala had already had to sell one of these large oxen in order to repay part of the huge credit debt he now faced. Worse, when I was able to make a brief return in April 1988, he had become even more depressed. Four more cattle, including the second ox, had died during the latter stages of the barren winter. Owing to compensatory calves, he still had eight animals, but this included no experienced draught animals. In the end, the remainder of his herd survived because of a grazing agreement negotiated with the commercial farmer across the Kwekwe river, referred to in Chapter 4, with whom an annual battle for grazing (even in wetter seasons) was the norm. Each owner had to pay Z$1 per head per month, and those who could not afford the fee had been offered piecework to earn it (Fieldnotes, 14 April 1988).

In Chirumhanzu, Silvester Mugarisi, ever forward looking, made a decision early in the drought to sell two large and experienced oxen for two good but smaller ones, 'because they eat less' (Fieldnotes, 7 August 1987).

Of the eleven middle and poor case-study households in Chiwundura, even before the bad winter of 1987, seven had insufficient cattle for their draught power purposes. This compares with four out of ten in Chirumhanzu. If farmers have to acquire cattle from others they may either borrow or use a combination of hiring and borrowing. 'Borrowing', it should be noted, in terms of the reciprocal obligations that may be attached, in the long run is not always the cheaper option.[16] It is cases of hiring that will be discussed here though.

In Chirumhanzu two case-study farmers who hired draught power returned labour in repayment, whilst three hiring in Chiwundura all paid in cash (or chickens). Whether the cattle owner is paid in cash or labour, the labour cost to the hirer is usually high. One of the Chiwundura farmers who hired draught power was Mrs Kumira. She hired Mr Nhonga and his oxen twice. It cost him probably 5–6 hours of time for which he ploughed about 0.55 ha of her land for Z$26. One day in mid-December I observed Mrs Kumira collecting red soldier termites near Muchakata business centre. She was pushing pieces of a round, juicy grass down termite holes. The grass came from the banks of the river below the centre. The ends she chewed to apply saliva in order to persuade the termites they were biting something alive. Some pokes were unproductive; others yielded up to three termites. Her tin was filling painfully slowly. In 15 minutes not even the bottom was covered. The termites had gone deep, she said, because of the rains. On a good day she can fill her tin within an hour. Then she goes home, roasts the termites and adds salt and piri-piri. Returning to the beerhall and bottle store at the centre, she sells the roasted termites at 20 cents a cup, fetching Z$2 for the tin. The production and sale of each tin must absorb on average over five hours of labour (the walk from home to centre alone is thirty minutes), costing her, by this method, upwards of 65 hours of labour to earn sufficient to pay for the hire of draught power.

In the Mavhaire area of Chirumhanzu, Constantine Tevera also hired oxen to plough the 1.4 ha that he and his wife cultivated that season. The wife and daughter of the owner came along with the animals – owners rarely allow others just to take their animals – the two mornings the Teveras used them. In return Tevera built a house for the owner. It took him two weeks to do so. The Manyongas in Maware also used cattle belonging to others. On three occasions Manyonga used oxen belonging to a secondary school headmaster, and on one occasion those belonging to a widow. In these instances he did the fetching and ploughing himself. In return Manyonga spent nine days ploughing and working in the headmaster's fields, whilst his wife spent four days assisting the widow with weeding. Thirteen days labour to repay the cost of obtaining draught power to plough 1.84 ha of land.

No cattle also means no manure. Whereas leading farmers can usually manure at least 0.4 ha of their land annually, poor farmers are fortunate if they can apply any organic fertiliser to their land.[17] There is much irony here. Alvord, back in the 1930s despaired of farmers ever overcoming their fear that the practices he recommended were rational and not magical (Floyd, 1961, p. 123). Yet now, in the age when the government research and extension organisations are solidly promoting inorganic fertilisers, it is the rotation system that Alvord encouraged that farmers consider the ideal fertilisation strategy.[18] On fields which have been manured farmers will grow maize for at least two if not three years, followed by groundnuts and then either millet or sorghum. The manure does not fully decompose until the second season, when it is reckoned its benefit to the crop is greatest.[19] The major advantage of manure, as Mrs Nhakuza from Mavhaire puts it, is that 'manure is a five-year plan' (Fieldnotes, 20 December 1986). In contrast, inorganic fertiliser is only effective for a single season. Moreover, manure retains moisture whereas fertiliser, 'without enough moisture is no good' (Nhakuza, fieldnotes, 20 December 1986). In 1986/7, among the case-study households, those fields with manure dried out least and, unless the crop was planted only after the second rains (planting period C), was invariably the household's field that produced the highest maize yield. All farmers bulk their manure with maize stover, and perhaps grass, leaves and groundnut stover. Antheap may also be used, although because it has a desiccating effect it is used less in drier southern Chirumhanzu than in Chiwundura. With respect to bulking, the leading farmers again have an advantage. More land, especially if it is vlei or wetland, means that more forage and maize stover are produced. Both of these provide dry season feed, enabling more livestock to be maintained. More livestock and stover means more manure, and more manure means higher yields and fields whose fertility is more sustainable. But, because of the ceiling on land availability, the contrast between leading and poor farmers in the communal areas is not so large that the leading can contemplate the poor with equanimity.

The Manyongas have a compost pit into which they put grass, food remains, maize stover and the fertility-raising leaves of a large *muwonde* tree (*Ficus sur*), which grows on the edge of their homestead area. In 1986, they applied compost to two-thirds of a 0.3 ha field. However, they left the task of carting the compost by wheelbarrow and then digging it in, until late November. Earlier the Manyongas had been fulfilling their labour obligations to those whose draught animals they were using, and Manyonga had also been undertaking piecework as part of a gang repairing a dam the local Catholic priest had financed. The germination rate of the maize the Manyongas planted in this field in early December was about 90 per cent, and the crop's early growth was the most promising of all their fields. But the crop was planted too late and it shrivelled with the drought. Still, two of the seven bags of maize the Manyongas produced in 1987 from the 1.05 ha they planted to maize came from this field. Amongst the other poor farmers mentioned, Teveras produced 4 bags of maize from 0.6 ha, Mrs Kumira 4 bags from 1.1 ha, and Mrs Mkucha, who worked extraordinarily hard, yielded just 5 buckets – under 1 bag – from 0.95 ha cultivated.

The official argument that farmers should use inorganic fertiliser in order to boost their production is advanced, of course, in large part because farmers do not have sufficient composted manure to fertilise all their fields every five years. But, as farmers all point out, chemical fertiliser is not a straight substitute for manure. Ecological and agronomic differences have been mentioned so far, but there are also tremendously significant economic ones too. These belong more to the discussion on agricultural credit, however, and so detailed reference to them will be deferred. Suffice to say that for those farmers who have little or no manure, the high cost of fertiliser prohibits them from using anything other than a token amount. The inviability of the agricultural production activities of most households is shown in Tables 5.5 and 5.6 which detail the economics of household maize production (Chiwundura) and overall crop production (Chirumhanzu) for the seasons 1984/5, 1985/6 and 1986/7.

Another resource constraint experienced by most middle and poor households, and even by some of the leading farmer housholds, is that of labour. Even if a hired labourer is only paid between Z\$30 and Z\$50 per month,[20] well below the legal minimum wage of Z\$100 per month, the annual wage of upwards of Z\$400 is more than any of the households I visited could afford to pay from purely agricultural returns. Labour can therefore only be hired if one's husband or one's children are remitting a regular and sizeable income. Thus, given a large enough land holding, one way of becoming a leading farmer is to have a husband with a good job. Mrs Skosana, who obtained her Master Farmer's certificate in 1987, is one farmer who has had this opportunity. Her husband is a supervisor on a Union Carbide chrome mine at Kwekwe and he pays the wages of two male labourers. The only other leading farmer houshold who employed permanent wage labour was the Mhenes in the Mavhaire area. Two of the Mhenes' sons, one of whom is a statistician with the Central Statistical Office and the other a secondary school headmaster, each pay the salary of one young male or female worker. Mr Mhene has lost one leg in an accident and they have no children still living at home, and so without help they could not continue to produce the crop surpluses they achieve.

All the other leading farmers make use of periodically hired labour to help particularly with weeding and harvesting. A teenage boy might be taken on to herd cattle during the school term.[21] These boys are often still of school age, but are from families whose parents can

Table 5.5   Maize expenditure and income: Chiwundura

	1984/5 Inputs Z$	Sales Z$	1985/6 Inputs Z$	Sales Z$	1986/7 Inputs Z$	Sales Z$
Leading farmers						
Takavada	446.00	2360.00	587.00	1073.50	527.50	768.00
Nhonga	374.00	1389.00	489.00	958.75	706.50	906.00
Mangwalala	342.00		494.50	295.00	398.30	32.00
Skosana		147.50	320.00	0.00	391.60	20.00
Total	1162.00	3896.50	1890.50	2327.25	2023.90	1726.00
Ave.	387.33	1298.83	472.63	581.81	505.98	431.50
Profit/loss		911.50		109.19		−74.48
Middle farmers						
K. Mugoni	238.00	841.25	248.00	221.25	198.00	0.00
Mrs R. Mugoni	208.00	870.25	294.60	162.25	185.40	0.00
Mrs T. Mabuku		330.00	162.00	0.00	186.50	0.00
Mrs Mangamba	238.00	325.75	170.30	0.00	215.90	0.00
Mathe			17.00	0.00	41.65	0.00
Total	684.00	2367.25	891.90	383.50	827.45	0.00
Ave.	228.00	591.81	178.38	76.70	165.49	0.00
Profit/loss		363.81		−101.68		−165.49
Poor farmers						
Komboni			201.50	15.00	5.00	0.00
Mrs Kumira	168.50	250.75	156.00	44.28	200.10	0.00
Hozheri			0.00	0.00	0.00	0.00
Mrs Mkucha			138.00	0.00	23.90	0.00
Moyo			50.50	44.25	6.50	0.00
Tangwena			0.00	0.00	0.00	0.00
Total	168.50	250.75	546.00	103.53	235.50	0.00
Ave.	168.50	250.75	91.00	17.26	39.25	0.00
Profit/loss		82.25		−73.75		−39.25

no longer afford the secondary school fees and the building fund payments that are ubiquitously required in the post-independence era of joint government and community funded educational expansion. Washington, the 15-year-old son of the Moyos in Phumelela, was one such boy. He spent three months herding cattle for relatives, ostensibly to earn money so that he could return to school. Earning Z$20 a month and with an annual secondary school fee of Z$100 plus a Z$30

Table 5.6   Crop expenditure and income: Chirumhanzu

	1984/5 Inputs Z$	Sales Z$	1985/6 Inputs Z$	Sales Z$	1986/7 Inputs Z$	Sales Z$
Leading farmers						
Nhakuza	330.00	2362.60	444.50	777.30	379.04	747.80
Mhene	228.00	1331.80	311.00	891.25	246.00	766.56
W. Mugwisi	438.50	2424.22	476.60	1105.34	750.70	1233.18
Mugarisi	200.00	3294.74	300.00	522.75	806.72	846.50
Total	1196.50	9413.36	1532.10	3296.64	2182.46	3594.04
Ave.	299.13	2353.34	383.03	824.16	545.62	898.51
Profit/loss		2054.21		441.14		352.90
Middle farmers						
Nhambeni	57.30	191.83	78.10	205.81	126.65	0.00
Ms Gonga	75.00	320.75	45.00	236.39	114.00	519.60
Mrs Jeke	94.00	229.40	143.85	116.30	52.40	52.25
K.Mugwisi		236.00	89.40	118.00	25.00	0.00
Mrs Jengwa		164.25		0.00	94.00	0.00
Machipisi		784.75	68.00	126.00	28.30	290.00
Total	226.30	1926.98	424.35	802.50	440.35	861.85
Ave.	75.43	321.16	84.87	133.75	73.39	143.64
Profit/loss		245.73		48.88		70.25
Poor farmers						
Masocha		0.00		0.00	86.50	0.00
Tevera		0.00	14.00	32.00	23.00	0.00
Manyonga	75.00	254.25	41.40	0.00	50.80	0.00
Rangwa		382.00		0.00	6.60	0.00
Total	75.00	636.25	55.40	32.00	166.90	0.00
Ave.	75.00	159.06	27.70	8.00	41.73	0.00
Profit/loss		84.06		−19.70		−41.73

building fund fee, this was a forlorn hope. The drought effectively ended any chance of its realisation.

Most of the leading farmers also have children and grandchildren who contribute to labour at peak periods of demand. In Chirumhanzu, both Nhakuza and Mugarisi, after I had spoken to them about methods of conserving soil moisture in the drought, decided to experiment with pot-holing and tie-ridging for a portion of their groundnut and maize crops, respectively. They were able to implement these methods, firstly, because they have draught power and a cultivator to create the necessary furrow between the plants, and secondly, the children to scoop out the pot-hole or construct the ties, using hoes. At harvest both felt the methods had helped improve their yields – the Nhakuzas for instance obtained eight bags of unshelled groundnuts from a 0.3 ha portion, which was excellent considering the season. But only those who have the labour, the draught power and the equipment can trial advice such as this.

Labour is scarce in many of the middle farmer households. In ten of the eleven case-study households in this category, women carried the labour burden. In nine, the husbands, if they were not migrant workers, performed local piecework jobs when they could find them, since food and money were clearly going to be scarce. In the tenth household, P. Gonga, an unmarried mother, was the farmer. Her main assistance was provided by an unreliable younger cousin. These women in the main are competent and strong; they manage. School-going children assist over weekends and during school holidays, and in loose reciprocal arrangements labour assistance is given by and returned to proximous female relatives – mothers-in-law benefiting more than daughters-in-law. One exception was Mrs Jeke from Mavhaire who, fragile to start with, had no one at home to provide support and became debilitated from bearing and caring for a son during the hot summer.

The poor households have the least land, but often still struggle to cultivate it through lack of physically fit adults. In Chiwundura, for instance, Kombini had TB and his wife did most of the work; Mrs Kumira was old and fragile and her daughter suffered blinding headaches exacerbated by the heat; Mrs Mkucha was elderly; Tachi Moyo was old and ill and his younger wife did the work; Tangwena was old and had TB, grumbled continuously and dreamt of having more money, but usually assisted his wife. Only the Hozheris were poor and young, but she was burdened with children, and Hozheri preferred welding to ploughing.

Most poor families in fact obtain their income, even in good years (as Appendix 2 shows), from sources other than their own crop production activities. Before turning to an examination of how households survive, given the lack of viability of much maize production, there is a final point to be made here on the subject of resource access. As an agency, Agritex, in the formal recommendations that extension staff are trained to pass on to farmers, simply assume that farmers have the resources available to put the cropping practices into operation. No farmer ever takes this access to land, labour, livestock or manure for granted.

INCOME AND SURVIVAL

By mid-February a drought seemed inevitable. My notebook entry for 16 February begins: 'Phumelela, 0705. A bright cloudless day, promising to be hot. Signs of rain as evasive as they have been over the last week or so.' The day after, accompanied by Aaron Nduku, the Agritex research assistant, I visited Mathe, one of the Phemelela farmers. Mathe sat under a tree stripping the bark from tree roots he had collected to make winnowing baskets. He tapped his head. 'This year is going to be a drought year and if you don't use your brains you are going to starve. You have to have plans. Hunger is what makes you cunning in this business' (Fieldnotes, 17 February 1987).

Mathe often exasperated his wife because whilst she weeded the maize crop in their homefield he sat under the tree and made winnowing baskets. Yet that season the Mathes harvested only between six and seven bags of maize and the other income was desperately important (Table 5.7). Between January and April, Mathe sold seventeen baskets. He was charging Z$3, but some people paid in chickens which were worth Z$5–6. Chickens, being small, are an important local currency. The Mathe's paid three chickens for 0.5 ha of their field to be ploughed in early November, and they paid another three for the same area to be autumn ploughed in April. In January and February when they were running short of maize, one bucket of maize (5–6 buckets = 1 bag) was purchased for Z$4 and another with a chicken.

The winnowing baskets were not the only non-agricultural activity the Mathes engaged in to earn income in 1987. Like Mrs Mkucha, Mrs Mathe earned a trickle of money through catching, roasting and selling termites. With the baskets this helped to pay for their frugal consumption of household groceries – tea, sugar and mealie meal. From Mbare Musika market in Harare, Mathe also purchased a sack of tobacco offcuts. These he resold at 10 cents per cup. A few women bought several cups from him to resell again at a slight mark-up. The sack cost Mathe Z$7.50 and the return transport to Harare Z$15. In March and April, Mathe sold two-thirds of the sack for Z$30, yielding till then a profit of Z$7.50. We discussed the economics. Purchasing three sacks at once would bring him a significant reduction in the unit cost of transport, but he lacked the capital for this.

In late April the government food-for-work scheme began. Mathe signed on and in April and May earned maize for his labour. In June the payment was switched to cash, a move popular especially with men because of the expenditure choice they now had. The first month he earned cash Mathe bought a pair of trousers.

Others, such as Takavada and Nhonga, who did not need the food, also signed on in June when the cash was offered. Nevertheless, after the perilous months from January to April, the government's introduction of food-for-work did indeed bring relief for many households. Appendix 2 provides a rough account of the income-earning activities of case-study households in Chiwundura during the fieldwork period, and profiles clearly enough the parlous economic state many household were in before drought relief commenced. There are three additional features of these activities and the size of the earnings they yield, to which attention should be drawn.

First, in this difficult agricultural period, which began with the adverse 1986 harvest, it is only two of the leading farmers, Nhonga and Takavada, who are earning any significant returns from maize production. Mrs Skosana, as the only other farmer producing a sizeable surplus of maize above household requirements in 1986 and again in 1987, would be if she were not squandering the surplus on feeding pigs in an ill-conceived and indecisively implemented pig-breeding experiment.

Second, the more lucrative income-earning activities outside dry land crop production, such as early season tomato production, and the hiring-out of draught power, are also undertaken predominantly by leading farmers because of their 'access qualifications' (Blaikie, 1985, p. 110) – wet land garden area, irrigation water, sufficient labour, draught power.

Third, the economic activities engaged in by poor households involve little capital and large amounts of labour. In some instances (like Mrs Kumira), the returns are marginal. If the entrepreneur can afford a slightly higher capital outlay (Mathe, Mrs Mabuku, Mrs Nhambeni) the profit margin and amount received is likely to be higher.

Nevertheless, even the incomes these middle farmers receive from these off-farm activities are negligible in comparison with the Z$2 per day drought relief earnings – which despite inflation, are still at the same rate they were in 1984 at the end of the 1982–4 drought.

Table 5.7 Mr and Mrs Mathe, Phumelela area: reported expenditure and income October 1986 to July 1987

	Expenditure activities	Cost[a]		Income-earning activities	
Nov 4/86	Ploughing of garden (for early maize) – 0.5 ha	3 chickens			
Nov 1986	Maize seed – 3×2 kg purchased on one trip to Gweru	9.35			
			Nov 1986	Intermediary in arranging a marriage (Mr N) (Income used for ploughing)	10.00
Nov 1986	Ploughing (for maize) – 0.3 ha	10.00			
Dec 3–4	Two portions ploughed by two relatives – 0.6 ha	No payment			
Dec 1986	Maize seed – 2×2 kg purchased in Gweru	7.30			
Dec 1986	Maize seed – 1×2 kg given by son	No payment			
Dec 1986	Maize seed – 1×2 kg bought from local farmer. Seed then replaced.	2.20 +seed	Dec/Jan 87	Weeding for son (mainly Mrs M)	No payment
Dec/Jan 87	Weeding assistance provided by '4 grandchildren of the Mathes Food – 1, 20 litre tin maize (Maize also to be replaced at harvest)	Food 1 tin rapoko			
Jan 1987			Jan 1987	Winnowing baskets – 3 sold (Mr M) (Income used to pay for maize)	9.00

Date	Inputs / Expenditure	Cost	Date	Output / Income	Value
Jan 1987	Food – 1, 20-litre tin maize (Maize from farmer with irrigation plot)	4.00	Jan 10/87	Red termites (roasted & piri-piri added) – sold at 10c per cup at beerhall (Mrs M)	2.50
Feb 1987	Food – 1, 20-litre tin maize	1 chicken	Feb/Mar 87	Winnowing baskets – 5 sold (Some money used to buy tea and sugar)	15.00
Feb 1987	Tobacco off-cuts – 1 bag purchased at Mbare Musika market + bus fare	7.50 +22.75	Feb/Mar 87	Winnowing baskets – 3 sold	3 chickens
			Feb 1987	Tobacco – sold at 10c per cup	9.70
			Mar/Apr 87	Tobacco – sales at 10c per cup incl $1.70 sold at field day and $1.50 sold to a woman who then resells (Mr M)	20.20
			Apr 1987	Food-for-work (Mr M)	2 tins of maize
			Mar 1987	Winnowing baskets – 6 sold	18.00
Apr 1987	Autumn ploughing – 0.5 ha	3 chickens	Apr/May 87	Tobacco off-cuts	12.00
			May 1987	Food-for-work (Mr M)	1 bag maize
			Jun 1987	Food-for-work (Mr M) (Purchased a pair of trousers)	44.00
			Jul 1987	Food-for-work (Mr M)	44.00
			Jun/Jul 87	Winnowing baskets – 3 sold	9.00

a Z$ unless indicated

The relative distress in which households in different categories find themselves in their struggle to produce food and money, depends on the household structure. Those households which have capital-consuming dependents – secondary schoolchildren, the long-term ill – are the most vulnerable. An obvious fact, but the consequences are tragic. Compare, for instance, two middle farmer households in Chiwundura, the Mathes and the K. Mugonis.

The Mathes were both over 60 years of age and no longer had child dependents. With children and grandchildren to help occasionally with resources such as seed, draught power and labour, they were content to manage with a low-risk agriculture, supported by informal income-earning activities. They did not gamble with seasonal variability and the chance of boosting yields in a good season by purchasing inorganic fertiliser. With no manure either, they were therefore resigned to a low-productivity agricultural system.

Middle farmers with children to support simply cannot afford to adopt this low-risk strategy. For those whose husbands are migrants and have permanent or occasional wage employment – three of the five middle farmer housholds in Chiwundura and two of the six in Chirumhanzu – the annual rainfall lottery is less traumatic. In the season following a drought, their husbands' salaries can help cover shortfalls in food, school fees, maize seed and fertiliser. For the K. Mugonis, the absence of the safety net of a remitted income has choked their children's futures. In the last six years the family has had one significant agricultural surplus. This was in the prolific season of 1984/5, the year the Agricultural Finance Corporation and Agritex launched a large promotion of credit. The scale of the success farmers like the Mugonis had in their use for the first time of large quantities of fertiliser, encouraged them to be more profligate in their spending than with experience they perhaps would have been. They harvested 72 bags of maize, of which 57 were marketed in various ways. Fifteen went on repaying most of the loan, twenty were used to purchase two heifers, one of which subsequently died, and twenty-two went towards buying building materials to build a two-roomed house for Mr and Mrs Mugoni. Until then the seven household members then living at home had all slept crowded in just two small rooms.

In 1986, though, they failed to produce another surplus, and then came the 1986/7 drought. Mugoni obtained only periodic piecework, firstly on a road-building project with the government District Development Fund (DDF), and then making bricks for classroom extensions to the local secondary school. His children he could not afford to send to the school. Sheila, aged 21, having completed only Form 1, had gone to Kadoma to stay with a relative, hoping to find employment and do Form 2 at night school. She obtained a child instead. In July, when I made my last visit, she was at home, 'in the process of getting married' (Fieldnotes, 14 July 1917).

Andrew, aged 17, had also not completed Form 1. Esnati, 15, started the year in Form 1 and determinedly kept returning to school, despite being 'chased away' on several occasions because none of the annual fee of Z$135 had been paid. In April she eventually lost the battle.

'*Chikoro*' [school] is our problem' said Mrs Mugoni (Fieldnotes, 17 January 1987). The little money Mugoni earns goes on food and household needs. In February he said his wife had been ill since December and he had had to sell one of their four goats to pay for a visit to the Gweru hospital and for tablets which had failed to help her (Fieldnotes, 11 February 1987). Ironically, in May, Mugoni obtained the temporary job with the DDF and consequently failed to get one of the quota of places each ward had for food-for-work. In July when I returned he was off seeking work on a commercial farm. 'We have no plans', said Mrs Mugoni (Fieldnotes, 17 January 1987), in stark contrast to the bravado of Mathe, who does not face the debilitating difficulties of having to school children.

Since independence a terrific expansion of primary and secondary education has occurred in the rural areas. But it is unmatched by any concomitant growth in employment opportunities,[22] and so children who are not able to complete Form 4 and attempt 'O' level are severely handicapped in their future options. Writing 'O' level is very expensive, for the exam fees raise the year's bill to over Z$250. Lincoln, the eldest son of the Mabukus, another of the middle farmer families, had also stayed at home in 1987 because of the extra cost of this fourth year. Mabuku was a self-employed painter who later in the year found jobs in Gweru, Kadoma, and on a commercial farm, but these were too late for Lincoln. With two-thirds of the rural population under twenty years of age,[23] even passing 'O' level is no guarantee for finding work – and most who write in the new rural schools fail. 'Those that have completed Form 4 are now the great thieves in town', commented Mugoni (Fieldnotes, 17 January 1987).

The lack of urban opportunities is a major reason for the reclaiming by established households of their former land husbandry arable land allocations. Reference was made in the previous chapter to a widely supported comment, made at a public meeting, expressing this sentiment. But such expansionary activities are a trade-off for there is no longer the land available for many sons to acquire allocations *and* for cattle to be grazed. On the possibility of the employment situation improving, Mugoni commented, 'For things to change it takes time. If everyone sees the weakness then things can be done. But some have enough to eat for them and their children and they don't see the problem' (Fieldnotes, 11 February 1987).

In sum, Chiwundura is very dependent on particularly the nearby urban economies of Gweru and Kwekwe, and the danger of this for rural welfare is becoming acutely clear with the current closure of the job tap in the urban areas.

In comparison with Chiwundura, people in Chirumhanzu have been settled in the area for longer and are more experienced in the art of drought survival. In the drought, southern Chirumhanzu appeared inhospitable; a harsh glare of stony, thorn-filled grazing wasteland, and stunted crops in parched, sandy fields. But as shown in the summary information on resource access (Table 5.2), in each of the three categories, farmers in Chirumhanzu cultivate more land than their counterparts in Chiwundura. Labour availability in the two areas is similar, but more farmers in Chirumhanzu have access to their own draught power. The Chirumhanzu case-study farmers, thus, as a rule have less intensive (or, in the case of leading farmers, more selectively intensive) and more diversified cropping systems than in Chiwundrua.

The less intensive nature of the cropping system means that once the drought loomed, many of the male heads of middle and poorer households sought piece-work employment, mostly in the lucrative rural building trade. Of the fourteen case-study households, two had male heads who were permanent migrant workers, whilst of the remainder, six had males who in the period between November 1986 and August 1987 carried out piece-work as builders. As the profiles in Appendix 2 show, all except Augustine Manyonga, who was a labourer not a builder, earned, or was engaged in earning upwards of Z$300. Even one of the leading farmers, Silvester Mugarisi from Maware, switched to building work in the winter of 1987, and in fact stood to earn over Z$800, as much as he had earned from cultivation that year. The remarkable fact about this is that in the whole of Maware ward, which has some 450 households, Mugarisi ranks as the best farmer. In April, as he has in several recent seasons, he won the prize for the best maize crop at the ward's annual field day.

As Mugarisi pointed out, compared too with food-for-work, the returns from building work were substantially higher – he earned Z$350 from one two-week job (Fieldnotes, 7 August 1987). In the case-study households, all of the males who were competent builders found building piecework in the winter for 1987, in preference to joining food-for-work. Those who employ them are, of course, predominantly urban wage earners.

Among the leading farmers, as Table 5.6 and Appendix 2 also show, the crop sales of the leading farmers despite the drought were surprisingly good. This is, in large measure, because of the rise in the local maize price due to scarcity. Compared with the official maize price of Z$180 per tonne, which once transportation is deducted yielded farmers Z$14.75 per 90 kg bag in 1985 and 1986, in 1987 farmers could sell maize from between Z$20 and Z$24 a bag.[24] Farmers also benefited from the greater diversification of their cropping system – mhunga, sorghum, groundnuts and sunflowers all providing income for the leading farmers. Although crop sales for these other crops are lower than for maize their profit margins in the drought season are higher, because of the minimal amount of inorganic fertiliser used on them. Straight comparisons are misleading here though, since crops such as groundnuts and sorghum benefit from being grown on fields previously manured for maize. These secondary crops are seen by most farmers as only complementing maize. An exception was the Machipisis, who short of capital, had adopted a low-input system focused on sorghum rather than maize. Their yields were low, but at the raised local prices they stood to make nearly Z$300, having paid a negligible amount for inputs.

A major use of small grains is in the production of home-made beer. Most of the case-study households brewed beer at least once during the period I was there, although only two, the Nhambenis and Teveras undertook beer brewing regularly as a money-earning venture. For women especially, beer brewing is carried out when immediate cash for household needs is required.[25] Significantly, in contrast with the return from building work that men can earn, women's non-agricultural earnings are often marginal.[26] Consequently it is women in particular – as was the case in Chiwundura – who joined the food-for-work scheme when it was introduced in mid-May.

A welfare contrast between Chiwundura and Chirumhanzu is that amongst the case-study households in the latter communal area, there were no children not attending school. Faced with the same problem of 'O' level exam fees as the Mabukus, the Machipisis sold one of their draught oxen to pay for their daughter Angela to write. The most horrific bill of all the households I worked with was faced by the Nhakuzas – Z$693 for three children. They were shrewd, experienced farmers. Nhakuza himself had become one of the first Master Farmers in the area, gaining his certificate in 1949, whilst Agnes, who was his second wife and half his age, was an astute business woman and energetic worker. Yet even with the high local prices, their profit from crop production in 1987 was just Z$370.

Mrs Machipisi, who came from Mashonaland, hated Maware. Their fields were stony, neighbours' cattle ate their young crops, and her husband had failed to find employment that year. Her husband's brother had already migrated to the Urungwe area in the Zambezi valley, opened up through the clearing of the tsetse fly. She had now persuaded her husband to make enquiries about undertaking a similar move.

HUMAN AGENCY AND SOCIAL STRUCTURE

The argument I have sought to present in this chapter is that those who speak of a 'farming miracle' having occurred in the communal areas since independence are deluded. For the bulk of the communal area population, such an optimistic picture is dangerously misleading. It leads only to an underestimation of the precariousness of the agricultural production systems of most rural households. Although few quantitative studies have been undertaken, there is no doubt that it is only a small minority of households and then mainly in the wetter natural region II part of the country who have participated significantly in the production increases achieved since independence. In a study of a 98 families in northern Wedza communal area (natural region II) in the poor season of 1981/2, Diana Callear (1984) records that only one-third of the sample were dependent on agriculture for the major part of their incomes. More tellingly, the majority of these were widows or elderly people, perhaps caring for grandchildren, and concerned only to subsist. Thus only 13 per cent of households were 'actively seeking to make their livelihood from agriculture' (p. 163). Callear states that despite the dearth of comparable data she has 'no reason to suppose this is unusual' (p. 163). I concur.

In the 1984/5 Ture Ward survey, questionnaire information showed an estimated 89 per cent of 449 households to have had maize yields *below* 1.75 tonnes per hectare for the excellent season of 1980/ 1. This is the target yield set in the First Five-Year Development Plan to be achieved by 1990. Jeremy Jackson *et al.* (1987) in a survey of 600 households for 1984/5, the only other good season since independence, found that the top 10 per cent of households produced 40.4 per cent of all cereal output and 56.8 per cent of cereal marketed. The top 25 per cent were responsible for 63.3 per cent of production and 83 per cent of marketed output (p. 69).[27] All these figures reveal that significant, though largely unacknowledged, social differentiation still exists in the communal areas, even if the incomes of the most productive households are still insecurely low.

In economic terms many household production systems are not currently viable – they are subsidised – and nor will they even be easily maintained at their present levels. The high cost of drought relief since 1982 shows this clearly. Social differentiation in the communal areas is underlain by differential access to production resource. However, the overwhelming problem of largely non-viable production systems is not so much a consequence of unequal distribution within the communal areas but of the smallness of the resource cake to which communal area households have access. One conclusion from this is that it is hopeless for agricultural research and extension agencies to thrust technical advice at farmers if there is no concurrent improvement in their capacity to assess and adapt that advice (see also Grant, 1981, p. 175).

At a national political level, removed from the seasonal drama of life in the communal areas, independence has, of course, brought formal recognition of the deprived status of the communal area population. The government points proudly to policies such as land resettlement and the increased provision of credit to peasant farmers. But it has already been shown in Chapter 3 that the present land resettlement policy, despite its achievements, cannot even cope with the population growth in the communal areas. And in the next chapter, when the impact of credit is examined, doubt will be cast as to whether many communal farmers in the Midlands have actually benefited from this.

If one takes, then, the non-viability and dwindling sustainability of communal area agriculture; if one takes the low and insecure rural incomes, even including non-agricultural sources; and if one takes the continuing overwhelming dependence of the communal area economy on migrant remittances, it is clear that the highly inequitable distribution of power within the relations of production of Zimbabwean society has not seriously altered since independence. The growing scarcity of land in the communal areas coupled with the lack of new urban jobs could well create a phenomenon Zimbabwe has not yet experienced – the growth of rural landlessness, escalating rural–urban migration, and a burgeoning, discontented, urban poor.

Whatever the validity of this argument though, in terms of my overall thesis it still leaves some unanswered questions. It explains inadequately the complex relationship between the state and the rural populace and the influence the more substantial, collective initiatives of groups might be having on social awareness. For instance, has the mobilisation that took place during the war had any residual effect on the consciousness of communal area societies? How much have forms of rural resistance, developed as a response to colonial subjugation, continued as part of rural responses to contemporary policies?

To answer these sorts of questions, what is required is a theoretical framework which can be used to examine what room people – as individuals or part of social collectivities – have to make their own world, within the context of the structural constraints that face them. Some such constraints have been referred to quite specifically or in passing in this chapter – limits to resource access, available production methods and technology, labour organisation options given the scale of production units, and permitted systems of land tenure and land use. All of these constraints are regulated through the media of power and money by the institutions of the state and capitalist economy. Consequently, although in part peasant households pursue economic strategies which utilise and are regulated by the formal state-regulated economic framework, their strategies also in part remain outside the embrace of the formal structures.

For example, people use the official Grain Marketing Board crop prices as a baseline. In favourable seasons when supply is plentiful farmers all sell to the GMB; in adverse seasons local prices rise and a large proportion of food crops marketed are sold locally. In 1987, rapoko, which is sold by the 20-litre tin for beer brewing, was selling in Chirumhanzu and Chiwundura for between Z$12 and Z$14 per tin – over Z$60 per bag compared with the official price of Z$27.27 per bag.

Another example is the means people use to circumvent restrictions on land availability. Land adjacent to communal areas, whether large or small-scale commercial or resettlement farming land, is commonly used by communal farmers for grazing their cattle or collecting firewood. Arrangements may be made with the farmers concerned, though the very nature of their informality makes them hard for farmers or community leaders to regulate, and thus leaves them open to abuse – as occurred on the Lot 5 of Debshan Ranch, adjacent to Ture Ward, in 1983. Members of established lineages, such as Nhonga and Takavada, are often likely to have relatives in resettlement areas whom they can use to safeguard cattle. Strategies such as these are generally limited in scope by their unofficial or outrightly illegal nature, and almost inevitably it is the poorest who have the least opportunity. But on occasion the peasantry have succeeded in successfully rebelling against the formal rules – their success in forcing the government to abandon the Land Husbandry Act being the best example. Even here though, with present land use policies echoing the past, a full transcending of land husbandry has yet to be achieved.

A theoretical framework appropriate for examining what room people have to resist, must be capable of being used to examine the actual interface relations between representatives of the state and the peasantry. But more than this, the reverberations of this interaction need to be captured – how it feeds back to influence future policy actions and how rural actors modify their behaviour.

The difficulty of achieving this in an analysis is that it requires a combination of a structuralist (systems-oriented) and an actor-oriented approach. Approaches in the tradition of Marxist critical theory have emphasised the former at the expense of the latter. Norman Long (1984), for instance, takes on a gamut of Marx-inspired models of rural social change which he believes are 'coloured by simple deterministic and centralistic thinking' (p. 168). Theories focusing on the penetration of rural society by capital and the state; or on the articulation of modes of production, whereby non-capitalist production relations are maintained as functionally useful adjuncts to the formal economy; or on the incorporation of periphery by centre; are all targets of Long (pp. 169–71):

These various general models of rural social change have in common the tendency to interpret the restructuring of agrarian systems and farming enterprise as resulting basically from the penetration of external forces. Hence changes in the organisation and activities of local populations are seen largely as responses to externally initiated change ... There is little room in these types of models for a full analysis of the interplay of local and extra-local forces. (p 171)

More appropriate therefore in Long's view, is an approach which 'recognises the interplay and mutual determinism of external and internal factors and relationships' (p. 171). The approach must take full account of 'human agency'. 'To avoid the determinism of existing general theories of social change' (p. 171), what is needed is 'to combine a structural analysis of political and economic processes with an actor-oriented approach that aims to understand how specific individuals and social classes responded to processes of intervention' (p. 175).

Cheater (1984), in the conclusion of her book on the emergence of class relations in an African freehold area in Zimbabwe before independence, also advocates an analysis which focuses on social process. She is, however, more firmly a Marxist than Long.

I would suggest that we are currently on the verge of a new theoretical understanding of the articulation of capitalism and pre-capitalistic modes of production in the developing world, but that before further advances can be made, we need much more detailed information on the processes of rural development and class formation at the local level. We must understand how people, including poor people, manage the resources available to them in order to shape their own world, socially and politically as well as economically ... Until we understand these issues, policies to generate growth with equity seem unlikely to succeed in the long term, precisely because they are based on existing theoretical analyses that concern themselves with structural generalities at the national level, and ignore process at the local level. (p.180)

Both these authors identify a deficiency in Marxist analyses of social change which critical theorists, beginning with the first generation of the Frankfurt School, have specifically set out to redress. As David Held (1980) notes, Habermas himself claims Marx to have had an 'unresolved tension in his work between the reductionism and positivism of his general theoretical approach and the critical, dialectical character of his concrete social investigations' (p.69).

In subsequent orthodox or 'scientific' interpretations of Marx by Engels, Lenin, Stalin, and recently Althusser, the tension is ignored and Marxism is reduced to an overly deterministic account of historical materialism. The Frankfurt School theorists, and Habermas in particular, have attempted to recapture the emphasis on the interplay between human agency and structure which is contained in the early Marx (Held, 1980, pp. 361–2).[28]

Certainly in Zimbabwe – and one may presuppose anywhere – the structural aspect cannot be ignored. The communal areas are the constructs of policy. The colonial government created them and they are only maintained as such because the post-independence government prevents communal area societies from undertaking their own land expropriation. All local initiatives are worked out in one form or another as part of an interactive process of response and counter-response to the imperatives of the state and capitalist economy. In analysing the political economy of rural Zimbabwe today, an actor-oriented account of the lineage form of production is unintelligible without reference to the nature of articulation with the overarching state-regulated capitalist mode of production. The two are deeply interpenetrated.

In this thesis I am attempting to lay the basis of such an integrated account through the application of Habermas's critical theory. In the next chapter I shall pick up and develop elements of critical theory introduced in Chapter 1. In particular I shall refer to Habermas's model of system and lifeworld and the distinctions he makes between the external world of culture and environment, the normative world of society and the internal world of personality. Habermas's intention with these conceptual tools is to construct a theoretical framework which steers between a structural perspective, such as that obtained if one uses the concept of mode of production as an analytical tool, and an actor-oriented perspective which views individuals and groups as active agents.

Nevertheless, Habermas's framework is not wholly satisfactory and some of the difficulties it provides will need to be identified and my own standpoint on them stipulated. This framework will then be made use of in an analysis of problems associated with forms of social organisation, and hence the integration, of communal area societies.

6 Cooperation, Credit and Social Integration

A critical social theory cannot remain satisfied with an ahistorical analysis of the constitution of our lifeworld through the agents' perspectives. It is also necessary to place this lifeworld within a larger picture of the social whole, its limits and possibilities. Such social constraints are not formed by tales but by the logic of those unintended consequences that escape the lifeworld perspective of social agents. In this sense, the perspectives of systemic and lived crises, of the structural contradictions of the whole and the felt experience of individuals, is fundamental. The task ahead is to think their unity, not to emphasize one at the expense of the other. (Benhabib, 1986, pp. 349–50)

It has been argued that an analysis of social change ideally requires a theoretical framework which can be used to analyse the scope that people, as individuals or part of social collectivities, have to make their own world, within the context of the structural constraints they face. The unit of analysis in the previous chapter was the household. It was shown that even leading farmers are constrained in their ability to enhance the viability of their production by the resource limitations they experience. If individual households by themselves cannot significantly improve their positions, then the onus falls upon the organisations that structure communal area societies. Accordingly, my concern in the empirical component of this chapter is to analyse the capacity of the two societies I worked in for effective, coordinated action at this supra-household level.

It will be shown that this capacity is limited. In large part this is because of the lack of legitimacy accorded to formal systems of social organisation in the communal areas, because they have been imposed rather than developed from within. Social integration, measured in terms of the degree to which members do coordinate their actions and adhere to agreed strategies and action-orienting norms, is deficient. There are, nevertheless, differences in what communities in Chiwundura and Chirumhanzu have been able to achieve. In Chiwundura, the smallholding land use pattern and the fencing of all arable land has alleviated the problem associated with livestock herding that is experienced in southern Chirumhanzu. On the other hand, as an organisational form for providing investment capital, the Chirumhanzu savings clubs have been more successful than the Chiwundura ward cooperatives, through which a group credit scheme has been implemented.

In *The Theory of Communicative Action*, Habermas wants to show how the polar sociological perspectives of, on the one hand, society as a complex system, and on the other, actors as creators of their world, each presupposes and is shaped by the other. The analytical task of combining an actor-oriented approach with a structural analysis is, however, more elusive than it might initially seem. For a start, as Benhabib indicates in the introductory quote above, 'thinking the unity' of human agency and structural constraint cannot be undertaken by a solitary observer.

This last point needs examining more fully for it will help to explain the status of the empirical material in the chapter. The brief summary presented above is neither entirely based upon, nor can it be validated by, merely my own observations. The actor perspective – the 'lifeworld perspective of social agents', as Benhabib calls it – although interpreted by the writer for the reader, must initially be presented to the writer by the participants themselves. The lifeworld, as I shall explain, because it is a resource rather than a material domain, can only be comprehended from the 'performative perspective' of those who draw from it. Thus combining an actor-oriented approach with a structural analysis entails combining 'the internalist perspective of the participant with the externalist perspective of the observer' (McCarthy, in Habermas, 1984, p. xxvi).

To fulfil such an approach requires a cooperative research enterprise. It reinforces Habermas's stance that the social scientist should be only a 'virtual' participant. If one becomes a full participant it is hard to retain the complementary externalist perspective, and if one remains only an observer one will fail to penetrate the internalist perspective. To unify the perspectives adequately suggests a research project in which the subjects cooperate as co-partners. And here I shall leave awhile the issue of the role of those who are the subjects of research. It is raised as a preface to the analysis in this chapter to indicate that it is only in a limited way that I will be able to present the actor perspective.

That a dual perspective is required is one of the more incontrovertible claims Habermas makes in his system–lifeworld model. The difficulty in making use of his model as part of an analytical framework is that it possesses features which lack clarity.[1] Three particularly controversial features of Habermas's model which require discussion here are: the dual conception of the lifeworld, the nature of the relation between the lifeworld and the system, and the relation between the economic sphere of production and the social sphere of interaction.[2] Taken as a whole, however, I believe that an effort to apply his theoretical framework in the Zimbabwean context is of value, precisely because one is forced to attempt to think the unity of perspectives which are generally retained as discrete.

In this chapter the first task I shall perform is to outline the system–lifeworld model and the distinction this allows Habermas to make between the dual possibilities for societal rationalisation in the modern world. The unresolved difficulties of this model identified above will also be explained and discussed.

Once complete this theoretical framework will then be used to explore key problems of social integration and organisation which directly affect farmers' production activities. These problems are connected with the imposition by the state of institutional structures, which in critical instances lack the legitimacy – and the office bearers, the competence – to obtain normative agreement on means for resolving conflict. Two examples will be discussed: in southern Chirumhanzu, the failure of people to reach a binding agreement on early season herding, and in Chiwundura the failure of a group credit scheme.

The first of these examples will be discussed largely from the internalist perspective of the participants, the second from my externalist perspective as an investigator. These two examples will then be contrasted with two further organisational initiatives. Again, the perspective adopted will shift during the presentation. In the first, that of the savings clubs in Chirumhanzu, an externalist perspective will be favoured, whilst in the second, an incipient form of group cooperation in Chiwundura, an internalist perspective will largely be used. These latter examples show operational success insofar as they meet personal needs and are under the control of members. Nevertheless, as will also be illustrated, the vulnerability of household production systems jeopardises even the more successful organisational forms. The relative health of exemplary savings clubs, such as the Maware club, has been due to the external advisory and auditing (in effect, monitoring) role of the Catholic Development Commission (CADEC).

In the final section of the chapter the threads of the analysis will be pulled together. The penetration of the capitalist economy and bureaucratic state threaten the social and economic reproduction of communal area societies. If institutions orchestrating further changes are to have any potential for improving the lives of the members of these societies and are to be accorded greater legitimacy by them, then these people must be more actively involved in the institutions. Yet the resources and ideas necessary to bring about economic improvement requires the intervention of outside agencies. This is the paradox of societal rationalisation as it applies to Zimbabwe: it is only the same economic and political-administrative sub-systems that have been responsible for the demoralisation of communal area societies which can help restore their vitality.

But this requires a change in the way decisions are taken and actions performed in these institutions – an ability to rationalise actions in the communicative as well as the purposive-rational sense. As shown in Chapter 7, some members of an institution such as Agritex have recognised the need for alteration in the organisational structure of decision-making, if the needs of communal farmers are to be better served. They have also acknowledged the formidable structural barriers to the achievement of such change.

THE LIFEWORLD AND SOCIETAL RATIONALISATION

There are two features of Habermas's theory of communicative action that are relevant to this chapter. The first feature is Habermas's insistence on the *necessity* of communicative action for the reproduction of social life. The second is the paradox of societal rationalisation – that the process of the rationalisation of the lifeworld, which marks the transition from traditional to modern attitudes, holds out the contradictory potentials for the realisation or the demise of human freedom. In order to explain the first of these features, it is necessary to clarify initially what Habermas means by the term 'lifeworld'. The second feature requires explanation of the distinction between purposive rationality and communicative rationality.

The way in which Habermas conceives the lifeworld is awkward because he equivocates between two meanings of the term (Baxter, 1987, p. 73). Most fundamentally, however, the lifeworld is the background *resource* that makes communication possible, and it is this meaning of the term that I shall introduce initially and adhere to in the analysis.

The three 'worlds' or domains of our experience – culture, society and personality – together constitute the lifeworld (McCarthy, in Habermas, 1984, p. xxv).[3] The domain of culture is the external or cognitive world of events and facts. The domain of society is that of normatively regulated social relations, in which acting, practical subjects are 'entwined in interaction with others'. The domain of personality is the inner world of our subjective feelings, desires and intentions, in which we relate as 'suffering and passionate' subjects to our own inner nature and subjectivity, and to the subjectivity of others (Habermas, in Dews, 1986, pp. 108–9; Roderick, 1986, pp. 96–7).

These domains exist in a formal rather than material sense (Benhabib, 1986, p. 391). They 'come into view' when one analyses communication processes from *the participants' perspective* (Habermas, in Dews, 1986, p. 109). Moments in the *attitude* the actor takes towards the one world can be distinguished, in terms of whether they be objectivating, norm-conformative or expressive (Habermas, in Bernstein, 1985, p. 208).

These three domains therefore come into being only as communicated experiences. In this sense the lifeworld is constituted *by* communicative action through the medium of language. It provides a source of 'situation definitions' (Habermas, 1984, p. 70), for the interpretation of the objective, social and subjective phenomena we encounter. Thus, the lifeworld is also constitutive of communicative action (Benhabib, 1986, p. 239). As a resource, the lifeworld is that 'which stands behind the back of each participant in communication and which provides resources for the resolution of problems of understanding' (Habermas, in Dews, 1986, p. 109). It remains, 'that background horizon of unthematized assumptions, implicit expectations and individual know-how within which communicative action unfolds' (Benhabib, 1986, p. 239).

The lifeworld is something that as members growing into a particular society we absorb and draw from rather than consciously learn. Habermas conceives that the three domains of the lifeworld – culture, society and personality – are symbolically reproduced through different types of communicative action:

> Under the functional aspect of *reaching understanding* communicative action serves the transmission and renewal of cultural knowledge; under the aspect of *coordinating action*, it serves social integration and the establishment of group solidarity; under the

aspect of *socialisation*, it serves the formation of personal identities. (Habermas, 1984, pp. xxiv–xxv)[4]

Impairment of these functions in a society gives rise to social and psychological disturbances such as loss of meaning, anomie, withdrawal of legitimation and psychopathologies (McCarthy, in Habermas, 1984, p. xxv; Roderick, 1986, p. 128).

The Bull and the Maize

An example illustrates one way in which this theoretical conception of the lifeworld can illuminate the empirical analysis. We return to Maware in November 1986:

> The local agricultural extension staff talk of the need for small-scale irrigation in the area to raise arable cultivation above the despairing venture it is now. The chairman of the local Ruware farming club has shown the possibilities. He has constructed a small dam on a stream below the hectare or so of land he has adjacent to his homestead. From this area he produced sizeable surpluses for each of the last two seasons by purchasing a small 4 hp engine which he used to pump water onto his fields. However, this year he will not be irrigating. The engine has been stolen; people are jealous he says.
>
> One night last week someone opened the gate to his field and let their bull in to eat his 15 cm high maize plants. 'It is too early for planting now', the wife of the owner said. 'We are waiting for December.'[5]

From this incident one can propose how the dimensions of the lifeworld are constituted for the actors concerned.[6] The world of events and facts (or existing state of affairs) is characterised by the following. First, the fact: a despair-inducing agricultural environment in which land and water are scarce. Second, events: a farmer – it is Silvester Mugarisi – fences his field, and then builds a small dam and purchases an engine in order to irrigate the field. He also plants early to maximise use of the first rains. Third, further events consequent upon the first set: the engine is stolen and a bull is let into the maize field.

In the domain of normatively regulated social relations two conflicting normative bases are drawn upon by the participants. The view of the modernisers, who are the agricultural extension staff and leading farmers such as Mugarisi, is that one must attempt to control and regulate the environment with the technology and resources that are available in order to create as favourable conditions as possible for economic production and social reproduction. The second group view the norms of the modernisers with suspicion. For them, technical control has undermined the social and normative structures that regulated their lives and gave them meaning. In particular they fear increasing social differentiation; that if those with adequate resource access are able to increase disproportionately their economic production and hence wealth, they will also increase their power over others. Thus the activist's reference to an in fact fictional norm, that one should not plant until the lineage leaders have judged it right to do so, is a means of expressing this fear.[7]

There is then the subjective domain of individuals' views of their own actions and intentions and those of others. Mugarisi believes others are jealous of his farming success. You are not showing solidarity with the remainder of your community, accuses the wife of the owner of the bull.[8]

Objectifying the components of the lifeworld in this way enables reference to and evaluation of the processes whereby the lifeworld is reproduced. Cultural reproduction, social integration and socialisation can be evaluated, states Habermas, 'according to standards of the rationality of knowledge, the solidarity of members, and the responsibility of the adult personality' (Habermas, *Theory of Communicative Action*, vol. 2 (*TkH* 2) p. 216, in Roderick, 1986, p. 128). But a central issue that has been raised is that of whose and what standards should be applied. On the subject here of early maize planting, I showed in the previous chapter how yield returns bear this out to be a desirable practice. Certainly few farmers would dispute that it is desirable to plant at least some maize after the first rains. The associated technical knowledge is nevertheless still regarded with suspicion because to implement it requires resources which many do not have – and thus favours the wealthier at the expense of the majority. However this particular action of letting the bull into the field was not so much, I would suggest, a result of conflict over technical knowledge – although this was conveyed in the women's statement – but over norms. The key evaluative criterion is that of the solidarity of members.

Local leaders in southern Chirumhanzu, as shall soon be shown through reference to the problem of the early season roaming of animals, themselves perceive this solidarity to be absent. They acknowledge that the lack of effective authority and social integration is a severe constraint to improving the viability of household production activities. By 'effective authority' I mean a legitimately accepted institutional structure which is able to bring about the consensual resolution of social organisational constraints to agricultural production. And as the leaders themselves emphasise, it is crucial that this problem of legitimacy is seen within the context of the resource constraints that the members of the society experience.

THE REPRODUCTION OF SOCIETY

If we continue the line of argumentation presented both in the example and in the preceding theoretical account, Habermas's most fundamental claim can now be comprehended. This is that *communicative action* and the coherence of the lifeworld are essential to the successful reproduction of society.[9]

If we assume that the human species maintains itself through the socially coordinated activities of its members and that this coordination has to be established through communication – and in certain central spheres through communication aimed at reaching agreement – then the reproduction of the species also requires satisfying the conditions of a rationality that is inherent in communicative action. (1984, p. 397)

The second feature of Habermas's theory of communicative action that I wish to refer to here, his reference to the 'paradox of rationalisation', now becomes explicable. So far the lifeworld has been described as a resource that actors draw from in social interaction, but which remains outside their discursive consciousness.[10] This does not mean to say that actors cannot thematise elements of their lifeworld: they can, but always only to a limited degree:

Individuals cannot 'step out' of their lifeworlds; nor can they objectify them in a supreme act of reflection. Particular segments of the lifeworld relevant to given action situations can, of course, be problematized; but this always takes place against an indeterminate and inexhaustible background of other unquestioned presuppositions, a shared global preunderstanding that is prior to any problems or disagreements. (McCarthy, in Habermas, 1984, p. xxv)

Thematisation of aspects of the lifeworld is, argues Habermas, an activity peculiar to modern societies. It is in modern societies that the potential for 'communicatively achieved understanding' has arisen, as opposed to that for 'normatively ascribed agreement' in pre-modern societies (Habermas, 1984, p. 79). And it is through the rationalisation of the lifeworld and the breakdown of religious–metaphysical worldviews that the potential for the former has occurred. Specifically this process involves a decentering of worldviews and a conceptual differentiation of the components of the lifeworld:

> Cognitive development signifies in general *the decentration of an egocentric understanding of the world*. Only to the extent that the formal reference system of the three worlds is differentiated can we form a reflective concept of 'world' and open up access to the world through the medium of common interpretive efforts, in the sense of a cooperative negotiation of situation definitions. (Habermas, 1984, p. 69)

It is in breaking the bonds of non-reflective forms of thought and action that the developmental potential of modernisation lies. This can only be realised, however, if *purposive rational* action is subordinated to decisions reached through unconstrained communication (McCarthy, in Habermas, 1984, p. xxvii). And herein lies the paradox of societal rationalisation.

By his thesis that society can be rationalised in more than one sense, Habermas offers an alternative to Weber's pessimistic thesis that the potential for rationality in the modern world is limited to that of purposive rationality. Not only did Weber see the spread and eventual domination of purposive rationality as inevitable, but he was horrified by what seemed to him the arbitrary – and therefore irrational – value choice that lies at its core. The 'disenchantment' with religion that occurred with the Englightenment has made the rationalisation of society possible. The cost though has been a world 'stripped of all ethical meaning', devalued and objectified as the material and setting for purposive-rational action (McCarthy, in Habermas, 1984, p. xvii). At the core, the choice of values that guide this purposive rational pursuit of interests is arbitrary because 'reason splits itself up into a plurality of value spheres and destroys its own universality' (Habermas, 1984, p. 247).

In its purest form, purposive rationality is merely means–end instrumental rationality in which the sole concern is the technical efficiency of an intervention. Strategic rationality accepts the involvement of human agency in technical interventions, but is concerned only with the manipulation of that agency in the name of means–end efficiency. Expansion of the realm of purposive rationality with the rise and spread of capitalism has made possible the autonomous development of economic and political-administrative sub-systems. In these, action is goal-oriented, or purposive-rational in nature, and coordinated not through language but through the media of money and power. With their growth, these sub-systems have reached into and 'colonised' the lifeworld. This has undermined the processes of cultural reproduction, social integration and socialisation which allow societies and the individuals within them to maintain their identities. In the scope for the domination of instrumental reason lies the potential for the demise of all human freedom.

On the other hand, insists Habermas, there are grounds upon which we can hope for a better future. This is because the rationalisation of the lifeworld also permits an expansion of communicative rationality in society, whereby members come to view the three dimensions of the lifeworld as distinct and open to rational reflection and cooperative, interpretive agreement. The spread of communicative rationality can thus be measured in terms of the success achieved in coordinating action and resolving conflict through unconstrained consensus (Habermas, 1984, p. 15). Tradition becomes critically appropriated, instead of merely accepted. This is the 'bright side of modernity' (Roderick, 1986, p. 133). In the scope for the spread of communicative rationality lies the potential for human emancipation.

Habermas thus answers Weber, as well as the early Frankfurt School theorists, Max Horkheimer and Theodore Adorno, who also held that purposive rationalisation was the only rationalisation process that modernisation has made possible. In believing it to be so, they had insufficiently realised that the reaching into all spheres of life of purposive rationalisation was a distortion of the potential of modernisation, caused by the uncontrolled growth of capitalism:

> Put in a nutshell, this is the thesis of *The Theory of Communicative Action*: rationalisation processes are paradoxical because they undermine the very rationality of the lifeworld which first made societal rationalisation possible. The rationalisation of the lifeworld, initiated by modernity, contains an emancipatory potential which is constantly being threatened by dynamics of societal rationalisation spurred on by capitalist growth. (Benhabib, 1986, p. 236)

This is, then, Habermas's system–lifeworld model, as it is connected to his conceptualisation of the three domains of the symbolically reproduced lifeworld and the distinction this subsequently allows him to make between purposive rationalisation and communicative rationalisation processes in modern society. There are, though, drawbacks to this conceptual schema which detract from its potential to enable one to 'think the unity' of a structural and actor-oriented perspective, the task, I have suggested, a social theoretical framework should help one achieve. The three primary interconnected ambiguities introduced earlier are: the double meaning Habermas imputes to the concept of lifeworld; the nature of the relationship between system and lifeworld; and the connection between the economic sphere of production and the social sphere of interaction in his theoretical framework.

Habermas first uses the concept of the lifeworld, in an expansion of Schutz's phenomenological formulation, to entail the background resource which actors draw upon in social interaction. The lifeworld is conceived as three-dimensional and it is *symbolically* reproduced through the processes of cultural reproduction, social integration and socialisation. In the second sense, where Habermas sets out to make the distinction between system and lifeworld, the lifeworld becomes conceived as a *sphere of action*. It is the *material* reproduction of the lifeworld (as civil society) with which he is now concerned. The key to the conception of this is, he holds, a 'methodological objectification' of the lifeworld as a system:

> Whereas social integration presents itself as part of the symbolic reproduction of the lifeworld – which depends not only on the reproduction of memberships (or solidarities) but also on cultural traditions and socialisation processes – functional integration amounts to a material reproduction of the lifeworld that can be conceived as system maintenance. The transition from one problem area to the other is tied to a change of methodological attitude and conceptual apparatus. Functional integration only comes into view when the lifeworld is objectified as a boundary-maintaining system. (Habermas, *TkH* 2, pp. 348–9)[11]

However, Habermas does more than just conceive of the lifeworld as system through methodological objectification. In addition, he substantively *separates* system from lifeworld (Giddens, 1984, p. 119). His argument is that in modern society the division of labour has resulted in the development of mechanisms to coordinate the diverse production activities and to facilitate the exchange of the products. Specialisation requires a delegation of authority and hence of *power* to those responsible for organisation, whilst product exchange requires the establishment of exchange relations (Habermas, *TkH* 2, p. 239).[12]

In this way the actions of individuals within the sub-systems of the modern political state and economy are coordinated with each other, not so much through understanding, but through the 'functional interlacing of unintended consequences' (Benhabib and Cornell, 1987, p. 6).[13] In modern societies, the operation of these systemic mechanisms becomes increasingly separate from that of the 'socially integrated' action contexts of the lifeworld. The economic and bureaucratic systems not only become independent from lifeworld structures, but penetrate them and cause their disintegration.

In this formulation the lifeworld is now clearly conceived as a sphere of action. A reason for this redefinition, as Baxter points out, is because the lifeworld as resource does not support the substantive system–lifeworld model:

> The lifeworld becomes not the *resources* of culture, society, and personality that serve as background to social action, but informally organised *spheres of action*, such as the family, voluntary associations, neighbourhoods, friendships, and the like ... Habermas must make this implicit redefinition, because as *resources*, culture, society, and personality are essential to all social action, not just communicative action. (1987, p. 73)

This problem of the double meaning of the lifeworld concept is connected to the second difficulty I wish to raise here about Habermas's model. In the modern world Habermas views social conflict as occurring primarily at the interface between system and lifeworld. In a material sense, it is conflict between institutions permeated by purposive rationality and 'civil' society, which they have penetrated. Yet clearly, those employed within economic and bureaucratic institutions do draw upon a lifeworld (as background resource) in their actions and have the competence to engage in communicative action. Contrarily, the family may often be a site of 'coercion and violence', rather than providing a haven from the system (Fraser, 1987, p. 37). Thus, as Benhabib asks, is it Habermas's conception that 'these categories correspond to institutional domains or do they permeate all institutions? Does the family belong to the lifeworld alone, whereas the factory belongs to the system?' (1986, p. 390).

My initial response to these questions is to accept the injunction of Baxter (1987, p. 78) and Ingram (1987, pp. 167–8). Rather than being specified as categorically distinct *spheres* of society, the life-world and system should be retained as different methodological *perspectives* on society. Spheres of action should not be construed as belonging to either system or lifeworld. So, for instance, government institutions *per se* are not 'the system', although they might be postulated as being structured as systems.

For the time being, therefore, I will refer to the lifeworld only in the sense of it being a background resource that is symbolically reproduced; it is society that is materially reproduced. Where the lifeworld is used as a sphere of action I shall refer instead to actual forms of social life, such as 'communal area societies'. Methodologically, the lifeworld perspective is that internalist perspective of a society which an outsider can only reach through the participants (or by becoming a full participant). It is the society as system perspective that can be achieved by an observer.

The third area of difficulty with Habermas's theoretical construction is his treatment of economic activity. Bottomore (1984, p. 81) and Roderick (1986, pp. 156–73) are among theorists who have argued that whereas in his initial work Habermas's intention is to *supplement* Marx's paradigm of production with a paradigm of communication, in his later theory of communicative action the latter *replaces* the former. A distinction between labour (work) and communicative action (interaction) in *Knowledge and Human Interests* (1972) becomes a subsumption of labour under communicative action. Giddens (1982) feels too that Habermas's theory of communicative action embodies insufficient account of contradiction and the significance of power and struggle in social development (p. 160). Habermas has leaned too much towards a Parsonian systems perspective and his critical theory has become over-functionalist. At the social level questions of 'power, sectional interest and struggle' are dealt with inadequately, and at the personal level 'the skilful and knowledgeable character of the everyday participation of actors in social practices' is undervalued (pp. 160–1).

Habermas's concern with conflict and struggle is better expressed in his earlier work. In Chapter 1, I defined communicative rationalisation through a quote from part of this earlier work in which his aim is to reconstruct Marx's concept of historical materialism:

Rationalisation here means extirpating those relations of force that are inconspicuously set in the very structures of communication and that prevent conscious settlement of conflicts, and consensual regulation of conflicts, by means of intrapsychic as well as interpersonal communicative barriers. (1979, pp. 120–1)

This emphasis on the role the relations of production play in sustaining 'systematically distorted communication' I have used so far and shall retain.

The theoretical framework can now be linked into the analysis of social change in the communal areas. I hope this will make both the empirical and theoretical material more explicable.

THE TRAUMA OF RATIONALISATION

In the book I have attempted to show how the agrarian policies of the colonial government initiated between 1930 and 1960 were formulated and implemented according to a purposive rationality. Similarly, I have shown how this rationality continues to underlie post-independent agrarian policies. Some of the adverse social and economic effects have been identified. Attention has also been drawn to the way in which the worldviews of communal area farmers have been totally alienated from the policy process; officialdom has ignored their voices throughout this century.

It is here that Habermas's model of the three-dimensional life-world, allied to his account of the conflicting possibilities of societal rationalisation, can add explanatory power to the analysis. As pre-capitalist modes of production are exposed to and penetrated by capitalism, becoming in the process only forms of production subsumed under a dominant capitalist mode of production, it is the whole organisational basis of society that changes. Local systems of authority based on alliances between lineage and religious leaders and backed by a holistic and naturalistic mythology, breakdown. Threats to the symbolic reproduction of the three-dimensional life-world encourage social and psychological conflict. Members of a society (or institution) view their culture, as it is being reproduced, with dismay; the rules laid down by institutions are not conceived as legitimate; individuals feel alienated and frustrated.

This loss of meaning occurs inevitably as part of the trauma of the 'decentering' of egocentric understandings of the world. This is the process that Horton (1971), to whom Habermas refers, describes as the shift from a 'closed' to an 'open' society. Socially and psychologically, the transition is 'painful, violent and partial' (p. 261).

> Here then we have two basic predicaments: the 'closed' – characterized by lack of awareness of alternatives, sacredness of beliefs, and anxiety about threats to them; and the 'open' – characterized by awareness of alternatives, diminished sacredness of beliefs, and diminished anxiety about threats to them. (p. 231)

Horton describes the open position as a *scientifically* oriented culture (p. 230), that is, one in which a purposive rationality predominates. He admits that the 'open' position has two problems: one, that it is accompanied by the depersonalisation of worldviews and an increasing obsession with material goods; and two, that it is rarely achieved (pp. 224–5, 229, 262). Horton's perspective here is somewhat positivist[14] and like Weber he fails to make the distinction between purposive and communicative rationality. He sees the lack of a pervasive scientific mentality as the major cultural problem of modernism. In contrast Habermas holds it to be the lack of a moral–practical grounding, through communicative action, of the values that orient people's actions.

Lawrence Vambe (1972) in his account of his Shona childhood, *An Ill-fated People*, provides a view that accords with that of Habermas. Vambe holds that the trauma created within his own society was because of the ignobility and baseness of the invading western values. 'In all my village upbringing' says Vambe, through the order and meaning imposed by people's faith in the power of the ancestral spirits, 'I never came across a case of an individual who cracked under the weight of social pressures and personal problems' (p. 21). The elders were convinced they had nothing of spiritual value to learn from what they viewed as a corrupt western materialism. 'They observed that the European was guided by power and wealth rather than by his Christianity' (p. 28).

This was still the 1920s that Vambe was writing about. Since then people have had no choice; rural society has been systematically opened up to the influence of western values. Vambe himself has come to condone the western values – he is now a director in several companies in Harare. But the social and psychological conflict of transition is a vivid part of contemporary rural Shona society. Wilson comments on this from his research. I quote his insight because his involvement in rural society was deeper than mine:

Underlying all these (ecological) problems, respondents mentioned two disrupting forces, forces so powerful that the community is
unable to weather them. The first is westernisation . . . My sense is
that the conflict is largely within people, rather than between them;
everyone wants westernisation and yet everyone endeavours to
hold it at bay. (1988a, p. 2)[15]

And the second disrupting force is the antagonism generated towards
modernising party or government officials, who are seen as 'upstarts
blocking the 'true' land rituals for their own ends' (1988a, p. 2).

It can be argued, then, that conflict – within society, between
lineage and modern forms of authority, and within people, between
egocentric and decentred attitudes towards the world – is thus
endemic to communal area societies. It is a conflict inextricably
linked, too, to changes in the nature of production and threats to
people's economic security. The nature of this general conflict is,
however, particularistic, depending on specific historical and social
factors pertaining to an area. And to illustrate such conflict, requires,
as has been emphasised, a focus on the lifeworld perspective of the
participants, as well as the society as system perspective.

Let us now return to southern Chirumhanzu and, from the
lifeworld perspective, look at the problem of early season livestock
herding.

CHIRUMHANZU: LIVESTOCK HERDING AND AUTHORITY

Compared with most farmers in Maware, Silvester Mugarisi is well
off. His early planted maize is adjacent to the house and protected by
fencing. Yet he still runs the risk of cattle eating the young plants.
Several among the case-study farmers found it infuriating that many
continue to allow their animals to roam after others have planted
their first crops. It is the lazy beer drinkers, said Mrs Jengwa, who do
not want to plough until December and do not herd their animals
until then. Only three families in her lengthy village 'line' plant with
the first rains (Fieldnotes, 17 December 1986, and 28 February 1987).
She had a mentally retarded daughter who during November and
early December spent large parts of her day sitting under a tree
guarding the early crops in their main fields, which were located
2.5 km from their home.

In mid-December, Mrs Machipisi complained of a bull belonging to

Rangwa, a sabhuku (and another of the case-study farmers), which had escaped from a cattle kraal and eaten some of her maize during the evening. Rangwa had been drinking and had not secured his kraal properly. This was the third occasion it had happened (Fieldnotes, 19 December 1986). Rangwa was a special case in that he had lost his wife and eldest son the previous year, through suspected poisoning, and now had little enthusiasm for life. However, during the considerable time he spent at local beer parties he certainly never lacked companions.

The scale of the herding problem encouraged me to question various local leaders on the subject. Many people were clearly being constrained from planting after the first rains, even though it was in the general interest to do so. Some farmers' fields were stony and needed heavier rain before they could be ploughed, but if these people were cattle owners they were in a position to autumn plough their fields, which would assist their planting early.

My questions about the herding issue were put to local leaders in the set of interviews referred to in Chapter 4. Simplicio Mugarisi, the VIDCO chairman for the area in which Silvester Mugarisi (his brother), Mrs Jengwa and the Machipisis live, responded as follows:

> We have that problem. What we do is when we have a meeting we tell the people it is time to herd the cattle. But even then they are not keen. Since I started farming here in '74[16] I have always had enough from my fields, but this year because of cattle I do not have enough . . . If cattle get into fields, between neighbours there is usually nothing that can be done. The owner says, since you are my neighbour there is nothing I can do. (Interview, 14 April 1987)

Mugarisi said that for years he had been the first to plant, but then people had said they should all plant at the same time. However, when he had done this he produced insufficient food and so had returned to using the first rains.

Mawindi, a sabhuku whose area falls within the same VIDCO, also confirmed Mugarisi's view, although in his attitude he was considerably more guarded than Mugarisi:

> In the reserve we are used to the cattle coming in to eat the crops. There is no way of avoiding that because our cattle need a grazing area, but even if you look around you will see there is no suitable place for grazing . . . After harvesting people will let their animals graze, and then will start herding again when people plant. It differs according to the families. Some prefer to start herding in November and some in December. (Interview, 14 April 1987)

Lineage, VIDCO and ZANU (PF) leaders were all agreed that the party (the councillor or party district chairman) was responsible for calling a meeting to discuss such a major problem. However, the leaders from the respective institutional structures clearly felt that having the two structures (lineage, on the one hand, and VICDO and party on the other) led to a displacement, confusion and, ultimately, absence of responsibility. Munyati, the party district chairman, said that they had called a special meeting to discuss the issue in March. Agreement had been reached that herding should be undertaking from the first rains and now the problem of enforcement had been referred to the vanasabhuku (Interview, 15 April 1987).

The lineage leaders denied, however, that they still possessed the influence to perform such a function. In a lengthy reply to my question, sadhunu Mutumiri spoke of the problem being a consequence of the breakdown of the clearcut responsibility of the vanasabhuku for the land, compounded by the shortage of land:

> It is true that those who planted earlier this year got enough maize for their families, but what happens is that there are some people who go for beer parties and don't plant early because they are drinking, and so when someone plants early they will let their cattle go into his fields, and they will say why don't you plant with us.
>
> It is a very crucial issue, because at times we have meetings with those people and at the meetings they will agree, but afterwards they will let their cattle into the fields again . . . The only possibility we see is that we have a big meeting with the people and tell them that if someone allows their cattle to go into someone's fields, then the owner of the cattle should pay something to the farmer.
>
> These days is not the same as before, because in the past the vanasabhuku had the power to say you should pay this, but now the people are no longer listening to the sabhuku. People stopped listening to the vanasabhuku after the liberation war. One of the reasons . . . was the VIDCOs were formed. In some cases people listen to what the VIDCO chairman is saying, but when we talk about the cattle going into the fields that is a problem even to the VIDCO chairman.
>
> Before, if someone found cattle in his field he would straight-away report to the sabhuku. The sabhuku would give him his policeman and he would go and look with the owner. Then the owner of the cattle would have to pay, depending on what the owner wanted . . . This would be mediated by the sabhuku. (Interview, 15 April 1987)

In an adjacent ward closer cooperation between the various leaders had apparently resulted in the institution of a system of fines. Mkata, a VIDCO chairman I interviewed from Chingwena ward, spoke wistfully of this (Interview, 15 April 1987). But in Maware and Chingwena wards, all leaders provided the impression that their authority was weak. The councillor and party leaders were recognised as the official leaders, but even they acknowledged that on the herding issue they could only obtain people's support with the active backing of the vanasabhuku. And this backing, from vanasabhuku such as Mawindi and Rangwa, was lacking, although on the other side of the valley the more active leadership of sabhuku Mazhlatini had brought about greater cooperation between households. His son, Robert, vice-secretary of the savings club and a member of the parish committee of the Catholic Church, called the non-cooperators 'barbarians', thus clearly seeing them as being non-modern and resistant to change.

The norm accepted by the more progressive then, is that, as in the Mazhlatini line, households should get together and arrange the sharing of herding duties immediately the first crops have germinated. This attitude conflicts, however, with those who believe, like the wife of the owner of the bull, that solidarity means planting (and herding) only in December.

The method of opposition the latter group use is that of passive resistance. Members of government or other outside agencies that work in southern Chirumhanzu know the people as a stubborn, suspicious and passive lot. As Wilson (1988c) notes, this method of resistance was well practised by many of the Shona peoples against the colonial authorities:

> A common view the Shona like to present of their methods of opposition is that they keep quiet or agree in meetings, refer to others whenever confronted, and generally use every possible obfuscating and delaying tactic in such a way as ultimately to outlive any authoritarianism.

Resistance in southern Chirumhanzu has not always been passive, however. We have seen that the implementation of the Land Husbandry Act in 1961 was met with active and violent opposition. This followed the disastrous years of the mid and late 1950s when the colonial authorities crippled the local economy, first by jamming people into the area from the Zinyaningwe purchase area and then by forcing through the devastating destocking exercise of 1958. Sabhuku

Mazhlatini, one of those who became a master farmer and was responsible for pegging fields in his area during land husbandry, described how he was chased by people wielding axes (Interview, 14 April 1987).

Once one is aware of this experience, it is not surprising that elders who lost land and cattle – their wealth and power – at this time, should still be suspicious of extralocal attempts to initiate change in the agrarian economy. Moreover, the resistance to herding suggests that there is also resistance to the imposition of a new local leadership structure, because many see it as being subject to the government's direction. In Chapter 4 reference was made to occasions when at the behest of the District Administration, VIDCO leaders have spoken about the introduction of grazing schemes, only to have had the idea rejected out of hand.

Another thorny resource issue is that of land allocation. Although formally the right is now delegated by the District Council to the VIDCO chairmen, in practice the chairmen accept that normatively it is the vanasabhuku that have the authority. One VIDCO chairman went so far as to say that, 'There is no VIDCO chairman who can do anything without the know-how of the sabhuku. The truth is the VIDCO is also under the sabhuku' (S. Hove, Interview, 16 April 1987). Since there can be up to six village areas within a VIDCO, each with its own sabhuku, by 'under' he clearly means in terms of legitimately accepted authority.

> When [the VIDCOs] were introduced, we were told they would work together with the vanasabhuku, and on land allocation, also with the extension workers. When we started operating as VID-COs we had problems because the vanasabhuku resisted it. They thought they had no power any longer. We tried to solve the problem on the land side by allowing the vanasabhuku to keep their authority over land. (Interview, 16 April 1987)

Two days after this interview, an incident occurred at the Maware Independence Day celebrations which also highlighted the friction that has been generated by this new structure.[17] During a speech the ZANU district chairman admonished 'those who do not believe in VIDCOs. They shall see what shall be coming to them next time.' This statement caused the inebriated son of a local sabhuku to sway forward from where he had been standing. 'You have a district chairman who is selling the people to ZANU', he shouted. Members of the audience eventually shut him up as he continued to make belligerent interventions, but his statements were not without support and are indicative of the confusion and conflict over authority. And much of this conflict is about the social norms that authority should uphold and who should be responsible for establishing them.

It is ironic that the vanasabhuku themselves were only given their own authority by the colonial administration, first as tax collectors and then as allocators of the land in their villages during implementation of the Land Husbandry Act (Weinrich, 1964, p. 18; Mazhlatini, interview, 14 April 1987). But the vanasabhuku still formed part of the lineage patriarchy which aimed to preserve what they could of the normative fabric of society against the inroads of the capitalist economy and colonial state. The VIDCO chairmen, on the other hand, have their positions foremostly because they are members of ZANU (PF), not because they are lineage leaders. Munyati, the party district chairman, in his speech at the Independence Day celebrations, ridiculed the uncooperative vanasabhuku as 'Smith's vanasabhuku'. However, whereas people do see the new government in an abstract sense as being theirs, when it comes to concrete issues such as the question of land, they do not trust the agrarian policies that are being promoted.

The lack of a local organisational structure that is accepted as legitimate by both the people and the state in Chirumhanzu, means that agreements reached about the herding of cattle are supported neither by normative nor formal sanction, and hence are valueless. As a consequence people fear to use the first rains for planting crops and they produce less food.

CHIWUNDURA: GROUP CREDIT AND DEBT

Farmers in the Mtengwa ward of Chiwundura do not share the problem of early season herding since all their arable fields are fenced. As many of the settlers have arrived within the last twenty years, they also do not have the bitter memories of the land husbandry era to inhibit an acceptance of social change. Culturally and psychologically, the development of the small-holding land use pattern means that families have developed a greater sphere of privacy around them. Resource exchanges have an extra edge and clarity to them. There is a keener interest in using scarce resources efficiently and land intensively. Without pushing the comparison too far, the Chiwundura economy is more distinctly privatised and commercialised than that of southern Chirumhanzu.

A factor that has helped this process along was the launching in 1984 of a group credit scheme. In the previous year Agritex had begun the pilot Training and Visit (T and V) extension project in Chiwundura and the other two communal areas in the Gweru region, Shurugwi and Lower Gweru. The T and V system with its emphasis on improving the efficiency with which agricultural 'messages' are passed down from extension agents to farmers has an inherent Green Revolution bias to it. The focus is on simple, replicable packages of recommendations, which are designed to increase farmers' yields – neither the sustainability nor the viability of their production, but the size of their output.

Most communal area farmers in the Midlands already use hybrid seed, and so the main change farmers were being urged to adopt was the increased use of inorganic fertiliser. In 1983, with the drought at its peak, Agritex was also promoting maize production, as it is both the staple food and a cash crop. It followed naturally, therefore, that as an adjunct to T and V there should be a drive to promote the use of credit for the acquisition of crop packs consisting of maize seed, fertiliser, and pesticide. With the support of Agritex, the Agricultural Finance Corporation (AFC) and a particularly enthusiastic Department of Cooperatives extension official set about the launching of credit in Chiwundura.[18] Through the efforts of the latter official a group credit scheme was implemented.

Since 1980, when few communal area farmers received credit, the AFC has considerably expanded this part of its service. Expansion occurred particularly between the 1983/4 and 1985/6 seasons. In 1983/4, 39 000 communal area farmers received loans totalling Z$13.24 million; two years later 85 700 farmers received Z$41.8 million (Government of Zimbabwe, 1986b, p. 107; Danida, 1985, pp. 14–15). A high proportion of these loans have been made, however, to farmers in the natural region II area of Mashonaland and Manicaland. In the Midlands, where the bulk of loans outside natural region II have been made, 15 000 loans were made to communal area farmers in 1984/5, out of the national total of 50 000 loans granted (AFC Western Region Manager, interview 21 March 1985).

This expansion of credit supply to communal area farmers, especially outside the more favourable natural region II area, was viewed with some trepidation by the AFC. Their recovery rate from individual farmers, especially during the drought, had been poor. Bratton

(1985, p. 22) comments that the AFC individual loans scheme was losing half of its capital stock each year through defaulting. For this reason, as early as 1980, the AFC had agreed to provide seasonal loans to 2600 farmers in 100 well-established Silveria House groups in Mashonaland East (Riddell Commission, 1981, para. 184; Bratton, 1985, p. 15).[19] In the Wedza area another experiment with group lending was launched in 1983/4.[20] The initiation of the Chiwundura group lending scheme in 1984/5 was, though, the first group scheme to be tried in the Midlands.

There were two reasons why the AFC viewed the concept favourably. First, since communal area farmers do not have freehold tenure, their lack of collateral is a constraint to the provision of credit. The AFC felt that lending through a group would engender a stronger loan discipline, 'in that the committee feels it has an obligation to ensure that the loans are repaid to the AFC' (AFC Western Region Manager, interview, 21 March 1985). Second, the scheme would cut down administration costs and allow them to reach larger numbers of farmers, since ostensibly the farmer groups concerned would be responsible for the vetting of applicants and the recovery of loans. Finally, farmer leaders themselves were in favour of the group scheme. The ward cooperatives administering the scheme would gain a 2 per cent discount on bulk ordering, but more important, the bulk transporting would lower the overall cost of the seed and fertiliser to farmers. Indeed, in 1984/5 the Chiwundura farmers saved Z$4.75 (8.2 per cent) on the price of a 0.5 ha maize package, as compared with the prices of the Somabhula Cooperative Union, which had previously delivered the inputs to those farmers receiving loans.

The Cooperative Union was unpopular with farmers particularly over handling charge deductions[21] and the late payment of cheques for crops marketed through the union. The Department of Cooperatives extension officer who registered the ward cooperatives had a terrific battle to overcome his provincial superior's sustained attempts to block the process. The Cooperative Union was administered by the government agency, and to farmers' annoyance the financial balance sheets of the union were never presented for their inspection. In 1983/4, when the drought resulted in farmers defaulting, the union somehow managed to acquire a lorry, although no authorisation was provided by members (Interview, 22 March 1986).[22]

It was only therefore through the persistence of the cooperative extension officer that the scheme was able to commence in 1984. It was a propitious season for it to do so, for after three years of drought, 1984/5 brought excellent harvests throughout the country. On the surface results, too, appeared encouraging and at the end of 1985 the then Midlands PAEO commented that, 'the Z$137 000 put out by AFC through seven leaders was completely repaid by mid-September – never been heard of before' (personal communication).

Of the seven cooperatives, which included three in the adjacent Masvori resettlement area and Gokomere small-scale commercial farming area, the Mtengwa ward cooperative was the flagship. Over 500 people received loans totalling Z$74 000, all of which was repaid. And yet three years later in 1988, the cooperative, without any theft of money having occurred, had collapsed and its committee was totally discredited.

There are two key factors to this collapse; one, the way the scheme was organised and managed, and two, the nature of the agricultural environment. The effects of the first on the scheme as a whole have exacerbated the implications of the second for individual households.

It might have been expected that the struggle to establish the cooperatives would have strengthened the cohesiveness of the organisations. This did not happen, certainly in the case of the Mtengwa ward cooperative, owing to awareness of the cooperative officer's struggle failing to penetrate beyond the small leadership. The Mtengwa ward cooperative has an executive committee of three, which is unusually small for a communal area organisation. The bulk of the work of managing the cooperation has fallen on the secretary, N. P. Zinduru.

In the first outwardly successful year of the group credit scheme's operation, three things went wrong with the organisation of the Mtengwa cooperative.[23] There was a dispute between the AFC and the executive over the vetting system for loan applicants. The executive received no training and has not done so since. And communication between the executive and members, poor at the outset, subsequently declined even further.

The seeds of the collapse of the Mtengwa cooperative were planted at the beginning of its life. The issue was the vetting procedure. According to Zinduru, the secretary, the AFC insisted on registering all those who wanted loans as they said credit should be accessible to everyone (Fieldnotes, 11 December 1986). The AFC staff concerned disputed this, saying that the cooperative committee members were vetting applicants entering the building in which they were sitting (Fieldnotes, 6 January 1987). But Zinduru was adamant they were restricted from performing this function.[24] As a consequence, many of those who received loans in the first year had no intention of repaying them. Some sold the fertiliser, others said the government should be providing it free as drought relief. One case-study farmer spoke of their VIDCO chairman having taken 18 bags of fertiliser in his name, 18 bags in his wife's name, 18 in his son's name, and another 18 for good measure (Fieldnotes, 10 April 1987). He was one of the 37 people who by 1987 still had an outstanding debt in excess of Z$100 from the 1984/5 season. Although Z$74 000 was reclaimed by the AFC through a stop order, when the ward cooperative marketed through the GMB in 1985, Z$34 000 worth of loans were still outstanding. Thus a full 40 per cent of the money recovered by the AFC was actually profit owed to farmers marketing surpluses.

These farmers were the leading farmers. By the time they eventually received payment for their surpluses at the end of 1986, they were fed up with the organisation and leadership of the cooperative. Attempting to recover the outstanding debts from 1984/5 has been Zinduru's nightmare. Lawyers were employed and the messenger of the court attempted to repossess furniture and even livestock from the debtors, all adding to the ward cooperative's bill. Zinduru estimates over ten of the debtor families have emigrated from Chiwundura. Six have fled to the newly opened up Urungwe area in the Zambezi valley. Others have gone to Gokwe, another family to Bindura, and several men working in Harare were reluctant to return home (Fieldnotes, 14 April 1988).

Amidst this disaster, the farmers who had marketed through the cooperative did not understand what was taking place. Rumours spread; Nhonga, the Takunda farmer who is chairman of both the Mtengwa ward farmers' committee and the Chiwundura area committee, being an instigator. He accused Zinduru and the cooperative's chairman of theft, but as the Z$1729 he had had to wait a year to receive is a small fortune by communal farming standards, he had cause to be dissatisfied. In 1985/6 the AFC relinquished control of the vetting procedure to the cooperative committee which immediately tightened control. The chairmen of the six farmers' groups in Mtengwa West and the equivalent groups in Mtengwa East became responsible for approving names in their areas and then submitting their lists to the cooperative committee. This was arranged successfully, but the chairmen continued to speculate rather than be accurately informed about the cooperatives overall financial position.

The Mtengwa cooperative disintegrated, therefore, not because the cooperative's management committee lacked any feeling of obligation to ensure that members repaid their loans, which was the concern of the AFC regional manager, but because many of the members themselves lacked such a sense of obligation.[25]

After the debacle of the 1985 marketing period, the cooperative continued to slide, but now largely because of the poor agricultural seasons. In 1985/6 farmers borrowed Z$60 000 through the cooperative. There was lengthy mid-season drought and crop returns were poor. Many farmers who did market made individual arrangements, as they did not trust the cooperative leaders. The cooperative committee, however, avoided the stop order system by using the chairman's own GMB grower's number instead of that of the cooperative. So those who did use the cooperative were paid out immediately in cash this time. The problem now was that when the loan came due on 31 December 1986, only a minimal amount had actually been collected by Zinduru and paid to the AFC. A further group loan of Z$40 000 had also already been taken for the 1986/7 season. Drought followed and the few leading farmers who did produce surpluses sold these informally to benefit from the escalation of local prices. The cooperatives debt was now Z$100 000 and rising at an annual compound interest rate of 14 per cent. The AFC refused to give any further loan in 1987/8 and would not even supply empty sacks for the farmers on the Mtorohuku irrigation scheme who wished to deliver to the GMB in 1987.[26]

This means no farmers received credit in Mtengwa ward in 1987. Instead, some of the leading farmers who had the cash available, raised Z$1200 between them and bought fertiliser as a cash group. Although this is not all the money that was spent on fertiliser use in 1987, it is fair to describe the life of the Mtengwa ward cooperative as the rise and fall of inorganic fertiliser use in the ward in the 1980s. For, in addition to the disaster of the ward cooperative, many farmers who have obtained loans through the cooperative and do not have access to an outside wage income, have become horribly indebted. These are farmers who repaid their original loans. They have thus succumbed in just two seasons – 1985/6 and 1986/7.

Taking an agricultural loan has one fundamental economic requirement. The recipient needs to have good reason to believe it possible to produce each season the minimum required to repay the loan. If there is no guarantee of this – and 1981/2, 1982/3, 1983/4, 1985/6, 1986/7 are seasons so far this decade that peasant farmers have defaulted in the Midlands – then loans are a trap.[27]

Of the fifteen case-study farmers, seven have fallen seriously into this trap. Table 6.1 provides a summary of their credit situations, as

Table 6.1 Chiwundura case study households: credit use 1984–7

	1984/5 (Z$)	1985/6 (Z$)	1986/7 (Z$)	Current debt (Z$)	Comments
Leading farmers					
Takavada	Loan: 446.00 Sales: 2360.00 Repayment: 446.00	Loan: 587.00 Sales: 1073.50 Repayment: Nil	Loan: 462.00 Sales: 768.00 Repayment: 200.00	85/6: 587.00 Int: 82.18 86/7: 462.00 Paid: 200.00 Debt: 931.18	Income from 85/6 sales to GMB banked with policeman son who then used part himself. Rmnder used on school fees. $200 repd in 1987 given by 2 other sons.
Nhonga	Loan: 374.00 Sales: 1389.00 Repayment: 374.00	Loan: Nil Sales: 958.75	Loan: 462.00 Sales: 956.00 Repayment: ?	86/7: 462.00 Paid: ?	Dispute with Coop Sec as to whether inputs ordered were collected in 85. Intended to repay 86 loan from local sales
Mangwalala	Loan: 342.00 Sales: Loan value + surplus	Loan: 449.00 Sales: 295.00 Repayment: Nil	Loan: 489.00 Sales: 32.00 Repayment: 300.00	85/6: 449.00 Int: 62.86 86/7: 489.00 Paid: 300.00 Debt: 700.86	Wife died in Jan 86 & income from 85/6 sales covered funeral costs. Bull sold to make payment in 87.
Mrs Skosana	Loan: Nil Sales: 147.50	Loan: 320.00 Sales: Nil Repayment: 320.00	Loan: 385.00 Sales: 20.00 Repayment: ?	86/7: 385.00 Paid: ?	Loan repd in 86 from husband's salary. 28 bags harvested and used mainly as pig feed. Debt in 87 to be paid by husband.
Middle-farmers					
K. Mugoni	Loan: 238.00 Sales: 841.25 Repayment: 221.75	Loan: 248.00 Sales: 221.25 Repayment: 221.25	Loan: 156.00 Sales: Nil Repayment: Nil	84/5: 16.75 85/6: 26.75 Int: 6.09 86/7: 156.00 Debt: 205.59	Part of surplus from 84/5 bartered for 2 cows & rmd used on building materials for a house. Now seeking to use antheap instead of fertiliser.
Mrs R. Mugoni	Loan: 208.00 Sales: 870.25 Repayment: 208.00	Loan: Nil Sales: 162.25	Loan: Nil Sales: Nil	Debt: Nil	84/5 used to buy some of materials for a house. Inputs for last two seasons remitted by husband.

					Notes
Mrs T. Mabuku	Loan: Nil Sales: 330.00	Loan: Nil Sales: Nil	Loan: 138.00 Sales: Nil Repayment: Nil	86/7: 138.00 Debt: 138.00	Husband had no work at time, so loan needed in 86/7. Debt to be paid by him.
Mrs Mangamba	Loan: 238.00 Sales: 325.75 Repayment: 238.00	Loan: 138.00 Sales: Nil Repayment: 50.00	Loan: 154.00 Sales: Nil Repayment: ?	85/6: 88.00 Int: 12.32 86/7 154.00 Debt: 254.32	Will attempt to repay loan gradually from money remitted by husband.
Mathe	Loan: Nil	Loan: Nil Sales: Nil	Loan: Nil Sales: Nil	Debt: Nil	Elderly couple whose cultivation is unintensive, as have no dependents. Have no d.p.
Poor farmers Komboni	Loan: 168.50 Sales: 250.75 Repayment: 168.50	Loan: 138.00 Sales: 15.00 Repayment: Nil	Loan: Nil Sales: Nil	85/6: 138.00 Int: 19.32 Debt: 157.32	Komboni has TB, wife does much of work, and looks after chid with TB.
Mrs Kumira		Loan: 141.00 Sales: 44.25 Repayment: 44.25	Loan: 156.00 Sales: Nil Repayment: Nil	85/6: 96.75 Int: 13.55 86/7: 156.00 Debt: 266.30	Has no draught power and an ill adult daughter who cannot do much work.
Hozheri	No land	Loan: Nil Sales: Nil		Debt: Nil	Young couple: land and seed given, draught power repaid with labour.
Mrs Mkucha	Loan: 104.00 Sales: 202.50 Repayment: 104.00	Loan: 138.00 Sales: Nil Repayment: Nil		85/6: 138.00 Int: 19.32 Debt: 157.32	Has no draught power.
Moyo	Loan: Nil	Loan: 44.00 Sales: 44.00 Repayment: 44.00		Debt: Nil	No longer wishes to use a loan.
Tangwena	Loan: Nil Sales: Nil	Loan: Nil Sales: Nil		Debt: Nil	

at July 1987. Those most straitened are the leading and poor farmers. Two of the leading farmers, Takavada and Mangwalala, had had debts of over Z$1000. Takavada, by drawing upon his working sons, had been able to reduce some of his arrears, but Mangwalala resorted to selling one of his prized draught oxen. Short of labour and alternative income sources, Mangwalala, one of those few who is committed solely to agricultural activities for his income, is likely to be handicapped by the debt for many years.

Three of the women farmers who have loans are not as worried as others by their situation as they have working husbands to bail them out. They are dependent, however, both on the security of their husband's job and upon his largesse. For other middle farmers, such as the K. Mugonis, the debt has prejudiced their children's chances of attending secondary school.

Some of those in the worst situation are the poor farmers who have been tempted into credit. Mrs Mkucha and Mrs Kumira, both widows, are two of those whose vulnerability has caused them great stress. Their debts are respectively just Z$157.32 and Z$266.30, but they are unlikely to ever produce enough to pay these off. Both work exceedingly hard and are proud women. Apart from the financial worry, it is also the indignity of becoming impoverished that they have to suffer.

The launching of T and V, and the introduction of credit brought about, as has been mentioned, an overwhelming emphasis on maize production. In 1986/7, 74 per cent of the cropped area in Chiwundura was under maize, and this was a decline over the previous two seasons, when crops such as sunflowers had not been grown. As late as the early 1970s, the small grains, rapoko, mhunga and sorghum, had still been grown widely on people's dryland fields. Maize cultivation had been restricted mainly to the wet land gardens, where it was intercropped with rice and often sold as green maize in the markets of Gweru and Kwekwe (Theisen, 1973, p. 15). The growing predominance of maize in the farming system took place as agricultural production intensified with the development of the smallholding land use pattern. An eventual consequence, as Mangwalala ruefully acknowledged, is that in droughts the reserves of the small grains that people previously had in their granaries are no longer there.[28] Credit had therefore helped bring about a weakening of households' food security.

The agronomic consequence of farmers' traumatic experience in the last few years with credit, is that they are using less inorganic

Table 6.2   Chiwundura and Chirumhanzu case study households: inorganic fertiliser usage 1984/5–1986/7

Farmer category	Type of fertiliser	1984/5 ave (bags)	Season 1985/6 ave (bags)	1986/7 ave (bags)	1986/7 Ave maize area	Bags of fertiliser per ha
Chiwundura						
Leading	Cmp D	14.0	12.5	12.3	3.79 ha	2.57
	AN	7.0	6.0	7.3		1.42
Middle	Cmp D	6.0	4.0	2.8	1.62 ha	1.85
	AN	3.0	2.6	1.8		1.11
Poor	Cmp D	3.0	2.2	0.5	0.91 ha	0.55
	AN	2.0	1.2	0.7		0.73
Chirumhanzu						
Leading	Cmp D	8.5	9.0	8.8	2.86 ha	2.58
	AN	6.5	5.8	6.5		1.57
Middle	Cmp D	1.3	0.8	1.2	1.34 ha	0.75
	AN	1.0	1.2	1.0		0.54
Poor	Cmp D	2.0	1.0	1.3	1.06 ha	1.18
	AN	1.0	0.5	0.6		0.59

Note: In the Mavhaire area of Chirumhanzu, both middle farmers and poor farmers received 1 bag Compound D and 1 bag AN as part of a Christian Care 'inputs'-for-work programme in 1986/7. As poor farmers were cultivating less land this increased their use of fertiliser relative to middle farmers. (Bags are 50 kg.)

fertiliser. Table 6.2 shows that in Chiwundura, among the case-study farmers, there was a slight decline in purchased fertiliser use even in 1986/7. In the 1987/8 season, although I do not have full figures, this decline was dramatic. Mangwalala, after obtaining 12 bags the previous year, purchased none in 1987. The three bags he used were part of a drought relief pack he obtained as a member of the National Farmers' Association of Zimbabwe.[29] He stated that in future he would only purchase fertiliser if he had cash on hand (Fieldnotes, 14 April 1988).[30]

If the adverse seasons have not been enough, the rate of increase of the price of fertiliser has also far outstripped that of the producer price for maize. Farmers use the ratio between the cost of fertiliser and the GMB price for maize (both per bag) as a comparative measure. In 1984/5, 1.2 bags of maize were required to pay off 1 bag of fertiliser. By 1986/7 the ratio was 1.8 and it has since risen again. The government is 'cheating' us, said one farmer.

This gloomy picture is not restricted to Chiwundura. In Shurugwi, where T and V was also implemented, in the 1987/8 season, leading farmers were moving out of credit to the extent they could scrape cash together to form a cash group for the bulk purchase of seed and more limited quantities of fertiliser.[31] But cash groups are only really an option for those few with a secure source of income.

For all farmers, but especially the less privileged, the Chirumhanzu savings clubs that possess depots provide a financial and input supply service that has several economic advantages over the use of credit. These allow farmers to adapt more successfully to environmental variability. But it is in the organisational differences that, in contrast with the Chiwundura ward cooperatives, the real strength of the savings clubs lies.

THE SAVINGS CLUBS AS INTEGRATIVE ORGANISATIONS.

The economic advantages the savings clubs offer over the use of credit are fourfold.[32] First, farmers obtain inputs more cheaply as they do not have to pay the 14 per cent interest on them.[33] Second – and very crucially – because they are using their savings farmers can gear their level of investment in inputs to their current financial status. If a season is poor and yields low returns they are able to reduce their fertiliser use the following season. Many Chiwundura farmers have become indebted because they cannot do this.

Third, the Chirumhanzu farmers are also able to adapt their levels of investment to the quality of the season at hand. For example, in 1986/7 the drought did not warrant the application of large quantities of top-dressing, which farmers therefore avoided purchasing. Chiwundura farmers, however, were left with unused bags of fertiliser on which they were paying interest.

Finally, through being able to delay the purchase of inputs until their time of application, farmers are able to accrue additional interest on their savings. The fact that the Chirumhanzu farmers are gaining interest on their savings whilst the Chiwundura farmers are facing accumulating compound interest on their debts, creates a tremendous psychological advantage. Southern Chirumhanzu is a drier region than Chiwundura, but it was amongst those farmers in the latter area who owed money to the AFC that the drought created greater anxiety.

Nevertheless, the economic factors, whilst central to the value of the service provided for members, are not those most central to a club's continuing health. These are, rather, organisational and managerial factors. The clubs that have functioned most successfully – and Maware has been one – have done so for two main reasons. First, they receive sound outside advice, training and auditing. This enables them to continue to manage their own affairs, even when the club expands its range of services and its operations become more sophisticated. But these services are available to all clubs and therefore it does not explain differences between them. It is the second reason that is club specific. This is the extent to which there has developed within the club's management a sense of responsibility towards members, and the extent to which members are able to hold the committee accountable for its actions.

The savings clubs, of which in 1987 there were 34 in the Gweru diocese of the Catholic Church (which covers Midlands and Masvingo provinces), were first begun in the mid-1950s. Then their aim was to enable people to pay school fees. Their agricultural role only began in the mid-1960s, when the Green Revolution idea of crop input packages first caught hold (Interview with G. Scheu, CADEC, 25 March 1985). During the liberation war the savings clubs went somewhat into abeyance, and it is only since 1983, with the takeover of a new CADEC coordinator in Gweru, that their most significant growth has occurred. In early 1984 members savings were collectively Z$175 489. By 1987 these had grown to Z$410 885, and in just the year between early 1986 and early 1987 membership grew from 4490 to 5375 people. The financial attraction for individual members is that the clubs pay interest on the basis of the highest level that members' balances stand at each month.[34] For the club itself, financial success depends on whether it can manage to establish a depot, from which it can sell to members bulk-purchased goods such as maize seed, fertiliser, maize, cement, chicken mash, plough parts, and so on. During the 1982–4 drought, for instance, one of the largest Chirumhanzu clubs, Chinyuni (membership 1150), turned over Z$2000 of maize meal each month at a government fixed profit margin of 9 per cent – 108 per cent annually (Interview with G. Scheu, 25 March 1985). The clubs with depots have established them with the aid of CADEC grants, but the management has to provide the necessary initiative and cohesion. Between November 1986 and August 1987, the membership of the Maware club grew from 84 to 187 members. And in the financial year between audits in February 1986 and February 1987 its invested savings grew from Z$9579–51 to Z$14 828–79 and its reserve fund from Z$4126–11 to Z$4840–02.[35] In 1986 the club paid out an interest rate to members of 10.9 per cent, and in 1987 of 14.2 per cent. These rates ranked as the best savings deal for small savers in the country.

During this same audit period the Mavhaire club was stagnating. Its membership grew from 154 to 167 people, but savings declined from Z$9028.83 to Z$7733.52. Situated midway between the St Josephs Hama and Maware depots, both about five kilometres distant, members travelled to these to obtain their inputs. Consequently, the club's returns were low and the interest paid in 1986 and 1987 was 1.3 per cent and 3.6 per cent, respectively. The chairman was unpopular. Concerned with his own status rather than the health of the club, he was prone to creating squabbles. Neither Maware nor Mavhaire has, however, been beset by the problems of theft and fraudulence such as experienced by two of the large clubs in Chirumhanzu, Chinyuni and Holy Cross (518 members). But these latter clubs are still functioning, and, following their experience, members are more likely to ensure that the committee is accountable to them and open in advising them of the club's financial position.

The successful testing of these clubs' resilience is fundamentally a tribute to CADEC's philosophy of being consistent in its supportive role, and in being firm that the clubs should be self-managing and serve an integrative and enabling role within their communities. On the basis of their audits, CADEC are able to monitor the progress of clubs and hence advise the clubs individually as well as assess overall training needs. When audits reveal financial malpractices, a meeting of members is called and their attention is drawn to these. But remedial action, if it is to be taken, has to be decided upon by the members.

To summarise, then, the insertion of an organisation, such as a ward cooperative or savings club, into a communal area society in which the normative structures required to sustain a modern institution are fragile and only partially developed, is a sensitive and difficult task. Such organisations are not part of people's experience and thus they will not emerge autonomously. Reference to Habermas's lifeworld concept can be made here. One can suggest that if members are able to internalise this experience of a more modern form of organisation this will assist the symbolic reproduction of a lifeworld in which the dimensions of culture, society and personality come to be differentiated out. Once committee and club members can evaluate efficiency, solidarity and individual responsibility as distinct criteria and act accordingly, the ability of the club to survive setbacks and offer a valuable service to members, will be considerably enhanced.

That these organisational and managerial factors connected with the development of a competent and responsible committee are foremost amongst CADEC's concerns, can be seen through reference to their annual report for 1987:

> Time and again we find some irregularities in some of the clubs but through regular auditing and through submission of monthly reports by the clubs, we manage to intervene in time so that no big losses occur. Since we started working with the Savings Clubs we emphasize that we are at their service and not running their clubs. This implies that they have the freedom to work with us and make use of our auditing services. This arrangement certainly helped the clubs to feel more responsible and self-reliant. Unfortunately it also happened in the case of Makanya and Gokomere, that the Executive refused auditing.
>
> . . . the Gokomere Club . . . wrote to us that they are not ready for auditing and would inform us when they are. Several appeals from our side have gone unheard and we will now have to inform the Parish Council and the people about this situation. We find this specially regrettable as Gokomere was one of the first and had a good record through all the years. We still have the problem in some of the very big and old clubs that the members use the Savings Club just like a bank and do not feel personally involved. Annual General Meetings are poorly attended and people only come forward when there is a problem.
>
> A very popular way has been found by some of the Clubs in the Takawira [Chirumhanzu] District. After the audit, they use part of the club fund to provide for a big feast with plenty of meat and drinks. On such an occasion, most of the members attend and it gives us, as the auditors, a valuable chance to give a report on our findings and other comments. (pp. 6–7)

Maware had such a party after their audit in January 1987. It was the most cheerful event in the area in an otherwise dry and depressing year. Membership soared afterwards – another 23 people joined within the next month (Fieldnotes, 24 March 1987).

SOCIAL ORGANISATION AND CHANGE

The organisations that have been mentioned so far have their roots in other non-lineage organisations. The Mtengwa ward cooperative committee were, or had been, members of the Mtorohuku irrigation committee.[36] The savings club executives usually had had experience as members of local church or parish councils, responsible for organising services and church affairs. In many instances too they were often teachers, although if trouble set in they were viewed with suspicion if they came from outside the area.

A different category of evolutionary organisation is the *mushandir-apamwe* (working together) farmer group. Traditions of labour cooperation are usually inherent in any rural society, though over-romanticised. Shona work group traditions, such as *nhimbe* (based on the provision of beer for labour) and *jangano* (based on the recipro-cation of labour) did and still do take place. However, these institutions, particularly the more generally found *nhimbe*, are often another form of labour extraction rather than being equity-oriented (Cheater, 1984, pp. 63–7; 1974). Some farmers in the study areas still claim they use *nhimbe* at periods of peak labour demand, but in practice the occasions on which they do are usually rare.[37] Payment in cash or grain for labour is much more common and, of course, it is only the better-off families who can afford this. In the last chapter it was shown, for instance, how poorer farmers, to pay for the hire of draught oxen, have to expend considerably more time in earning the cash than is spent by the owner performing the work. Clusters of households, usually kinship based, but not necessarily entirely so, may also exchange resources on a loosely reciprocal or sub-economic basis (that is, below the going rate). Reference to this type of exchange was also made in the last chapter.[38]

The mushandirapamwe group, in contrast, incorporates house-holds from the area of an entire farmer group and cuts across the usual network of resource exchange relationships and systems. To function, the group has to offer participants clear individual benefits and to derive an acceptably equitable method of resource sharing. Such a group developed in Phumelela in 1985/6. The wife of Mangwalala, the farmer group chariman, was instrumental in starting it and encouraging people to join. 'She used to sing, and stayed cheerful and hard working' (Mrs Skosana, fieldnotes, 17 March 1987). Mrs Mangwalala died in January 1986 and the continued organisation of the club by Mangwalala, supported by Mrs Skosana, was spurred probably by the desire to make something of her initiative, as well as their own Christian ethic, to which both referred.[39] The group thrived in 1986/7. Its membership grew from seven to sixteen households, of which ten had draught power units. Each member of the group had between 0.5 and 1.0 ha of maize ploughed and planted in the period after the first rains. Having seven or more draught teams available all at once meant that, even in a one-hectare field, the final harrowing could be completed within three hours of the first furrow being cut.[40] This maximised moisture conservation, vital to ensuring reasonable yields in the drought season. Mrs Mkucha, the elderly widow, swore that she would 'live the mushandirapamwe to death' (Fieldnotes, 6 December 1986).[41] The role of women in the success of the group was fundamental. In group discussions and decision-making they were particularly vocal and influential.[42]

The mushandirapamwe group's activities were not welcomed by all farmers in the area. Some leading farmer non-members complained about the reduced earnings from hiring out draught power they had experienced since the group's inception. For instance, in the 1986/7 season, the poor farmer, Tangwena, had one hectare of his land ploughed voluntarily by the group,[43] and he subsequently became a member assisting in other group operations elsewhere. As comparative newcomers and without relatives in the area, his family had formerly been rather isolated. Others who had previously hired draught animals were also in the group and a few non-members were able to hire the whole group at a rate lower than that charged by individual farmers. Mangwalala deliberately intended that these people should be cut out – 'they can go on crying in the wind' (Fieldnotes, 21 April 1987). In the autumn of 1987, the group agreed to help members with activities such as winter ploughing and the carting and spreading of antheap and manure. But the drought exercised its own power. Members' animals died and people worried that their remaining animals would be too weak to plough even their own fields. Mangwalala said that when they ploughed someone's field as a group, the next day the draught animals would have little strength. People consequently went back to ploughing individually. Mangwalala was discouraged, but hoped the group could be resuscitated before the next growing season (Fieldnotes, 14 April 1988).

The two researchers who have written most on farmer groups in Zimbabwe since independence, Bratton and Truscott, have differing views on the subject. Truscott (1987) believes 'that farmer groups can develop into production units in their own right, at least in certain areas and under certain conditions' – the conditions being appropriate advice and resource access for each stage of a market-oriented production operation (p. 3). On the contrary, Bratton (1984) argues that the type of labour and draught power sharing activities undertaking by groups such as Phumelela are likely to be ephemeral. Some groups may form marketing cooperatives, providing services for member households. But, 'the general trend in Zimbabwe, government strategy for socialism notwithstanding, is from group to individual rights of ownership and towards the commercialisation of property and work relations' (p. 21). In Chiwundura the mushandirapamwe group functioned, however, precisely because the demarcation of smallholdings has taken place. In southern Chirumhanzu, where arable holdings are still in open blocks, producer cooperation stumbles over the basic issue of herding.

Agricultural cooperation is inhibited further by the overall scarcity of resources in the communal areas; the increased vulnerability to drought hinders economic cooperation and social integration. This I have tried to show through an account that draws upon both the internalist perspective of the participant and the mediated interpretation of the virtual participant. Habermas's framework provides directions for integrating the lifeworld and system perspectives, but as Benhabib suggests, this provides only a starting-point for methodological praxis.

The literature on participation and organisation in rural development stresses some of the points that have been made in this chapter. For instance, Uphoff and Esman (1974), in their classic study of local organisations in Asia, state that: 'On the whole, rural people are more capable and responsive than the paternalistic model of social change suggests, but less able to change their lives autonomously than the populistic model suggests.' The latter occurrence they attribute to the ubiquitous fact of 'entrenched local interests' (p. xiii).

At a conference in Leiden in 1982, on participation of the poor in development, the rather rhetorical view was stressed that the promotion of members' interests requires the commitment and involvement of all, and the development of and adhesion to organisational norms, procedures and decisions (Bujis, 1982, p. 13). This conference is referred to because its proceedings provide a good summary of the mainstream ideas on rural participation through organisation. But what I have intended to show, using Habermas's theoretical concepts of the lifeworld and the paradox of societal rationalisation, is that any evolution of modern organisational forms in rural communities is a historically and culturally contingent project. This is much more akin to Freire's (1972) concept of 'cultural synthesis' (as opposed to cultural invasion), which he defines as 'a mode of action for confronting culture itself' (p. 147). Strong, broadly representative institutions are required at the local level if people are to improve their access to resources, but there is no model which can be implemented as a universally applicable panacea. If the organisations are to be sustainable, in each instance their struggle to reach maturity must be worked out by people themselves. Outsiders are necessary as facilitators, as CADEC has been in the last few years. More commonly, however, external institutions have at best created dependency (as the Catholic Missions have tended to do) or fostered new forms of control and despair, as took place with the group credit scheme.

It is the reproduction of the three-dimensional lifeworld of rural societies that is at issue. This requires, as societies are rationalised, that systems of economic reproduction, social integration and educatory processes of socialisation are continued and transformed, but in a manner that is coherent to, rather than induces anomie in, participants. It is a process that cannot occur autonomously or through purposive-rational policies. Habermas's theory of communicative action, allied to the Marxist paradigm of production, helps us to see this.

There is a convincing argument, I believe, that the improvement of the quality of economic and social life in the communal areas will only occur if the technical and economic relations between government (and parastatal, non-governmental and commercial institutions) and communal area societies, are conducted on the basis of value priorities and norms which are agreed beforehand through communicative action. But as we have seen in this chapter, there is the *a priori* question of with whom. Communal societies are structured by complex forms of social organisation. There is a historically embedded form of social organisation, but this has undergone massive upheaval and transformation during the colonial period and the war and so its legitimate form today is often uncertain. And then there is a form of social organisation that has been imposed since independence but has some grounding in the ZANU (PF) village committees established during the war. This means that despite the formal legality of the latter, in affairs concerning the land the councillor–WADCO–VIDCO system has yet to gain thorough acceptance at the local level. Variations between areas depend upon both recent history and the specific characters of leaders. Thus communicative action is required not only to set priorities for policy action, but also to establish even a form and structure of social organisation in the communal areas, which is acceptable to both the people and the state, and hence can serve as the method of communication between them. As Agnes Heller (1984) argues, in any social organisation there has to be a system of representation. Thus we have to choose to submit ourselves to a *relative authority*, but for such personal relationships of dependency to be non-authoritarian, the values that guide the organisations action need to be agreed democratically (pp. 177–8).

In the next chapter, I will examine the relations between Agritex and farmers in the two study areas. During my fieldwork the above thesis was put to extension staff in various guises, and also expounded on by them with or without prompting, in discussions of the issues that arose from my analysis. An evaluation of the response of Agritex staff to my review of their activities will then allow me to conclude the overall analysis of the impact of government policy on agrarian change in the communal areas, carried out through an exploration of critical theory.

7 Democratic Ideas and Technocratic Practices in Agricultural Extension

Regional Agricultural Extension Officer:
I think we are confining training to downward showering of theoretical knowledge by the officer to the extension worker. I believe we must be flexible ... Because the learning atmosphere itself, once you don't treat it well, you are already killing the whole plan of training.

Acting Provincial Agricultural Extension Officer:
The principle of adult education, to add onto what he is saying, is that everybody in a training situation has got some experience of some kind, and has got a contribution to make to the overall learning situation. So we should not assume that the one we say to be above everybody else is the one who has got more knowledge. He should be looked at more as a facilitator rather than as a trainer. And if we pursued that attitude in a training environment, I think we would all learn a little bit more.
(Extract from discussion meeting, Gweru, 13 April 1987)[1]

In the previous two chapters, the production systems and economic situations of the poor, middle and leading case-study households have been examined, as have the social contexts in which the households are embedded. I have sought to show in these accounts how the resilience of both household economies and rural social organisation is under severe strain, in the face of environmental fluctuation and the policy pressures exerted by the state. For many poor households, most of their income comes from non-agricultural sources; for many middle and even leading farmers, agricultural production is subsidised by wage-income remittances; and for even leading farmers, the struggle to keep their production activities viable is perilous.

The scope of this chapter's discussion is restricted, but specifically related to these factors. Two failures of Agritex are explored. One is why Agritex, in their agricultural extension work, have not addressed more directly the economic and social constraints to agricultural production. And two, why the agency has not sought to negotiate extension strategies with its peasant farmer clientele.

The information used in the analysis is predominantly that gained from my interaction with Agritex staff in the Midlands province. This interaction was of two forms. At the primary level my aim was to understand what staff were doing and how they explained their actions. At a secondary level, through more active engagement, I sought to elicit responses to my ongoing analysis of key issues concerning Agritex's activities.

The notion of engagement, as utilised here, has two characteristics. These characteristics are the latter two of the three tasks that Fay (1975) outlines for a critical social science. The first is that of intersubjective critique – of probing to induce reflexive thought in order to promote understanding. But in addition, engagement, in the context of critical theory, embodies a concern for change towards more satisfying human relationships and a more just and rational society (Gibson, 1986, p. 2). Alternatively, as Heller (1984) says in her *Radical Philosophy*, it is change towards the true, the good, and the beautiful. These three values correspond to the different action orientations – objectivating, norm-conformative, expressive – that one can take towards the world. In the first two value areas, questions regarding truth and normative rightness – the latter category including issues of social justice – can, in terms of Habermas's theory of communicative action, be clarified and tackled through argumentation.

The practice of engagement, then, was a method of testing Habermas's theory. At the level of praxis, the outcome of the interaction with Agritex staff is used to clarify requirements and barriers to improving communication between the state (in the specific form of the extension agency) and farmers. But the engagement experience also provides an empirical basis for evaluating the concept of communicative action itself. This is only undertaken in Chapter 8, but it is because I was concerned to use and test the notion of engagement that the scope of my examination of Agritex's activities is relatively narrow in content. There are limitations to this, such as the comparative lack of emphasis in this chapter on how local political issues may affect the quality of communication with extension staff. Some of these limitations will be raised later in the chapter and in Chapter 8.

In most cases my interaction with Agritex staff was carried out within the two study areas. Recorded discussions, usually of a relatively informal nature, were held with groups ranging in size from two to over forty people. In addition, two discussion meetings were held at Agritex's provincial offices in Gweru. These were arranged to discuss issues relating to the nature of the organisation's activities, which I had identified in two 'progress reports' written during the fieldwork period. These meetings were attended by staff from all levels of Agritex's organisation – district, provincial and national. After the completion of the fieldwork, a full working paper was presented and discussed in a seminar in Gweru. In the text these events are referred to as the first and second discussion meetings, and the Gweru seminar.

On all these occasions the debate was lively and stimulating. This was true too of the few interviews conducted with individual staff members. Conflicting views naturally did emerge, but overall there was a remarkable degree of consensus on what people perceived to be the significant weaknesses in Agritex's approach to agricultural extension. The statements quoted at the chapter's outset sum up a standpoint expressed in different ways by many staff members. This is that they would be more effective in their work if they interacted with farmers in a cooperative atmosphere, in which not only their own knowledgeability but that also of farmers was formally recognised. Taken to its logical conclusion, in such an approach, farmers would cease to be viewed as the ignorant receptacles of extension advice and instead would be treated as thoughtful beings, capable of articulating and debating their experience and needs. They would become partners in a 'responsive' model of agricultural extension and research, which would start in the farmer's field rather than on the research station (Assistant Director, Gweru seminar, 22 July 1987).

This is not the agricultural extension model that Agritex adheres to in practice. With only limited adaptation, this model remains a conventional, thoroughly technocratic, and diffusionist one. Moreover, despite the widespread recognition, especially at the operational end of Agritex's structure, of the need for significant change in operational policy, there are few indications that this will take place. Thus, the lasting impression I gained of Agritex as an agency was of the discrepancy between potential and actuality.

In this chapter the nature of this gap between potential and practice will be explored, so that the factors which explain it can be identified. There are three main sections to the investigation.

The first section summarises my evaluation of Agritex's extension practices in the two study areas. This evaluation is conducted in terms of the degree to which the practices are meeting the organisation's principal national and provincial objectives. Some of the reactions of staff to the issues raised in my research will be noted in this summary. A more complete picture of the views on what should and can be done to improve the agency's performance is then presented in the section that follows. Finally, the analysis turns to consider the constraints to substantive change, again largely as identified by people within Agritex. These constraints are contextual to Agritex's role in the communal areas and location in the government bureaucracy.

EVALUATING AGRITEX'S PRAXIS

The term 'praxis' as originally employed by Aristotle refers to the sphere of moral–practical action (McCarthy, 1978, pp. 2–3). This means praxis can be evaluated not only through reference to the goals to which it is directed, but also in terms of its consistency with an underlying value system (Habermas, 1984, pp. 171–2). In the following evaluation of Agritex's activities in 1986–7 in Chiwundura and Chirumhanzu I shall show the relevance of taking inherent value priorities as well as goals into account.

The overall operational goal of Agritex is: 'To stimulate the adoption of proven agricultural practices leading to increased, sustained and profitable production.'[2]

This statement contains, however, more than a goal. There *is* a goal – 'increased, sustained and profitable production'. But included also is the means whereby it is to be achieved – 'the adoption of proven agricultural practices'. Thus, so long as it adheres to this so called 'goal' statement, Agritex is condemned to a diffusionist approach. The phrasing of the statement permits no alternative.

What will be shown in the following discussion is that in Agritex's praxis the goal itself has become largely forgotten. Instead the means has become the sole object of extension policy and operations, its link to the goal simply being assumed. There are problems to this. The link is unproven and the means statement itself is contentious.

Let us conside these two observations further. In the way Agritex operates, 'proven agricultural practices' are translated into packages of practice recommendations, which are passed down the organisation's hierarchy from subject-matter specialist (SMS) to agricultural extension officers (AEOs) to extension workers (EWs) to members of farmer groups, sometimes through farmer training leaders (FTLs).

This operational method is thoroughly institutionalised. Yet no one I spoke to in the agency, from two Assistant Directors downwards, was prepared to state categorically that these recommendation 'packages' are appropriate for the majority of farmers, especially in natural regions III, IV and V.

In what way are these practices 'proven', then? The defence for the packages is listed in an introduction to the handbook *Crop Packages: Midlands Province*, produced in January 1987:

> Production recommendations found in Agricultural Handbooks today are based on research done for Commercial production. Most of these have been directly 'transplanted' onto the communal situation and have proved to be unsatisfactory. Modifications have been done over the years and have been seen to produce better results with the communal farmer, considering his environment and the resources available to him. (p. 1)

The 'modifications' referred to are primarily ones of degree only. Fertiliser recommendations are tailored down for each natural region as they become successively drier – for example, 300 kg compound D per hectare for natural region III is reduced to 200 kg for natural region IV – and by a further 50 kg if manure is used. Manure is treated as a partial supplement, not as it really is, the basis of farmers' crop rotations to the extent they can deploy it. Behind these packages there is only research to show how yields can be raised in the short term under optimal conditions. There is a research lacuna on how to *sustain* yield levels and on how production activities can become viable under communal area conditions. There is even little research on how farmers, especially the non-leading, can *increase* yields in anything other than seasons of good rainfall. Farming systems research (FSR) was introduced to Zimbabwe after Independence. Improvements have occurred. Some contact between researchers and farmers takes place where none did previously. A few improved white sorghum and millet varieties are emerging. Some trials on reduced tillage and on water conservation strategies for maize and sorghum have begun. But these trials have all occurred without decisive farmer participation. And here the process falls down. For instance resource constraints, especially shortage of animals (manure and draught power) and labour, have a critical bearing on a house-hold's ability to practice moisture conservation techniques.[3] But little real modification of the conventional technocratic approach to re-search has yet occurred in the FSR Unit's activities. Social, economic and even ecological considerations which impinge directly on raising, sustaining and the viability of production *under fluctuating environmental conditions*, have yet to be integrated in research activities, beyond the analytical stage.[4] In Chiwundura, thirteen FSR and Agronomy Institute field trials were carried out during the 1986/7 season. For these the researchers concerned could not even provide basic information on the costs of the huge array of inputs that were applied.[5]

There is, then, nothing proven about the agricultural practices that Agritex recommends, in terms of the three requirements of the agency's overall goal. Why then does Agritex still adhere to such an approach? The answer that the extension supervisor in Chiwundura provided echoes probably a general view. The crop packages, in terms of set amounts of seed, inorganic fertiliser and pesticide, to be applied per unit area in prescribed ways, provide a standard against which the 'correctness' of farmers' actual practices can be measured. But this standard is a false idol. It has nothing to do with what the agency is supposed to be achieving.

The assumption that this diffusionist approach of passing down messages is linked to the three elements of the goal is, upon examination, empty. The approach is authoritarian – at best paternalistic – in nature. What Agritex is committed to is not a goal, but an authoritarian value system founded in a purposive rationality and, to quote Heller (1984), an 'ethics of duty' (p. 163).

In the light of Agritex's commitment to a method of operation which has no proven capacity to achieve the organisation's goal, we can now examine whether the new initiatives launched in the Midlands since independence have brought about any significant reform in praxis. In Chapter 3 it was explained that in the Midlands there has been an attempt to shift away from a purely top-down and technocratic extension approach. After Agritex's formation in October 1981, the intention of the first new Provincial Agricultural Extension Officer (PAEO), as referred to in Chapter 3, was to create 'an attitude of mind which would enable people to think for themselves' (Interview, 21 March 1985). The 'people' were both the staff within Agritex and the farmers themselves. The means by which independent thinking was to be stimulated amongst agency staff was through a 'teams within teams' approach. Amongst farmers the agency's aim was to institutionalise dialogue between itself and farming communities through the organisation of the latter into groups. For such an aim to be realised and a responsive model of extension instituted, an ethics of duty needs to be replaced by an 'ethics of the personality', in which an individual responsibility to uphold the true and the good is assumed (Heller, 1984, p. 163).

The launching of the pilot T and V project in the Gweru region[6] provided an opportunity to initiate this new emphasis. The two principal objectives of the project were stated by the Gweru Regional Agricultural Extension Officer (RAEO) as:

(i)   To develop a team of Extension Workers that are highly trained in knowledge and skills and timeously service the relevant needs of their farmers.

(ii) To develop through this team of Extension Workers farmers who are self-reliant and able to play a major and increasing role in the training of fellow farmers. (1984, p. 1)

And although the RAEO did not stress it, the PAEO was emphatic that the reason for developing teams and farmer groups represented by leaders, was to improve the nature of communication up the system:

whilst we are pumping information one way down this pipeline, we want to be receptive to the fact that there is a hell of a lot of innovation going on in those groups . . . So it is not an agency which sees itself as the master of all knowledge, but rather as [an encourager of] true dialogue, in which the progression is shared as much between ideas up from the field as it is with ideas down. (Interview with PAEO Midlands, 21 March 1985)[7]

These three objectives then, to develop teams within teams, self-reliant groups, and to facilitate the processes through dialogue, represent an intention to reform the autocratic aspects of the diffusionist extension model. How much has this intention been fulfilled? In answering this, the training component of the T and V system in Chiwundura shall be considered first.

Training and Messages: Chiwundura

The T and V system focuses narrowly on EWs and farmer leaders. Herein lies its strengths and weaknesses. The major strength of T and V is that there is a system and EWs are enabled to maintain a high-contact profile with farmer groups. For instance, as one of the seven EWs operating in Chiwundura and the adjacent resettlement and small-scale farming areas commented in a staff meeting, 'Before T and V there was no system at all' (Fieldnotes, 17 February 1987). On another occasion a second EW remarked: 'This T and V, one of the advantages I see is that the extension worker is always in touch with the farmers' (Fieldnotes, 13 January 1987). And indeed, such contact was not occurring in Chirumhanzu.

On the other hand, a major weakness of T and V is that the AEO operating as the principal training officer for the team of EWs, may have only a tenuous link to the team. If this occurs, the upward transmission of information is blocked at this level in Agritex's organisational hierarchy (see Figure 3.1). In Chiwundura this was what was happening.

Since independence Agritex has increased its educational requirements for its technical staff. The majority of staff at nearly all technical levels are new. With their qualifications they are often quickly dissatisfied with Agritex's salary structure and move on. Internal transfers are also high.[8] Thus amongst technical staff, experience is low and turnover high. This applies not least at the AEO level. One consequence is shown by the following account.

The AEO serving Chiwundura in the 1986/7 season had been there less than a year; he was the fifth AEO in the area in seven years. He assured me that his training programme with the EWs had been drawn up with the participation of farmers. But when I queried this assertion he explained in detail how the programme was formulated – and in so doing supplied four reasons why farmers' priorities were not seriously considered or even elicited. First, groups are likely to derive different training priorities so that there is no joint consensus (and no joint meeting is held to obtain one). Second, there is a need to 'remind' farmers of various practices, such as stalk-borer control, winter ploughing and so on. Third, there is also a need to ensure a 'balanced' training schedule by, for instance, including aspects related to livestock management and conservation, which farmers themselves might not include in their programmes. Finally, there are new subjects to be introduced, originating from national or departmental policy. In the 1986/7 season these included a drive to promote oilseed crops (national policy) and savings clubs and projects (provincial policy). Consequently, to meet all these requirements, the training programme is drawn up by the region. Even the EWs denied that they were actively involved in the process.

One result was that many 'messages' passed to the EWs were wrongly timed, and, for the drought season, totally inappropriate. The most ironical example of the latter was a lesson on fish-farming held in mid-March. By then there had only been two or three storms for the whole of the previous two months. The land was parched, most small ponds and pools were already dry – and the rainless winter was still ahead.

An example of both a wrongly timed and inappropriate lesson was that on maize top-dressing and stalk-borer control. The initial AEO–EW session was scheduled in the week between Christmas and New Year but was postponed as part of the bureaucratic inertia that takes hold during this holiday period. For farmers, though, the bulk of maize top-dressing that is done is carried out between mid December and the end of January. If stalk-borer is a nuisance and any pesticide applied, this takes place even earlier. Eventually the combined lesson was given to EWs in mid-January. By this time the drought had ensured that no further top-dressing was feasible. The EWs did not bother to hold training sessions of their own. Mrs Mazonde, whom I worked with, simply remarked that if she had tried farmers would have said, 'Where have you been?'.

As well as being late, the lesson was also inappropriate for the prevailing dry conditions. The advice for maize top-dressing on the handout sheet given to EWs read:

Heavy textured soils – 4–6 weeks after emergency [*sic*]
Light textured soils – splitting gives better results
First application – 4–6 weeks after germination
Second application – 8–10 weeks after germination

Most of the leading case-study farmers, in their use of ammonium nitrate top-dressing, time their application by the height rather than age of the crop. If they are prepared to make two applications, the first is made when the crop is about knee height and the second at waist height. If only one is to be made it is applied between knee and waist height. Whether one or two applications are used depends on the time of planting and the nature of the season. In 1986/7, the only crops top-dressed twice were wetland (garden) maize (planting period A) and a limited amount of early planted maize (planting period B).

In the drought, the real issues concerning top-dressing, according to two extension workers, were whether it should be applied at all taking into account the nature of the season, the cost and the comparative benefit that could be expected, and if it was applied, when (Fieldnotes, 13 January 1987). The lengthy dry spell in the latter half of December and then from mid-January, meant that soils were often dry at the times when farmers wanted to apply the AN. They therefore faced the twin dangers of the fertiliser being ineffective and of it potentially 'burning' the crop. At Z$27 per 50-kg bag this advice was of no small importance to them. Mrs Mazonde, in her first season as an EW, was first asked for advice on 19 December, a month before the AEO–EW training session was held.[9] Her response was to arrange for one of the six groups in her area to hold a reminder demonstration on 2 January. She observed the methods the group used and decided what aspects could be improved upon. After this, she was able to respond to queries from farmers in other groups.

In Chiwundura, then, the diffusionist model of passing down messages had not been ameliorated with the introduction of the T and V system. If anything it had been strengthened, with the AEO providing regular lessons from previous years' lessons, technical literature and other external sources. Conditions prevalent on the ground were not considered. The extension workers, however, faced a demand by farmers for advice specific to the season and their individual farm conditions. As this demand was not catered for in the training they received, the EWs had to improvise. The two extension workers referred to above commented that they found their college diploma notes more useful than their fortnightly training sessions (Fieldnotes, 13 January 1987).

Another point is that because wet planting must wait for the rain, the rhythm of more and less intense agricultural activity periods during the season is not wholly predictable. Farmers have to schedule their activities in a flexible and incremental manner, and EWs must follow suit. The T and V system requires EWs to have a fixed programme for the month ahead. In practice, the only dates that can be filled in so far in advance are those such as AEO-EW training sessions, workshops and field days. Within this framework the contact time with the farmer groups is gradually arranged. Mrs Mazonde only had a full schedule for the week to come, thereafter the gaps still to be filled in increased through two, three and four weeks ahead.

If extension workers are to provide a service for farmers they must be innovative, organised and adaptable. But in Chiwundura they are not supported in these roles by the hierarchy above them.

Groups: Chiwundura and Chirumhanzu

A knock-on effect of the inadequate training the EWs were receiving was that attendance by farmers at EW–farmer training sessions was falling off. For crops like maize, farmers were being passed the same message for the third year running. The group membership figures that Agritex put in their returns were gross overestimates of the active membership of any of the groups I encountered. The average number of households per group in Chiwundura was reported in November 1986 as 37.[10] However, the only group activity I witnessed at which there were more than 20 people, were the self-organised *mushandirapamwe* operations of the Phumelela group.

A claim of staff which is at root of the inflation of numbers, is that group members are not exclusively master farmers as they were before independence. Membership now embraces the range of farmers in the communal areas. My own conclusion was that whatever the paper memberships of the groups were, the training and other activities Agritex was promoting amongst them still catered only for a privileged proportion of farmers.[11] Furthermore the type of resource-sharing activities carried out by the Phumelela group, which did involve all categories of households, was an initiative of the group itself rather than Agritex. The groups were formed through Agritex's encouragement, but the ideas that some groups have of how they can benefit their own members are often more appropriate than those currently employed by the extension agency. Agritex, which views the groups paternalistically – staff regularly speak of them 'maturing' – has difficulty seeing this.

The actual functions that Agritex was encouraging groups to perform in Chiwundura were threefold. The first is the role fundamental to the T and V system of farmer leaders learning to train other farmers. As they become more 'mature', the groups should, secondly, be encouraged to establish income generating projects. Thirdly, in their annual good-farming competitions and field days, farmer leaders should be responsible for as much of the judging and organising as possible. If each of these aspects is considered it can be shown why, despite Agritex's intentions and the initial flush caused by the introduction of T and V and the group credit schemes, the active members in groups are still largely leading farmers.

The idea behind farmer leader training was that the role should not be performed by an exclusive few, but that for different subjects members of the group should rotate as trainers (Interview, PAEO Midlands, 21 March 1985). In 1986–7 farmer leader training was, however, not occurring in this way. In fact it was hardly occurring at all. One reason was distance. Even though distances within an EWs area in Chiwundura are probably shorter than in most other communal areas in the Midlands, for farmers from all six groups in Mtengwa West to gather at a central place means a walk of over six kilometres for those furthest away. As a result crop lessons are often given individually to groups, or with farmers from adjacent groups attending, so that altogether two to three lessons on that subject is given by an EW.

Apart from the physical constraint, when farmer leader training is held, for social reasons there is minimal rotation of training leaders. Three of the extension workers in Chiwundura, when questioned on the subject commented among other things:

- Some illiterate farmers resent attending farmer leader training sessions for fear of being unable to impart the lesson to the group.
- There is a tendency among FTLs to delay report-backs to suit their liking.
- The capability of FTLs is doubtful considering that
  (i) many farmers are illiterate, and
  (ii) there is a lack of confidence in their teaching by most fellow farmers. [12]

Mistrust and conflict caused by 'domestic quarrels and disputes over social status' or 'personality complexes' as another EW phrased it, exacerbate matters. Examples of these abound. Kwaedza group in Mtengwa West was extremely poor at organising training sessions or report-back demonstrations, because of disagreement between the chairman and vice-chairman. If she had any message for the group, Mrs Mazonde would inform the two men separately. Another group, Vukuzenzele, with a predominantly female membership, had however elected a male leading farmer as chairman because he refused to be led by the women. Some of the women were also at loggerheads in a dispute over money. Mr Murasi, the chairman, was a jovial personality but his forgetful and argumentative character hardly made him an appropriate trainer.

Faced by the problem of members' dwindling enthusiasm and attendance at meetings, because of message repetition and disillusionment with fertiliser and credit, Agritex adopted a new strategy in 1986–7. This was the promotion of group projects. According to Agritex's extension supervisor responsible for the overall training of groups in the province, the aim was to persuade groups to establish projects for the generation of income, the production of food, and as a method of improving group cohesiveness and membership (Field-notes, 7 January 1987). However, the only group in Mtengwa West that was conducting such a project consisted of twelve farmers, all with plots on the nearby Mtorohuku irrigation scheme, and thus with some of the highest incomes in the area. The twelve had a poultry project sited in the homestead area of the group's treasurer. To start it they had obtained a Z$520 grant from the Ministry of Community Development and Women's Affairs. If run efficiently, according to the treasurer's figures, each member could receive up to Z$40 every three months or so. For poorer families in Chiwundura this would be a significant income, for most of these people it would not.

As Agritex was encouraging the establishment of projects through-out the Midlands, it is appropriate to include here consideration of three projects in southern Chirumhanzu and the issues they raise. The first is a gardening project in Mavhaire. Fifteen women and five men were members. As the project had been non-operative in 1985/6, for the 1986/7 season members had each contributed Z$2 for seed. Each person, once the seeds were transplanted, was allocated rows and was responsible for tending these and for selling the produce (Fieldnotes, 2 March 1987). From the proceeds Z$20 then had to be returned to the club. Profits were possible. Mrs Nhakuza made Z$30 surplus to the Z$20 she returned in 1986/7. But she is a dynamic and resourceful woman – and a member of a leading-farmer household which has fewer resource constraints than most. Few others are able to make her type of profit.

Another gardening project near Maware School was stagnating because a promise of aid had robbed the members of initiative. The group was operating as a cooperative of about thirty people. Most work was carried out on the *chisi*[13] day of Thursday. The location of the 0.4 hectare site was good as it was adjacent to a borehole. However, the only intensive cultivation was a few lines of tomatoes, which by early February had yielded around Z$40 from sales. This was not going to go far towards helping members pay for their children's school fees, as was the project's 'target'. If more extensive watering was to be carried out a storage tank was needed. The Maware savings club was in a position to provide a loan for such. But a local community advisor informed me that a representative of some donor organisation – name unknown – had visited the project and raised the possibility of providing fencing. The extension worker shook his head. Now the members will not organise themselves, he said. 'They won't make their own plan' (Fieldnotes, 28 January 1987, 4 February 1987).

The third project did draw a loan from a savings club. This project was a source of much sensitivity with Agritex, first, because of the considerable capital invested in it, and second, because the local extension worker and the AEO for southern Chirumhanzu had tried extremely hard to provide assistance.

The project was a large piggery at Chinyuni. The debate I had with Agritex staff, particularly at the regional and provincial level, was whether this project could be viewed a success and 'on track'. Their attitude initially tended to be that it was so. The income generated from sales in 1987 was held out as evidence of this: 68 pigs sold (mainly to Colcom, a national cooperative and the main producer of pork products in Zimbabwe) for Z$4977.23. If one looks, however, at the full balance sheet of the project's operations for 1986 and the first seven months of 1987 (Table 7.1), a more complete financial picture emerges. The figures are not comprehensive, but in the absence of a complete and accurate set of records, they were the best that could be obtained from the account books.

The main points to be noted from the accounts can be summarised as follows. To begin with, from 1984, when construction work started, to the end of 1986, the major funding for the project had consisted of two loans totalling Z$10 000 from Chinyuni savings club, and individual contributions of Z$400 each from seven of the sixteen members and Z$350 each from the remainder. Of these investments the loans from the savings club in fact covered the major capital costs of construction (Z$7656) and the purchase of ten sows and one boar (Z$2300). Thus the members' contributions were covering only running costs and not capital expenditure. By August 1987 the project had been operational for two years. In 1986 sales had been worth Z$3210.89 compared with (under-)estimated running costs of Z$10 101.08. For the period January–July 1987, which saw the sales referred to above, expenditure, at Z$6142.23, was still running significantly higher. Furthermore, for the remainder of the year the cooperative faced escalating costs for maize because of the drought and a wait of several months before they could expect to sell another large batch.[14] In addition, interest payments on the Z$10 000 loan from the Chinyuni savings club were still outstanding for the whole of 1986 and 1987.[15]

At this juncture, too, management was beginning to deteriorate. Mutual dissatisfaction between the previous manager, who through

Table 7.1   Tangamoise piggery project, Chinyuni: income and expenditure estimates 1986/7

	Income	Expenditure	Balance
1986			
Interest	300.00		
Loan from Chinyuni savings club (April)	4000.00		
16 members paid $100 each	1600.00		
16 members paid $5 each	80.00		
(for thatching grass)			
Pig sales to Colcom −37	2298.89		
Pigs sold locally −3	132.00		
Boar sold	140.00		
Sows sold −3	640.00		
Building materials and labour		2167.01	
Building labour		1583.91	
Maize feed		2139.95	
Grinding of maize		744.00	
Feed concentrates		1646.50	
Water		122.50	
Transport for feed		44.21	
Transport for marketing pigs		50.00	
Part of Colcom registration fee		100.00	
Salaries		1440.00	
Visitors		39.00	
Meetings and auditing		24.00	
Interest on loan – unpaid		–	
	9190.89	10101.08	
January–July 1987			
7 members paid $100 each	700.00		
9 members paid $50 each	450.00		
Pigs sold to Colcom (Jan) – 3 baconers	355.39		
Sow killed and meat sold (Jan)	120.00		
Pig sales to Colcom (5 March) – 40	2615.02		
Pig sales to Colcom (12 May) – 24	1886.82		
Maize		3033.00	
Grinding of maize		591.10	
Pig mash and concentrates		1651.05	
Salaries		840.00	
Building repairs		27.08	
Transport for marketing pigs – free		–	
Interest on loan – unpaid		–	
	6127.23	6142.23	−15.00

Agritex had received some training, and the other members, caused his resignation. He felt that the others undersupported him, whilst they were after a speedier return on their investment than seemed likely. His replacement was nowhere near as competent, and the project's chances of attaining viability receded further.

Agritex claimed they had investigated the economic feasibility of the project. The provincial farm management specialist had conducted an internal rate of return (IRR) calculation for the scheme in 1986. This was held up to show that a positive net annual return could only be expected in the third year of operation – which, from the start of construction, was 1987 (Discussion meeting, Gweru, 13 April 1987). On checking the calculation errors of assumption, fact and calculation could be ascertained, all of which undermined the positive conclusion.[16] It seemed to me highly likely that the scheme would remain unprofitable unless management – which had not been incompetent under the first manager – could develop a significant level of sophistication. The initial capital investment was certainly unlikely to be recouped.

At this point, though, Agritex managed to obtain assistance for the project. The Mvuma District Administrator agreed to supply the project with its own borehole, and an EEC micro-project grant was secured. These impending subsidies meant that it was acknowledged the project could not become economically viable by itself.

This somewhat detailed account on projects has been included to illustrate clearly two factors. First, the cost of participation of many projects can be afforded only by leading farmers. Second, to enable a project to become 'income-generating' is usually a difficult and intensive task, accentuated as the economic scale of the project rises. Extension workers in Chiwundura cover an average of around 475 households (RAEO, 1985, p. 2), whilst in Chirumhanzu the number can be in excess of 800 – the EW covering Maware and the adjacent Chingwena ward had at least 830 households. AEO's provide technical support for upwards of six EWs. Even with the best will, it is beyond Agritex's capability and competence to deliver timely, ongoing and sophisticated advice and back-up support as such projects may require.

The third area where Agritex is attempting to mobilise groups is in the organising of preliminary judging in the good-farming competition held in each EW's area, and of the field day held at its conclusion. These competitions provide the means whereby Agritex extension staff are able to evaluate whether farmers are adopting the practices being recommended. The field day is then an occasion when the winners are held up as examples to other farmers. And if the group whose field day it is has been largely responsible for the organisation, then an encouraging example of group development can be shown to visiting officials and farmer leaders from adjacent areas. But again I found it difficult to ascertain, especially in Chiwundura, how these occasions performed a positive function for any but a narrow band of leading farmers.

Mtengwa West had a three-stage judging procedure for their competition in 1987. Problems occurred at each stage. At stage one committee members from each of the six farmer groups judged members of an adjacent group, selecting three farmers to proceed to stage two. This initial selection was disrupted and delayed by two funerals. The second round judging then had several false starts, since Nhonga, who as area chairman was responsible for the organisation, was more concerned to complete a house building contract. He tried to delegate duties, but did so through Kwaedza group, and the non-communication between their chairman and vice-chairman meant nothing happened. Eventually, after the judging had taken place, the area chairman, who successfully remained uninvolved, then made the arbitrary decision of giving the name of one farmer from each group to the visiting extension worker conducting the final judging, instead of the best six overall as had been agreed.

The results of this final stage were then disputed by the area committee because the farmer judged third had proceeded straight into the finals as the only entrant from his group. He was the chairman of Vukuzenzele, the nearly-all-female group. The women had boycotted the competition as a protest against the high entry fee. The move to prevent this person coming third was, however, vetoed by Mangwalala, the Phumelela chairman, and Mrs Mazonde. An hour-long debate was held on the issue. What remained unsaid during it were the names of the two farmers competing to benefit from a disqualification. These were the farmer placed fourth, and the farmer third overall on marks, but who had been excluded from the final judging because he was only second in his group. Respectively, these two were the area chairman and the area secretary, both of whom were present (Fieldnotes, 7 April 1987).

At the field day, on checking marks I noted another discrepancy. The person placed second overall had only come second in his group. The group's winner, a woman, had also been screened out of the final judging by the area chairman.

The field day itself was characterised by a low attendance. This was in large part because the area chairman had been insistent on a high entry fee – Z$5 per crop, or Z$10–Z$15 per farmer, as to do well two or three crops have to be entered. Such a sum was a larger fee than any I encountered elsewhere in Chiwundura and Chirumhanzu. The fee was necessary, the chairman said, if there was to be enough money for prizes – and group members not entering should be fined. Farmers were unimpressed. Before the actual day, when another 13 people paid to partake of the food, only 37 people out of over 500 households in Mtengwa West had paid an entry fee.

In a speech the Chiwundura Extension Supervisor rebuked farmers for not attending:

> Where are all the Mtengwa people? You say T and V improves production, but how can you do it when you are absent on such occasions as today when we expect a large gathering? By not attending field days and other farmers' gatherings, a farmer reaps nothing but starvation, which is a danger to his family and the country. (Fieldnotes, 8 April 1988).

But what does happen on these occasions? Men and women gather to hear the lectures of outside officials. Then all the also-ran farmers who have entered the competition receive token prizes, before the winners are announced and held up as examples to the others. Finally begins the event to which all who have paid look forward: the feasting. But even here participation is not as equals: the 'chefs', who do not pay, obtain the choicest cuts.

As a form of evaluation good-farming competitions and field days reinforce the current message system. The winners are the few farmers who have adequate access to production resources – land, labour, draught power, capital and equipment – and hence can produce the best crops. The fact that the extension messages are inappropriate for the bulk of farmers – the also-rans and the failures – is passed by.

In Chiwundura, the area field day is held within the winner's homefield area. However, in southern Chirumhanzu, where the bulk of cultivation is still performed in the open arable blocks established during the land husbandry era, field days are held out in these blocks. Prizes are still awarded to individuals, but the event is hosted by the group – not the individual – adjudged as having attained the highest overall level of achievement. Thus as affairs they are less oriented to the individual household than in Chiwundura. In the way marking is carried out, however, the farming competition still functions mainly as a means of evaluating farmer adoption of Agritex's recommendations.[17]

In general terms, the farmers' groups in Maware and Mavhaire were less cohesive than in Chiwundura. There were no resource-sharing activities, such as the Phumelela *mushandirapamwe*, and even interaction for training purposes was restricted. Between November 1986 and April 1987, the two groups I was working with in the Maware and Mavhaire areas received only one reminder lesson each. Extension workers were hampered by the large number of groups they had to serve – the Maware EW had twelve groups in his area, the Chinyuni EW fourteen groups. Nevertheless, the lack of clear principles to guide the nature and form of contact contributed to reduce the degree and quality of interaction. In improving the organisation and effectiveness of contact between EWs and farmer groups, the T and V system had certainly brought about a significant change in Chiwundura. This was one of three main contrasts between the extension systems operated in Chirumhanzu (which falls within the Mvuma region) and Chiwundura (Gweru region). In the other two areas the Mvuma region system displayed comparative strengths. These positive contrasts will be examined in the final part of this evaluation.

Meetings and Follow-ups: Chirumhanzu

The first of the comparative strengths of the extension system as operated in the Mvuma region lay in the greater amount of relatively unconstrained communication that occurred between staff members within the region. This was because of the different way staff meetings were structured and conducted. In the Gweru region, the only regular staff meetings attended by the Chiwundura extension workers were monthly affairs held in the communal area. The purpose of these meetings was form-filling – travelling and subsistence claims, monthly itineraries, monthly reports, quarterly reports, crop estimates, and so on. The meetings, chaired by the extension supervisor, dragged on for three to five hours. His task was to elicit the answers required by the forms. The extension workers spelled each other at being sufficiently alert to prevent the trickle of replies from altogether drying up; their stamina in surviving the torpidity was impressive. These meetings were infrequently attended by the AEO, whose preferred strategy was clearly to avoid the tedium if he could. He never lasted a whole meeting. The only staff member from Chiwundura who attended meetings at the regional level was the Extension Supervisor.

The Mvuma region had three types of staff meeting.[18] One of these three, the senior staff meeting, was similar to the second of the two types of meeting held in the Gweru region. The others, however, were very different. Quarterly meetings involved all the region's personnel. These affairs were chaired by an AEO, rather than the senior person present, the RAEO, as a deliberate strategy to invite freer participation. And indeed meetings, although long, were at least lively, with a wide range of the extension staff contributing to the discussion.[19]

The third type of Mvuma region staff meeting was a zonal meeting, held monthly and attended by all the staff in an AEO's area. This is the only occasion the AEO meets all the EWs in a month, for there are not the fortnightly training sessions of the T and V system. In the period between meetings, what the AEO did do was to spend at least one day per month in each EW's area. In Chiwundura EWs complained that the absence of such follow-up visits reduced their motivation and led to declining farmer interest in the groups. If messages are to be 'kept relevant to farmers' problems and particular situations', technical staff 'need to check up and face farmers directly' (Fieldnotes, 13 January 1987).

The greater contact that AEOs have with EWs and farmers is the second comparative strength of the Mvuma region extension system. For instance, with the advantage over his compatriot in Chiwundura of several years' experience in his area, the AEO in southern Chirumhanzu was able to identify problems during his follow-ups and then discuss these with the EWs in the monthly zonal meetings. Two such problem areas pinpointed in 1986/7 were the production of the oilseed crops, groundnuts and sunflowers. It is worth discussing these for they throw light on the limits of the extension system at the technical level as it is presently constituted, even given a highly competent and conscientious AEO.

The problem with groundnut production in southern Chirumhanzu, according to the AEO, is that yields have declined in recent years.[20] Consequently, at their January 1987 staff meeting, the AEO agreed with the extension staff on a set of groundnut demonstrations to be performed the following season. The hypothesis for the demonstrations was that the decline in yields is because 'there are some aspects of groundnut production which are being neglected by the farmers'.[21] The twelve demonstrations the staff wished to carry out would investigate the effects of four types of fertiliser: lime and manure, both of which are ploughed into the soil prior to planting; compound S, which is applied at planting; and gypsum, a top-dressing. Of these four types of fertiliser, one is organic, two are cheap, and only the fourth, compound S, is an expensive fertiliser to purchase. The rationale behind the proposal was, therefore, that if farmers can see from this type of local trial that they can raise their yields in a relatively inexpensive and cost-effective way, then there is a greater likelihood that they will do so.

This proposal can be compared with the groundnut nutrient trial carried out as part of the FSR and Agronomy Institute on-farm trials in the Gambiza area of Chiwundura in 1986/7. The trial was investigating treatments of seed innoculem, potash, phosphorus and nitrogen (in the form of AN). But in addition, blanket applications of manure, nematacide, trace elements, gypsum and lime were applied to all plots (Fieldnotes, 13 January 1987). The economics of the trial were considered irrelevant by the research staff concerned (Fieldnotes, 12 March 1987). To the local Agritex staff, however, it was senseless carrying out such a trial in a communal area, if it ignored completely communal area conditions.

The case of groundnuts thus provides an example where an AEO was trying to respond to farmers' problems, conveyed through EWs and noted from his own observations. Problems that occurred with sunflower production in 1986/7 were, however, of a different ilk. Although some farmers had grown the crop before, the 1986/7 season was the first in which sunflowers had been extensively grown in Chirumhanzu. Of the fourteen extended case-study households in the Maware and Mavhaire areas, nine of them grew the crop this season. With 12.1 per cent of the total area cultivated by the case-study farmers given over to sunflowers, it replaced rapoko as the second most extensively grown crop (Table 5.1). Previously only five of the households had grown even small areas of the crop.

This expansion in sunflower production was consequent upon a call by the Minister of Lands, Agriculture and Rural Settlement, shortly before crop planting began, for increased oilseed production. The intention was to reduce the hectarage of maize because of the national surplus that had accrued over the 1984/5 and 1985/6 seasons (see Chapter 3). An improved producer price for sunflowers meant that communal area farmers heeded this call. Agritex staff regarded as a success the fact that even at late notice additional farmers had been persuaded to grow the crop, thus meeting government policy (Interview, AEO Chirumhanzu South, 9 March 1987).

In their haste, though, to implement the Minister's call, Agritex staff were unconcerned that they had broken the agency's procedural norms. In one discussion with extension staff in Chiwundura on the benefits of manure, the Extension Supervisor concluded, 'We have no results from research on nutrient levels etc. so we cannot recommend, because our training is backed by research' (Fieldnotes, 17 February 1987). Yet when it came to sunflowers, farmers were urged to grow them in the absence of advice on techniques. In the Mavhaire area farmer group members received a combined lesson on all oilseeds in October, in which minimal information was provided on sunflowers. In the Maware area, the lesson was aborted as no farmer in the group was prepared to provide seed for a demonstration.

Commercial farmers in Zimbabwe mistrust sunflowers as a crop because it has 'inconsistent yield, removes too much from the soil and is susceptible to nematodes' (*Financial Gazette*, 12 December 1986). Hand-out literature on the subject which Agritex has available stresses the importance of fertilisation to increase yields and because the crop is a scavenger. The importance of liming soils with a ph of less than 5.3 (which is the case with many of the worked-out granitic sandveld soils) is noted because of sunflowers' negative sensitivity to acid soils. Lime is a cheap agricultural input, yet currently Agritex do not widely recommend farmers to use it. Nor are farmers encouraged to test their soils, although the cost was only Z$2 per sample. Manure can also be used, or compounds L, C, or B. Yet if farmers use any fertiliser it is compound D, which they use on maize. Sunflowers are susceptible to boron deficiency; compounds L, C, and B contain boron, D does not. Because sunflowers are high nutrient consumers, thinning of the crop and weeding are both important as means of preventing wasteful competition for water and nutrients. Few farmers knew these facts or performed the practices.

The point of all this is that unlike groundnuts, the other oilseed crop communal farmers grow widely, sunflowers are not nitrogen-fixing. They deplete soil fertility drastically. In 1987 two farmers who had grown sunflowers before, indicated this to me by pointing out extremely poor crops in fields where sunflowers had grown the previous season. Many farmers were due for a nasty surprise in 1987/8. In fact, when I visited Mangwalala, the Phumelela chairman, in April 1988, he had already dropped the crop after planting two hectares of it in 1986/7. Disappointed at harvesting only four bags from that area, he observed curtly, 'the next season the maize can't do well' (Fieldnotes, 14 April 1988).

During 1987, the southern Chirumhanzu AEO had observed the problem and discussed it with the EWs at their February staff meeting. Yet subsequent to this meeting neither the Mavhaire nor the Maware EW returned to speak to farmers on the subject. Throughout the remainder of February and March they were busy arranging and conducting crop judging and field days.

The AEO acknowledged that it was not presently possible to tackle problems arising in the course of a season during that season. The best that could be hoped for was an improvement the following year (Interview, 9 March 1987). Having been urged to grow the crop, farmers I worked with were irate at the subsequent lack of advice. The Assistant PAEO admitted later that the agency had not been careful enough. 'It must not be a short-term effect that we are putting across', he said (Discussion meeting, 13 April 1987).

In summarising this evaluation of Agritex's extension practices in Chiwundura and Chirumhanzu, the following conclusions can be reached. Shortcomings in the diffusionist approach of passing on packages of recommendations can be seen in two respects. First, there are deficiencies in meeting the technocratic values that underlie the diffusionist model itself. This is seen in the case of sunflower production in 1986/7, when in the rush to promote the crop specific agronomic requirements and dangers were ignored. Second, and more crucially, the diffusionist approach fails because it is under-pinned merely by a purposive rationality. The sole concern is to persuade farmers to adopt technical messages. There is no active questioning of the appropriateness of their content or source, or even whether it is justified to believe that the approach can achieve the agency's operational goal.

At the outset of the T and V pilot project in the Gweru region, the Midlands PAEO identified the instrumental activity of blindly passing on technical advice as stifling initiative and creating dependence among extension staff and farmers. It was intended the T and V project would engender greater dialogue between levels in the extension hierarchy: technical specialists, extension workers and farmers. Since then improved EW–farmer leader communication has been achieved, but further advances in dialogue have been blocked at the technical specialist level. In Chirumhanzu, the reverse has occurred. Specialist staff in the region have improved the quality of interaction among the region's staff members, but the system is constrained by infrequent and poorly organised EW–farmer contact.

Agritex's group development initiative is the second of the agency's new policy foci in the Midlands. Even in the diffusionist model, the need for developing groups is obvious. Extension messages are aimed at farmers and therefore the element of strategic action – the manipulation of farmers – needs to be considered in addition to the instrumental action of passing down messages. In execution, the use of farmer groups has remained true to the diffusionist model. The extension system is not receptive to farmer group initiatives that may actually conflict with the organisation's own priorities. Hence training programmes are 'fixed' and field days, the organisation of which consumes weeks of an extension worker's time, are the showpiece of the extension agency rather than of the farming communities themselves. Agritex states that it aims at group 'self-reliance', but in practice this means something like, 'we would like you to organise yourselves, thereby reducing our work, to do the things we would like you to do'. In 1987, Robinson Gapare, Chairman of the National Farmers' Association of Zimbabwe, informed Agritex's Gweru regional office that he was accepting an invitation to attend a field day in the Masvori resettlement area. The immediate response of the Gweru office was to summon the Chiwundura Extension Supervisor. He was asked to explain why an invitation by a farmers' area committee to the national chairman of the farmers' own organisation had not been routed through the government extension agency.

Group development is occurring, then, entirely within the paradigm of purposive rationality. Dialogue between agency and communal area farmers and the encouragement of self-reliant (that is, non-dependent) farmer groups, can only take place once a 'talk-down' relationship between government agency and communal area farmers has been suspended. Until then the formal advice provided by the extension agency is likely to remain inappropriate for the socio-economic conditions and specific agro-ecological conditions (that is, taking into account landform, soil types, vegetation cover, and other physiographic features, in addition to the natural region), with which the vast majority of communal area farmers have to contend.

It is now time to see how Agritex staff responded to this evaluation, and in turn, contributed to the process of intersubjective critique that I was testing.

DISCOURSE WITH AGRITEX

Habermas makes a distinction between critical and discursive forms of argumentation. For him the term 'critique' applies 'when arguments are employed in situations in which participants need not presuppose that the conditions for speech free of external and internal constraints are fulfilled' (Habermas, 1984, p. 42). On the contrary, discourse occurs when controversies concerning validity claims of truth, normative rightness (justice) and sincerity are adjudicated collectively through (relatively) unforced argumentation.

> I shall speak of 'discourse' only when the meaning of the problematic validity claim conceptually forces participants to suppose that a rationally motivated agreement could in principle be achieved, whereby the phrase 'in principle' expresses the idealizing provisio: if only the argumentation could be conducted openly enough and continued long enough. (Habermas, 1984, p. 42)

In working with staff in a bureaucratic institution where actions are regulated through a hierarchical system of power, conditions of free speech are obviously rarely likely to prevail. Nevertheless, if one is using a critical research method, then one should be prepared to take the process of engagement as far as is constructively possible. By seeking forums in which issues arising from the research could be presented and responses elicited, my intention was to sound boundary limits within people and within the institution, and hence to seek the conditions for discourse.

That the technique of engagement was successful at all says much for the more democratic atmosphere that has been engendered in relations between Agritex staff within the Midlands since independence. At the Gweru seminar which completed the engagement process, the first Midlands PAEO, by then promoted to head office, articulated his acceptance of the democratic value priorities behind my method:

> I don't see that this type of critique reflects too seriously on us in any personal sense . . .
>
> We are an organisation that invites criticism . . . because if we are to be . . . the agency that advances agriculture in this country, and we do not have the attitude that we want to accept constructive criticism then we will never put Zimbabwean peasant agriculture on the map of the world. Whereas, if we are prepared to accept this

kind of objective criticism then I reckon we've gone a long way towards getting to that point. (Assistant Director, Field, Gweru seminar, 22 July 1987)

But, as will be made clear later, this positive acceptance of engagement needs to be qualified. It is people within Agritex who may accept constructive criticism, not necessarily the institution itself. Furthermore, in this instance, the critique was initiated by a researcher extralocal to the institution. Thus the reactions of staff in discussions cannot be taken as a measure of how institutional relations are conducted. On the other hand, my position of honorary attachment allowed staff, in discussion situations generated by my presence, to relax inhibitions that might otherwise be in place in their institutional interactions. Consequently the ideas expressed by staff in these situations can be treated with reasonable assurance as truly theirs.

The subject headings under which the discussion of the previous section was organised – training and messages, follow-ups and groups – will be implicitly used again as the basis for examining the reactions of Agritex personnel. This will enable eventual linking back to the overall aim of the agency, 'to stimulate increased, sustained and profitable production'.

First, the subject area of training and extension messages will be considered. Let us recap. The Training and Visit extension system operates on the assumption that the world of agricultural research has the technology required to boost the production levels of small-scale farmers. What is needed is an efficient extension system which maximises two factors:

(1) training contact time of extension workers with technical specialists, and farmers with extension staff and each other;
(2) the number of farmers that can be 'reached' by the messages, through the organisation of farmers into groups and the use of contact farmers for training purposes. (Benor and Harrison, 1977)

These are the efficiency factors. Effectiveness requires the messages from the knowledgeable to be clear and uncomplicated, so that in the passing the unknowledgeable do not become confused. At the Gambiza ward field day in Chiwundura, as this was the ward in which the FSR on-farm trials had been conducted, there were research and agricultural training personnel present. The principal of the Mlezu Agricultural College, which abuts Chiwundura to the north-west, summarised in a speech the principles on which this system functions. There are four bodies in agriculture: researchers, educators, extension agents, and farmers. Researchers produce the knowledge, educators pass it to trainees, trainees are employed by Agritex, the knowledge is passed to farmers. This completes the full team in agriculture (Fieldnotes, 12 March 1987).

The principal's speech was shortly followed by that of the coordinator of the FSR team. 'The purpose for us is to try things before the extension workers can teach you. We try, try, try for many years first' (Fieldnotes, 12 March 1987).

Finally the Chiwundura Extension Supervisor spoke: 'Researchers should try and start where the people are and modify their research to the tools the farmer has' (Fieldnotes, 12 March 1987).

If these three personalities can be taken as representative of their institutions, it is then only staff within Agritex who are yet questioning the total reliance on the technocratic diffusion model. I would suggest this representation does have considerable currency. In Chiwundura, two of the poorest of the extended case study households produced their largest yields in 1986/7 from a rather surprising crop – cucurbits. *Mashamba, mapfudzi, mananga, mavisi* – there are a wide range of indigenous pumpkins and melons which all farmers grow. The Tangwenas, who, as referred to in Chapter 5, received assistance from the mushandirapamwe group, still only produced 6.5 bags of maize. But in April, in one 0.5-hectare area I counted 137 ripening *mashamba* (Fieldnotes, 21 April 1987). Mrs Mkucha, who produced just 5 buckets of maize, also had a significant haul of cucurbits. At the Gambiza field day I questioned a FSR agronomist on whether cucurbits could be researched, say as part of an intercropping programme. He responded: 'We can't do research on these – how can you measure the plant population of melons?' (Fieldnotes, 12 March 1987).

With respect to the crop-packs, the packages of recommendations which are the products of research, no one in Agritex, at the time or subsequently, disputed the point made by the Assistant Director (Technical) in the first of the Gweru discussion meetings, held in February 1987. Asking the question, 'Have we a technology which we can offer the poorer farmer in natural regions III, IV and V?', he then supplied his own answer: 'I don't think so' (Discussion meeting, 6 February 1987). Other senior officers in the Midlands acknowledged the inappropriateness of the packages for the majority of farmers and the undesirability of perpetuating existing praxis. The Gweru RAEO, whose extension teams, through the T and V system, were promoting these packs probably more than any other region in the province, commented:

> On these packages ... I think something has got to be done. I agree ... that we give farmers packages ... which can be appropriate to those who have got the resources. We know that the farmers are forced by circumstances to modify those packages but we don't follow up and evaluate those modifications. (Gweru seminar, 22 July 1987)

But if consensus existed that the crop-pack approach was an unsatisfactory method of meeting farmers' extension needs, no one could explain who was responsible for the continuance of the approach. Agritex staff said the Agricultural Finance Corporation wanted a fixed set of recommendations to make the administration of loans and the delivery of inputs easier.[22] To the contrary, AFC officials said the packs were not particularly suitable but came from Agritex (Meeting, 6 January 1987). Regional and provincial Agritex staff stated the packages originated from Head Office's production and training branches; Head Office staff said the provinces and regions were supposed to adapt the packages to their own situations. With responsibility thus duly apportioned by all concerned to all others concerned the crop-packs live on.

As well as acknowledging the problems associated with the confinement of training, as put in the chapter's introductory quote, to the 'downward showering of theoretical knowledge', extension staff also had ideas on how to tackle them. This leads onto the twin subjects of groups and dialogue.

On the topic of how to make extension training more appropriate, two of the Chiwundura extension workers expressed their feelings emphatically:

> If the decision was given to everyone, including farmers, to say how T and V could be improved, the decisions would be pouring ... (1st EW)

> Because the real problems are lying on the EW and the farmer. Those people in the office are just imagining things, and not knowing things practically. (2nd EW)

Their feelings were strong, but in fact their argument was recognised by at least some people right throughout the Agritex hierarchy. At the Gweru seminar, the Assistant Director (Field) put the view succinctly: 'But the focus in my view is not the research station anymore, it is the farmer's field' (Gweru seminar, 22 July 1987). Such a shift would remove the narrow focus of research on yield per hectare, and lead to stronger consideration of 'overall production from the household's area'. Two requirements had to be met for the basis to be laid of an altered approach. First, the 'weak link' in the agency's upward communication channel required strengthening. The AEO needed to add a diagnostic role to his portfolio. To this end CIMMYT[23] was being brought in to help train trainers, who could then introduce AEOs to this more definite and rigorous method of follow-up and diagnosis of key farmer problems. Second, some readjustment of resource allocations within the agency was necessary to ensure that the key staff for reaching farmers through this diagnostic approach could operate relatively unfettered. These were the extension workers, AEOs, and then the subject-matter specialists responsible for back up the AEOs (Gweru seminar, 22 July 1987).

Other region-based staff agreed with the intentions of this altered approach, but highlighted especially the second of the constraints to making it operational. Both the Gweru and Mvuma RAEOs, faced continually with the problem of managing on limited operational resources, especially for travel purposes, stressed that to implement a diagnostic approach they would require more resources. 'I believe there is really . . . very little dialogue between us and farmers and this is why the information flow is not adequate. [But] in communal lands dialogue is very expensive and the same applies to evaluation' (RAEO Mvuma, Gweru seminar, 22 July 1987).

It was also noticeable that if a diagnostic approach was implemented a great many local extension staff already have good ideas of problems that farmers face, almost none of which are tackled by the present message system. In an interview, the Chirumhanzu South AEO reeled off a whole series of such needs. It is worth identifying them because of the degree of shift from present practice that addressing them entails. The problem with declining groundnut yields and the plan for local demonstration trials, has already been referred to in the chapter. On maize, echoing the Chiwundura extension workers, he said that in the drought it was wrong to reiterate the standard message. Of more importance to farmers than the information on set application rates was advice on whether or not they should fertilise. He highlighted too the central role of organic fertiliser:

> People know they have got to use manure, they have got to use compost. But . . . if you want to use organic manure, for example, you have got to find where you will get the grass, where you will get the materials to make compost. These may not be available . . . [So] it is now a question of addressing ourselves to the problems which arise. (Interview, 9 March 1987)

The AEO referred also to the need for more attention to be paid to moisture conservation techniques in the drier seasons. Techniques such as tied-ridging and pot-holing they did not yet know enough about. As an agency, they stressed the importance of autumn ploughing, but conveniently ignored the fact that the gravelly soils found on the upper parts of slopes in southern Chirumhanzu were by harvest often already too hard to plough. Such soils needed also more than brief early rains for germination to occur. In sum, for him, 'the main problem is that we are mainly emphasising on technical know-how, but we should also be looking strongly into management . . . I think we want to . . . try and be more of managers than just advisors' (Interview, 9 March 1987). But this would require Agritex to increase the scale of their intervention into communal area farming and so could scarcely be described as a recommendation for turning round the technocratic nature of the current approach.

Farmer groups and related issues such as field days, projects and the range of farmers who were active members of groups, were subjects that always elicited a depth of feeling and frequently provoked defensive reactions among Agritex staff. One experienced Chiwundura EW did point out that, 'They won't change drastically as most people might want' (Fieldnotes, 17 February 1987), but generally the groups were seen as the vehicles for change. Nevertheless the route to strengthening groups was regarded unimaginatively; for most it was merely a more effective version of the current practices. The only innovative idea that the Chirumhanzu South AEO advanced for groups was an adaptation of the T and V concept of training contact farmers. His proposal was rather to include farmer leaders at zonal staff meetings (the cost of transporting them withstanding), 'so that when we discuss a problem of groundnuts, a problem of sunflowers, a problem on cattle . . . the group leaders actually get in and give us their views on what we think. Then maybe they can go back and hold

meetings and pass on whatever we have agreed onto the farmers . . .'
(Interview, 9 March 1987).

The question of projects, and especially that of the Chinyuni
piggery project, aroused vehement debate in the meeting held in
Gweru to discuss the second progress report. After an extended
argument had ensued from my query as to whether an inviable
project was better than no project, the Gweru RAEO raised the issue
which goes to the core of the problem with projects. This was the role
of donor assistance. 'When the donor comes with the money, what do
you want? His short-term money, or the short-term viability of our
farmers?' After a brief and inconclusive scrutiny of what constituted
viability the Assistant PAEO (Field) interjected:

> the question of donors . . . Before you have even worked out your
> cost analysis, the donor has got the carrot and he is pushing the
> farmer . . . if you don't do this [rapping table] the money is going
> next door. This is what is happening in Mberengwa.[24] They are
> coming out with saying we have got this money, if you don't use it
> within the next six months it will be gone. The farmer gets mad and
> he works day and night putting up fences, just fencing off, so that
> he can get this money . . . We are in an unfortunate position that
> before we have even worked out the viability of any project, the
> farmer has constructed a structure . . . The moment they see that
> . . . the agent is not responding fast enough, the farmers will go
> ahead with the plans without you, and help themselves. And you
> will be asked to correct that situation. (Discussion meeting,
> Gweru, 13 April 1987)

Proposals tentatively put forward in the meeting for tackling the issue
of projects, received little support. In the end the provincial land use
planning specialist merely turned to the need for monitoring and
evaluation. But a research officer from the agency's head-office-
based monitoring and evaluation unit refined this to say that it was
internal monitoring of a project by those people actually engaged in
it, that would be most effective.

The issue of field days was another where extension staff had little
new to offer. Because they are the showpiece days for the agency,
generally Agritex staff – apart from the extension workers that have
to organise them – like field days. The Chiwundura Extension Supervisor offered a riposte to my critique of the events: 'Field days would
probably be ideal to categorise farmers into three groups . . . But we
know farmers do not like to be classified as poor.' The reply of the

Assistant Director (Field) was that it was precisely this type of impasse that should be the subject of dialogue with the farmer groups. 'Put the challenge to the group ... Look, we perceive you don't seem to be expanding and attracting this category of member. How are we going to do it? Perhaps they have the ideas anyway' (Gweru seminar, 22 July 1987).

The ideas that farmers have, such as the *mushandirapamwe* resource-sharing, may, though, have nothing to do with field days. They may be generated from priorities entirely different from those of the agency.

What, then, of the future of dialogue – in formal terms the advancement of communicative action within the agency and between the agency and farmers – in order to generate mutual understanding and action grounded in an expanded sphere of consensus?

BARRIERS TO CHANGE

A range of Agritex staff within the Midlands province and even at the national level recognise the need for the organisation to change its praxis, have ideas on how that change might take place, and indeed, with for example the introduction of the CIMMYT training, have even initiated some change. Yet this is a long way from representing any significant transformation in institutional style and value priorities. In the first part of an interview held at the end of my research with the Assistant Director (Field), he acknowleged that his preference for a democratic style ran against the bureaucratic grain. He sought enhanced collaboration and commitment amongst staff and valued people who were prepared to sit and exchange ideas. 'We are in the business of ideas here, to be encouraged and developed ... I will take an idea from anybody from a field orderly upwards, if the idea has something for the organisation' (Interview, 10 June 1987).

One idea the Assistant Director had which would help to answer positively the question asked above on the future of dialogue, was that from the farmer groups might evolve farmer extension leaders. The emergence of such paraprofessionals could lead to the 'bottom-up capture' by farmers of the lower levels of the extension service. This type of idea, although in the spirit of the Prime Minister's Directive of February 1984, whereby the VIDCOs were established, otherwise runs counter to so much of current thinking ... but if current solutions are not solving things, we must be part of the problem. If we can't see ways out of these things, we'll never solve problems in a hundred years. (Interview, 10 June 1987)

Yet, the Assistant Director acknowledged a series of formidable constraints. For instance, even with the introduction of training in a diagnostic approach to extension, there was no guarantee that the AEOs would effect a more rigorous method of conducting follow-ups with farmers. They had to fulfil other responsibilities too – the training of teams of extension workers and that of land use planning (Gweru seminar, 22 July 1987). These various roles not only have to be balanced in terms of their time demands, but they are also potentially conflicting. How AEOs and other technical specialists resolve these demands and conflicts depends not only on them and departmental policy, but also on the policy of the Ministry of Lands, Agriculture and Rural Settlement as a whole. Thus, if a higher priority is placed on the internal land use reform policy, AEOs are going to be pushed to become more purposive rational in their actions, not less so.

This means that even though Agritex has the best developed extension network in the communal areas of any government agency, the question can still be asked as to whether the agency actually does have the capacity to develop a relationship based on dialogue with farmer groups. I asked the Assistant Director how much he thought a democratic style could be institutionalised in a way that could be sustainable despite changes in leadership.

We are an instrument of government policy to implement agricultural policies, which at times are not the policies from the bottom up but the top down. And so long as we are in that situation, I have nagging doubts about an effort or a determined commitment to make ourselves more responsive than the bureaucracy allows us ... If we start moving a little bit out of line with policy, sooner or later we are going to be brought back into it again. So I think that is one of the most important questions you've asked me ... Previously I would have answered you differently. Now that I have got to this level, I see just what we are up against. (Interview, 23 July 1987)

The phrase 'what we are up against' seems to be referring to the way power is deployed in the bureaucratic and political system as a whole. But to grasp more explicitly the content of this expression, a greater theoretical clarity is needed. Here I think Anthony Giddens in

The Constitution of Society (1984) provides more assistance than does Habermas. There are three concepts that Giddens employs that I wish to introduce. The first is that of the *duality of structure*:

> The structural properties of social systems are both medium and outcome of the practices they recursively organise. Structure is not 'external' to individuals: as memory traces, and as instantiated in social practices, it is in a certain sense more 'internal' than exterior to their activities in a Durkheimian sense. Structure is not to be equated with constraint but is always both constraining and enabling. (p. 25)

A *social system*, then, is that 'in which structure is recursively implicated'. It comprises 'the situated activities of human agents, reproduced across time and space' (p. 25). And finally, to understand the *structuration of social systems* requires analysis of 'the modes in which such systems, grounded in the knowledgeable activities of situated actors who draw upon rules and resources [that is, the lifeworld] in the diversity of action contexts, are produced and reproduced in interaction' (p. 25).

We can now return to Agritex. Agritex forms part of the bureaucratic system of the Zimbabwean government. This bureaucracy is structured on the basis of a set of values which, despite the surface populist concessions, upholds a belief in the wisdom of a political and professional elite, and thus justifies central political and governmental control. A 'teams within teams' approach within the Midlands has provided a freeing-up of internal relations within the province, but staff members have no illusions that this has altered the structuration of the system. In a bureaucracy, 'structuration' is grounded in actors' knowledge of how the organisation rewards and punishes actions.

> And make no mistake, the system tends to reward those who respond to directives that come down the line and punish those who feel that they have got something more important that concerns the farmer that they should be engaged in. And you all know this. You are civil servants like myself. (Assistant Director, Field, Gweru seminar, 22 July 1987)

The only way that an approach more responsive to farmers' needs and contexts could be developed, the Assistant Director believed, was by staff becoming more 'inwardly introspective'. 'We needed to be monitoring what we were doing more actively than we were' (Gweru seminar, 22 July 1987). This accords with the point, referred to in the previous section, which the research officer made in the discussion on projects.

The structural properties of a bureaucratic system can only be changed if somehow the structure itself becomes an object and subject of consciousness – an object that can be viewed cognitively and then as a subject brought into the arena of communicative action. Giddens differentiates between 'practical consciousness' and 'discursive consciousness'. This is a distinction that Habermas handles awkwardly in his concept of the lifeworld. Practical consciousness is distinct from the latter in that it is 'what actors know (believe) about social conditions, including especially the conditions of their own action, but cannot express discursively' (1984, p. 375).

Discursive consciousness is often more shallow within us than we realise. We also compartmentalise and in certain instances suspend our knowledge. For example, despite a positive acceptance and response to my evaluation, when called upon at the end of 1987 to produce a formal report on the activities of the Field Division of Agritex, the Assistant Director (Field) used only 'official', uncritical information in his remarks on subjects such as the development of technical messages, land use planning and the Training and Visit programme. Even reports written for the government such as that by Collinson (1982), which showed that extension recommendations are geared solely to resource-rich farmers, and that by Sandford (1982), which debunked much mythology on the environmental impact of livestock, are ignored in official reports. Yet in my interaction with extension staff they could and did verbalise understanding of their actions which previously they had held only at the practical level.

To conclude, although we may have an inherent capacity to change the properties of the structures that entangle our lives (to the extent that we are as individuals able to engage together in unforced communication), this capacity is deeply constrained. In 1988 the Assistant Director was passed over for promotion and soon after left Agritex for another post in agriculture. Most structural change occurs through the undemocratic use of power, and in Zimbabwe those that control the party-state institutional system hold most power.

This brings us back to the land. For it is in the land that the roots of central control lie, as they did during the colonial period. And as discussed in Chapter 2, this process has been only an accentuation of an earlier process when those that held the land, especially the wetlands, held power.

We can now return to a larger theme of the book. In this chapter, the barriers to change within the extension agency that have been explored are largely constraints to communicative action. They are those that prevent the expansion within the institutional structure of a communicative rationality that will counterbalance the purposive rationality of the diffusionist model. But I have argued that there is also another set of constraints to meaningful change at the level of rural society. This set, which although interrelated cannot be sub-sumed under the paradigm of communication, are the constraints to production consequent upon inequalities within the relations of production. It is these inequalities that act as the generators of distorted communication within bureaucracy and society.

At the end of the Gweru seminar, the research officer from the monitoring and evaluation unit who had been present at the second of the discussion meetings, intervened with an incisive speech:

> We have been looking at the aims of Agritex. I notice that in the kind of environment in which we operate it is not easy to attain them. But the problem I think is more fundamental. It is because of overpopulation in those areas. Now the challenge tends to shift away from extension . . . for extension can no longer actually help to achieve the desirable objectives . . . The groups can exist, but to what extent can they share the resources that exist within a parti-cular area? Now there is a problem. Can we actually say a person should have so many cattle or so many whatever?
>
> So . . . despite the fact that we are looking at improving groups, how would we do it to perhaps raise the level of food production, perhaps make it profitable at certain levels, while we have these inequities in access to the land, access to grazing area, access to arable area, access to resources?
>
> Secondly, there is the problem of the quality of the soil. For how long can we sustain this population in that sandy soil, carrying out arable activities and perhaps animal production? To what extent can the extension worker improve their position?

The research officer in this statement is confirming the conclusion I drew earlier: Agritex, in their extension activities, do not address the goal they have set for themselves. The problem is, as the research officer implicitly states, that in the end Agritex's goal is highly political and not merely technical. I have attempted to show in Chapter 4, with regard to land use and land use planning, that the questions of land access and use are inseparable even if the state attempts to enforce land 'reform' projects independent, in the specific instances, of the access issue. In Chapter 4 the subject of environmental resilience was also broached in order to argue that a technocratic approach, which bases all techniques around the assumption of a 'normal' season, is wholly wrong for savanna environments.

Given the social and economic constraints to improving the viability and sustainability of household agricultural production in the communal areas, is it realistic to hold out any hope that Agritex's goal, 'to stimulate increased, sustained and profitable production', can be fulfilled? Certainly, if the goal is to be seriously tackled, the scale of change that is required is enormous. For, as will be argued in the final chapter, the finding of appropriate policies depends on initial change in official attitudes and institutions.

8 The Duality of Structure

We underestimate our farmers, gentlemen, simply because we
have no dialogue. Thank you very much. (Shurugwi Extension
Supervisor; the final speaker, Gweru seminar, 22 July 1987)

In general, it is a mistake to connect linguistic understanding with a
necessary (even if only potential) agreement among speakers and
hearers of particular speech acts. (Fay, 1987, p. 190)

There are two tasks to be performed in this concluding chapter. The
main substantive, theoretical and methodological themes of the book
need, firstly, to be drawn together. This synthesis will then provide
the basis for a final discussion on the aim stated in the opening
paragraph of the book, that of finding a means of linking an analysis
of past and present change with a practical interest in the future.

One intention of the chapter's second section is to indicate ways in
which the ability of critical theory to provide an adequate analytic
and normative basis for the consideration of agrarian change, can be
improved. One evaluative point already stressed is that Habermas's
paradigm of communication, as outlined in his *Theory of Communicative Action*, is valuable only as a supplement to a Marxian
paradigm of production. If this is accepted, then there is much that
Habermas's critical theory can contribute to an analysis of agrarian
change.

A key task that Habermas has performed, with implications for
method and hence the content of an analysis, is to shift much more
firmly than did Marx, from a positivist to a critical epistemology. In
distinguishing between the three attitudes (or action orientations)
that we can take towards the world, he helps displace earlier
theoretical and methodological misconceptions that a researcher who
seeks only to objectivate (the cognitive orientation) is capable of
penetrating the lifeworld perspective of those under investigation. A
deeper understanding of others can only take place through interpretive accomplishments based on unforced interaction (the social
orientation). But there is yet a further orientation, the subjective,
which in the *Theory of Communicative Action* Habermas underplays.
As shown in the previous chapter and emphasised by Fay in the quote
above, the reaching of understanding does not mean there is an
agreed commitment on what to do. Between understanding and

commitment, as it were, lies the subjective dimension of individual responsibility: how do we as individuals relate to ourselves and to the world?

Giddens's concept of the 'duality of structure' captures how we as human agents do exercise choice, even if always under pressure. The rationalisation of such choice, according to Habermas in later work of his (as yet unpublished in English), can be evaluated in terms of an aesthetic or expressive rationality. An explantion of what this entails, and some conceptualisation of its linkage to the paradigms of production and communication – and hence the linkage of theory, method and substance – will be provided after the synthesis that now follows.

AGRARIAN CHANGE AND GOVERNMENT POLICY IN ZIMBABWE'S COMMUNAL AREAS

In Chapter 1 an argument was set out on the nature and impact of past, present and future policy in Zimbabwe's communal areas. Use was made in the argument of Habermas's exegesis on the differentiation of the lifeworld that has occurred with the process of societal rationalisation in the modern era. Of particular importance is the distinction Habermas makes between purposive and communicative rationality.

It was posited that there are strong similarities between pre- and post-independence agrarian policies in the communal areas, and that these policies have had a radical but adverse overall effect on household economies and on the integration of rural societies. Consequently agrarian policies have long been opposed by the rural population. Why then have the continuities occurred? The explanation lies in the institutionalisation of a purposive rationality in the modern state system that was developed during the colonial period, and the wedding of this rationality to the imperatives of an expansionary state and capitalist economy.

It was then argued that a more effective basis for policy actions than the present authoritarian – at best paternalistic – relationship between state and peasantry requires the counter-institutionalisation of a communicative rationality. A greater commitment to dialogue would enhance mutual understanding. Such a commitment is, however, obstructed by the 'relations of force' that are entrenched in the institutional structures of the state and capitalist economy. This means the fundamental constraints to the improvement of rural social welfare lie at the level of the state rather than within rural societies.

Information related to the claims made in this two-stage argument was advanced in Chapters 2 to 7. The case was made in Chapters 2 and 3 that, although the main legacy of colonialism is commonly portrayed as the economic divide between white and black, the process of colonialism has in fact been more total and insidious than this. For the new political and bureaucratic leadership of independent Zimbabwe has been internally colonised by ideas of progress and development that arise from the one-sided and distorted process of societal rationalisation that has taken place with the spread of capitalism.

The focus within Chapter 2 was on an analysis of the nature, impact and ideological justification of the four main technical development policies implemented between 1930 and 1960. The argument was put forward that, notwithstanding the colonial economic interests that were being served, these policies were founded in a teleological view of social development. In this view 'progressive' western culture was seen as superior to the presumed backward and mythology-based nature of agrarian African culture.

It was argued that this ideological presentation, which colonial officials actually believed in, obstructed their ability to understand real rural economic and social trends. Most crucially, and as developed thematically in Chapter 4, it was not understood that agrarian survival in the savanna environment of the Zimbabwean plateau was a symbiotic affair between humans and the environment. This relationship was not teleological but cyclical. The rhythm of life was geared to the inevitability of seasonal fluctuation and to the cycle of birth, growth, desiccation and decay. Wetland cultivation provided the most reliable food supply, but differential access to this land led also to the uneven accumulation of women, children and cattle.

From 1900, after the cessation of the First Chimurenga of 1896–7, the developing colonial society created new opportunities for accumulation. The establishment of towns and mines generated a demand for migrant labour and the supply of grain and meat. In the area of the southern Shona, people moved down from their hill-top strongholds and away from the tightly controlled wetlands. The adoption of the plough, especially after 1914, led to an expansion of dryland cultivation and the era of the 'plough entrepreneurs'. These were often younger men, who became a new group of *hurudza* or land barons. They traded grain, accumulated cattle and engaged periodically (particularly before first moving onto the land) in wage labour. This way they sought to free themselves from the control of the old male patriarchs.

Cattle, after their appropriation in the nineteenth century first by the Ndebele and then by the white settlers, consequently regained their importance in the rural economy. *De jure* holdings were distributed extremely unevenly. This was, however, indicative of the different process of rural social differentiation now taking place, rather than of a continuity of late-nineteenth-century lineage production relations.

The exact changes in and nature of social differentiation in this early colonial period still requires much clarification. This is largely because of the yet further drastic changes wrought by the technical development phase of colonial policy. This phase was launched because the administration felt its policy of land segregation to be threatened. The growth in livestock numbers on the land and the extensive methods of cultivation used in the expansion of maize production, fuelled fears that the reserves, into which the African population was being pushed, would not support the growing human numbers.

As far as rural peoples themselves were concerned, though, the technical development policies of agricultural demonstration, centralisation, destocking and land husbandry, were simply designed to make them poorer. Their land and cattle were taken, and the use of wetland areas for intensive cultivation was prohibited. Even when a modern technical idea was gradually accepted as beneficial, such as the idea of a manure-based dryland crop rotation, it was also perceived as having the strategic purpose of raising yields so that the government could justify the taking of more land.

These policies reduced not only rural economic and social welfare but also the extent of rural social inequalities. In so doing a redistribution of local power was once again experienced. The *vanasabhuku*, the 'keepers of the book' from their early colonial role as tax collectors, became, with the implementation of land husbandry, in some places almost like landlords. The Land Husbandry Act formalised the concept of a land market, and even though this was legally abandoned at the end of 1961, the practice has since grown with, in the study areas, the *vanasabhuku* the main regulators and beneficiaries.

The technical development phase ended when opposition to the implementation of the Land Husbandry Act became overt and

violent. Nevertheless, thirty years later, the internal land resettlement policy that is currently being promoted in Zimbabwe closely
resembles this notorious policy. A clue as to why this is so may be
found in the brief period of reflection that took place in the early
1960s. With the then international spread of the community development model, the Native Affairs Department (from 1962, the Ministry
of Internal Affairs) took up the concept and promoted it as a less
authoritarian and technocratic form of development. This policy was
never implemented in any significant form because of the coming to
power of the Rhodesian Front. More important to my thesis, though,
is the reaction of government officials to the early enthusiasm for the
concept. Those who came into direct contact with the rural population largely welcomed the idea of removing coercion and granting
greater local autonomy. However, more senior officials did not
perceive a need for either since their model of a backward and
inferior rural population had remained unchanged.

In Chapter 3 it is argued that in the post-independence period, this
conception has only altered marginally. The social Darwinist ideology
of the pre-RF period has been replaced in the rhetoric of ZANU (PF)
by a claimed adherence to principles of Marxism-Leninism. But
ZANU (PF) is a mass-based nationalist party, rather than a vanguard
party, and few senior members have any real commitment to
socialism. Consequently in practice the new government's development policy is populist rather than socialist. The planning and
political framework that has been established allows for the so-called
representation of people's interests through an administrative rather
than political structure. This process is thus tightly controlled by the
party-state, and, as shown by the example presented in Chapter 4 of
the 'land reform' proposal for Ture ward, it acts more as a system for
transmitting downwards policy imperatives than as a system of
democratic representation.

The discussion of the Ture ward project proposal drew together
one other theme introduced in Chapter 2. This is the fact that the
misunderstanding that has continued between rural peasantry and
government administration is based upon the two holding altogether
different perspectives on the communal area environment and economy. Through their education and training, government officials
have a faith in western science, technology and a purposive rationality. Within the ministries responsible for implementing agrarian
policies, a consequence of the dominance of a purposive rationality is
that technical issues are seen as distinct from the often highly political

nature of the proposals concerned. In Ture, local government officials were promoting a rural housing scheme together with the internal land use reform policy proposals. The idea that local people had accepted the government proposal was promoted through the district planning committee to the provincial level, because of acquiescence by the ward councillor. However, his interest and that of other local leaders lay not in land reform but in the acquisition for pastoral purposes of commercial ranchland adjacent to the ward. The interplay of different strategic interests in the subsequent development of the case history hides the crucial substantive issue. This is that the model of a reified livestock 'carrying capacity', used by the government since the introduction of destocking in the mid-1940s, is totally at odds with the variable nature of the environment and accordingly the preferred land use strategies of peasant farmers.

Recent research for the first time has begun to provide empirical evidence that the peasant livestock management model does have validity. It has been shown that the 'key resource' wetland areas are the most productive areas of the communal area environment and that if used carefully environmental degradation need not result. However the pressures of too many people on the land in the communal areas, coupled with the restrictive nature of land use policies, has led to the unavoidable abuse by peasant farmers of the type of grazing management strategy which most accept as suited to the environment and the nature of the production system. Consequently decrease in the primary productivity of the land has occurred. What is not known is whether this decline is ongoing and irreversible.

Within Agritex, cognisance of the fact that neither peasant farmers nor the extension workers who had immediate contact with farmers were 'idiots' has led to a shift in extension strategy in the Midlands province since 1983. The key principle of the change, according to the Provincial Agricultural Extension Officer who initiated it, was that extension staff and farmers alike should be encouraged to think for themselves and the latter enabled 'to stand on their own feet' (PAEO, interview, 21 March 1985).

The predominance of a purposive rationality might well have created within Agritex, as the PAEO argued, an 'attitude of mind' whereby staff are not motivated to think for themselves. But amongst farmers dependency is more than just an attitude; it is also resource-based. This was shown in the analysis in Chapter 5 of the agricultural production systems and economic activities, during the 1986/7 drought season, of the 29 case-study households.

In the drought, the ability of households to produce a net economic gain from their maize crop was dependent largely on their ability to make full use of the early rains that fell at the end of October. This ability required either wetland, or soils with sufficient organic content to be soft enough to plough and plant before the arrival of heavy rain. It also required access to draught power and a labour supply sufficient to cover not only planting but also the herding of animals and the protection of the new crops from the still-roaming animals of others.

If households lack land, livestock or labour, it has a negative self-reinforcing effect on the whole production system. The proviso to this is that the possession of a regular migrant wage remittance can raise the level of household security significantly. In Chiwundura, an experienced and still energetic elderly farmer leader had sunk into debt because he lacked labour support and a non-agricultural income. Across the road his neighbour, a middle-aged woman, is wealthier and more comfortable and has a new Master Farmer certificate. Her more favourable position is by virtue of the good urban job her husband possesses. In both Chirumhanzu and Chiwundura even the leading farmer households who live predominantly on their agricultural earnings still have the insurance of income-earning children who can cover an emergency expense, school fees, or the hiring of wage labour. Migrant incomes have thus largely replaced wetland cultivation and cattle accumulation as the means of coping with unfavourable agricultural seasons.

It was also shown in Chapter 5 that because of the fragility of many household agricultural production systems, household members ensure their production and reproduction through diverse activities. In the drought, even reported off-farm incomes were higher than on-farm incomes for most poor and middle households. Agriculture was thus the supplementary rather than the main activity. In good seasons this situation may be reversed – but during the 1980s, only two seasons have qualified as such. This means that household labour and capital have to be allocated between the different economic activities. In February 1987, once the certainty of the drought was established, men especially, but also women if they were the household head, began to divert a larger proportion of their labour to non-agricultural activities.

In Chirumhanzu, as the household economic profiles in Appendix 2 show, the divide between households whose main rural income came from crop production or off-farm activities, was more clear-cut than in Chiwundura. This is because of the wider range of crops grown in Chirumhanzu. Apart from maize, households had larger areas of crops such as groundnuts, rapoko, sorghum, and sunflowers, from which they produced marketable surpluses. But, in addition to land, and particularly access to wetland, the analysis highlighted the importance of cattle to agriculture. The leading case-study farmers had on average 5.48 ha of land in Chiwundura and 6.01 ha in Chirumhanzu, compared with 1.51 ha and 2.55 ha in the two areas respectively for poor farmers. Notwithstanding the importance of this land access, however, the only households that produced crop surpluses above household needs in 1987 were those which had their own draught power. Cattle, by providing manure and by being immediately on hand for ploughing, cultivating and the transporting of harvests, permit arable activities to be carried out with a timeliness and return to labour that cannot be attained by households managing (except at planting) largely by hand labour. Remove cattle from a household agricultural production system, therefore, and it ceases to have a chance of being viable.

The centrality of cattle to the farming system, and the premium placed on the scarce grazing resources available in a dry season, has led to controversy which spills over into the social arena. An issue particularly sensitive in southern Chirumhanzu was examined in Chapter 6. Here there still exists the pattern of unfenced blocks of arable land that was established during the implementation of the Land Husbandry Act. Those farmers who plant early to catch the first rains face an endemic problem of keeping the cattle of their tardier neighbours away from their germinating crops. Local leaders have been unable to bring about a binding community resolution on the issue. Broad agreements acquiesced to in meetings are not kept by people afterwards. Leaders themselves attribute this problem to the lack of clear-cut, legitimate social authority.

The lifeworld of the rural peoples draws its inspiration from the natural environment. In this way social institutions too depend on the land. Their legitimacy is anchored in the relations they allow between society and environment; the relations of access, as it were. Here the impact of colonialism, followed by the party and local government structures that arose during the liberation war and since independence, have resulted in much confusion. Party leaders, VIDCO leaders and the *vanasabhuku* form a leadership melange. Institutional dynamics vary widely between and even within communal areas. In southern Chirumhanzu, the lack of an authority able to back agreement with normative as well as formal sanction means that people fear to use the first rains for planting crops. They thus produce less food.

In Chiwundura, the smallholding land use pattern that has developed spontaneously since the late 1960s, independent of any government regulation, has resulted in the fencing of all arable land. But if roaming animals early in the growing season are less of a problem in Chiwundura, an issue that is proving deleterious to agricultural production is the provision of credit. A large group credit scheme launched in Mtengwa ward in 1984 has fallen apart after three seasons. The Mtengwa Ward Cooperative itself owes the AFC Z$100 000, whilst individual farmers are in debt for sums up to and exceeding Z$1000. The reasons for the failure of this scheme are economic and social. They are economic in one sense, in that an over-reliance on inorganic fertiliser and dryland maize production is not a sustainable basis for an intensive peasant production system under the variable climatic conditions of natural regions III and IV. And they are economic and social in that the cooperative was provided with no administrative, financial or training support from the outside agents responsible for its establishment. This led not only to problems of economic management but also to the inadequate acceptance of the cooperative into local society. Integrational problems were exacerbated by the leaders of the farmer groups within Mtengwa not being involved in the conduct of the cooperative's affairs. The lack of active local support led to the cooperative's demise for it increased both the extent of defaulting and the use of marketing channels other than the cooperative itself.

In contrast with this credit scheme, a savings club operation in southern Chirumhanzu, supported on the basis of a quite different philosophy by the Catholic Development Commission, has been relatively successful. CADEC performs a training and auditing function, and therefore helps identify and advise on problems in the clubs. But the management of the clubs and decisions regarding issues such as theft of club funds, are the sole responsibility of members. In some clubs there has begun an evolution of competence and solidarity among the committee and whole membership respectively, because people perceive the clubs as being of benefit to them. This has seen them through experiences that would have resulted in the dissolution of more fragile organisations.

Another local initiative analysed in Chapter 6 was the *mushandir-apamwe* operation of the Phumelela farmers' group in Chiwundura. This group functioned successfully as a resource-sharing organisation over the 1985/6 and 1986/7 seasons, before foundering after the drought of 1987 had considerably weakened members' cattle. The basis of the group's early support was that individual members were clear as to how they would benefit and were expected to contribute. Problems that arose were aired in discussions held after each session. In 1986/7 most members benefited from having a large area of maize planted early in the season. The quick operation maximised moisture conservation and hence germination rates.

This type of group activity contrasts with the type of group activity that Agritex encourages. As detailed in Chapter 7, Agritex still caters principally for a communal area elite. This is seen in their promotion of capital-intensive crop packages, projects of uncertain viability, and field days to herald those farmers with the resources to follow extension advice (albeit, if only on some of their *dryland* fields). Moreover, the organisation's extension activities are still administered in a largely technocratic manner. In spite of the policy initiative to stimulate dialogue and the 'bottom-up' transmission of farmers' training priorities, no significant institutionalisation of this has occurred within the study regions.

In Chiwundura a T and V pilot project has assisted the efficiency of extension workers, but left them frustrated with the barrenness of the technical support they receive. In southern Chirumhanzu, a competent technical officer is able to provide some immediate support. But he is hampered by the general failure of the agricultural extension and research organisations in Zimbabwe to address the agricultural problems in the form and at the time they are actually perceived and prioritised by different categories of farmers.

In terms of the research methodology, the second part of Chapter 7 deals with the response of Agritex staff to my evaluation of their activities in the study areas. The main point noted here is that staff fundamentally agreed with the evaluation and many were able to identify means of improving the agency's praxis. In general these ideas were in support of greater dialogue with farmer representatives and a democratisation of both agency–farmer relations and intra-agency relations.

Yet despite this widespread agreement on the weaknesses of Agritex's current diffusionist extension approach, the actual change that was occurring was minimal. People by and large simply followed well-established work routines. In the concluding section of Chapter 7 the barriers to change within Agritex were discussed. Two main factors were raised. First, that the institutional system exerts a power over staff so that individuals tailor their actions to what they feel their superiors will accept. This means that only individuals in senior positions will conceivably take responsibility for initiating change. Further, even where widespread agreement exists that policy change is required, for instance on the whole approach of disseminating packages of practices, the fact that no one within the organisation's diffuse hierarchy assumes responsibility for the specific manner of implementation, makes the likelihood of change more remote. An individual's quest to translate a personal commitment to reform institutional practices into reality proved unachievable, even once he reached the level of the Directorate.

The second factor brings us back to the point raised earlier. If Agritex attempts to change its praxis, for instance with regard to land use policy, it will as an agency almost immediately have to face the fact that it cannot divorce technical from political considerations. But as the organisation's remit is purely technical, senior staff wish to avoid having to admit this. This root cause of the continuity of Agritex's technocratic approach is likely to remain.

This last point can be vindicated and spelled out a little further, if reference is made again to the final interview I held with the Assistance Director (Field).[1] In the interview the subject of the T and V pilot project and the inappropriateness of the crop packages was raised. The Assistant Director agreed that the service provided to extension workers and farmers was unsatisfactory. He then commented further:

> Worse still, when you see what research has to offer, it is totally bankrupt for natural regions III, IV and V. We are almost going to have to be generating appropriate technologies. So you don't know what to say ... you are not going to say too publicly because people start to get a bit worried when you want to start acknowledging things. So on the one hand you want to half admit it, to shake these guys up, but on the other hand you don't want to admit it, because you're pulling the mat out from under your feet. (Interview, 23 July 1987)

In this way the Assistant Director summed up his feelings of the formidability of the task of instituting a balance between a purposive and a communicative rationality within Agritex. This task he had been committed to since his appointment to the post of Midlands PAEO in 1982, but in 1988 he finally acknowledged that it was beyond his capacity.

Notwithstanding his own inability to affect it, the Assistant Director still believed that significant change in communal area land use policy had to take place. Echoing the concern expressed by the research officer at the end of the Gweru seminar[2] and indeed expressed by communal area farmers themselves, he stated towards the end of our interview:

> But you can't just have burgeoning populations, no matter what system you've got. You meet the limits; there are finite limits. It's going to happen. There has to be a policy then which accommodates an identification that there are too many people and too many animals. But that's the other thing, it is people *and* animals. People and animals are inseparable components. (Interview, 23 July 1987)

The first sentiment expressed here has of course motivated what has been done to the rural population since the late 1920s. There are too many people in the communal areas, but as has been shown here, the fluctuating nature of the environment means that there are no fixed 'finite' limits. Rather, there are too many people now in the communal areas because they can no longer adjust particularly their pastoral land use requirements to the nature of the season. So farmers themselves would certainly agree with the Assistant Director in saying that people and animals must be considered together.

How then might a more beneficial redirection of policy occur? In the last section of this study I wish to examine briefly the type of substantive, theoretical and methodological tasks that lie ahead if the economic and social welfare of Zimbabwe's communal area peoples is to improve.

SOCIAL STRUCTURE AND INDIVIDUAL RESPONSIBILITY

The discussion in this section will lead from theory to method to substance before being finally drawn together. I shall begin by returning to the issue of subjective responsibility raised at the outset of the chapter, initially in the context of Agritex's operations.

It was concluded that through argumentation controversial aspects of the activities of Agritex staff can be debated and a broad agreement reached on the need for change. The proviso to this is that an agreement that change is required provides no guarantee that either change in policy or in individual actions will take place.

The theoretical consequence of this is that the few people in

Agritex who were actively committed to the actual change of policy actions were motivated by more than agreement. They were motivated by a commitment to an individually held value system and driven by an acceptance of their individual responsibility to pursue that in which they believed. In this commitment, external ideology is irrelevant. As the Assistant Director (Field) stated in the first part of our final interview, 'I am looking for commitment in the staff, and the only way to achieve this is by being exemplary' (Interview, 10 June 1987). In his own case, the Assistant Director resigned because, through the constraints which came to be placed on his ability to be exemplary, he believed his commitment to be rejected.

Using the attitude and actions of the Assistant Director as a model, I wish now to develop the theoretical argument further. In it I shall draw upon other social philosophers concerned with critical theory.

First, if one analyses the Assistant Director's actions, the realm one is concerned with is that of the subjective relation of the individual to the world. This is the expressive or aesthetic dimension. Within this dimension, Habermas states we can evaluate action according to the sincerity with which we believe the actor has related this action to earlier performances and to linguistically stated intentions. More than this though, in recent work of his on modernity, politics and aesthetics, Habermas acknowledges that we can speak of an expressive or aesthetic rationality.[3] With regard to the attitude an individual subjectively takes towards the world, *aesthetic rationality* is measured in terms of the interpretation of desires and feelings with respect to culturally established standards of value and the reflection upon the adequacy of these values as authentic expressions of an exemplary form of experience (Ingram, 1987, p. 181).

Such a concept of rationality is required if one is to understand the position the Assistant Director was in and the role he was performing within Agritex. The problem is, once a concept of rationality is accepted which is grounded in subjective value choice and the assumption of an individual's responsibility for her or his own actions, a difficulty is acknowledged for both the understanding and coordination of the action of individuals.

At the level of understanding, the historical contextualisation of human action now has to be penetrated. In his theory of communicative action Habermas holds that we can communicate our experience through understanding – and that perfect understanding should logically be possible. Habermas can make this claim because he possesses a passionate commitment to the power of reason. The concept of communicative action is grounded by him in the pre-supposition of an 'ideal speech situation'. Contentious validity claims of truth, normative rightness or sincerity he believes could be resolved through discourse, 'if *only* the argumentation could be conducted openly enough and continued long enough' (1984, p. 42). He speaks too of a 'claim to reason', intrinsic to the rationality of purposive action and linguistic understanding, but which, because of the pervasive use of power within production relations, is most often distorted:

> Again and again this claim is silenced; and yet in fantasies and deeds it develops a stubbornly transcending power, because it is renewed with each act of unconstrained understanding, with each moment of living together in solidarity, of successful individuation, and of saving emancipation. (1982, p. 221)

Such a commitment to reason can easily allow one, though, to underestimate the difficulty of attaining understanding in human communication. An early opponent of Habermas, the hermeneuticist Hans-Georg Gadamer, counter-claims persuasively that understanding is *always* limited because of our historicity:

> The real meaning of a text [or social situation], as it speaks to the interpreter, does not depend on the contingencies of the author [or actors involved] . . . For it is also always co-determined by the historical situation of the interpreter and thus the whole of the objective course of history . . . The meaning of a text [or social situation] goes beyond its author [or the actors involved] not occasionally but always . . . Understanding is not merely a repro-ductive procedure but also always a productive one. It suffices to say that one understands differently when one understands at all. (Gadamer, 1975, p. 264; and 1976, p. xxv)

Through the potential power of reason, it is not only the basis for understanding that Habermas wishes to lay, but also that for the coordination of action through the attainment of binding agreements among individuals. But if understanding is always limited by the histories of communicants, if understanding and agreement are not synonymous, and if, as I have shown, to agree is not necessarily to act, then Habermas's theoretical basis for the coordination of action is prejudiced. Fay (1987) has recently argued that Habermas's theoretical account of communicative action presupposes and draws upon an 'excessive rationalism of the ontology of activity' (p. 212).

He suggests that in the context of social action, an account of reason 'needs to be modified to unravel the mysteries of human identity and to make the hard choices with which humans are inevitably faced' (p. 212).

Moreover, as Heller (1984) recognises, complete consensus is not an ideal. For we may hold what she terms 'true values', which involve morality but may nevertheless oppose each other (p. 95). This leads to the *dilemma of morality*. A true value is one for which we can claim universal validity; however, because we have often to make value *choices*, we cannot claim universal moral validity for our actions:

> if I proclaim justice to be a value but then as the occasion arises show mercy instead of justice, or in the name of justice show no mercy to a person pleading for mercy, then in neither of these cases can I wish my action to have any claim to universal validity. Neither the choice of values nor value rational action can exclude the aspect of personal responsibility . . .
>
> Morality . . . realises itself in action, and the process of realisation cannot be wished away from morality . . . The dilemma is a dilemma, *because it has no theoretical solution.* For anyone who makes a moral judgement . . . it is their duty to differentiate between the realisation of a value, the incoherence of a value system and the rationalisation of their own particularity. *There is no general formula which could release them from this responsibility.* (Heller, 1984, pp. 85, 87)

We cannot avoid the dilemma of morality because we must make value choices. And we cannot avoid personal responsibility for these choices and our actions. The integrated personality is one that acknowledges and accepts this responsibility.

To summarise this theoretical discussion, then: as individuals and societies, our different historical experiences obstruct our understanding of ourselves and others; nevertheless, if we are to be whole people our past is no excuse for what we do.

Let us lead now from theory to method. Habermas's conception of aesthetic rationality, David Ingram (1987) believes, is an attempt by him 'to reinvest his theory with hermeneutic content, thereby bridging the gap between discursive reflection and lived experience that had bothered so many of his critics' (p. xii). One consequence of recognising the aesthetic dimension and accordingly one's responsibility

when exercising power through the making of value choices is, I argue, to make us aware of what I term our hermeneutic responsibility
– whether one is a politician, government officer, NGO practitioner or researcher. It is this hermeneutic element, therefore, that requires to be developed in research methodologies.

This hermeneutic responsibility occurs furthermore at two levels because there is a 'double hermeneutic' (Giddens, 1984, p. 374). The first level is the interpretation required of actors' presentation of their world – the internalist lifeworld perspective. The second is the interpretation of the author's presentation of that presentation. If one holds an awareness of these hermeneutic requirements, then one cannot relapse into a positivist epistemology, which acknowledges only an objectivating viewpoint, and in which thrives a purposive rationality and hence the desire to manipulate humans and nature.

In the conduct of these hermeneutic tasks, an issue that arises is the distinction Giddens makes between mutual knowledge and common sense (pp. 334–43). This requires us not only to interpret but to critique, and as I have argued in the book, mutual knowledge can only be arrived at through an intersubjective process of critique, in which internalist and externalist perspectives are engaged. A barrier that critique seeks to overcome is that within a social context much mutual knowledge is tacit, carried on at the level of practical rather than discursive consciousness (Giddens, 1984, p. 336).[4] For instance, the grazing scheme management strategy adhered to by most communal area pastoralists is held largely at this practical level of consciousness. It is fully revealed to the outsider only if farmers are engaged in a dialogue in which they are treated as equally human.

In my fieldwork, the link between critical theory and method was influenced by Fay's threefold characterisation of a critical social science. These characteristics were those of interpretation, critique and the enabling of change. Since then, Fay (1987) has come to lay greater stress on human differentness and on the constraints to understanding. He thus agrees that a much greater methodological emphasis needs to be placed on interpretation.

The case-study method employed, especially if seen in terms of the type of extended case study or situational analysis that Manchester School social scientists such as van Velsen and Turner introduced, can be imbued with much hermeneutic and critical sensitivity, if the idea of a researcher as active virtual participant replaces the concept of participant observation. In the context of not only Zimbabwe but also other peasant farming environments, and indeed any society which historically lacks an orthography, research of this nature is particularly essential if the arrogant misunderstanding of those who exert power is to be superseded.

If one accepts the double hermeneutic, then this hermeneutic sensitivity has to occur at two levels. More especially, if the understanding and knowledge of outsiders of rural societies (or government bureaucracies) is to be improved, part of the methodological challenge is to negotiate the double hermeneutic. This is an area where both Habermas and Gadamer agree. Gadamer speaks of understanding being a process of the 'fusion of horizons'. For Habermas, if mutual understanding is to take place, the explanation offered by an outsider for a phenomenon has to be located within the same 'universe of discourse' as that within which the actors involved provide theirs (1985, p. 205). Social scientists or bureaucrats, if they use language esoterically, block their ability to understand and communicate with others. Nevertheless Habermas is insistent that even if in a social science one has to establish 'hermeneutic access' to an object domain, one does not have to renounce the idea that through engagement we can strive towards a more objective (or consensual) understanding of history.

As far as Zimbabwe is concerned, colonial presentations of Shona history, and indeed the normative counter-accounts of the Shona themselves, have in the last few years rapidly begun to be overturned. In this study the internalist perspective of those I worked with in the communal areas is drawn from and framed within the externalist perspective I have constructed from the paradigms of production and communication. This means that at the farmer level, although the research was focused on production activities, I did not attempt specifically to 'fuse' my horizon of understanding with those with whom I interacted.[5] I would suggest then that my presentation is most vulnerable from the internalist perspective.

Accepting this limitation, two paths emerge, I believe, from the historically embedded analysis that has been presented. The first derives from the fact that the rural economy is not founded solely on agriculture. Migrant incomes have provided a more secure base for rural social welfare since at least 1930. Moreover, the experience of the case-study households suggests that, in adverse and perhaps in all but very favourable seasons, off-farm activities are more important internal sources of income than are farm activities for especially poor, but also many middle and even a few leading farmers.

The government, however, lacks policies which support the

diversification of rural employment and the absorptive capacity of the rural and urban informal sector. As one local commentator cogently points out, in the 1985–90 First Five-Year National Development Plan it is acknowledged that the most favourable employment growth rate will only take up 15 per cent of school leavers during the plan period. Nevertheless, the question of how the other 85 per cent of job seekers are expected to earn their livelihoods is totally ignored (*Moto*, 1986, no. 46 pp. 5–7). It is not surprising then that communal area farmers speak as anxiously about jobs as they do the land itself.

The need for off-farm employment support is thus one substantive requirement that emerges from the analysis. The second is with reference to the land itself. The starting-point here is that the land cannot support the burgeoning school leaver and school drop-out population, even if a more flexible land resettlement policy were to open up additional land for small-scale farmers.

A brief reference is useful here to a visit I made to the Masvori resettlement area north of Chiwundura in April 1987. With their 5 ha (Model A) arable land allocations, farmers here have landholdings more than double those in the adjacent communal area. Upon entering a village I was struck by the sight next to one home of an enormous storage container constructed from wooden poles, full of maize cobs waiting to be shelled. There were over 100 bags worth of maize in that container, and the woman farmer present estimated their final harvest would be nearly double (Fieldnotes, 23 April 1987). In Chiwundura, among the four leading farmers I worked with, each of whom had 5 ha of land, although in split locations, the highest output produced in 1987 was under 60 bags. The resettlement farmers were probably benefiting from several advantages. The arable allocation of each household was in one unit close to the village. The soils having been worked only a few years still had a higher natural fertility than in the communal area and the greater vegetation cover in the area allowed farmers to bulk up their livestock manure considerably with plant litter, in order to maintain this fertility. Finally, the granting of loans by the AFC for the purchase of draught oxen meant that all households had draught power.

Notwithstanding the greater productivity of many of these resettlement farmers compared with their communal area counterparts, villagers estimated that 60 per cent of farmers in the village would still be in debt by the end of that year's marketing period (Fieldnotes, 23 April 1987). In a sample survey of 111 resettlement farmers in natural regions II, III and IV (the bias towards region II) that he conducted in 1986–7, Kinsey (1987) found that in March 1987 the average level of debt was Z$1043. Only 8 per cent of farmers had no debt, and over 16 per cent had debts exceeding Z$2000 (pp. ii, 16–19). Still 55 per cent of these farmers had had a farm income of over Z$1200 for 1985/6. This suggests that the resettlement area farmers are involved to a greater extent in cash crop farming, with concomitantly larger cash flows, than are most communal area farmers in the Midlands, but the robustness of their household economies is still in doubt.

Furthermore, as indicated in Chapter 3, whilst 20 per cent of the large-scale commercial sector has been subsumed since 1969, mostly for resettlement purposes (Table 3.1), no alleviation of communal area population densities has occurred. And, on the basis of the evidence above and experience in the communal areas, if the current resettlement models are retained but population densities in the resettlement areas increased, this will not enhance the viability of agricultural production within them.

This means that an expansion of the land horizon of most communal farmers is not currently a likely proposition. Nevertheless, if the government were to be less concerned with the tight control of the resettlement programme, particularly in its prevention of any peasant purchase of commercial ranchland, there is land suitable for pastoral purposes adjacent to many communal areas in natural regions II, IV and V. This could, under the control of peasant farmer groups, at least help alleviate the acute scarcity of grazing land in the communal areas. Even if such marginal expansion of the communal areas occurred however, a process which thus far the government has been dead against, there is still a need for the intensification of agricultural production within the communal areas. Unless AIDS came to decimate the rural population, peasant farmers and government officials alike agree on this need for intensification. And it can only be achieved through the assurance of a more secure water supply and the maintenance of the soil's organic content.

In the book it has been contended that the late-nineteenth-century agricultural system of the southern Shona was based on a wetland cultivation system. In this century indigenous irrigation methods have been stamped out ruthlessly. The methods were condemned for generating erosion, although no evidence has been advanced to support this claim, and in fact what evidence does exist shows their value (e.g. Theisen, 1973; Grant, 1981; Wilson, 1986a and 1989a; Bell,

1988). The result, as Theisen (1976) argues, has been 'retrogressive' psychologically and physiologically. People have become more vulnerable to seasonal variability, and, turning their energy 'inward for survival', they have no energy or incentive left to protect vlei areas over which they have inadequate control (p. 8).

The replacement technocratic path in the communal areas has been through the capital-intensive development of irrigation schemes, on which farmer holdings vary from 0.1 ha to 2 ha.[6] However, in the communal areas this capital-intensive development of irrigation is not a viable proposition. Until now the schemes have been heavily subsidised, and as net returns have decreased with rising construction costs, this situation is unlikely to be turned around (World Bank, 1983). Besides, as shown for Chiwundura, the paucity of these schemes leads only to a small percentage of farmers benefiting.

A relevant comment on the Mtorohuku scheme in Mtengwa West, Chiwundura, to which I have referred earlier, is provided by Hughes (1974), on the basis of personal communication from Theisen. Hughes discusses the 'negative attitudes' towards the scheme of especially those living near it:

> In this instance the scheme had been established on vlei land which people in the area had been accustomed to cultivate. Such land is highly regarded in this area, as it permits the cultivation of winter crops and provides an assured supply of summer crops, even in drought years.
>
> First, the cultivation of this vlei land had been forbidden in terms of Natural Resources legislation. Then the scheme had been established on land the cultivation of which had been forbidden. Finally, the people (including those who had previously been cultivating this land) were invited to take up plots on the scheme, provided that they paid considerable sums of money 'to the government' annually and submitted to a host of irksome restrictions.
>
> The expression of negative attitudes towards the scheme by these people is not completely inexplicable in circumstances such as these. (p. 216).[7]

An alternative to these schemes would be a return to the careful and strategic use of the key-resource vleis, riverine strips, wells and gardens, through combining nineteenth-century methods and knowledge with the twentieth-century ability to research and improve technology. Farmers themselves believe these key resources could serve as a pivot for a more sustainable agriculture. In sandveld areas such as Chiwundura this would complement the smallholding land use pattern that has developed.

Towards the end of the fieldwork I held a meeting in Mtengwa West to find out from a range of farmers their views on their deteriorating debt situation. Most of these farmers, including the poorer, had either in their homefield or in a separate garden, a shallow well, used mainly for watering vegetables. At this meeting a proposal that these might be deepened a little so as to provide supplementary irrigation, through gravity feeding, to one or two contour strips of their field (from 0.2 ha to 0.5 ha), received much consideration (Fieldnotes, 9 April 1987). But for most, the digging, lining and even a simple pump would require another loan.

Agritex staff in Gweru withheld serious comment on the idea because of lack of knowledge of the underlying geology and how the hydrology of a system like this would work (Gweru discussion meeting, 13 April 1987). From the vlei area research that he conducted in Chiwundura, however, Theisen (1973) was able to state that cultivation and the provision of a crop cover prevented the evaporation of the capillary water from the soil surface during the crucial October–December period before the main rains. If the vleis were only left for grazing this did not occur. Theisen concluded that if further trials did confirm the trend, 'then it is obvious that cultivation will improve the water reserves of the vlei thus confirming the local people's belief that vlei cropping, "raises up the moisture" to improve the springs, sponges and wells' (p. 50).[8]

Wilson (1988c) from his research in the south of the Midlands province suggests that on the rather different clay soils of Mazvihwa a wetland cultivation system would be as appropriate:

> This would mean a reversion to farming small productive areas near (not necessarily always on) rivers with supplementary irrigation (rather than full-scale irrigation works which are too expensive and use too much water). The bulk of the land could then support a combination of livestock and game . . . [with] soil conservation work . . . recreating heterogeneity in the land surface, and ensuring a rapid increase in vegetation cover and soil organic matter. (p. 15)

This is a long way from the present communal area land use system in the drier natural regions, which generally owes its form to the exercise of technocratic coercion rather than farmer ingenuity. Many local-level extension staff agree with the Shurugwi extension supervisor, quoted at the outset of the chapter, that farmers' capabilities are underestimated because of the lack of dialogue between peasantry and bureaucracy. Agritex certainly requires dialogue with farmers if it is to find policy directions which are consistent with its goal as an organisation. Dialogue, however, as the post-independence history of Agritex has shown, cannot easily be institutionalised. Social history, and embedded within this, individual histories, provide formidable barriers to the effective institutional change that is the prior requirement for radical substantive change. If things are to be changed, 'then things must be changed, not least in precisely the relationships between people' (Heller, 1984, p. 136).

Theory, method and substance can now be drawn together. For, overriding them all, is the duality of structure. At the centre of any consideration of the sphere of human action, *praxis*, is the agent, the person who would be a whole personality, to paraphrase Heller. An agent has needs, and as a social creature these needs are fulfilled through social circumstances. Resource scarcity ensures that all needs cannot be fulfilled, but human weaknesses and unreason aggravate the failure. For in addition to needs, we also have interests, which unlike needs, require the exercise of power over others for their achievement (Heller, 1984, pp. 185–6). Social structure constrains and enables, we are formed by it and in turn reproduce the social systems in which structure is 'recursively implicated' (Giddens, 1984, pp. 25, 304). How much then as agents can we 'make a difference' to a state of affairs or course of events? Giddens holds the strong view that in fact, 'an agent ceases to be such if he or she loses the capability to "make a difference", that is to exercise some sort of power' (p. 14).

The final element to be considered then is power and its relation to need. The ability to make a difference cannot be considered out of the context of the paradigm of production and the social inequalities which are the outcome of differentiated access to production resources and outputs. But although these inequalities are often the outcome of purposive-rational actions, that is actions of a strategic or instrumental nature, they may be tackled through communicative action. Communicative action is contingent upon the use of power, but social norms eschewing asymmetries of power and divisions of interest in society persist because there are always those who stubbornly oppose 'those relations of force that are inconspicuously set in the very structures of communication' (Habermas, 1979, p. 119). In this context those who hold power can perhaps best be appealed to through the conviction of feeling born from experience. This conviction is that of an aesthetic rationality.

There remains the dilemma of morality. Quite clearly in the bureaucratic and economic systems of the modern era, attempts at democratic communication are by themselves inadequate as a means of mitigating the overdominant institutionalisation of a purposive rationality. The strategic involvement of others is essential even if one's commitment is to seek the spread of a communicative rationality. What values underpin the strategic action and how an individual combines the two types of action are no more and no less than the responsibility of that person. At the social level this individual responsibility remains, for, as Ingram (1987) concludes his synthesis of Habermas's recent work: 'There are no criteria of rational argumentation to which we can appeal in disputes over how this balance, so central to our utopian understanding of the good life, should be construed' (pp. 178–9). Ingram suggests that once more we must return to Max Weber:

> The naive pre-Socratic reliance on a pure aesthetic ethos – a rhetoric of life, if you prefer – in which humanity is handed over to a fate that is at once both beautiful and tragic is no longer a real possibility for us. But neither is that equally naive confidence in the power of reason to soar above the historicity of substantive tradition. And so we return once again to Weber, for to be caught up in the eternal conflict between the gods of critical reflection and those of living tradition is the only fate possible. Any attempt to extricate ourselves can only lead to nihilism. (pp. 187–8)

We may indeed be forever condemned to misunderstand because we cannot remove the inhibiting depth of our personal and social histories. But critical social theory has come a long way from the pit of theoretical despair into which Weber cast himself. Whereas for Weber the advance of reason could lead only to the paradoxical repressiveness of *Zweckrationalitat*, Habermas re-establishes reason as the defender of choice and alternative possibilities. The eternal struggle between reason and the prejudice of tradition is the essence of life itself. For me, Habermas and Zimbabwe's rural peoples are alike in that they show that however despairing objective circumstances might seem, the reproduction of life lies in not surrendering to the bleakness.

Appendix 1: Extended Case Study Households: Resource Access 1986/7

A. CHIWUNDURA – TAKUNDA AND PHUMELELA AREAS

Farmer(s)	Arable land (ha)		Labour		Livestock and draught power	Income sources for investment in agriculture	Comments
Category 1: Leading farmers							
T1. Takavada (& Mrs) Chairman, farmer group	Homefield: Garden: Dryland Arable:	1.45 0.5 3.5 5.45	Full: Part-time: Piecework for weeding and harvesting	6 6	Cattle: 22, of which 8 with son in resettlement area, and 6 with daughter locally.	Credit and previous maize sales.	Sons contributed $200 after 1987 harvest to paying off of $1131 AFC debt.
T2. Nhonga (& Mrs) Vice-chairman, farmer group, Chairman, area and district committees	Homefield: Garden: Dryland Arable:	2.7 0.7 1.65 5.05	Full: Part-time: Piecework for harvesting	2 4	Cattle: +45, of which 32 with nephew in resettlement area	Credit, maize and tomato sales, building piecework.	Wealthiest and most entrepreneurial of case study farmers.
P1. Mangwalala Chairman, farmer group, area committee member	Homefield: Garden: Dryland Arable:	3.0 0.6 2.75 6.35	Full: Part-time:	2 1	Cattle: 10, all at home.	Credit and maize sales.	AFC debt of $700 at end of 1987.

Appendix 1 (*continued*)

Farmer(s)	Arable land (ha)		Labour		Livestock and draught power	Income sources for investment in agriculture	Comments
P2. Mrs Skosana Vice-chairwoman, farmer group	Homefield: Garden: Dryland Arable:	0.75 0.55 3.75 ––––– 5.05	Full: incl. 2 male employees Part-time:	3 5+	Cattle: 16, all at home.	Credit, remittances from husband, maize, tomato and groundnut sales.	Husband invested $1000 in well, water tank, hand pump & piping – can irrigate 0.5ha. Unsuccessful pig project draining maize and cash.
Category 2: Middle farmers							
T3. K. Mugoni (& Mrs)	Homefield: Garden: Dryland Arable:	1.35 0.25 0.8 ––––– 2.40	Full: Part-time:	3 2	1 Cow, 4 Donkeys. Latter used for draught power.	Credit.	Mugoni is seeking to substitute antheap for fertiliser, to avoid credit.
T4. Mrs R. Mugoni	Homefield: Garden: Dryland Arable:	0.85 0.3 1.85 ––––– 3.00	Full: Part-time:	2 3	Cattle: 5	Remittances from husband. Some use of maize sales.	Used credit once only.
T5. Mrs T. Mabuku	Homefield: (incl. small garden) Dryland Arable:	0.85 0.95 ––––– 1.80	Full: Part-time:	2 3	Cattle: 4, but incl. no oxen. Draught power hired and borrowed.	Occasional remittance from husband, credit, some use of maize sales.	

Name	Landholding (ha)		Labour		Cattle / Draught power	Other income	Notes
P3. Mrs Mangamba	Homefield: 0.9 Garden: 0.3 Dryland Arable: 1.05 2.25		Full: Part-time:	1 5	Cattle: 4	Credit, remittances from husband.	
P4. Mathe (& Mrs)	Homefield: 1.65 Garden: 0.25 Dryland Arable: 0.25 2.5		Full: Part-time:	2 2	1 Heifer. Draught power hired and borrowed.	Piecework and craft sales.	
Category 3: Poor farmers T6. Komboni (& Mrs)	Homefield: 1.2 (incl. small garden)		Full: Part-time:	2 2	Cattle: 2, both oxen.	Credit, piecework, social welfare.	Komboni has TB. He lends Hozheri, his neighbour, his oxen, in return for help with ploughing. Their wives aid each other with weeding.
T7. Mrs Kumira	Homefield: 1.1 (incl. small garden)		Full: Part-time:	1 2	No cattle. Draught power hired or borrowed.	Craft sales.	
T8. Hozheri (& Mrs)	Homefield: 0.65 (incl. small garden)		Full: Part-time:	1 2	No cattle. Draught power borrowed.	Given.	Young couple: given seed by relatives & repay use of draught power with labour.
P5. Mrs Mkucha	Homefield: 2.0		Full: Part-time:	2 1	No cattle. Draught power borrowed and mushandirapamwe.	Credit and temporary employment.	

Appendix 1 (*continued*)

Farmer(s)	Arable land (ha)	Labour		Livestock and draught power	Income sources for investment in agriculture	Comments
P6. Moyo (& Mrs)	Homefield: 1.0 (incl. small garden)	Full: Part-time:	2 2	Cattle: 6	Piecework and hire out of draught power.	Three children of secondary school age engaged in temporary work to try and earn school fees.
P7. Tangwena (& Mrs)	Homefield: 1.6	Full: Part-time:	2 1	No cattle. First contour strip hoe planted, then assistance given.	Limited remittances from son-in-law.	Tangwena joined mushandirapamwe group after being given assistance to plough and plant 1 ha.

Note: All garden areas possess at least one open well, and except for Mrs R. Mugoni all gardens are attached to either the homefield or the dryland arable areas.

B. CHIRUMHANZU – MAVHAIRE AND MAWARE AREAS

Category 1: Leading farmers

Farmer(s)	Arable land (ha)	Labour		Livestock and draught power	Income sources for investment in agriculture	Comments
MV1. Nhakuza (& Mrs) Area committee member	7.85	Full: Part-time:	2 5	Cattle: 17	Crop sales.	
MV2. Mhene (& Mrs) Treasurer of savings club	3.55 (+1.9 under migrant sons)	Full: (incl. 2 employees) Part-time:	4 3	Cattle: 31, of which 14 belong to sons.	Crop sales and remittances from sons.	Mhene is one-legged; two of his sons pay the salaries of the two employees.

Farmer		Labour		Livestock	Income sources	Notes
MV3. Mugwisi (& Mrs) Chairman, farmer group and savings club.	8.80	Full: Part-time: Extensive piecework	2 2	Cattle: 37	Crop sales.	
MW1. Mugarisi (& Mrs) Farmer group chairman	4.00	Full: Part-time: Piecework for harvesting	2 4	Cattle: 6, incl. 2 oxen	Credit, crop sales and building piecework.	Constructed small weir and engine used for supplementary irrigation in 83/4 and 84/5. Engine stolen in 85/6.
Category 2: Middle farmers						
MV4. Nhambeni (& Mrs)	3.00	Full:	2	Donkeys: 4	Crop sales and building piecework.	
MV5. Ms Gonga	4.55	Full: Part-time:	1 2	Cattle: 18	Crop sales.	
MV6. Mrs Jeke	4.85	Part-time:	3	Cattle: 9, incl. 2 oxen	Crop sales and remittances from husband.	Mrs Jeke had a child in December and could only do limited agricultural work.
MW2. K. Mugwisi	3.45	Full: Part-time:	2 2	Cattle: 3, 1 ox and 1 cow used for draught power.	Building piecework undertaken by son.	Son after a period in Harare decided that it was more profitable and easier for him to be a rural builder.
MW3. Mrs Jengwa	2.10	Full: Part-time:	1 2	Cattle: 7, incl. 3 oxen	Remittances from husband.	

Appendix 1 (*continued*)

Farmer(s)	Arable land (ha)	Labour		Livestock and draught power	Income sources for investment in agriculture	Comments
MW4. Machipisi (& Mrs)	4.30	Full: Part-time:	1 5	Cattle: 8, incl. 4 oxen (1 sold towards end of season)	Crop sales.	
Category 3: Poor farmers						
MV7. Masocha (& Mrs)	1.95	Full: Part-time:	1 2	Donkeys borrowed from brother-in-law for draught power	Building piecework.	Mrs Masocha is crippled and can only contribute in a limited way to the agricultural work.
MV8. Tevera (& Mrs)	1.80	Full:	2	Cattle: 1, draught power hired.	Beer sales, craft sales and various types of piecework.	
MW5. Manyonga (& Mrs)	1.85	Full: Part-time:	1 1	Draught power hired (paid for with labour)	Piecework as a labourer.	
MW6. Rangwa	4.60	Full: Part-time:	1 2	Cattle: 5, incl. 3 oxen	Nil	Wife and eldest son died suddenly the previous year and in 86/7 Rangwa took little interest in farming; he planted late and scarcely weeded.

Appendix 2: Extended Case Study Households: Income Profiles, November 1986 to July 1987

A. CHIWUNDURA – TAKUNDA AREA

Household	Income from crop sales		Other sources of income	
1. Takavada	Maize sales from 1986 harvest:			
	1986 – 50 bags to GMB at $14.75 net	$737.50	6&7/87 Food-for-work at $44.00/month	$88.00
	1986 – 16 bags locally at $15.00	$240.00		
	1&2/87 – 3 bags locally at $3.00/tin	$54.00		
	3&4/87 – 1 bag locally at $4.50/tin	$27.00		
	4/87 – 0.5 bag locally at $4.50/tin	$15.00		
		$1073.50		
	Maize sales from 1987 harvest:			
	5/87 – 2 bags locally at $24.00/bag	$48.00		
	Est further sales – 30 bags at $24/bag	$720.00		
	Groundnut sales: 1 bag at $30.00	$30.00		
		$798.00		

Appendix 2 (continued)

Household	Income from crop sales	Other sources of income

2. Nhonga	Maize sales from 1986 harvest:
	1986 – 68 bags to GMB at $14.75/bag $958.75
	2&3/87 – 5 bags locally at $18.00/bag $90.00
	  $1048.75
	
	Crop sales from 1987 harvest:
	2&3/87 Tomato sales in Gweru $50.00
	3&4/87 Sales of early maize crop,
	19 bags at $20.00/bag $380.00
	Est further sales – 24 bags at $24/bag $576.00
	  $1006.00
		11&12/86 Draught power hire $16.00
		
		87 Building work $200.00
		4/87 Winter ploughing $40.00
		6&7/87 Food-for-work at $44.00/month $88.00

3. K. Mugoni		Income: Mugoni 11/86 Draught hire (donkeys) $40.00 Goat sold to buy medicine for Mrs M. $32.00 3&4/87 Brickmaking for school $47.00 Income: Mrs Mugoni 12/86 Weeding piecework $37.00 (incl. children) 5&6/87 Crochet work (sold Kadoma) cotton $13.50 – net 2nd hand clothes +$11.50
4. Mrs R. Mugoni		Remittances – these vary depending on requirements, monthly range: $30–$100 (incl. goods e.g. fertiliser, building materials for house)

5. Mrs Mabuku

Income – 1986:

Crochet mats – 7 sets (of 3) at $7.00 cost $6.30/set – net	$4.90
Clay pots – 30 at $1.00 each	$30.00

Income – 1987:

1/87 Clay pots, 6	$4.50
2/87 Weeding piecework	$16.20
4–6/87 Knitted gloves, 14 pairs wool $18.15, gross $54.00 – net	$35.85
6/87 Collected from husband (self-employed painter, undertaking piecework in Kadoma)	$200.00

6. Komboni

Social welfare provide 20 kg mealie meal, 5 kg powdered milk, 2 kg beans per month because of child with TB (Komboni also has TB)	
11/86 Draught power hire	$16.00

Income: Mrs Komboni

Resale of 8 large bars of soap (bought Gweru) – net	$5.80
6&7/87 Food-for-work at $44.00/month	$88.00

7. Mrs Kumira

1/87 Red termites collected & roasted	$3.00
Goats sold at $20.00 each	$40.00
3&4/87 Grass brooms – net loss	–$5.00
7/87 Grass brooms – net	$3.70

Appendix 2 (*continued*)

Household	Income from crop sales		Other sources of income	
8. Hozheri			From 4/87 was able to obtain social welfare because of adult daughter's disability, $40.00/month	$120.00
			Income from piecework on commercial farms, amount unknown	

A. CHIWUNDURA – PHUMELELA AREA

Household	Income from crop sales		Other sources of income	
1. Mangwalala	Crop sales from 1986 harvest: Maize – 20 bags to GMB	$295.00	Chickens – 20 at $5.50 each costs – $62.50, net	$48.50
	Crop sales from 1987 harvest:			
	Maize – 1.5 bags locally	$32.00		
	Groundnuts – 1 bag locally	$35.00		
	Sunflowers – 4 bags locally at $5/tin	$120.00		
		$187.00		
2. Mrs Skosana	Crop sales from 1986 harvest: Groundnuts – 7 bags at ?		Remittance income: min. of 2 wages/month at $50.00 each	$100.00

Crop sales from 1987 harvest:
Tomatoes – Gweru market at $3.50/tin — $185.00
6–7/87 G'nuts – 4 tins locally at $7/tin — $28.00
Est further sales:
Groundnuts – 6 bags locally at $35/bag — $210.00
$423.00

3–5/87 Chickens – 50 purchased but 25 died. Gross sales $124, net — $13.00
6–7/87 Pigs – 4 killed and meat sold locally — $76.00
6–7/87 Pig – 1 sold locally (alive) (cost of feed for pigs +$1000.00) — $50.00

3. Mrs Mangamba
Crop sales from 1986 harvest:
Rapoko – 1&2/87 2 bags at $10.00/tin — $120.00
Monthly remittance from husband — +$30.00
4/87 Goat sold — $40.00

4. Mathe
Income: Mathe
Winnowing baskets – 17 sold at $3 (some paid for with chickens) — $42.00
Tobacco-offcuts, net — $11.65
3,5/87 Food-for-work – maize — 1.3 bags
6–7/87 Food-for-work at $44/month — $88.00
Income: Mrs Mathe
1/87 Red termites (roasted) at 10c/cup — $2.50

5. Mrs Mkucha
winter/86 Temporary employment as a domestic at $50/month — $100.00
12/86 Meat of half a pig sold — $24.00
5/87 Food-for-work – maize — 1 bag
6–7/87 Food-for-work at $44/month — $88.00

6. Moyo
Income: Mrs Moyo
1–2/87 Weeding – maize — 1.5 bags

Appendix 2 (*continued*)

Household	Income from crop sales	Other sources of income	
		Income: Moyo	
		3/87 Food-for-work – maize	5 buckets
		5/87 Food-for-work – maize	1 bag
		6–7/87 Food-for-work at $44/month	$88.00
		Income: Children	
		2 Teenage children had temporary jobs of from 2–4 months, earning from $20–$23 per month	
7. Tangwena		1–2/87 Maize-meal remitted by son-in-law	
		Income: Tangwena	
		3/87 Food-for-work – maize	5 buckets
		5/87 Food-for-work – maize	1 bag
		6–7/87 Food-for-work at $44/month	$88.00
		Income: Tangwena's son	
		6–7/87 Building piecework	$147.00

B. CHIRUMHANZU – MAWARE AREA

1. Mugarisi

Crop sales from 1986 harvest:		
Maize – 18 bags to GMB	$265.00	
Sorghum – 15 bags to GMB	$221.25	
	$486.75	

Crop sales from 1987 harvest:		
Green mealies – 3 bags sold in Mashava	$325.00	
Maize – 4 bags at $20.00/bag	$80.00	
Maize – 3 bags at $22.50/bag	$67.50	
Maize – 3 bags at $24.00/bag	$72.00	
Groundnuts – 8 tins at $7.50 each	$60.00	
Sunflowers – 15 bags to GMB	$242.00	
	$846.50	

11–12/86 Sale of chickens in Mashava, net	$146.52	
7–9/87 Building work – House 1	$350.00	
House 2	$475.00	
	$825.00	

2. K. Mugwisi

Maize sales from 1986 harvest: – 8 bags locally	$118.00	

Income: Mrs Mugwisi		
2/87 Beer brewing, net	$19.00	
6–8/87 Food-for-work at $44/month	$132.00	
Son's income:		
(He lives at home, and is a builder)		
11/86 Blair toilet built	$30.00	
12/86–1/87 Outside plastering	$35.00	
1987 House built	$230.00	
5–8/87 Another house built, school ceilings put in, house in Masvingo completed	?	

Appendix 2 (continued)

Household	Income from crop sales	Other sources of income	
3. Mrs Jengwa		Remittances – monthly range $50–$60	
		12/86 Herbalist treatment	$30.00
		2/87 Beer brewing, net	$11.00
		1987 Table mats, 1 set at $7.00	$7.00
4. Machipisi	Crop sales from 1986 harvest: Rapoko – 5 bags to GMB $126.00	Manure – 4 lorry loads sold to mission 4 × 5 tonnes at $30.00 each	$120.00
	Crop sales from 1987 harvest: Sorghum – 5 bags locally at $20.00/bag $100.00 Rapoko – 2 bags locally at $10.00/tin $120.00 Sunflowers – 4 bags to GMB $70.00 $290.00	Draught ox (sold to pay daughter's 'O' level fees)	$220.00
		Mrs Machipisi: mid 5–8/87 Food-for-work at $44/month	$154.00
5. Manyonga		Income: Manyonga 12/86 Building – hut, pd set of overalls	
		Dam repairing piecework – 50 kg mealie meal – 8 days work	$40.00
		Labourer in building cooperative constructing church	$100.00
		8/87 Working at Driefontein Mission for building cooperative	?
		Income: Mrs Manyonga 8/87 Food-for-work at $44.00/month	$44.00
		2 Goats sold (for mealie meal) at $26.00 each	$52.00
6. Rangwa		mid 5–8/87 Food-for-work at $44.00/month	$154.00

B. CHIRUMHANZU – MAVHAIRE

Household	Income from crop sales		Other sources of income	
1. Nhakuza	Crop sales from 1986 harvest:			
	Maize – 28 bags to GMB at $14.75/bag	$413.00	Goats – 3 sold for $40.00 each	$120.00
	Rapoko – 8 bags to GMB at $27.00/bag	$216.00	Group garden – sales by Mrs Nhakuza	
	Sunf'rs – 3 bags to GMB at $16.10/bag	$48.30	$20.00 rtd to group for seed – net	$30.00
	Maize – 4 bags locally at $4.00/tin	$96.00	Women's group uniform making	
	Mhunga – 1 tin locally at $4.00/tin	$4.00	repaid joining fee of $40.00 – net	$60.00
		$777.30		
	Crop sales from 1987 harvest:			
	Maize – 20 bags locally at $24.00/bag	$480.00		
	G'nuts – 3 bags locally at $21.00/bag	$63.00		
	(sold cheaply to relatives)			
	Sweet potatoes – 2 tins at $12.00/tin	$24.00		
	Sorghum – 2 bags locally at $20.00/bag	$40.00		
		$747.80		
2. Mhene	Crop sales from 1986 harvest:			
	Maize – 38 bags to GMB at $14.75/bag	$560.00	Remittances – 2 sons $50.00 each	
	Rapoko – 5 bags to GMB at $25.75/bag	$96.00	per month for 2 wage labourers	
	Mhunga – 5 bags to GMB at $21.20/bag	$128.75		
	G'nuts – 4 bags locally at $24.00/bag	$106.00	Beer brewing – 3 occasions gross	$120.00
		$891.25		

Appendix 2 (*continued*)

Household	Income from crop sales		Other sources of income	
	Crop sales from 1987 harvest:			
	Maize – 16 bags to St Josephs Mission at $180.00/tonne	$261.76		
	Maize – 12 bags locally at $20.00/bag	$240.00		
	G'nuts – 1 bag locally at $8.00/tin	$48.00		
	Mhunga – 4 bags locally at $24.00/bag	$96.00		
	Sunf'wrs – 8 bags to GMB at $15.10/bag	$120.80		
		$766.56		
3. W. Mugwisi	Crop sales from 1986 harvest:		1–3/87 Milk and sour milk sales	$150.00
	Maize – 68 bags to GMB	$991.60		
	Sorghum – 5 bags to GMB	$67.26		
	Sunflowers – 3 bags to GMB	$46.48		
		$1105.34		
	Crop sales from 1987 harvest:			
	Maize – 45 bags locally at $24.00/bag	$1080.00		
	Sorghum – 1 bag locally at $20.00/bag	$20.00		
	Sorghum – 4 bags to GMB	$62.50		
	Sunflowers – 4 bags to GMB	$70.68		
		$1233.18		
4. Nhambeni	Crop sales from 1986 harvest:		Income: Nhambeni	
	Maize – 4 bags to GMB	$55.76	Building work – 12/86–5/87	$125.00
	Sorghum – 5 bags to GMB	$68.05	3/87	$100.00
	Maize – 4 bags locally at $18.00/bag	$72.00	7–9/87	$150.00
		$205.81	Income: joint	
			Beer brewing – 7 occasions net	$140.00

5. Ms Gonga

Crop sales from 1986 harvest:
Maize – 13 bags to GMB	$191.75
Sunflowers – 2 bags to GMB	$44.64
	$236.39

Crop sales from 1987 harvest:
Maize – 20 bags (?) locally at $24.00/bag	$480.00
Sun'frs – 3 bags to commercial fmr at $13.20/bag	$39.60
	$519.60

Income: Mrs Nhambeni
Knitting baby-suits – 3 sold – net	$105.00
Beer brewing	?
Pottery sales	?

6. Mrs Jeke

Crop sales from 1986 harvest:
Sorghum (red) – 4 bags to GMB	$59.00
Sorghum (white) – 3 bags to GMB	$39.30
Sunf'rs – 1 bag locally at $18.00/bag	$18.00
	$116.30

Crop sales from 1987 harvest:
Sunf'rs – 3 bags (to GMB)	$52.25

Remittances – approx. $45.00/month	
Chair covers – 2 sets of 4 at $35.00 each, materials $28.00, net	$42.00

7. Masocha

Income: Mashocha
Building work – late 86 – house 1	$75.00
late 86 & early 87 – house 2	$135.00
6&7/87 – house 3	$180.00
Bicycle repairs – 12/86	$25.00
6&7/87	$15.00
	$430.00

Appendix 2 (continued)

Household	Income from crop sales	Other sources of income	
		Income: Mrs Masocha	
		Beer brewing – 1/87	$18.00
		Knitting jerseys – 2 at $3.00 each net	$6.00
			$24.00
8. Tevera		Income: Tevera	
		1986 Brickmaking – 5000 unburnt brks	$100.00
		1986 Plastering – 1 round kitchen	$15.00
		1986 Hoe handles – 12 at 70c each	$8.40
		1986 Ox yokes – 2 at $7.00 each	$14.00
		1987 Hoe handles – 7 at 70c each	$4.90
		1987 Axe handles – 2 at $1.00 each	$2.00
		1987 Set of whips	$10.00
		5–7/87 Brickmaking – 2000 burnt brks	$80.00
		6&7/87 Building – 1 round hut	$120.00
		Income: Mrs Tevera	
		1986 Beer brewing – 3 occasions, net	$75.00
		1987 Beer brewing – 2 occasions, net	$55.00
		1986/87 Resale of snuff, 3 occasions	
		tin $2.00, gross sales $2.50, net	$1.50
		7/87 Beer brewing, net	$22.00
		6/87 Food-for-work, 3 days infilling	$6.00

Notes

Chapter 1 Introduction: The Past, Present and Future in Zimbabwe's Communal Areas

1. Habermas is pre-eminent amongst the second generation of Frankfurt School social scientists. The first generation, who included Max Horheimer, Theodore Adorno and Herbert Marcuse, were those at the Institute of Social Research (founded 1923), University of Frankfurt, during its most active years from 1933 to 1944. Nazism forced the Institute's leading members to flee to the United States and it never regained its pre-eminence. Habermas is associated with the Institute as he launched his career working as an assistant to Adorno between 1956 and 1961. He taught philosophy and sociology in Frankfurt from 1964 to 1971, then became director of the Max Planck Institute in Starnberg, and in 1983 returned to teaching at the Johann Goethe University in Frankfurt (Dews, 1986).
2. World Bank (1989) *World Development Report 1989*.
3. Oral accounts formed an invaluable part of the work of another researcher, Ken Wilson, whose work elsewhere in the Midlands province was begun slightly after mine. His research, conducted primarily in the Mavihwa communal area, south of Zvishavane, although it spilled over into the Mberengwa and Runde communal areas (Midlands province) and Chivi communal area (Masvingo province), I shall draw from on occasion in this study. Wilson was joined by a co-researcher, Ian Scoones, whose work on livestock I refer to in Chapter 4.
4. The work of the Centre for Applied Research in Education (CARE) at the University of East Anglia, since the time Lawrence Stenhouse was Director, exemplifies this.
5. This is a probable answer to an oft-made criticism of Habermas himself: why he has not applied his critical theory in practical work when it is supposed to be a theory concerned with praxis.
6. The term 'form of production' is appropriated from Rello, in R. L. Harris, 'Marxism and the agrarian question in Latin America', *Latin American Perspectives*, vol. 4 (1978) p. 4.
7. Some Shona and Dema peoples in the Zambezi valley in the north of Zimbabwe, and other Shona groups in the east of the country had had contact with Portuguese traders. These traders operated trading posts, and in the north even riverine farms from the fifteenth to early twentieth century (Lan, 1985, p. 17; Newitt, 1973, pp. 21–31). The cultural influence of the Portuguese was limited and more subtle than that of the British; there was a greater fusion of indigenous and exotic cultures.
8. Just how bureaucracies have changed in the post-colonial period is of course a complex issue. Hyden suggests that as a response to colonial experience African leaders have found it natural to replace an impersonal, economic market place by more direct and personal political interventions – the political market place:

These may be called bureaucratic measures, but they are not the impersonal, regulatory interventions of the modern type of bureaucracy. It is an approach in which the political ends of the regime are employed by the leaders to justify the use of the state machinery regardless of what the formal rules and regulations prescribe. (1980, p. 220)

Nevertheless patronage politics in any form is still a type of strategic action. The value system according to which political decisions are made may have altered, with less political emphasis being given to the credo of technical efficiency, but this does not mean the model of purposive-rational action is seen any less as the institutional ideal.

9. In the book I use the term 'policy action' to refer to the whole political and administrative process of policy formulation and implementation.

10. Hyden (1983) defines the 'economy of affection' as denoting 'a network of support, communications and interaction among structurally defined groups connected by blood, kin, community or other affinities, for example, religion' (p. 8).

11. See chapter 4.

12. For the Ture ward survey, the interviewees were local paraprofessional village health workers and community development workers, together with government agricultural extension workers. These people were involved in the drawing-up of the questionnaire and contributed to both the what and how of questions.

Chapter 2 The Colonial State and the Penetration of Purposive Rationality

1. Arrighi's (1967, 1973) pioneering articles of their time on the political economy of, and labour supplies in, Rhodesia, are the archetypes of this approach.

2. The British South Africa Company was established by Cecil John Rhodes to conduct the 1890 Pioneer Column into Zimbabwe and to provide the administrative services required by the new settlers.

3. The word 'chief' is placed in inverted commas because during the colonial period the whole concept of who and what a chief was became so much a colonial creation that it confuses entirely what actually were the pre-colonial roles, powers and titles of lineage leaders (see Wilson, 1986a, 1986c; and Cheater, 1988).

4. The *makuvi* derive their water from run-off from the granite outcrops which characterise the terrain of this sweep of central and south-eastern Zimbabwe. The run-off is unable to percolate far, unless the underlying granite bedrock is very jointed, and hence it may re-emerge as a spring, or coalesce as a stream, to form a vlei. The formation of the latter is often assisted by the existence of a clay hardpan layer.

   The oral history research conducted in Shurugwi communal area confirmed that the wetland agricultural system had predominated in this area, as well as the Runde–Mazvihwa areas to the south, where Wilson conducted his research. It can be proposed then that vlei areas were cultivated through most of this dry, granite country.

5. In Shurugwi communal area in 1988, whilst engaged on a Common-wealth Science Council agroforestry training and research project, I was shown *mipanje* ridges which had survived virtually intact since their owners had been forced to abandon them in 1929, when centralisation was introduced to the area. In this instance, ridges were constructed in four parallel lines down the slope. On the ridge, *shezhe*, a variety of sweet potato known elsewhere as *tsenza*, were grown, and in the channels between the ridges, rice (*mapunga*) was cultivated. After being abandoned for 50 years the only erosion I observed was near the bottom of the valley. Here the ridges had broken down in one place allowing lateral and then headward erosion. A belief that the system caused erosion was why the colonial authorities forced the abandonment of the practice.

6. Until 1957 what is now the Zvishavane district (formerly Shabani) was part of the Mberengwa district (formerly Belingwe).

7. In 1988 the Belingwe native commissioner guessed there were 1145 head in the district, but Zachrisson (1978, p. 214) states this was an underestimate. Another note is that the rinderpest epidemic, which decimated herds elsewhere in the south and west of Zimbabwe, does not seem to have affected the Mberengwa area.

8. Arrighi, 1973, pp. 189–91; van Onselen, 1976, pp. 100–1; Palmer, 1977a, p. 96; Mosley, 1983, p. 34, all discuss labour trends during this period. This was the time, following the establishment of the Labour Bureau in 1899 (there were three between 1899 and 1933), when the notorious *chibaro* system of forced labour was at its peak (van Onselen, 1976, p. 114). However, the major proportion of recruits, not least in the Mberengwa–Zvishavane area, were foreign workers (Mosley, 1983, p. 135; Zachrisson, 1978, p. 159).

9. Arrighi (1973, p. 203) records that the number of African-owned cattle increased at an average compound rate of 12.5 per cent per year between 1905 and 1921; this then fell to 6 per cent between 1921 and 1931, and 1 per cent between 1931 and 1945.

10. These comments continue and include the serious drought of 1946–7, which was the worst drought experienced until the 1982–4 drought (NC Belingwe, Annual reports, 1927, 1930, 1942, 1946, 1947).

11. Until the granting of responsible government in 1923, the colonial 'state' was controlled by both the Imperial government and the British South Africa Company.

12. Boserup's (1965, 1981) thesis is that agricultural innovation is induced by increases in population pressure on the land.

13. For example, Zachrisson (1978, pp. 247–55) describes this process for the Belingwe district.

14. The NC Belingwe first described the Runde communal area (then Lundi Reserve) as 'poor and overstocked' in his annual report for 1925 – although he did mention that 6000 transport cattle had used the area for pasture whilst outspanned along the Shabani–Selukwe road.

15. Some of these comparable predictions, including one made as recently as 1985, are referred to in Chapter 3.

16. C. Palley, *The Constitutional History and Law of Southern Rhodesia, 1888–1965* (Oxford, 1966) referred to in Holleman, 1968, p. 19.

17. CNC, Annual Report 1932; in Palmer, 1977a, p. 202.

18. From 1934 there was a slight improvement in the maize price. In the district, following the 1934 Amendment Act which removed the monopoly of traders, the huge Central Estates offered peasant producers the maximum price of 5/- that they were now permitted to offer for maize they would directly consume (as livestock feed) (NC Chilimanzi, Annual Report 1934; Keyter, 1978, p. 11). The Maize Control Board, which had a depot at Mvuma, 30 km north of Chirumhanzu communal area, then paid a direct delivery price of 6/6 in 1937, and although this dropped the following year (Keyter, 1978, p. 15), the period during which the traders could hold the prices very low, was over.

19. Specifically, it was in 1921 that the maize price was half that of 1920 and sales from peasant farmers were 78 per cent down (Palmer, 1977a, p. 48). Cattle prices slumped during the drought year of 1922 – one farmer in the Zvishavane area recalled that prices fell from £5 per head to £1 per head during the year (Interview with Wilson, 21 March 1987, at which I was present; also Zachrisson, 1978, p. 195).

20. Floyd continues the passage I have drawn from: 'There was also the conviction that only fundamentally different methods drawn from Western agriculture would suffice to overcome a rapidly deteriorating situation' (p. 290).

21. Derived from a policy statement made by Sir Godfrey Huggins in November 1941.

22. In fact during the first twenty years in which black agricultural demonstrators were deployed in the communal areas there was no rise in the average yields of demonstration plotholders or of 'ordinary' farmers, as the following figures for peasant farmer yields (all crops) show:

10-year period	Demonstration plots Ave yield per acre (bags)	All other fields Ave yield per acre (bags)
1926/7–1935/6	9.7	1.3
1936/7–1945/6	10.0	1.3

Source: Annual Report of the Director of Native Agriculture, 1948.

23. Yudelman (1964) provides the following estimates:

Utilising the available data and adjusting the figures on the basis of the demographic sample survey of 1954, one can say that the de facto farm population of African areas rose from 514 000 in 1901 to 1 224 000 in 1950 – an increase of something like 140 per cent at a time when output rose by 140 to 150 per cent and cultivated acreage was extended by 260 to 270 per cent. [Thus]
(a) Population increased more rapidly than did the expansion of the

African areas. .... Available acreage per head declined from around 40 acres to 15 acres.

(b) Output per acre declined. A 260–270 per cent increase in cultivated acreage was required to produce a 140–150 per cent increase in output.

(c) Acreage cultivated per family rose considerably, with a population 140 per cent greater cultivating 260–270 per cent more acreage.

(d) Output per family did not increase much, for a 140 per cent increase in rural population was accompanied by only a 140–150 per cent increase in output. (pp. 237–8)

If one combines Yudelman's figures with those from note 9, then it may be surmised that the significant drop in yields occurred in the period prior to the late 1920s, which was the period when the most rapid adoption of the plough was taking place.

24. These two crops are still important in the Chirumhanzu area today – because they are still the two crops most directly under women's control. Rapoko meal is more nutritious than maize meal, and if produced, as I have witnessed, is still eaten in preference to maize meal by farmers. Rapoko is also highly valued in local beer production and fetches a very good local price (see Chapters 5 and 6). It is, however, a labour-intensive crop to produce.

25. The NC Chilimanzi made this estimate on the basis of Tax Advice Forms sent from other districts. He obtained the figure of 34 per cent in 1942 and 39 per cent in 1943.

26. See note 22.

27. Oral history interviews conducted in 1988 by Ian Scoones and myself during the Commonwealth Science Council agroforestry training and research project, confirmed that the consumption of grazing land by those expanding their arable areas had been a large problem. This problem the centralisation scheme had helped to resolve. But the interviews also revealed that Nema had not been an important local leader until he had used the colonial authorities to gain local power and influence.

28. The rainfall for the 1946/7 season was 15.69″ (392 mm). In the 1986/7 season there was a very similar rainfall total. At Chaka in the north of the Chirumhanzu communal area 393 mm was recorded. Less than this was received in the south.

29. In a footnote Holleman (1968) specifies that Pendered became Under Secretary of the Division of Native Affairs, ranking second (together with the Assistant Chief Native Commissioner) in the NAD hierarchy (p. 53).

30. These figures are in fact borne out by those provided by Alvord in his 1948 annual report (note 22).

31. This figure is a rough estimate only, but it makes the point. The number of plotholders in 1942/3 was 843. The total African population in the communal areas in 1941 was 854 000 (Mosley, 1983, p. 26). Using an estimate of five persons per household – the Annual Report of the Director of Native Agriculture only uses an estimate of four

people – this means the communal areas contained 170 000 'house-holds' and equating 1 farmer with 1 household (which in itself can be a misleading assumption) this provides the figure of 0.5 per cent.

32. It was. Johnson (1964, p. 195) and Yudelman (1964, p. 243) record that the average yield per acre for the 'ordinary' farmer between 1948 and 1958 for all grain crops was 2.0 bags per acre. Yudelman attributes much of this rise in yield compared with the previous 20 years to improved weather conditions rather than the impact of the Land Husbandry Act.

33. The CNC recorded that 212 000 of 313 931 cultivators could be accommodated (Annual Report 1959, p. 11); Bulman (1973, pp. 15–16) cites 204 046 of 346 261 eligible farmers.

34. 1 Large Stock Equivalent = 500 kg. Today Agritex use an average weight of approximately 300 kg (Cousins, 1987, p. 30), although more exactly this is 312.5 kg (that is, 1 animal = 0.625 Livestock Units [LU]), to convert number of head to LU for carrying capacity calculations.

35. The reason for this change in assessment is that the northern and southern parts of Chirumhanzu communal area lie in different rainfall regions (NR III and NR IV respectively). As the whole area was being accorded a standard carrying capacity this meant that in all assessments a decision had to be made how to weight the respective part.

36. The Serima communal area also lay in the Chilimanzi district at that time.

37. The NC estimated that 76 200 acres were being used in the Chirumhanzu and Serima communal areas at that time, compared with 41 000 acres in the early 1920s. The Land Husbandry Assessment Committee had adjudicated that this acreage of 76 200 acres should be reduced to 72 000 acres.

38. Weinrich (1964, p. 18) also refers to the events of this year in Chilimanzi. She mentions that several small riots broke out and that nationalist leaders were jailed

> for inducing people to return their grazing rights to the NC, for stoning dip tanks and burning hide shades, and for inciting people not to allow land allocation. Allocation was stopped, and the Agricultural Officer satisfied himself with merely circumscribing for each headman his village lands, leaving the individual allocation to him. (p. 18)

39. The African National Congress only survived from 1957 to 1959 before it was proscribed. It was the first black nationalist movement in Zimbabwe. Its successor, the National Democratic Party, was formed in 1960 and banned the following year (see Astrow, 1983, and Mandaza, 1987).

40. The NAD's retort was that no new legislation was required to impoverish the African and deprive him of land; he had been doing it 'very effectively by himself without the assistance of any legislation' (in Floyd, 1961, p. 268).

41. Following the end of the period of peak prosperity, a qualitative change took place in the rural economy in the 1930s. Migration for wage employment became much more a necessity rather than a mechanism resorted to most often in times of drought. Arrighi (1973) terms this the development of a 'structural disequilibrium between means of production and subsistence requirements of the peasantry' (p. 214).

As far as employment is concerned, a substantial rise from 16.7 per cent to 28.9 per cent of the total Zimbabwean black population in employment occurred between 1931 and 1951 (calculated from Mosley, 1983, pp. 112, 115). From 1932, for the first time since the drought years of 1911–12, the supply of labour to the mines exceeded the demand, and this continued regularly until 1948 (Mosley, 1983, pp. 126–7). In the 1950s employment growth slowed (from 85.7 per cent between 1941 and 1945 to 17.7 per cent between 1951 and 1961), as an outcome of black trade-union demands for improved wages. This was the time when the government was threatening to use the LHA to create a large landless class of young men in the rural areas.

42. Sample surveys in two wards in the Mangwende Reserve revealed that 40 per cent of even the adult males who were registered as taxpayers had been registered landless by the land allocations made under the LHA (Mangwende Commission, 1961, para. 411).

43. Harold MacMillan, then British Prime Minister, made his famous 'winds of change' speech, which heralded the era of African independence, on 3 February 1960.

44. Mangwende Commission: *Mangwende Reserve Commission of Inquiry*. Robinson Commission: *Commission of Inquiry on Administrative and Judicial Functions in the Native Affairs and District Courts Departments*.

45. Paterson's *First Report on the Organisation and Development of the Southern Rhodesian Public Services* was published in 1962. The report of the Philips Advisory Commission, *The Development of the Economic Resources of Southern Rhodesia with particular reference to the Role of African Agriculture*, appeared in 1962 (Holleman, 1968, p. 219).

46. The Native Affairs Department had been renamed and restructured.

Chapter 3 The Socialist State and The Peasantry

1. Interview with a government and party official, 20 April 1988.
2. The Ministry, of which Chidzero is still the head, is now that of the Ministry of Finance, Economic Planning and Development.
3. Interview with a government and party official, 20 April 1988.
4. The breakdown of land by natural regions is as follows:

Natural region	Designation	Land area (million ha)	% of total
I	Specialised and diversified crops	0.705	1.8
II	Intensive	5.857	15.0
III	Semi-intensive	7.290	18.7
IV	Semi-extensive	14.770	37.8
V	Extensive	10.450	26.7
Total		39.072	100.0

Source: Cole, 1981, in Moyo, 1987, p. 182.

5.　　Zimbabwe Conference on Reconstruction and Development.
6.　　The government's 1980–5 socio-economic review (Government of Zimbabwe, 1986b, p. 1) puts the overall annual population growth rate at an estimated 2.9 per cent, whilst the 1986–90 National Development Plan document (Government of Zimbabwe, 1986a, p. 47) has an even more optimistic estimated annual growth rate of only 2.84 per cent for 1982–5 and 2.76 per cent for 1985–90. World Bank estimates have always placed the 1980s growth rate at least at 3.6 per cent – for instance the 1989 World Development Report lists the 1980–7 population growth rate at 3.7 per cent and suggests that might slow to 3.0 per cent in the period to 2000.
7.　　The delivery period is from April to March.
8.　　Mugabe affirmed this principle for instance, at ZANU (PF)'s second congress in August 1984 (*The Financial Gazette*, 17 August 1984), and at the interparliamentry union conference on African agricultural development held in Harare in 1986 (*The Herald*, 9 December 1986).
9.　　The Ministry of Agriculture was amalgamated with the Ministry of Lands, Resettlement and Rural Development after the June 1985 general elections to form the Ministry of Lands, Agriculture and Rural Settlement.
10.　　The distribution of communal areas and commercial farming areas by Natural Region in 1982 was as follows:

Natural region	Large-scale commercial farming area	Communal farming area
I	3.0	0.7
II	28.6	8.7
III	17.5	17.1
IV	25.2	47.6
V	25.7	25.9
	100.0	100.0

Source:　Weiner *et al.*, 1985.

11.　　This pilot programme was perhaps not articulated as clearly as this, although political pressure was exercised for it to be so. This pressure emanated in particular from the Ministry of Public Construction and National Housing, which had substantial funds for rural housing programmes. Thus this ministry was urging District Administrators to promote the villagisation component of the programme, and the Ministry of Local Government, Rural and Urban Development was exerting pressure on Agritex to replan entire village land use areas. A case study of this political and bureaucratic process is discussed in Chapter 4. Although policy details still remain imprecise, internal land use reform has now become a catchphrase within many government ministries of what is required within the communal areas.
12.　　This figure for black ownership is undoubtedly an underestimate, for

one because of the disguised forms ZANU (PF)'s leadership code has occasioned the registration of ownership to take. Palmer (1990), 'Land reform in Zimbabwe, 1980–1990', *African Affairs*, 89, 355, p. 175, raise this estimate to at least 500.

13. Table 21 in the Chavunduka Commission (1982, p. 40) report provides comparative production statistics for the communal and commercial sectors between 1964/5 and 1980/1. For the last two seasons mentioned, 1979/80 and 1980/1, average yields for maize in the communal sector were 0.8 and 1.0 tonnes per ha respectively, and for the commercial sector 4.0 and 5.6 tonnes per ha. The communal sector averages would be subject to greater variation both within and between regions.

14. One such counter-claim is presented by Weiner *et al.* (1985). They attempt to use 1974–82 Central Statistical Office material to show that the output–input ratio in the communal areas is on average six times greater than that in the commercial areas (pp. 282–3). However, from the detailed work that Jackson *et al.* (1987), among others, have been carrying out on communal area costs of production since 1984–5, it is clear that any CSO estimates, especially in the pre-independence period, are only guesswork. Labour and draught power are often heavily under-costed resources – labour time itself is extremely difficult to calculate. Moreover, as Weiner *et al.*'s table (p. 283) does illustrate, the lower resource input levels make communal area production more vulnerable to environmental fluctuation. On the commercial sector side, although his statistics cover only the period until 1960, Mosley (1983, pp. 172–3) shows that commercial agriculture was not uniformly less efficient than elsewhere in the world, including the USA, as is frequently presumed. There was, however, a greater range in farmer efficiency in colonial Rhodesia, less competent farmers being kept on the land by protective government measures (Mosley, 1983, pp. 234–5). Arguments about efficiency – and especially potential efficiency – are difficult to sustain because of the contrasts in situational circumstances between sectors and the variations in performance which have historically occurred within them.

15. Commission of Inquiry into Incomes, Prices and Conditions of Service, chaired by Roger Riddell.

16. Iterated for instance, in the opening paragraph of the 'Growth with Equity' policy statement (Government of Zimbabwe, 1981, p. 1), and again in the 'Economic Programme of the Central Committee of ZANU (PF)' at ZANU's second party congress in August 1984 (Government of Zimbabwe, 1986a, p. 2).

17. Richard Bernstein (1976) wants to make the point that an ideology is not any set of moral, social or political attitudes. The particular feature of an ideology is that it is a set of beliefs '*which purport to be a true or valid*' interpretation of historical circumstances (pp. 107–8: my emphasis). Accordingly Robertson (1984) states that populism, 'Pragmatic, eclectic, and notably devoid of long-term social ambitions . . . might better be described as a set of attitudes rather than an ideology' (p. 230).

18. The two guerrilla armies, the Zimbabwe African National Liberation Army (ZANLA) and the Zimbabwe Peoples Revolutionary Army (ZIPRA), owed for most of their histories allegiance to the political leaderships of, respectively, the Zimbabwe African National Union (ZANU) and the Zimbabwe African Peoples Union (ZAPU). In October 1978 these two parties were united by the frontline state leaders to form the Patriotic Front (PF), but this split before the March 1980 elections. After bitter conflict during the early 1980s, the leaders of the two parties eventually agreed to remerge in 1987.

19. The information in this paragraph is taken from the interview with a government official and party intellectual, 20 April 1988.

20. Thesis 5 of the resolutions passed at ZANU (PF)'s Second Congress states that the party must lead the state.

21. Cheater (1983) develops an argument which complements that presented in this section, although it is constructed differently. Her purpose is also to show that when it comes to the peasantry, the government has a rhetorical rather than genuine commitment to socialism. Cheater begins by stating that the 'primary contradiction' in post-independence Zimbabwe is the relationship between peasantry and the state. She then backs this claim by showing how rates of appropriation of crop surpluses, even since independence, have continued to be high – in some cases, higher for communal farmers than commercial farmers. Her conclusion is that the government's cynical attitude towards the peasantry will backfire by negatively affecting the national economy at least as much as it does the rural population.

22. One argument that might be put forward to at least partially explain post-independence policy continuities is that there has been a continuity in government staff. However there has been both a rapid expansion of and changeover within the civil service. By the end of 1983 the bureaucracy had been approximately doubled and one-third of the former staff had left, so that two-thirds of the bureaucracy by then already consisted of people appointed after independence. Weitzer (in Mandaza, 1987) provides figures for this: from February 1980 to January 1983 the number of white officers in the civil service dropped from 7202 to 4495 and the number of non-white officers increased from 3368 to 17 693 (p. 45).

23. Model 'D' is intended to be implemented in the drier Natural Regions IV and V. It is based on the rotational utilisation of purchased ranch-land for group livestock ranching, each group to have access to the ranchland one year in four, on the theory that this would allow their own grazing land to recover and be replanned into a paddock system (Agricultural and Rural Development Authority, 1983, pp. 35–6).

   Model 'F' refers to a single scheme near Karoi (NR II/III), 'more along the lines of the former African purchase farms than resettlement', where 106 plots of a minimum size of 100 ha have been allocated to 'master farmers' – the colonial term for farmers who had successfully undertaken agricultural training (*The Herald*, 4 October 1984, and 6 February 1985).

24. Callear (1982, pp. E3–5) describes a case of 70 farmers in the Wedza communal area who established a collective on an adjacent farm acquired by the state. The reason was that the MLRRD coerced them into it – they were informed they could settle on the land only on the condition that they formed a collective. 'Reluctantly they were forced to agree but in fact the seventy farmers who decided to go were giving little up; all of them retained their rights to land in the communal area in the following season' (p. E5). In Chirumhanzu, whilst I was there, one project group – its members teachers or leading farmers – were offered the use of state-purchased land on the same condition.

25. The report was only released in 1984 after the government had examined the report's recommendations.

26. The Secretary for Lands had been a member of the Chavunduka Commission.

27. Before an inter-ministerial meeting hosted at a tourist hotel to discuss the draft plan, it was well publicised in three newspaper articles in *The Herald* on 20 March and 21 March 1985. This was an unusual procedure for a draft government document which till then had been solely an inhouse exercise.

28. In illustration of this similarity, the objectives of the two documents are juxtaposed below. First are listed four of the five objectives of the LHA as laid down in the 1955 Government of Southern Rhodesia document, 'What the Native Land Husbandry Act means to the Rural African and to Southern Rhodesia'. Second, three recommendations are extracted from the 1985 draft communal lands development plan:

1. The main objects of the Native Land Husbandry Act are:-
   (1) to provide for a reasonable standard of good husbandry and for the protection of natural resources by all Africans using the land: the Act contains powers to enforce these provisions:
   (2) to limit the number of stock in any area to its carrying capacity and as far as is practicable, to relate stock holding to arable land holding as a means of improving farming practice:
   (3) to provide individual security of tenure of arable land and individual security of grazing rights in the communal grazings.
   (Government of Southern Rhodesia, 1955, p. 4)

2. The following land reform measures should be pursued:
   — arable and grazing land be held by individual legal persons, group members or by cooperative members on a long term leasehold basis over 99 years . . . in order to safeguard economic continuity and legal security as preconditions for effective land use, profitability and for land improvements;
   — land for arable and grazing having been assessed as an economic long-term viable minimum farm entity and size may neither be subdivided nor sold by the landholder except to the Government for purposes beneficial to the State and the community;
   — leasehold titles for the entire land holding only, may be passed on to the heirs of the farming family, to the successors of the

group or to the cooperative members during the leasehold
period, provided a high standard of productivity can be maintained. (MLRRD, 1985, pp. 79–80)

29. The conference was held at the Brondesbury Park Hotel, Nyanga,
from 19–23 October 1987.

The three farmers' unions referred to are the Commercial Farmers'
Union, the Zimbabwe National Farmer's Union (representing small-
scale commercial farmers), and the National Farmers' Association of
Zimbabwe, representing communal farmers. Periodic attempts since
independence to seek the amalgamation of the three unions have so
far failed.

Chapter 4 Alternative Strategies for Managing Livestock on the Land

1. The nine member countries of the Southern African Development
Coordination Conference are Angola, Botswana, Lesotho, Malawi,
Mozambique, Swaziland, Tanzania, Zambia, and Zimbabwe.

2. Cliffe quotes Zishiri, now Agritex's Midlands PAEO, who states 'any
land reform programme or land tenure system has to consider the
grazing areas first'.

3. Hardin's theory of the 'tragedy of the commons' assumes that each
owner's interest is independent of the interests of other owners whose
animals make use of the same communal grazing areas. Thus individual owners will allow the environment to be degraded, because it is
against their independent interests to act collectively to regulate
grazing. As Routley and Routley (1980, pp. 30–1) express, the theory
presumes not a system of communal usufruct, but rather 'the operation of private individuals in no-man's land'.

4. Village Development Committees and Ward Development Committees were established under the Prime Minister's Directive of February
1984. This Directive laid down the national planning structure now in
operation. The Provincial Governors were appointed shortly after and
the system of provincial councils and provincial development committees, paralleled by local authorities and district development committees at the district level, was brought into being.

5. Agritex's 1984 Midlands Annual Report notes:

> The delineation of Village and Ward development areas was initi-
> ated by the Ministry of Local Government and Town Planning in all
> Districts in this Province, assisted by the Regional Topographic staff
> of Agritex. However, as a result of undue haste, many of the
> boundaries do not follow recognisable physical features and have in
> consequence been impossible to accurately map. (p. 29)

6. Holleman (1968) says of the land hsubandry implementation procedure:

> in mapping out the new arable and grazing division, the physio-
> graphical nature of the land received first consideration, the recog-
> nised boundaries of chiefdoms second, but those of the tribal wards
> (*dunhu*) hardly any consideration or none at all. (p. 55)

A discussion of the administration's various definitions of lineage boundaries and the disputes on the ground these created is also in Scoones and Wilson (1988, pp. 48–50).

7. I was able to read some of Agritex's reports on these schemes.

8. There was one veld management scheme in the southern Chirumhanzu area at Murarugwa, to the east of Maware ward.

9. The 1982 census records Chirumhanzu as having a population density of 40.4 people per square kilometre. The population density in the south of Chirumhanzu is however higher than in the north – at the end of land husbandry two-thirds of the areas population lived in the drier southern part (Weinrich, 1964, p. 11).

10. This is why farmers who have extensive wet 'garden' areas are extremely favoured, for they can plant earlier and more leisurely – see the discussion on arable cultivation in chapter 5.

11. The actual labour committed varies enormously between households, depending on the household constitution, the resources they have access too, and peoples' characters and physical capabilities.

12. Weinrich (1964, p. 31) corroborates this. She states that in the early 1960s all the cattle in a village were herded together. Each family in turn was responsible for herding the sometimes over one hundred animals.

13. This occurred during 1985/6. Two of the case-study farmers I worked with had cattle impounded and were forced to pay Z$50 fines. Along his farm boundary, across the Kwekwe river from the communal area, the commercial farmer had allocated land to 'border' farmers, and given them cattle, so that they would have a stake in keeping the communal area animals out.

14. For example, see Scoones' (1987) seasonal calendar for pastoral management in Mazvihwa communal area.

15. In this calculation of density, so that it is consistent with the remainder of the density calculations in Tables 2.1 and 2.2, no allowance for class VIII land is made, although this has no grazing value.

16. Scoones (1987, fig. 2) lists figures collected from the Department of Veterinary Services that show that in the Mberengwa and Chivi communal areas cattle numbers reached their highest ever level in the mid-1970s, whilst in the Runde communal area this peak was reached in 1981.

17. These figures can be compared to the much lower average of 2.3 head per family in Chirumhanzu in 1958, after the drastic destocking that had taken place that year.

18. The Central Statistical Office 1983/4 sample survey for the communal areas in the Midlands listed 40.6 per cent of households as having no cattle and 33.2 per cent as having between one and five animals.

19. Interview with Garfield Todd, 10 December 1984, and with D. Tredgold, Managing Director of Debshan, 20 December 1984. On the stock losses, those in Rumhasa VIDCO, nearest to the De Beers land, were only 17 per cent compared with the 43 per cent for Dambashoko, the VIDCO furthest from the commercial ranchland. Even at the end of the drought in December 1984, at least 20 per cent of the Rumhasa

herd were still being taken daily to the De Beers land, which lay in the Ngezi river valley.

20. My thanks to Nick Abel, Mike Stocking and Ken Wilson for their comments on this section.

21. As an example, Wilson (1988, personal communication) refers to the Serengeti short grass which, although it has a comparatively low plant biomass, supports a very high livestock biomass.

22. Agritex's Midlands 1986 annual report includes the following statement:

Denudation is still a problem in Communal areas as organised grazing systems have not started to function properly. The farmers continued to restock after the three dry seasons and one good season left some farmers with little or no cattle, plenty grazing and hence worsening situation which had been naturally corrected. (p. 14)

23. Within the Ministry of Lands, Agriculture and Rural Settlement.

24. Soil erosion within the Save catchment area has been controversial because of the extensive silting of this wide river that has taken place. As Campbell *et al.* (1986) note, some of the soils in the catchment area are more susceptible than most to erosion. They refer to 'the tunnel erosion that occurs in sodic soils in illuvial zones'.

25. Rainfall fluctuations also have a political and cultural element, since the land spirit guardians of the autochthonous clan are held to control rainfall and hence environmental fertility (see D. Lan, 1985, *Guns and Rain*; K. Wilson, 1986, *History, Ecology and Conservation in Southern Zimbabwe*).

26. Letter from the ANC Que Que to the NC Gwelo, 7 June 1950.

27. This report was produced for the Ministry of Lands, Resettlement and Rural Development in 1982. It received a hostile reception. It was not published in Zimbabwe and was not used by the Ministry.

28. Cousin's reference is to B. Mombeshora, (1985), 'Livestock production research', in M. Avila, (ed.), *Crop and Livestock Production Research for Communal Areas*, Harare, ZAJ Special Report No. 1, DR&SS, p. 84.

29. Interview with D. Tredgold, 20 December 1987. This portion (Lot 5) of Debshan had already been offered to the government for purchase.

30. In a plenary discussion on land reform at Agritex's 1986 Midlands provincial conference (referred to at the end of the chapter), the district agricultural extension officer for Zvishavane supported this interpretation that the councillor had lost his position because he had recommended land reform.

31. The total cost was Z$120 000.

32. The basic unit of the ZANU (PF) party structure is the village committee. This incorporates about 100 people and is headed by a village chairman. About five village committees, approximately 500 people, form a branch so that there are about two branches per VIDCO area. These branches are then affiliated to a party district, which in the study areas included from one to two-and-a-half wards.

33. Interview, 23 March 1987.

34. Transferred from the Ministry of Lands, Resettlement and Rural Development when it was merged in 1986 with the Ministry of Agriculture.
35. See Chapter 3, note 22, for an explanation of Model 'D'.
36. Densities for Runde and Mberengwa communal areas.
37. These reasons were cited to me by Mangwalala, Phumelela farmers' group chairman (Fieldnotes, 16 February 1987).
38. The discussion on this conference is taken from my notes, 26–7 November 1986.
39. Transcription of tape of meeting, 13 April 1987.
40. For this meeting my tape malfunctioned. This comment was taken from brief notes.
41. 'Harare works farming miracle' was the headline of an article on the increased production output of the 1984/5 season in *The Guardian*, 15 March 1985.

Chapter 5   Maize Production and Household Survival

1. According to the 1982 population census, over 22 per cent of the population lived in the major urban areas, 56 per cent lived in the communal areas, and 21 per cent lived in the commercial farming areas (Government of Zimbabwe, 1986b, p. 1).
2. Nevertheless, if one has the research funding available, I believe it preferable to employ research assistants from the area on a full-time basis. A rapport can be developed between researcher and assistants, which allows the latter to assume a more responsible and rewarding role in the exercise. I observed this, for example, with the work of Wilson and Schoones in the Mazvihwa area of the Midlands province.
3. The discussion, during which I took notes, was held at my request to reflect on the subject of field methodology.
4. Some of the people Wilson and Scoones worked with acknowledged this too – that the research had forced them to think 'everything through' (Wilson, 1987, p. 18).
5. 'Sunday at Maware', Spring 1987 Newsletter of the Norwich Third World Centre.
6. NC Belingwe and ANC Shabani, Annual Reports 1923–48.
7. In the higher, hill areas of the Shurugwi communal area, some early rain fell in late September/early October 1987 which fostered the best maize and groundnut crops obtained during the season. This crop was sufficiently mature to avoid the worst effects of the heavy February rains. But generally periods of heavy rain on sandveld soils tend to be damaging to crops through the effects of leaching and waterlogging. However, in areas of heavy red soils, such as in Mazvihwa, there is a marked increase in yields with rainfall until truly exceptional falls are received (Wilson, 1988b; and personal communication).
8. The practice of autumn ploughing is commonly called winter ploughing in Zimbabwe, since autumn is not a distinct season. The timing of the activity, in April–May, after harvest and before the soils have become too hard to take a plough, is however pre-winter.

9.   In referring to the case-study households I have adopted a practice employed by Patrick White in his novel *Tree of Man* (1956). In this, White referred to the home of the husband and wife, or that which was done jointly by them, as 'Parkers'. The added 's' denotes the unit and the lack of gender exclusivity in possession. In the thesis I have added the 's' if both husband and wife are living at home and contribute to the agricultural work or activity being mentioned. Wives do not, however, enjoy equal possession of the home as Amy Parker did.

10.   The dates provided by Mangwalala on when the area was centralised and Gokomere became a purchase area are corroborated by the district annual reports of the time.

11.   Theisen (1973) carried out a sample survey of 84 farmers in 1969–70 and recorded that 98 per cent of families already cultivated fenced home-fields, whilst 67 per cent and 45 per cent, respectively, still retained separate 'arable block land' and separate 'vlei gardens' – another 11 per cent had gardens within one of their other arable areas (p. 15a).

12.   Theisen (1973) states that in 1970 people were paying the controlling sabhuku from 50c to Z$2.00 for access to a portion of vlei land (p. 14).

13.   Interview with Chidagwa, ward councillor, 14 January 1987.

14.   Information from Commonwealth Science Council training programme.

15.   The 1982 census showed Chiwundura to have a population density of 71.2 people per sq km and Chirumhanzu 40.4 people per sq km (Central Statistical Office, 'Report on demographic socio-economic survey: Communal lands of Midlands Province, 1983/84').

16.   In Shurugwi one young farmer, dependent on his father for draught power, estimated that he had carried out piecework worth about Z$150.00 for his father. In return he borrowed animals to plough 0.4 ha of land (CSC training programme).

17.   In a sample of 30 households in Shurugwi communal area, the leading farmers were applying manure bulked with antheap, maize stover, grass and compost, to between 0.8 and 1.0 ha of land annually, whilst middle farmers had sufficient for 0.2–0.4 ha annually, and poor farmers 0.2–0.4 ha on an irregular basis (CSC training programme).

18.   The rotation Alvord recommended was:

Season 1.   Maize with manure
      2.   Maize or sorghum, or other inter-tilled, farinaceous crop.
      3.   Groundnuts, beans or other legume crop.
      4.   Rapoko, or other close-growing millet crop.

(in Floyd, 1961, p. 8).

19.   Nhonga and Mrs Mazonde, Agritex extension worker, Fieldnotes, 20 February 1987.

20.   In a survey of 135 rural wage labourers in Masvingo province in 1986/7, Adams (1988) records 43.0 per cent as earning between Z$21 and Z$30 per month, 26.7 per cent as earning between Z$31 and Z$40 per month, and 12.6 per cent between Z$41 and Z$50 per month (table 2).

21.   Mhene and Mugwisi hired boys of school-going age to herd livestock for them, and sons in the Mabuku and K. Mugoni households sought employment through herding.

22. Estimates of the likely number of school-leavers between 1986 and 1990 vary between 500 000 (*Moto*, 1986, no. 46, p. 5) and 750 000 (*Financial Gazette*, 22 July 1988, p. 13). In 1985 there were about 71 500 leavers and in 1986, 85 000 leavers. In addition to school-leavers, the 'officially recognised' unemployment back-log was 255 000 in 1986, and this does not take into account people within the communal areas who may be forced out to seek employment. Moto estimates the total seeking jobs within the period 1986–90 will be in excess of one million, whilst the plan job-creation target in the First Five-Year Development Plan is only 144 000.

23. In the census survey carried out in Ture ward in 1984/5, of the total resident population, 54.4 per cent were below the age of fourteen, and 65.1 per cent below twenty years. Males formed only 44.29 per cent of the ward's resident population, and of these 40.4 per cent were under ten years and 71.6 per cent under twenty years. Women formed two-thirds of the adult population (Drinkwater, 1985).

24. The resale price of GMB maize was Z$21 per bag. But many poorer families purchase only a tin – one-sixth of a bag – of maize at a time, both because they cannot afford the whole bag and also because they cannot carry it from the few stores where it is available. For these reasons the local price of grain can rise above the official selling price.

25. An alternative lucrative activity which some women perforce engage in, is prostitution.

26. In Ture ward in 1984/5 I spoke to women's group members involved in a series of projects – three bakery projects, a school-uniform-making project, a gardening project, a poultry project and a consumer cooperative. None of them were making any profit (Fieldnotes, 13 December 1984).

27. In contrast with the drought season of 1986/7, most maize sold in 1984/5 was marketed formally through the GMB because of insignificant local demand.

28. Roderick (1986, pp. 142–5), following Gouldner (1980), also makes on the same lines this distinction between the 'scientific' Marxists and the 'critical' Marxists.

Chapter 6   Cooperation, Credit and Social Integration

1. Habermas himself readily admits this. He has always presented his critical theory as something that is being constructed, partly in response to the criticisms and suggestions of others, and never as something that is complete. For example, see Habermas, 'A Reply to My Critics' in J. B. Thompson and D. Held (eds) (1982) *Habermas: Critical Debates*, pp. 219–20.

2. Baxter (1987), Benhabib (1986), Giddens (1984), Ingram (1987), and some of the articles in Thompson and Held (1982) all examine elements of these controversial features. The issues and the standpoint I shall adopt on them will be explained as part of the overall outline of the theoretical framework.

3. The concept originates in the phenomenology of Husserl and Schutz.

Later hermeneuticists, such as Gadamer, have also employed it, but only to explain how the lifeworld, as a shared social horizon, contributes to cultural transmission. It is only with Habermas's construction that the concept has been made three-dimensional, to incorporate also the symbolic reproduction of the structures of society and personality (Benhabib, 1986, pp. 238–9).

4. This quote is taken from Volume 2 of Habermans's *The Theory of Communicative Action*' (referred to as *TkH* 2).

5. 'Sunday at Maware', Spring 1987 Newsletter of the Norwich Third World Centre.

6. In this explanation I am following Habermas's principles of adopting a methodological attitude and objectivating the lifeworld. As a researcher I am theoretically able to take an objectivating attitude and discuss aspects of the social and subjective domains, through *thematising* what has been expressed to me and what I have observed about actors' attitudes to these domains of the lifeworld. In other words, what is first experienced by participants as something subjective, or first encountered as something normative, is objectivated and turned into a state of affairs by the researcher and hence opened up to analytical discussion (Habermas, in Bernstein, 1985, p. 208).

7. My thanks to Ken Wilson (personal communication) for his comments on these subjects of early planting and the invention of 'traditional' norms.

8. The reaction of the woman is a comparatively mild response to the disruptive effect on social and psychological integration that the change generated by colonialism has had in Africa. Other common responses have included that of religious innovation, and often connected with this, witchcraft accusation. In the context of rural Zambia, van Binsbergen (1981) describes forms of religious innovation as 'an attempt to reconstruct the integrity of the local rural community assaulted by these various incorporation processes' (p. 50).

9. The normative grounding that Habermas attempts to establish for his theory of communicative action formally lies in his modification of speech act theory. 'Reaching understanding is the inherent telos of human speech' (1984, p. 287), he asserts. 'Our first sentence expresses unequivocally the intention of universal and unconstrained consensus' (1972, p. 314). Even if we seek to manipulate or deceive people, he argues, our strategic intention relies on others understanding us and accepting our speech claims. If mutual distrust becomes pervasive, social interaction breaks down.

10. Giddens (1985) employs the term 'discursive consciousness'. His definition, which is appropriate here, is:

> What actors are able to say, or to give verbal expression to, about social conditions, including especially the conditions of their own action; awareness which has a discursive form. (p. 374)

11. In McCarthy's introduction to Habermas, 1984, p. xxvii.

12. In McCarthy's introduction to Habermas, 1984, p. xxix.

13. See also *TkH* 2, p. 226, in Baxter, 1987, p. 52.

14. Horton acknowledges in his footnotes a considerable debt to Popper (pp. 263–5).

15. Wilson provides an example to illustrate this statement:

> One of the old headmen who reported in the survey that rainfall decline was caused by failure to organise the *mutoro* (rain-making ceremony) properly, told a different story earlier in the year. When I asked him why I had not seen him at the *mitoro* he asked me whether I really thought that drinking beer was going to make the rain fall. He said rainfall patterns were created by land forms and meteorological conditions (he is a great believer in the deforestation hypothesis). (1987, p. 2)

Two of the older people I worked with in Chiwundura also attributed the drought to *mitoro* not being conducted properly.

16. Previous to this he had been a migrant worker.

17. The account of this day is taken from my fieldnotes, 18 April 1987.

18. Discussed in more detail in a seminar paper, 'Loans and manure: the dilemma of access', presented in the Department of Sociology, University of Zimbabwe, and now produced as a working paper (2/87) by the Department of Agricultural Economics and Extension.

19. Silveria House is a Catholic institution regarded as being the initiator of the savings club movement in Zimbabwe. The savings clubs in the Midlands, now advised by CADEC, were however started independently of the Silveria House movement.

20. See Truscott, 1985, *The Wedza Project*, Agritex.

21. Members of cooperative unions in Zimbabwe, which were first formed in 1965, have always disliked handling-charges, since if as a local group they bulk order inputs directly from fertiliser companies they can inevitably obtain them more cheaply than through the unions (see Cheater, 1976; Hughes, 1974, p. 269).

22. There was eventually a court case over financial and administrative malpractices in the union this year, which resulted in the jailing of two provincial staff.

23. Some of the factors listed, such as the training aspect, obviously apply to all the ward cooperatives, but I do not have details of their case histories beyond the first year.

24. He has constantly reiterated this point in conversations I have had with him, including the last on 14 April 1988.

25. Hughes (1974) presents an interesting case study of a locally controlled cooperative known as the African Farming Development Company, which operated in the Chiweshe communal area from 1965 to 1969. The reasons he provides for the organisation's collapse echo those provided here. The company had insufficient capital to cover overheads; people were provided with loans although having no interest in becoming cash crop farmers; after the 1965/6 drought a great deal of loan defaulting took place and in subsequent seasons many farmers became increasingly indebted; and participants, through various means, avoided the stop-order system of crop marketing and loan recovery. All these factors made the financial management of the company impossible.

26.   Notes from discussion with N. P. Zinduru on 14 April 1988.

27.   The single previous period when a significant amount of agricultural
      credit was extended to communal area farmers was between 1964 and
      1967. In this period there was a drought in 1965/6 and in 1967 the
      scheme was sharply scaled down because of increasing indebtedness,
      as is occurring in Chiwundura now. (Hughes, 1974, pp. 276–7, 286).

28.   The small grains, with their hard husks, have a storage life of several
      years, whereas maize has to be stored very carefully in a granary to be
      still edible by even the next harvest.

29.   Members of farmers' groups who pay both an annual membership and
      contribute to an annual affiliation fee for the club are members of the
      National Farmers Association of Zimbabwe (NFAZ), the organisation
      which is supposed to represent the interests of communal farmers. As
      it is only leading farmers that are members of the NFAZ, it is only they
      who received the drought relief packs, which consist of seed and
      fertiliser for 0.4 ha of maize.

30.   In Chirumhanzu, Silvester Mugarisi was the only case-study farmer
      who was using AFC credit in order to obtain inputs. This was in large
      part because he had fallen out with the Maware savings club and been
      disbarred as a member. However, in August 1987, he also stated his
      intention to stop using credit. For the 1987/8 season he intended to use
      the income he had earned through building work (see Appendix 2) to
      purchase inputs, and thereafter he hoped he would be allowed to
      rejoin the savings club (Fieldnotes, 7 August 1987).

31.   Information from the Commonwealth Science Council rapid appraisal
      training programme, a research report from which is still to be
      published.

32.   These factors were first outlined in the working paper, 'Loans and
      Manure: The dilemma of access' (1987).

33.   In 1986/7, the Chirumhanzu savings club depots charged Z$22 and
      Z$25 respectively for compound D and ammonium nitrate, compared
      with the Chiwundura cooperative prices of Z$24 and Z$27. Chiwun-
      dura, being nearer major centres has cheaper transport rates.

34.   In the Midlands, Agritex has also organised savings clubs, but through
      a stamp-book system for which no successful method of paying interest
      has been devised. There were two such savings clubs in Mtengwa
      ward. One in Phumelela performed a marginal role only in members'
      financial lives. At one session I attended, 11 people deposited
      Z$24.20. This can be compared with the fortnightly banking sessions
      at Maware, conducted after Sunday mass, at which often upwards of
      50 people were depositing upwards of Z$400 (e.g. on 23 November
      1986, 49 people deposited Z$800.60; on 8 March 1987, 88 people
      deposited Z$551.70; on 22 March 1987, 59 people deposited
      Z$381.10). The second Mtengwa club, Vukuzenzele, had disinte-
      grated because of conflict among the largely female committee. The
      chairwoman was suspected of taking money.

35.   The reserve fund is obtained through the investment of savings in paid-
      up permanent shares (PUPS) at 11.25 per cent in one of the national
      building societies, and from the sale of goods.

36. Some of the hostility of leaders from other farmer groups was because the cooperative's management committee all came from the farmer group in whose area the irrigation scheme was located, a source of jealousy.
37. I have rarely observed it being practised, and farmers who claim to use it, if pressed can provide few actual instances.
38. Wilson and Scoones in their work used these resource-sharing clusters, organised in Mazvihwa primarily around the sharing of the costs and benefits of stock, as a basis to delineate the households they had in their research sample (Wilson, 1988d, p. 1).
39. They were, respectively, members of the Seventh Day Adventist and Anglican churches. Mrs Skosana referred for instance to the Christian ethic of helping others: 'if you are a Christian your deeds should be shown by work and so we should help him' (Fieldnotes, 12 December 1986).
40. I observed the group in operation on four occasions. In all instances the group began work with first light and were complete before 9.00 am.
41. She unfortunately did not benefit from the potential of the group operation to ensure maximum moisture retention. When her land was ploughed she had not yet obtained maize seed. As a result she only planted the maize, using a hoe, several days later. By this time the soil had dried out. From one hectare of maize she harvested just one bag.
42. This was analysed by A. Nduku, Agritex research assistant.
43. My presence had an influence, however, as Mangwalala, the group chairman, accompanied me on my first visit to Tangwena and was struck by his family's abject situation.

Chapter 7 Democratic Ideas and Technocratic Practices in Agricultural Extension

1. Extracts from the discussion meeting held in Gweru on 13 April 1987 and the Gweru seminar held on 22 July 1987 are taken from transcripts of tape recordings.
2. PAEO Midlands, 1986, p. 1; and reiterated by B. M. Ndimande, then Director of Agritex, at a National Extension Framework Study Workshop, Harare, 12 May 1987.
3. Agronomic research on millet varieties is another area where detailed local-level research has shown that appropriate varieties and cropping practices cannot be developed without farmer participation. Wilson (1987) records over 60 indigenous varieties of finger millet and bulrush millet in a detailed investigation he carried out into the subject. On the clay soils of Mazvihwa he found farmers to 'consider desirable certain agronomic properties defined as "weedy" by conventional agriculturalists'. Varieties adapted to rainfall *variability*, not *low* rainfall, are preferred, and it is their ability to tiller (that is, to produce side-shoots from the base) that is valued (1988, personal communication). They reap a good harvest and store it – so that optimising food production in poorer years, which crop breeder researchers often assume is the goal

of small-scale farmers, is of much lower priority to them (Wilson, 1988b). Researchers cannot therefore take it for granted that they know what varieties farmers in different micro-environments want.

4. Reports read include the 1983–4 Annual Report of the Farming Systems Research Unit, the unit's solitary annual report, and a draft report produced in July 1987, 'The Zimbabwe Case Study: The organisation and management of five on farm research programs in the Department of Research and Specialist Services'.

5. Most of these 13 trials ended up providing a single salutary lesson. Because the Department of Research and Specialist Services (DR & SS) had had insufficient funds to pay travel and subsistence allowances to deploy field assistants in late October, the early rains were missed. Planting consequently only took place in early December, once the rains had returned. Most trials yielded extremely poorly – and so proved only the value of early planting.

6. When compared with that employed by other ministries, Agritex's terminology is confusing. Some Agritex regions are the equivalent to an administrative 'district', but in this case the Gweru region comprises the Gweru and Shurugwi districts. The senior civil servant in a district is the District Administrator.

7. The PAEO, in later commenting on the transcript of this interview, admitted that in terms of how the institution conducted its affairs, 'true dialogue' represented a goal not a concrete realisation.

8. These points reoccur in several of the discussion meeting and interview transcripts.

9. This information is taken from diarised notes of her activities written by Mrs Mazonde, as part of the research exercise.

10. RAEO Gweru, 26 November 1986, at Agritex's Midlands Provincial Annual Conference.

11. As mentioned in note 29 to Chapter 6, the organisation that purportedly represents communal area farmers, the National Farmers Association of Zimbabwe (NFAZ), also only caters for the interests of this elite, since it is only the leading farmers who usually find it worthwhile (and can afford) to be fully paid up members of the organisation. In an interview I had with Robinson Gapare, chairman of the NFAZ, he emphasised that his organisation sought to promote only the interests of the 'good' farmer (Interview, 12 June 1987).

12. Fieldnotes, A. Nduku, April 1987.

13. This is a day of rest on which people should not work the soil in any way, in honour of ancestral land guardian spirits (Bourdillon, 1982, p. 66).

14. By July the number of pigs in the piggery had declined to 63 from the highpoint of 103 in March. Of these 63, there were 9 sows and 2 boars. This meant that feed quantities could not be cut back significantly during the high prices of the drought until the young pigs were fattened and sold.

15. This loan, granted because members of the piggery project were on the executive of the savings club, had been set initially at the rate of 12 per cent per annum. CADEC, in their audit at Chinyuni in January 1987, advised the club to halve this.

16. These errors were as follows:

— The calculation was carried out after the project was under way and yet actual costs and statistics were not used in the calculation.
— A 16-sow unit was assumed in the calculation, whereas the project was in fact a 10-sow unit.
— A mistake in the IRR calculation of the cost of feed meant that the total variable costs had been underestimated by 4.4 per cent.
— Actual feed costs were significantly higher than in the calculation.
— An assumption was made that the mortality rate (MR) would decrease from 13 per cent to 5 per cent over 5 years. At the end of March 1987 of a total litter of 77 piglets born in February–March, 19.5 per cent had died. More deaths occurred subsequently.
— Each sow was expected to produce two litters of 16 piglets per year, resulting in 32 pigs sold annually as baconers (for which prices of over Z$90 could be received compared with the Z$60 to Z$75 for different sizes and grades of porkers). In practice two litters from each sow were not being sold per year; the average litter size was nearer 8 than 16; and of the 64 pigs sold in March and May only 9 were classified as baconers.
— The number of pigs classified as grade 1 is assumed to rise to between 60 and 70 per cent. In March, 42.5 per cent were grade 1 and the remainder grade 2, but in May, after the change in manager, 42 per cent were grade 2 and the remainder grade 3.

17. In Mavhaire ward I was enrolled by one group as one of their first round judges. The best maize crop I saw was in a field where the woman farmer had intercropped rice with the maize. She did not want to enter this field because the intercropping was not recommended and the group chairman I was with was reluctant to judge it when I suggested it should be entered (Fieldnotes, 26 January 1987).

18. The form of these meetings was discussed in an interview with the Chirumhanzu South AEO on 9 March 1987.

19. Fieldnotes, 14 April 1987, on the quarterly meeting I attended.

20. This is a general trend countrywide. Makombe, Bernsten and Rohrback (in Rukuni and Eicher, 1987) suggest that on average groundnut yields have declined by over 50 per cent over the last ten years. (They actually state that area planted has fallen by 60 per cent and gross output by 80 per cent, which amounts to this.)

21. Minute for Chirumhanzu South, mid-January 1987 staff meeting.

22. For example, this was stated by the Assistant Director (Technical) at the Gweru discussion meeting of 6 February 1987.

23. International Maize and Wheat Improvement Centre.

24. A grazing scheme was being implemented in Mberengwa, reference to which was made in Chapter 4.

Chapter 8   The Duality of Structure

1. This interview was first referred to in the last section of Chapter 7.
2. See the quote at the end of Chapter 7.

3. The term 'aesthetic rationality' is one that I have found most people to be uncomfortable with. What I am unsure of is whether a more suitable term could be employed (I have not thought of it), or whether the unease is simply because people have not considered the concept thoroughly before.

4. For the distinction between the two, see the last section of Chapter 7; or Giddens, 1987, pp. 374–5.

5. At the level of the agricultural extension agency, however, I did undertake this since my evaluation of the activities of staff was conducted in terms of the agency's goals.

6. Most of these schemes are under 50 ha in size and nearly all are under 100 ha (Hughes, 1974, p. 187). In 1983 some 2800 ha of land in the communal areas was under irrigation (World Bank, 1983).

7. Hughes provides other examples of schemes where the original cultivators were extremely dissatisfied. Moyana (1984) also refers to people's anger at what they felt was the exercise of 'government trickery' in the implementation of three irrigation projects in the Save valley (pp. 120–2).

8. This notion still lacks empirical verification.

References

1. ZIMBABWE AND AGRARIAN CHANGE

ADAMS, J. (1988) 'Wage labour in rural Zimbabwe', unpublished seminar paper, African Studies Association UK conference, Cambridge.

AGRICULTURAL AND RURAL DEVELOPMENT AUTHORITY (1983) 'Project Proposal for Resettlement, Rural Development and Environmental Rehabilitation: Gwanda District, South Matabeleland', Harare, ARDA.

ALLAN, W. (1965) *The African Husbandman*, Westport, Connecticut, Greenwood Press.

ALVORD, E. D. (1928), 'The great hunger', *NADA*, 2, 6, pp. 35–43.

———. (1929) Agricultural Life of Rhodesian Natives', *NADA*, 2, 7, pp. 9–16.

ARRIGHI, G. (1973) 'Labour supplies in historical perspective: A study of the proletarianisation of the African peasantry in Rhodesia', in ARRIGHI, G. and SAUL, J. S. (1973) *Essays on the Political Economy of Africa*, Monthly Review Press, New York.

———. (1973; orig. 1967) 'The political economy of Rhodesia', in ARRIGHI, G. and SAUL J. S. (1973) *Essays on the Political Economy of Africa*, Monthly Review Press, New York.

ASTROW, A. (1983) *Zimbabwe; A Revolution That Lost its Way?*, London, Zed Press.

BATES, R. H. (1983) *Essays on the Political Economy of Rural Africa*, Cambridge, Cambridge University Press.

BEACH, D. (1971) 'The rising in south-western Mashonaland, 1896–7', Ph.D. thesis, University of London.

———. (1977) 'The Shona economy: Branches of production', in Palmer, R. and Parsons, N. (eds), *The Roots of Rural Poverty in Central and Southern Africa*, London, Heinemann.

———. (1979) '"Chimurenga": The Shona rising of 1986–7', *Journal of African History*, 20, 3, pp. 395–420.

———. (1983) 'The Zimbabwean plateau and its peoples', in Birmingham, D. and Martin, P. M. (eds), *History of Central Africa: Volume One*, New York, Longman.

———. (1986) *War and Politics in Zimbabwe 1840–1900*, Gweru, Mambo Press.

BEINART, W. (1984) 'Soil erosion, conservationism and ideas about development: a Southern African exploration, 1900–1960', *Journal of Southern African Studies*, 11, 1, pp. 52–83.

BELL, M. (1988) 'Irrigation on dambos in Zimbabwe', unpublished seminar paper, African Studies Association UK conference, Cambridge.

BENOR, D. and HARRISON, J. Q. (1977) *Agricultural Extension: The Training and Visit System*, Washington, World Bank.

BLAIKIE, P. (1985) *The Political Economy of Soil Erosion in Developing Countries*, London, Longman.

BLAIKIE, P. (1989) 'Environment and access to resources in Africa', *Africa*, 59, 1, pp. 18–40.

BOSERUP, E. (1965) *The Conditions of Agricultural Growth*, London, Allen & Unwin.

——. (1981) *Population and Technology*, Oxford, Basil Blackwell.

BOURDILLON, M. F. C. (1982) *The Shona Peoples*, Gweru, Mambo Press.

BRATTON, M. (1984) 'Draft power, draft exchange and farmer organisations', Working Paper 9/84, Department of Land Management, University of Zimbabwe.

——. (1985) 'Financing smallholder production: A comparison of individual and group credit schemes in Zimbabwe', Working paper 2/85, Department of Land Management, University of Zimbabwe.

BUIJS, D. (1982) 'On admittance, access, cooperation and participation: The basic concepts of the "Access and Participation" research', in GALJART, B. AND BUIJS, D., *Participation of the Poor in Development: Contributions to a Seminar*, Leiden, Institute of Cultural and Social Studies, University of Leiden.

BULMAN, M. E. (1973) *The Native Land Husbandry Act of Southern Rhodesia: A Failure in Land Reform*, Salisbury: Tribal Areas of Rhodesia Research Foundation.

BUSH, R. and CLIFFE, L. (1984) 'Agrarian policy in migrant labour societies: Reform or transformation in Zimbabwe', *Review of African Political Economy*, 29, pp. 77–94.

CALLEAR, D. (1982) *The Social and Cultural Factors Involved in the Production by Small Farmers in Wedza Communal Area, Zimbabwe, of Maize and its Marketing*, UNESCO.

——. (1983) 'Land and food in the Wedza communal area', *Zimbabwe Agricultural Journal*, 81, pp. 163–8.

CAMPBELL, B. M., du TOIT, R. F. and ATTWELL, C. A. M. (eds) (1986) 'Relationship between the environment and basic needs satisfaction in the Sabi catchment, Zimbabwe', draft report, University of Zimbabwe.

CATHOLIC DEVELOPMENT COMMISSION (1987), 'CADEC Gweru Office – Annual report for 1987: Literacy programme and savings clubs', Gweru.

CHEATER, A. P. (1974) 'Aspects of status and mobility among farmers and their families in Msengezi African Purchase Land', *Zambezia*, III, ii, pp. 83–6.

——. (1976) 'Co-operative marketing among African producers in Rhodesia', *The Rhodesian Journal of Economics*, 10, 1, pp. 45–57.

——. (1983) 'Socialist transformation and rural development: Reflections on selected aspects of the Zimbabwean conundrum', unpublished paper.

——. (1984) *Idioms of Accumulation*, Gweru, Mambo Press.

——. (1988) 'The ideology of "communal" land tenure in Zimbabwe: Mythogenesis enacted?', unpublished seminar paper, African Studies Association of U.K. conference, Cambridge.

CLAY, E. J. and SCHAFFER, B. B. (1984) (eds) *Room for Manoeuvre: An Exploration of Public Policy in Agriculture and Rural Development*, London, Heinemann.

CLIFFE, L. (1977) '"Penetration" and rural development in the East African context', in CLIFFE, L., COLEMAN, J. S. and DOORNBOS, M. R. (eds), *Government and Rural Development in East Africa: Essays on Political Penetration* , The Hague, Martinus Nijhoff.

——. (1986) *Policy Options for Agrarian Reform in Zimbabwe*, Harare, FAO.

——. (1987) 'The debate on African peasantries', *Development and Change*, 18, 4, pp. 625–35.

COLLINSON, M. *et al.* (1982) 'A diagnostic survey of the south of Chibi District, Zimbabwe, for adaptive research planning', draft final report, CIMMYT/Department of Research and Specialist Services, Zimbabwe.

COUSINS, B. (1987) 'A survey of current grazing schemes in the communal lands of Zimbabwe', unpublished report, University of Zimbabwe, Harare.

DANISH INTERNATIONAL DEVELOPMENT AGENCY (1985) 'Zimbabwe: Assistance to the Resettlement Credit Scheme', Copenhagen.

DANKWERTS, J. P. (1975) *A Socio-economic Study of Veld Management in the Tribal Areas of the Victoria Province*, Salisbury, Tribal Areas Research Foundation.

DRINKWATER, M. J. (1985) 'Ture Ward, Zvishavane District: Exploring the issues of a land reform proposal in natural region IV', Gweru, Midlands Provincial Development Committee.

——. (1987a) '"Exhausted messages" – Training and groups: A comparative evaluation of Zimbabwe's Training and Visit system', Working Paper AEE 2/87, Department of Agricultural Economics and Extension, University of Zimbabwe.

——. (1987b) 'Loans and manure: The dilemma of access', Working Paper, AEE 3/87, Department of Agricultural Economics and Extension, University of Zimbabwe.

ELWELL, H. A. (1985) 'An assessment of soil erosion in Zimbabwe', *The Zimbabwe Science News*, 19, 3/4, pp. 27–31.

FINUCANE, J. R (1974) *Rural Development and Bureaucracy in Tanzania: The Case of Mwanza Region*, Uppsala, Scandinavian Institute of African Studies.

FLOYD, B. N. (1961) *Changing Patterns of African Land Use in Southern Rhodesia*, Lusaka, Rhodes Livingstone Institute.

GAIDZANWA, N. R. B. (1981) 'Promised Land: Towards a Land Policy for Zimbabwe', M. Dev. Studies thesis, The Hague, Institute of Social Studies.

GARLAKE, P. (1985) *Great Zimbabwe: Described and Explained*, Harare, Zimbabwe Publishing House.

GESCHIERE, P. (1984) 'Segmentary societies and the authority of the state – problems in implementing rural development in the Maka villages of south eastern Cameroon', *Sociologia Ruralis*, xxiv, 1, pp. 10–29.

GIBBON, P. and NECOSMOS, M. (1985) 'Problems in the political economy of African socialism (Tanzania)', in BERNSTEIN, H. and CAMPBELL B. K. (eds), *Contradictions of Accumulation in Africa*, Beverley Hills, California, Sage.

GRANT, P. M. (1981) 'The fertilisation of sandy soils in peasant agriculture', *Zimbabwe Agricultural Journal*, 78, 5, pp. 169–75.

HAYWARD, J. W. (1984) 'Agritex work plan: NAER programme 1984–85', *Second Annual Review Meeting of National Agricultural Extension and Research project*, Kariba, Zimbabwe.

HOLLEMAN, J. F. (1968) *Chief, Council and Commissioner*, Assen, The Netherlands, Koninklijke Van Gorcum.

HORTON, R. (1971) 'African traditional thought and Western science', in YOUNG, M. F. D. (ed.), *Knowledge and Control*, London, Collier-Macmillan.

HUGHES, A. J. B. (1974) *Development in Rhodesian Tribal Areas: An Overview*, Salisbury, Tribal Areas of Rhodesia Research Foundation.

HYDEN, G. (1980) *Beyond Ujamaa in Tanzania* , London, Heinemann.

——. (1983) *No Shortcuts to Progress*, London, Heinemann.

——. (1986) 'Discussion: The anomaly of the African peasantry', *Development and Change*, 17, 4, pp. 677–705.

——. (1987) 'Final rejoinder', *Development and Change*, 18, 4, pp. 661–7.

ILIFFE, J. (1979) *A Modern History of Tanganyika*, Cambridge, Cambridge University Press.

IVY, P. (1981) *A Guide to Soil Coding and Land Capability Classification for Land Use Planners*, Harare, Agritex.

JACKSON, J. C., COLLIER, P. and CONTI, A. (1987) *Rural Development Policies and Food Security in Zimbabwe: Part II*, Geneva, Rural Employment Policies Branch, Employment and Development Department, International Labour Office.

JEATER, D. (forthcoming) 'Bridewealth and conflict in the African community 1894–1920s', draft chapter from forthcoming Ph.D. thesis, University of Oxford.

JOHNSON, R. M. W. (1964) 'African agricultural development in Southern Rhodesia', *Food Research Institute Studies*, iv, 2, pp. 165–223.

KASFIR, N. (1986) 'Are African peasants self-sufficient?', *Development and Change*, 17, 2, pp. 335–57.

KELLY, R. D. (1973) 'A comparative study of primary productivity in different kinds of land use in south-east Rhodesia', Ph.D. thesis, University of London.

KEYTER, C. F. (1978) *Maize Control in Southern Rhodesia 1931–1941*, Salisbury, Tribal Areas Research Foundation.

KINSEY, B. H. (1983) 'Emerging policy issues in Zimbabwe's land resettlement programme', *Development Policy Review*, 1, pp. 163–95.

——. (1987) 'Agricultural extension in intensive resettlement schemes: A case study within the framework of the National Extension Framework Study', unpublished paper for the National Extension Framework Study, Zimbabwe.

LAN, D. (1985) *Guns and Rain: Guerrillas and Spirit Mediums in Zimbabwe*, London, James Currey.

LEONARD, D. (1977) *Reading the Peasant Farmer: Organisation Theory and Practice in Kenya*, Chicago and London, University of Chicago Press.

LESSING, D. (1957) *Going Home*, London, Michael Joseph.

LONG, N. (1984) 'Creating space for change: A perspective on the sociology of development', *Sociologia Ruralis* , xxiv, 3/4, 168–83.

MAKOMBE, G., BERNSTEN, R. H. and ROHRBACH, D. D. (1987) 'The economics of groundnut production by communal farmers in Zimbabwe', in RUKUNI M. and EICHER, C. K. (eds), *Food Security for Southern Africa*, Harare, Department of Agricultural Economics and Extension, University of Zimbabwe.

MANDAZA, I. (ed.) (1987) *The Political Economy of Transition 1980–1986*, Harare, Jongwe Press.

MBWANDA, C. (1985) 'Problems and conflicts of the resettlement and the expansion of state marketing and credit programmes in Zimbabwe since Independence', M.Sc. dissertation, University of East Anglia.

MOSLEY, P. (1983) *The Settler Economies*, Cambridge, Cambridge University Press.

MOYANA, H. V. (1984) *The Political Economy of Land in Zimbabwe*, Gweru, Mambo Press.

MOYO, S. (1987) 'The land question', in MANDAZA, I. (ed.), *The Political Economy of Transition 1980–1986*, Harare, Jongwe Press.

MUNSLOW, B. (1985) 'Prospects for the socialist transition of agriculture in Zimbabwe', *World Development*, 13, 1, pp. 41–58.

NEWITT, M. D. D. (1973) *Portuguese Settlement on the Zambesi: Exploration, Land Tenure and Colonial Rule in East Africa*, London, Longman.

PALMER, R. (1977a) *Land and Racial Domination in Rhodesia*, London, Heinemann.

——. (1977b) 'The agricultural history of Rhodesia', in PALMER, R. and PARSONS, N. (eds), *The Roots of Rural Poverty in Central and Southern Africa*, London, Heinemann.

PASSMORE, G. (1972) *The National Policy of Community Development in Rhodesia*, Salisbury, University of Rhodesia.

PHIMISTER, I. (1986) 'Discourse and the discipline of historical context: Conservationism and ideas about development in Southern Rhodesia 1930–1950', *Journal of Southern African Studies*, 12, 2, pp. 263–75.

PRATT, C. (1979) *The Critical Phase in Tanzania 1945–1968: Nyerere and the Emergence of a Socialist Strategy*, Cambridge, Cambridge University Press.

RANGER, T. (1985) *Peasant Consciousness and Guerrilla War in Zimbabwe*, Harare, Zimbabwe Publishing House.

REYNOLDS, N. and IVY, P. (1984) 'Proposals for a National Land Use Programme', unpublished report, Agritex.

RIFKIND, M. L. (1969) 'The politics of land in Rhodesia', M.Sc. dissertation, University of Edinburgh.

ROBERTSON, A. F. (1984) *People and the State: An Anthropology of Planned Development*, Cambridge, Cambridge University Press.

ROUTLEY, V. and ROUTLEY, R. (1980) 'Social theories, self management and environmental problems', in MANNISON, D. S., McROBBIE, M. A. and ROUTLEY, R. (eds), *Environmental Philosophy*, Monograph Series No. 2, Australian National University.

RUKUNI, M. and EICHER, C. K. (1987) (eds) *Food Security for Southern Africa*, Harare, Department of Agricultural Economics and Extension, University of Zimbabwe.

SANDFORD, S. (1982) *Livestock in the Communal Areas of Zimbabwe*, London, ODI.

——. (1983) *Management of Pastoral Development in the Third World*, London, John Wiley & Sons.

SAUL, J. S. (1979) *State and Revolution in Eastern Africa*, London, Heinemann.

SCOONES, I. (1987) 'Economic and ecological carrying capacity: Implications for livestock development in the dryland communal areas of Zimbabwe', unpublished seminar paper, Department of Biological Sciences, University of Zimbabwe.

SCOONES, I. and WILSON, K. (1988) 'Households, lineage groups and ecological dynamics: Issues for livestock research and development in Zimbabwe's communal areas', position paper for the workshop on *The Socio-economic Determinants of Livestock Production in Zimbabwe's Communal Areas*, Masvingo, Zimbabwe.

SCOTT, J. C. (1985) *Weapons of the Weak*, New Haven and London, Yale University Press.

SEDDON (ed.) (1978) *Relations of Production: Marxist Approaches to Economic Anthropology*, London, Frank Cass.

SHIVIJI, I. G. (1976) *Class Struggles in Tanzania*, London, Heinemann.

SIMON, D. (1985) 'Agrarian policy and migration in Zimbabwe and Southern Africa: Reform or transformation?', *Review of African Political Economy*, 34, pp. 82–9.

STOCKING, M. (1984) *Erosion and Soil Productivity: A Review*, Norwich, School of Development Studies, University of East Anglia/FAO.

TAMBO, O. (1986) 'Racism, apartheid and a new world order', *Third World Quarterly*, 8, 3, pp. xiii–xx.

THEISEN, R. (1973) 'The cultivation of vleis in the Que Que Tribal Trust Land: An ecological study showing the importance of vlei arable to development', unpublished report.

——. (1976) 'Principles of vlei conservation', Gweru, unpublished paper.

TRUSCOTT, K. (1985a) *The Wedza Project: Its Impact on Farmer Households, Agricultural Production and Extension*, Harare, Agritex.

——. (1985b) 'Socio-economic factors related to food production and consumption: A case study of twelve households in Wedza communal land', unpublished paper produced for the FAO, Harare.

——. (1987) 'Farmer groups in the communal areas: The impact of farmer groups on the extension service', unpublished paper for the National Extension Framework Study, Zimbabwe.

UPHOFF, N. T. and ESMAN, M. J. (1974) *Local Organisation for Rural Development: Analysis of Asian Experience*, New York, Cornell University.

VAMBE, L. (1972) *An Ill-fated People: Zimbabwe Before and After Rhodes*, London, Heinemann.

van BINSBERGEN, W. M. J. (1981) *Religious Change in Zambia*, London, Kegan Paul International.

van BINSBERGEN, W. M. J. and GESCHIERE, P. (1985) (eds) *Old Modes of Production and Capitalist Encroachment*, London, KPI.

van ONSELEN, C. (1976) *Chibaro: African Mine Labour in Southern Rhodesia 1900–1933*, London, Pluto Press.

van VELSEN, J. (1964) *The Politics of Kinship*, Manchester, The University Press.

WALKER, B. H. and NOY-MEIR, I. (1982) 'Aspects of the stability and resilience of savanna eco-systems', in HUNTLEY, B. J. AND WALKER, B. H. (eds), *Ecology of Tropical Savannas*, Berlin, Springer-Verlag.
WALLIS, J. P. R. (ed.) (1954) *The Southern African Diaries of Thomas Leask*, London, Chatto & Windus.
WEINER, D., MOYO, S., MUNSLOW, B. and O'KEEFE, P. (1985) 'Land use and agricultural productivity in Zimbabwe', *The Journal of Modern African Studies*, 23, 2, pp. 251–85.
WEINRICH, A. K. F. (1964) 'The social background of agriculture in Chilimanzi Reserve', *Rhodes Livingstone Institute Journal*, 36, pp. 7–39.
———. (1975) *African Farmers in Rhodesia*, London, Oxford University Press.
———. (1979) *Women and Racial Discrimination in Rhodesia*, UNESCO.
WILLIAMS, G. (1982a, orig. 1976) 'Taking the part of peasants', in ALLEN, C. and WILLIAMS, G., *Sociology of "Developing Societies": Sub-Saharan Africa*, London, Macmillan.
———. (1982b) 'Equity, growth and the state', *Africa*, 52, 3, pp. 114– 20.
———. (1987) 'Primitive accumulation: The way to progress', *Development and Change*, 18, 4, pp. 637–59.
WILSON, K. B. (1986a) 'History, ecology and conservation in southern Zimbabwe', unpublished seminar paper, Department of Sociology, University of Manchester.
———. (1986b) 'The human ecology of Zvishavane District, Zimbabwe: The problems of woodland and veld', unpublished paper.
———. (1986c) 'The human ecology of Zvishavane District, Zimbabwe: A preliminary account of rainfall and peoples' perceptions of it', unpublished paper.
———. (1986d) 'Aspects of the history of vlei cultivation in southern Zimbabwe', unpublished workshop paper, Dambo research project workshop, Harare, 1986.
———. (1986e) 'The African peasant experience in Zimbabwe: Some peasant views', unpublished paper.
———. (1987) 'The indigenous genetic resources of the Karanga crop production system', unpublished report, prepared for ENDA-Zimbabwe.
———. (1988a) 'Patterns of constraint interaction and peoples' perceptions of the future', unpublished paper.
———. (1988b) 'Relationship between savanna production dynamics and human welfare vulnerability', unpublished seminar paper, Department of Zoology, University of Oxford.
———. (1988c) 'Indigenous conservation in Zimbabwe: Soil erosion, land-use planning and rural life', unpublished seminar paper, African Studies Association of U.K. conference, Cambridge.
———. (1988d) 'Access to arable land', unpublished paper.
———. (1989a) 'Historical dymanics of the farming systems in Mazvihwa in relation to coping with rainfall variability', Appendix to forthcoming Ph.D. thesis, University of London.
———. (1989b) 'Trees in fields in southern Zimbabwe', *Journal of Southern African Studies*, 15, 2, pp. 369–83.
WORLD BANK (1983) *Zimbabwe Agricultural Sector Study*, Southern Africa Agricultural Division.

WORLD BANK/GOVERNMENT OF ZIMBABWE (1985) *Zimbabwe: Land Subsector Study*, Southern Agriculture Division, Eastern and Southern Africa Projects Department.

WORSLEY, P. (1984) *The Three Worlds: Culture and World Development*, London, Weidenfeld & Nicolson.

YUDELMAN, M. (1964) *Africans on the Land*, Cambridge, Massachusetts, Harvard University Press.

ZACHRISSON, P. (1978) *An African Area in Change: Belingwe, 1894–1946*, University of Gothenburg.

2. CRITICAL THEORY

ARATO, A. (1982) 'Critical sociology and authoritarian state socialism', in THOMPSON, J. B. and HELD, D. (eds), *Habermas: Critical Debates*, London, Macmillan.

BAXTER, H. (1987) 'System and life-world in Habermas's *Theory of Communicative Action*', *Theory and Society*, 16, 1, pp. 39–86.

BENHABIB, S. (1986) *Critique, Norm and Utopia: A Study of the Foundations of Critical Theory*, New York, Columbia University Press.

BENHABIB, S. and CORNELL, D. (eds) (1987) *Feminism as Critique: Essays on the Politics of Gender in Late-Capitalist Societies*, Cambridge, Polity Press.

BERNSTEIN, R. J. (1976) *The Restructuring of Social and Political Theory*, Oxford, Basil Blackwell.

_____. (1985) (ed.) *Habermas and Modernity*, Cambridge, Polity Press.

BOTTOMORE, T. (1984) *The Frankfurt School*, Ellis Horwood/Tavistock Publications, London.

DEWS, P. (ed.) (1986) *Jurgen Habermas: Autonomy and Solidarity – Interviews*, London, Verso.

FAY, B. (1975) *Social Theory and Political Practice*, London, George Allen & Unwin.

_____. (1987) *Critical Social Science: Liberation and its Limits*, Cambridge, Polity Press.

FRASER, N. (1987) 'What's critical about critical theory? The case of Habermas and gender', in BENHABIB, S. and CORNELL, D. (eds), *Feminism as Critique: Essays on the Politics of Gender in Late-Capitalist Societies*, Cambridge, Polity Press.

FREIRE, P. (1972) *Pedagogy of the Oppressed*, Harmondsworth, Penguin.

_____. (1976: orig. 1974) *Education: The Practice of Freedom*, London, Writers and Readers Publishing Cooperative.

FRIEDMANN, J. (1973) *Retracking America: A Theory of Transactive Planning*, New York, Anchor Press.

_____. (1978) 'Innovation, flexible response and social learning', in BURCHELL, R. W. and STERNLIEB, G., *Planning Theory in the 1980's: A Search for Future Directions*, New Jersey, Centre for Urban Policy Research.

_____. (1979) 'Basic needs, agropolitan development and planning from below', *RAPI Journal*, February.

GADAMER, H. G. (1975) *Truth and Method*, London, Sheed & Ward.
——. (1976) *Philosophical Hermeneutics*, Berkeley, University of California Press.
GIBSON, R. (1986) *Critical Theory and Education*, Sevenoaks, Hodder & Stoughton.
GIDDENS, A. (1982) 'Labour and interaction', in THOMPSON, J. B. and HELD, D. (eds) (1982), *Habermas: Critical Debates*, London, Macmillan.
——. (1984) *The Constitution of Society: Outline of the Theory of Structuration*, Cambridge, Polity Press.
——. (1985) 'Reason without revolution? Habermas' *Theorie des Kommunikativen Handelns*', in BERNSTEIN, R. J. (ed.), *Habermas and Modernity*, Cambridge, Polity Press.
——. (1987) *Social Theory and Modern Sociology*, Cambridge, Polity Press.
GOULDNER, A. (1980) *The Two Marxisms*, New York.
HABERMAS, J. (1972) *Knowledge and Human Interests*, London, Heinemann.
——. (1979) *Communication and the Evolution of Society*, London, Heinemann.
——. (1982) 'A reply to my critics', in THOMPSON, J. B. and HELD, D. (eds) (1982), *Habermas: Critical Debates*, London, Macmillan.
——. (1984) *The Theory of Communicative Action, Volume One*, Cambridge, Polity Press.
——. (1985) 'Questions and counterquestions', in BERNSTEIN, R. J. (ed.), *Habermas and Modernity*, Cambridge, Polity Press.
HELD, D. (1980) *Introduction to Critical Theory: Horkheimer to Habermas*, London, Hutchinson.
HELLER, A. (1982) 'Habermas and Marxism', in THOMPSON, J. B. and HELD, D. (eds) (1982), *Habermas: Critical Debates*, London, Macmillan.
——. (1984) *Radical Philosophy*, Oxford, Basil Blackwell.
HERON (1981) 'Philosophical basis for a new paradigm', in REASON, P. and ROWAN, J. (eds), *Human Enquiry: A Sourcebook of New Paradigm Research*, Bath, John Wiley & Sons.
HORKHEIMER, M. (1968) *Critical Theory: Selected Essays*, New York, Herder & Herder.
INGRAM, D. (1987) *Habermas and the Dialectic of Reason*, New Haven, Yale University Press.
McCARTHY, T. (1984; orig. 1978) *The Critical Theory of Jurgen Habermas*, Polity Press, Cambridge.
OUTHWAITE, W. (1985) 'Hans-Georg Gadamer', in SKINNER, Q. (ed.), *The Return of Grand Theory in the Human Sciences*, Cambridge, Cambridge University Press.
RODERICK, R. (1986) *Habermas and the Foundations of Critical Theory*, Basingstoke, Macmillan.
THOMPSON, J. B. and HELD, D. (1982) *Habermas: Critical Debates*, London, Macmillan.

3. GOVERNMENT OF ZIMBABWE

Commissions

GOVERNMENT OF SOUTHERN RHODESIA (1925) *Report of the Land Commission*, Chairman: W. Morris Carter.
_____. (1944) *Report of the Native Production and Trade Commission*, Chairman: W. A. Godlonton.
_____. (1961) *Mangwende Reserve Commission of Inquiry*, Chairman: J. S. Brown.
_____. (1961) *Commission of Inquiry on Administrative and Judicial Functions in the Native Affairs and District Courts Departments*, Chairman: V. L. Robinson.
_____. (1962) *Report of the Commission of Inquiry into the Maize and Small Grains Industry of Southern Rhodesia and Northern Rhodesia*, Chairman: A. W. O. Bock.
GOVERNMENT OF ZIMBABWE (1981) *Report of the Commission of Inquiry into Incomes, Prices and Conditions of Service*, Chairman: R. Riddell.
_____. (1982) *Report of the Commission of Inquiry into the Agricultural Industry*, Chairman: G. Chavunduka.

National Archives of Zimbabwe (NAZ)

S1051, Agriculturalist, Native Affairs Department, Annual Report 1943.
S1051, CNC, Annual Report 1943.
S1051, NC Belingwe, Annual Report 1943.
S1051, NC Gwelo, Annual Report 1943.
S1563, CNC, Annual Reports 1945–6, 1948.
S1563, Director of Native Agriculture, Annual Reports 1946, 1948.
S1563, NC Belingwe, Annual Reports 1936–8, 1940–2, 1944–8.
S1563, NC Chilimanzi, Annual Reports 1936–8, 1940–8.
S1563, NC Gwelo, Annual Reports 1936–8, 1940–2, 1944–8.
S1563, ANC Shabani, Annual Reports 1942, 1945–8.
S160 LS 106/1/50, ANC Que Que to NC Gwelo, 7 June 1950.
S160 LS 106/1/50, 'Land survey': Natives occupying Crown land, Rhodesdale, 1948–51.
S235, NC Belingwe, Annual Reports 1923–35, 1939.
S235, NC Chilimanzi, Annual Reports 1923–35, 1939.
S235, NC Gwelo, Annual Reports 1923–35, 1939.
S235, ANC Shabani, Annual Reports 1926–7, 1931, 1934–5, 1939.
SRG3/INT4, CNC, Annual Reports 1949, 1952–3, 1957–62.
SRG3/INT4, Director of Native Agriculture, Annual Reports 1950–61.
SRG3/INT4, Secretary for Agriculture, Annual Report 1962.
SRG3/INT4, Secretary for Internal Affairs, Annual Reports 1963–7.
Unreferenced, NC Belingwe, Annual Report 1955.
Unreferenced, NC Chilimanzi, Annual Reports 1951–2, 1955–9, 1961.

Unreferenced, NC Gwelo, Annual Reports 1951–2, 1955–9, 1961.
Unreferenced, ANC Shabani, Annual Reports 1951–2, 1956.
Unreferenced, NC Shabani, Annual Reports 1957–9, 1961.

Reports

ASSISTANT DIRECTOR (FIELD) (1986) 'Communal land grazing: An holistic perspective', Paper prepared for the Zimbabwe Society of Animal Production Conference, University of Zimbabwe, 5–6 June.
DEPARTMENT OF AGRICULTURAL TECHNICAL AND EXTENSION SERVICES (1984) 'Annual report, Midlands Province', Gweru.
——. (1986) 'Annual report, Midlands Province', Gweru.
——. (1987) 'Crop packages: Midlands Province', Harare.
DEPARTMENT OF RESEARCH AND SPECIALIST SERVICES (1984) *Farming Systems Research Unit Annual Report 1983–84*, Harare.
DEPARTMENT OF RURAL DEVELOPMENT, MINISTRY OF LANDS, RESETTLEMENT AND RURAL DEVELOPMENT (1983) 'Progress report on the intensive and accelerated resettlement programme', Harare.
GOVERNMENT OF SOUTHERN RHODESIA (1955) *What the Native Land Husbandry Act Means to the Rural African and to Southern Rhodesia: A Five-Year Plan that will Revolutionise African Agriculture*, Salisbury.
GOVERNMENT OF ZIMBABWE (1981) *Growth with Equity: An Economic Policy Statement*, Harare.
——. (1982) *Transitional National Development Plan 1982/83 – 1984/85*, Harare.
——. (1986a) *First Five-Year National Development Plan 1986–1990*, Harare.
——. (1986b) *Socio-economic Review of Zimbabwe 1980–1985*, Harare.
MINISTRY OF LANDS, AGRICULTURE AND RURAL SETTLEMENT (1987) 'Impact of various reform policy options on the agricultural sector', paper presented at the National Symposium on Agrarian Reform, Nyanga.
MINISTRY OF LANDS, RESETTLEMENT AND RURAL DEVELOPMENT (1981) 'Intensive resettlement: Policies and procedures', Harare.
——. (1983) *Government Policy on Co-operative Development*, Harare.
——. (1985) 'Communal Lands Development Plan: A 15-Year Development Strategy', draft.
MINISTRY OF LOCAL GOVERNMENT, RURAL AND URBAN DEVELOPMENT (1987) 'Resettlement progress report as at August 31, 1987', Harare.
MINISTRY OF NATURAL RESOURCES AND TOURISM (1987) *The National Conservation Strategy*, Harare, Ministry of Information.
REGIONAL AGRICULTURAL EXTENSION OFFICER, GWERU (1984) 'First report of the Midlands Province Training and Visit pilot project', Gweru.
——. (1985) 'Second report of the Midlands Province Training and Visit pilot project', Gweru.

4. INTERVIEWS AND MEETINGS

The following are a list of the interviews and formal meetings conducted as part of the research with people resident outside of the study areas. The many informal meetings and discussions conducted with Agritex staff at regional level and below are not included.

Interviews

Sen. G. Todd, owner Hokonui Ranch, 10 December 1984 (partial tape transcription).

D. Tredgold, Managing Director Debshan Ranch, 20 December 1984 (tape transcription).

J. M. Dondo and Mr Chikasha, AFC Western Region staff, Gweru, 5 February 1985 (notes).

J. Ngwenya, Agricultural Finance Corporation Western Region Manager, Gweru, 21 March 1985 (tape transcription).

Midlands PAEO, Gweru, 21 March 1985 (tape transcription).

Interview with Cooperative Extension Officer, Department of Cooperatives, Gweru, 22 March 1985 (tape transcription).

G. Scheu, Catholic Development Commission, Gweru, 25 March 1985 (tape transcription).

AEO Chirumhanzu South, Chaka, 9 March 1987 (notes and tape transcription).

Community leaders, Maware and Chingwena wards, Chirumhanzu, 14–16 April 1987 (8 interviews) (notes).

R. Gapare, Chairman National Farmers Association of Zimbabwe, 12 June 1987 (tape transcription).

Assistant Director (Field), Agritex, 10 June 1987 (notes).

Assistant Director (Field), Agritex, 23 July 1987 (tape transcription).

Under Secretary, Ministry of Local Government, Rural and Urban Planning, Harare, 20 April 1988 (notes).

Meetings

Meeting attended by provincial and regional Agritex staff, offices of the RAEO Zvishavane, 13 December 1984 (tape transcription).

Meeting with AFC Western Region staff, AFC offices, Gweru, 6 January 1987 (notes).

Meeting attended by national, provincial and regional Agritex staff, Gweru, 6 February 1987 (First Gweru discussion meeting) (tape malfunctioned, some notes).

Meeting attended by national, provincial and regional Agritex staff, Gweru, 13 April 1987 (Second Gweru discussion meeting) (tape transcription).

Seminar and discussion of my evaluation of Agritex activities in the study areas, Gweru, 22 July 1987 (tape transcription).

Index